ORTHODOX CHRISTIANITY AND CONTEMPORARY THOUGHT

SERIES EDITORS
George E. Demacopoulos and Aristotle Papanikolaou

This series consists of books that seek to bring Orthodox Christianity into an engagement with contemporary forms of thought. Its goal is to promote (1) historical studies in Orthodox Christianity that are interdisciplinary, employ a variety of methods, and speak to contemporary issues; and (2) constructive theological arguments in conversation with patristic sources and that focus on contemporary questions ranging from the traditional theological and philosophical themes of God and human identity to cultural, political, economic, and ethical concerns. The books in the series explore both the relevancy of Orthodox Christianity to contemporary challenges and the impact of contemporary modes of thought on Orthodox self-understandings.

ORTHODOX CONSTRUCTIONS OF THE WEST

ORTHODOX CONSTRUCTIONS OF THE WEST

EDITED BY
GEORGE E. DEMACOPOULOS AND
ARISTOTLE PAPANIKOLAOU

FORDHAM UNIVERSITY PRESS
New York • *2013*

Fordham University Press has no responsibility for the persistence or accuracy of URLs for external or third-party Internet websites referred to in this publication and does not guarantee that any content on such websites is, or will remain, accurate or appropriate.

Fordham University Press also publishes its books in a variety of electronic formats. Some content that appears in print may not be available in electronic books.

Library of Congress Cataloging-in-Publication Data

Orthodox constructions of the West / edited by George E. Demacopoulos and Aristotle Papanikolaou. — First edition.
    pages ; cm. — (Orthodox Christianity and contemporary thought)
    Includes bibliographical references and index.
    ISBN 978-0-8232-5192-6 (cloth) — ISBN 978-0-8232-5193-3 (paper)
  1. Orthodox Eastern Church—Relations—Catholic Church. 2. Catholic Church—Relations—Orthodox Eastern Church. 3. Orthodox Eastern Church—Doctrines.   I. Demacopoulos, George E.   II. Papanikolaou, Aristotle
    BX324.3.O774 2013
    281.9—dc23

                                                                    2013003548

Printed in the United States of America

15 14 13   5 4 3 2 1

First edition

CONTENTS

Acknowledgments

The content of the present volume was introduced at a three-day conference in June 2010. That conference belongs to a triennial conference series, initiated in 2007, dedicated to a historical and theological investigation of the Eastern Orthodox and Roman Catholic schism. In 2008, Solon and Marianna Patterson of Atlanta, Georgia, provided the Orthodox Christian Studies Center at Fordham University with a generous gift that established a permanent endowment for the conference series and its subsequent publications. It is their goal and ours that this series will slowly chip away at those things that academic research can demonstrate to be false barriers to Christian unity. We are profoundly moved by the Pattersons' generosity and indebted to their guidance for the center's endeavors.

In addition to the Pattersons, the 2010 conference had several other patrons. Four founding members of the center's advisory council—Drake Behrakis, John Grogan, Kenneth Hickman, and Gus Poulopoulos—made generous donations. Within the university, we received support from the Offices of the Dean of Faculty, the Dean of the Graduate School of Arts and Sciences, the Dean of Fordham College Rose Hill, and the Dean of Fordham College Lincoln Center. The Center for Medieval Studies, directed by Maryanne Kowaleski, offered essential clerical and staff support. And the Department of Theology served as a cosponsor.

We would like to thank the many Fordham doctoral students who helped to staff the conference, including Michael Azar, Matthew Briel,

Jennifer Jamer, Ian Jones, Matthew Lootens, Lindsey Mercer, John Penniman, Ashley Purpura, Jon Stanfill, and Nate Wood. Lindsey Keeling offered additional service in anticipation of the conference (including the selection of the image for the book jacket). Andrew Steffan and Matthew Baker provided keen editorial assistance in the preparation of the manuscript.

In some ways, the idea for this project was born during the sessions of Fordham Faculty reading group, sponsored by Mike Latham, Dean of Fordham College Rose Hill. We would like to thank Ben Dunning, Brad Hinze, Michael Lee, and Brenna Moore for their ideas and friendship. We would like to thank Peter Bouteneff, Demetrios Katos, Brad Hinze, Mary-Jane Rubenstein, and William Baumgarth, who served as session chairs during the conference. Finally, Fred Nachbaur and everyone at Fordham University Press are to be commended for their expeditious work on this volume and for their continued support for the Orthodox Christianity and Contemporary Thought series, to which this volume belongs.

ORTHODOX CONSTRUCTIONS OF THE WEST

ORTHODOX NAMING OF THE OTHER: A POSTCOLONIAL APPROACH

George E. Demacopoulos and Aristotle Papanikolaou

Who is Western? Who is Eastern? Am I "Eastern" if I commune in an Eastern Orthodox parish in Toledo, Ohio? Am I "Western" if I commune at an Eastern-Rite Catholic parish in Kiev? What if I was baptized into the Eastern Orthodox faith as a child, but I've never learned an Eastern language or traveled outside of the United States—am I Eastern or Western? What if I am a convert to an Eastern or Western faith? In short, what is the link between religious confession and location, and how do the considerations of confession and location impact the construction of self and its other(s)?

Perhaps even more problematic are the questions that surround the actual location of East and West. Is it a physical location? If so, it certainly is not a static one. What is more, wherever it is that East and West belong on the map, it would seem to shift according to perspective. Is the location of East and West linked to a linguistic and/or cultural distinction? For the Christians of late antiquity and the Middle Ages, it is possible to locate with some confidence those Christians who worshipped in Greek versus those who worshipped in Latin. So too, the division of the Christian world into five autonomous patriarchates (a division often known as the *Pentarchy*) does follow along certain linguistic—though not ethnic—distinctions (though even this seemingly clear distinction is thrown into some confusion by the Balkans). And while it is true that the Greek/Latin binary might help to explain why the competition for converts in the Balkans was so critical for the projection of East and West in the ninth century, it does not account for the significant percentage of Christians who spoke neither Greek nor Latin (particularly in Egypt, Palestine, and Syria).[1]

Whatever the situation may have been in the premodern world, however, the linguistic distinction has virtually no meaning in the present because Christians of Eastern and Western traditions have moved all over the globe.[2] In short, however often Christians in the past and present employ the categories of Eastern and Western in their narration of self and other, there has been and continues to be an inherent ambiguity and an embedded paradox of location in these constructions of place. The categories of East and West are always fluid, always multiform, and almost always projections of an imagined difference.[3]

And, yet, the category of the West has played an important role in the Orthodox imagination. It has functioned as an absolute marker of difference from what is considered to be the essence of Orthodoxy, and, thus, ironically, has become a constitutive aspect of the modern Orthodox self. We will attempt to unravel how the East has constructed the West and, through the use of critical theory, suggest some possible ways to make sense of why the West is so important to the East.

Historical Rupture and the Naming of Otherness

While some readers will, no doubt, be familiar with the basic parameters of Eastern Christian history, it is nonetheless important to highlight those transitions that stand out as pivotal for the way that Eastern Christians came to view themselves in relation to the Western Christian or the Western secular "Other."[4] These pivotal points provide some indication of how Christian self-identification emerged within the East/West binary, especially since the initial identification markers, which were not oppositional, were Latin and Greek: In other words, the Greek-speaking Christians did not self-identify against the Latin-speaking Christians. For our present purposes, it does not so much matter whether Eastern Christians were conscious of a historic transition at the moment of occurrence or if it was only later that they consciously identified a particular sequence of events as a significant moment in East/West relations. And while the following survey is admittedly both incomplete and cursory, it is enough to provide some sense of when the East started to construct both the West and itself.

From Constantine to the Fall of Constantinople

Since the fourth century, the Roman emperor Constantine (d. 337) has served as a romanticized model for Eastern Christian authors who believe that the Christian experience is, or should be, an imperial one. As is well known, Constantine was the first Roman emperor to legalize Christianity and to convert to the faith. He also famously moved the capital of the Roman empire from Rome to Constantinople (modern-day Istanbul), in order to situate his government and its armies more effectively between Persian and Germanic threats. When the Western half of the Roman empire began to slip from Constantinopolitan control at the end of the fifth century, the Eastern empire continued on a path of imperial and Christian symbiosis.[5] Even the rapid loss of territories in Egypt, Palestine, and Syria in the middle of the seventh century did little to diminish the imperial setting for most Chalcedonian Christians in the East.[6] The categories of Western and Eastern in the Constantinian era only served to identify the two halves of the empire. In fact, according to the present-day East/West division, Constantine is an enigma: a Latin-speaking Emperor who knew little-to-no Greek and who is revered as a saint in the present-day East but not in the West.

For several centuries after Constantine's conversion, any difference between the Eastern and Western elements of the Roman world were primarily linguistic and reflective of the political borders drawn by the Roman provincial network. Western writers (such as Ambrose of Milan and Jerome) freely borrowed from Eastern sources and Eastern clerics routinely sought the political and theological assistance of Western leaders.[7] Even on the eve on the seventh century, we find a prominent figure like Pope Gregory I (bishop of Rome from 590 to 604) maintaining extensive political and ecclesiastical contacts in the East.[8] Gregory found no doctrinal difference between himself and the Greek bishops of the East with whom he corresponded. While it is true that modern scholars have sought to identify theological schools or trajectories according to an imposed Greek/Latin or East/West paradigm (the most famous being the exaggerated scholarly narrative of Cappadocian/Augustinian incompatibility), there is simply no surviving evidence that anyone in the late-ancient Roman world understood such linguistic or geographical paradigms to be a marker of theological difference.[9]

But during the seventh and eighth centuries, new geopolitical realities forced the Roman world into permanent structural changes that would eventually estrange the Eastern and Western Christian communities. In the East, Islamic armies not only seized Egypt, Palestine, and Syria, but also laid siege to Constantinople itself in 674. Though the city weathered the attack, the loss of the southern territories was devastating to the Byzantine economy and the empire would never again be in a position to be a viable political force in the West. As a consequence, by the middle of the eighth century, the bishops of Rome who were desperate for military assistance turned to the Franks for help. The papal-Frankish alliance not only transformed European and Mediterranean political dynamics, but also opened the door for Frankish theologians to become permanent players in the Christian discourse. The papal turn away from Byzantium would also, eventually, fuel an antipapal theological discourse within certain Orthodox circles, which, as John Manoussakis's essay illustrates, is not without its own theological problems.

It is the *filioque* controversy that evokes the formation of the contemporary East/West divide. As is well known, the *filioque* refers to the theological claim that the Holy Spirit proceeds from the Father "and the Son." Theologically, it is often attributed to Augustine, though it is clear that Greek-speaking Christian thinkers theologized about the role of the Son in the procession of the Holy Spirit.[10] In other words, Augustine was not alone in attempting to understand further the mystery of the Trinity, especially the interrelations of the *hypostases* (persons) of the Trinity.

Historically, what eventually became known as the Nicene-Constantinopolitan Creed did not contain the phrase "and the Son"; rather, it reads "And in the Holy Spirit . . . who proceeds from the Father, who together with the Father and the Son is worshipped and glorified." It is often thought that the first interpolation of the *filioque* in the Nicene-Constantinopolitan Creed occurred at the Council of Toledo (589).[11] Though the scholarly consensus supports a later interpolation of some version of the *filioque* in the acts of the Council, "it is clear that within a few short years of the council the interpolated Creed was firmly established in both the liturgy and the theology of the Spanish Church."[12] It is also agreed that the *filioque* was meant to counter an Arian Christology. Its inclusion in the Creed was reaffirmed by nine subsequent councils in Toledo throughout the seventh century, such that its absence from the Creed would have, ironically, seemed to the Christians of Spain a betrayal of the ancient councils.[13]

Although there is evidence of theological discussions of the *filioque* in the seventh and eight centuries, it would not be until the coronation of the Frankish king, Charlemagne, that the inclusion of the *filioque* in the Nicene-Constantinopolitan Creed would become a major point of contention between Latin- and Greek-speaking forms of Christianity. An event catalyzing the magnification of this division occurred in 807 in Jerusalem when the monks of St. Sabbas in Jerusalem heard Frankish monks recite the interpolated Creed, and, subsequently, tried to evict them from the Church of the Nativity during Christmas celebrations, accusing them of heresy.[14] It is at this point in the history of the *filioque* controversy that the question must be raised whether the reactions of Frankish and Roman monks to each other over the interpolated Creed are simply the result of sincere interest in theological fidelity, or were fueled by growing awareness of Frankish/Latin-Roman/Greek difference. Although the Latin/Greek difference had not previously been used for the purpose of theological self-identification vis-à-vis the proximate other, this difference became magnified as opposition with the emerging difference between Franks and Romans. The Greek Romans did not consider the Franks as Romans, and the Franks were primarily identified with Latin. The theological difference, thus, gets caught up in the oppositional identification difference between Franks and Romans, which was facilitated by inclusion of the *filioque* in the Creed. In short, the so-called East/West difference started to take its initial shape as a Frankish-Roman difference, which mapped onto the Latin-Greek difference, even if there is no evidence that the latter was used for oppositional identification. Grounding this oppositional identification difference was, thus, until the ninth century, a muted theological debate on the *filioque*.

Examining the Eastern actors in the *filioque* dispute, Tia Kolbaba has recently demonstrated the extent to which Byzantine authors, sensing ethnic and political difference between themselves and the Latins, drew on the traditions of heresiology to mark the Latins as the heretical other—a distant but familiar enemy that was infected by evil and had to be countered in every way.[15] To be sure, Western protagonists were equally engaged in a process of exclusion and demonization. It is well beyond our purpose to attempt to adjudicate the ninth-century dispute, but we can simply observe that international religious-political conflict in this period was intimately tied to a sophisticated and deeply invested program of identity formation that was simultaneously focused on both the formation and naming of an internal audience and also a concern with demonizing the other. Kolbaba also demonstrates in her essay included in this volume that many of same factors were in play in the tenth-century Byzantine condemnations of the Azymes.

It was the centuries-long experience of Western crusades in the East, however, that likely marked a permanent turning point in Eastern attitudes toward the West. Historians have argued for generations that the pillaging of Byzantium's financial and religious treasures between the eleventh and fourteenth centuries did far more than weaken the political viability of the Byzantine empire—it embedded a heretofore unprecedented animosity within the Eastern Christian consciousness against a collective "West."[16] It was in this period, in fact, that the ever-increasing polemical assault on Western theological "errors" (especially the papacy and the *filioque*) were creatively connected to the political and economic exploitation of Eastern populations by Western colonists.[17] The penetration of Latin "heresy" into the heart of Byzantine territory was perceived to be so calamitous that even Orthodox writers living beyond crusader-occupied lands began to insist that Orthodox Christians guard their "purity" by rejecting any sacramental interaction with Western Christians (e.g., receiving the Eucharist from a Latin priest, marrying a Frank, or asking a Frank to serve as a godparent).[18]

Even today, it is not uncommon to find modern Orthodox polemicists—interestingly, many of them Roman Catholic and Protestant converts to Eastern Orthodoxy—referring to the Fourth Crusade as though it were an act of religious violence that had been perpetuated against them personally. Indeed, the attachment that modern Orthodox Christians feel (or at least describe) with respect to the victimization by the Latins during the Fourth Crusade is fascinating due to the degree in which this attachment has become a marker for self-identity in the belief that they possess the true faith. For many, the East/West or Greek/Latin binary becomes one of Victim/Aggressor. An example of the importance of the Fourth Crusade to the Orthodox mindset is the apology given by Pope John Paul II in 2001 to Archbishop Christodoulos of Greece for the Crusades, to which Archbishop Christodoulos started to applaud. The apology occurred after the Archbishop read a list of thirteen offenses perpetrated by the Roman Catholic Church against Eastern Orthodox Christians, including, of course, the Fourth Crusade.

While some scholars are beginning to revise previously exaggerated narratives by questioning the extent to which lay populations in the Greek-speaking provinces would have actually possessed the animosity against the Franks they are often said to have harbored, the state of Frankish-Greek Roman (Byzantine) relations during the Crusader era still lacks a theoretically informed analysis.[19] For example, no one has yet explored in detail the extent to which the Byzantine empire effectively underwent a period of colonization at the hands of the Franks and Venetians in the period between the eleventh and the fifteenth centuries. Byzantine writings need to be scrutinized from this period to assess whether or not the experience of Latin-Frankish-Western hegemony (political, economic, and religious) left traces of cultural ambivalences, antagonisms, and hybridities similar to those that can be found among populations (Orthodox or not) that have more recently experienced colonial oppression.

There is little doubt, for example, that Venetian and Frankish settlers brought Western-style political and religious practices with them. It is also clear that these colonists and their traditions remained prominently in place even after Byzantine armies reclaimed lost territories. While the spread of Western political, economic, and religious practices in the East have been traced by others, no one has yet explored the ways in which the Byzantines developed ambivalences toward, and may have subtly resisted the imposition of, cultural and religious colonialism that coincided with Venetian and Frankish outposts in Byzantine lands. Nor, conversely, has anyone really explored the ways in which the experience of colonizing and subjugating a Christian other may have disrupted the religious convictions and/or sensibilities of the Latin Crusaders.[20]

The sharp ambivalence among Byzantine intellectuals for Scholastic authors, as pointed out in Marcus Plested's essay, offers an excellent case in point. Why is it, for example, that certain late Byzantine thinkers (in some cases men regarded as bastions of Orthodox purity[21]) offered such glowing praise for Scholastic authors but decried certain Scholastic methods, such as the use of philosophical syllogism? Certainly the answer cannot be that Aristotelian-styled syllogisms are incompatible with Eastern Christian theological reflection—the model is repeatedly employed by the Cappadocian Fathers and John Damascene, to name only the most obvious examples. Rather, it would seem, the emphasis on syllogism and the explicit appeal to pre-Christian authors (such as Aristotle) that was current in Latin theology during the fourteenth and fifteenth centuries offered tangible markers of theological difference and, thus, became a means for narrating both what one should and should not do in the process of theological reflection.[22]

The utter reliance of the Byzantines upon Frankish armies and Venetian merchants in the final decades of the empire likewise produced a significant ambivalence in Eastern attitudes toward the West. On the one hand, the Franks and Venetians were the religious other—the heretic, the papist.[23] In the early generations of Crusader and Venetian colonization of Byzantium, Western cultural and religious customs rarely drew opposition from the indigenous, lay population. But this peaceful coexistence began to fracture when monks arrived in the years after 1204 with the task of subordinating the Eastern Church to the papacy. That shift in Latin policy was soon exploited by the exiled Byzantine elite who used Orthodox identity as a vehicle to advance their own political and economic aims.[24] Eventually the combination of growing lay resentment (fueled, no doubt by the introduction of ecclesiastical tithing) and Orthodox activism on the part of the elite led the average Byzantine Christian to recognize that he was subject to a foreign regime, one that was both political and religious. Michael Angold observes that it was the Constantinopolitan elite in exile who were the first to beat the drum of Orthodox unity, linking the Greek faith to a form of Byzantine "nationalism." According to Angold, this elite faction had the most to lose with the partitioning of the empire, and so they assumed the role of the defenders of Orthodoxy as a way to retain their political viability.[25]

At the same time, Western merchants, intellectuals, and armies had been in Byzantium for centuries, and without their support, there was no possible hope of preventing the Ottoman advance. Perhaps it was for this reason—the disgrace of relying upon a castigated and heretical other—that the late Byzantines are sometimes characterized as preferring the "sword of the sultan to the miter of the pope." The dependence of Eastern Christians upon the Western "Other" did not cease with the fall of Constantinople in 1453. If anything, it increased in both scope and complexity, as did Orthodox Christian ambivalence toward the West.

Ottoman "Captivity" and the Reliance upon the West

During the nearly four hundred years of Ottoman occupation of former Byzantine and Slavic Orthodox lands, the Christian East suffered a prolonged intellectual and economic decline. In large part, this was due to the oppressive policies directed at Christian communities by the Ottoman empire. Those policies included the suppression of Christian printing, the imposition of a Christian tax, and the closure of Christian schools. The Ottoman occupation of the Byzantine and Slavic territories magnified the well-established and deepening divide between Western and Eastern Christians. As Norman Russell indicates in his essay, the Ottomans often gave control of the Christian Holy Land sites in Jerusalem according to whatever served their political and economic interests: In 1675, the Church of the Nativity was in the hands of the Greeks; by 1690, it was in the hands of the Franciscans due to Ottoman need for French support against the Austrians. In short, East/West Christian divisions allowed the Ottomans to play the Christians against each other.

The Ottoman prohibition of printing by Christians within its territories also served to magnify the growing divide between Western and Eastern Christians. As Russell demonstrates, books printed in non-Ottoman-occupied territories were specifically written in order to "convert" the Greek and Slavic Christians to an allegiance to the Pope—i.e., to the form of Christianity that is today called Roman Catholicism. One book in particular, the *Targa*, was written in the seventeenth century in Greek by a French Jesuit, François Richard, against the Greek "schismatics." Such books provoked fear in the Christians of the Ottoman occupied territories, a fear that was exacerbated by the memory of the conversion of Eastern Christians to the Roman faith (a conversion that was largely enabled through the creation of an Eastern-styled liturgical rite). Given the aggressive proselytism that occurred during this period, by Jesuit missionaries in particular, one could understand Patriarch Dositheus of Jerusalem's persistence in establishing a printing press in Moldavia, a territory with autonomy within the Ottoman empire. Added to the memory of the Crusade was now the memory of Roman proselytism, which would only fuel the anti-Western rhetoric within the East. But it is precisely because those memories are so important for the Orthodox self-narrative that Robert Taft's contribution to this volume is so valuable, since he reminds us that the "crimes" of the past were in no way one-sided.

The Orthodox attitude to the West, however, was not all negative. As in the late-Byzantine period, during the Ottoman occupation there were elites who were extremely sympathetic to all that was Western. Eastern Christians would continue to make appeals to the West for assistance. Until 1600, nearly all Orthodox theological and liturgical printing took place in Western print shops, mostly in Italy. Even after printing was established in Russia, the vast majority of Greek texts continued to be produced in territories that were not traditionally Orthodox. Perhaps even more significant, Christian clerics within the Ottoman zone who received formalized theological education in this period did so as resident aliens in Western seminaries. The impact that this situation had upon the Eastern Christian intellectual tradition has not been sufficiently examined. To be sure, this interaction produced a variety of easily discernable and anecdotal responses (ranging from cooperative to hostile), but even more significant and difficult to untangle is the great number of complex ambivalences toward the West that can be traced to Orthodox authors who remained under Ottoman control in this period.[26]

What is more, the consequences of the Orthodox reliance on the West during the Ottoman occupation did not end with the wars of independence in the nineteenth century. By the time of these independent movements, a growing elite within the Ottoman territories were being influenced by liberal political philosophy of the Enlightenment, and the American and French revolutions, in calling for a restricted influence of Orthodox Christianity in the newly emerging nations of Greece, Romania, Serbia, and Bulgaria. For many of these elites, religion was useful only insofar as it solidified a national identity. The idea of the West would now be expanded beyond its Christian referents—Roman Catholic and Protestant—and include Western, secular political and philosophical thought, which would come to shape post-Ottoman life for Orthodox Christians.

In political terms, one could also view the "independence movements" in Greece and the Balkans as the exchanging of one foreign sovereign for another. Indeed, many of these movements, however popular they may have been, were in many ways orchestrated by Western European colonial figures who were eager to spread Western influence into the Balkans and beyond. Their efforts were facilitated by Orthodox elites who were often just as eager to Westernize the newly formed Orthodox nations. The kings of Greece, Romania, and elsewhere were in fact drawn from the royal courts of Germany and reflected a form of proxy colonization by the Western European powers. The Westernization of Orthodoxy was visibly evident in both liturgical art and music of this period. Thus, the story of Western colonization of the nineteenth and twentieth centuries must be expanded to include the once-Ottoman-colonized eastern European countries. The Orthodox postcolonial story includes both the Ottomans and the Western European empires who would come to occupy most of the tricontinental area.

It remains one of the great paradoxes of modern Orthodoxy that a faith with such universalist theological claims could have its ecclesiastical structure fracture so severely along political and ethnic lines in the past century and a half. To be sure, the division of episcopal jurisdictions has, since antiquity, mirrored the borders of secular provincial governance. But whereas the political boundaries within the Roman and Byzantine provincial system were based primarily upon economic and military considerations (not linguistic or religious associations), the modern splintering of Orthodox Christianity into national churches is quite unlike its ancient, medieval or early-modern precedents. The origins of the ethnic division, of course, can be traced to the Ottoman millet system, as well as the emergence and cementing of national imaginations across Europe and the Balkans during the nineteenth century.[27] Orthodox scholars are only now coming to terms with the reality of national churches (and rarely with the same conclusions!). To be sure, the formation of Serbian or Bulgarian or Russian or Ukrainian Orthodox identity had a great deal to do with the construction of sameness and otherness as it relates to the most proximate of neighbors (in other words, Orthodox communities differentiating themselves from one another). It often goes unnoticed by the Orthodox that the very idea of "nation" is itself a Western construct of imagination that was imposed on formerly occupied Ottoman territories so as to better integrate Eastern Europe into Western Europe. Orthodoxy and national identity have become so fused in the Orthodox imagination that a philosophy professor from the University of Athens who is a self-admitted atheist is identified as Orthodox; that an American Orthodox visiting Greece was once asked by an uncle if they shared the same religion. The nationalist identity, which, again, in the modern Orthodox imagination, is inseparable from the religious identity, is now the primary lens through which Orthodox view one another.

This nationalist lens becomes especially evident when considering the Orthodox diaspora—Orthodox immigrants from the traditional Orthodox countries who immigrated either to Western Europe, North America, or Australia (i.e., non-Orthodox territories). Institutionally, these jurisdictions are divided along nationalistic borders, in clear violations of Orthodox principles of ecclesiology, which, basically, demand that all Orthodox within a given geographical region be united in one jurisdiction. The very

Western notion of nationalism is currently structuring, ironically, Orthodox attitudes toward the Western diaspora. At the same time, some Orthodox in traditional Orthodox territories are increasingly labeling the Orthodox in the diaspora as "Western Orthodox," especially when the Orthodox in the diaspora espouse views that promote seemingly Western values, such as nonprivileging, unconditional religious pluralism. The category of West in such a labeling is often used to demonize and dismiss an Orthodox voice that could potentially disrupt more traditional Orthodox understandings of something like church-state relations.

The Emergence of Russian Ecclesiastical Identity vis-à-vis the West

Beginning in the sixteenth century, religious authorities in Russia began to envisage the See of Moscow as a "Third Rome,"—the center of a final incarnation of the Christian empire. While scholars have increasingly called into question the extent to which this concept was widespread in early-modern Russia, one of the more interesting features of the initial sixteenth-century claim is the implicit role of Western influence in the transferal of "Roman" status from Constantinople to Moscow.[28] In other words, to the extent that the See of Moscow's claim is an ecclesiastical one and not a political one, Moscow's usurpation of Constantinopolitan privilege is predicated upon the purity of Muscovite adherence to the traditions of Orthodox Christianity by contrasting it with the late-Byzantine capitulation to Latin theological positions at the controversial Council of Florence in 1438–39 and final years of the empire.[29] There is little denying the fact that the monk Filofei (the person typically credited with the first Third-Rome proclamation) believed that the Latins were heretics and that the late Byzantines, save Mark of Ephesus, had committed apostasy.[30] Indeed, one of the most frequent claims of post-1453 Orthodox narratives (Russian or otherwise) was that the collapse of Byzantium had been a punishment from God because the Greeks had abandoned the Orthodox truth and conspired with heretics.[31] In such a narrative, anyone who could be painted with the brush of Latin collaboration was tarnished; only those who remained true to the faith were authentically Orthodox. Given these factors, embedded in the Third-Rome claim is an anti-Western dimension, both in its initial iteration in the sixteenth century as well as in its active promotion in the nineteenth century.

Of course, many early-modern Russian rulers were pro-Western. Students of early-modern European history are familiar with the vigorous attempts of Peter I (1672–1725) and Catherine II (1729–96) to modernize Russia according to Western standards. Among their initiatives, perhaps the most significant for our purposes was the creation of an educational system that was modeled upon Western academies.[32] These educational reforms, in fact, introduced the first unified seminary system in the Orthodox world. In part, because Peter's and Catherine's priority was to train an elite bureaucratic core (rather than an educated priesthood) and, in part, because they saw the seminary program as a means to further other pro-Western agendas, these schools adopted a decidedly Western curriculum, which replaced the traditional Orthodox canon with scholastic and enlightenment authors.[33] By 1700, Latin replaced Old Slavonic and Greek as the intellectual languages of Russia and the most respected of the theological academies, Kiev, Moscow, St. Petersburg, and Kazan, taught in Latin rather than Russian for much of the eighteenth century.[34] While it would not be possible to attempt to quantify the impact of these educational reforms for the subsequent Russian theological tradition in the present essay, it is certain that the Latinizing and pro-Western push by Peter and Catherine fueled the nineteenth century's reactionary movement in Russia against the West and, especially, the Western Christian traditions.

Indeed, the pro-Western policies of the state were resisted in many quarters, including the Church where alternative models stressed the ascetic/monastic dimension of Eastern Christianity and promoted a return to "authentic" Orthodox textual sources. As the papers in this volume by Paul Gavrilyuk and Vera Shevzov note, a more extreme version of the anti-Westernization afoot in Russia was the so-called Slavophile movement, which interpreted the theology and cultural ethos of the West as fundamentally flawed and alien to Orthodox truth. It was in this context and from this perspective, for example, that St. Augustine of Hippo was first condemned unilaterally by Eastern authors, who saw in him Western Christianity's unmistakable slide into heresy.[35] Although the Slavophile movement did not dominate the Russian theological outlook, it did provide an important trajectory within the Russian intellectual tradition, especially as it pertained to the issues of religious self-identity vis-à-vis the West.

Slavophilism, however, was not the only trajectory within nineteenth-century Russia. An alternative intellectual current was flowing in which

"Western" philosophy was not slavishly imitated nor was it unilaterally condemned. The iconic figure of this current is Vladimir Soloviev, in whose thought one can trace clear influences of a variety of Western sources, especially German Idealism. Soloviev was the father of a movement known as sophiology, which reached its theological apex in the work of Russian Orthodox theologian Sergius Bulgakov. It is common to refer to the thinkers associated with sophiology as Russian religious thinkers, and not as theologians.[36] This label is given, in part, because the sophiological thinkers are thought to have unjustifiably mixed the Orthodox theological tradition with Western philosophical influences. Such a designation does not do justice to the fact that there were a great variety of positions within Russian sophiology. It is particularly inaccurate when applied to Bulgakov, who can be interpreted as offering the first "neo-patristic synthesis" well before Georges Florovsky coined the phrase. The dismissal of the Russian sophiological tradition, in particular the Orthodox theology of Bulgakov, is clearly grounded in an anti-Western sentiment that came to view any association with philosophy as a betrayal of the purity of thought of the Greek patristic authors.

The most visible representative of the contemporary Orthodox theological antipathy to Western philosophy and reason is Vladimir Lossky (1903–58). Lossky cannot be identified with the form of extreme anti-Westernism that characterized many of his theological disciples, especially John Romanides and Christos Yannaras. He did, however, delineate a clear theological dividing line between the East and the West. The criterion for the point of demarcation had to do with the role of reason in theology. For Lossky, the West, by which he meant modern neo-Scholasticism, subjected the truths of dogma to external, philosophical criteria of justification. In addition to subjecting the revelation of the living God to human reason, a philosophically justified theology reduces knowledge of God to propositional truths rather than an encounter of mystical union. Theology understood in terms of knowledge as mystical union must necessarily be apophatic, since its role is simply to express the truth of the revelation of divine-human communion in Christ in antinomic expressions that would guide the ascetical struggle toward an experience of *theosis*. The other hallmark of Lossky's theology is the essence/energies distinction, which, he argues, is the antinomic way of expressing divine-human communion, and which he uses to base his attack against the Neo-Scholastics. As Sarah Coakley rightly indicates in her essay, Lossky presents a certain diametrical opposition between West and East in terms of method in theology, and, yet, he does so in Paris in the midst of a patristic revival occurring among Lossky's Catholic counterparts, many of whom he knew well and considered as friends. Lossky and the *ressourcement* theologians shared a common enemy—neo-Scholasticism.

What Vladimir Lossky shares with all the notable Orthodox theologians of the twentieth century—Sergius Bulgakov, Georges Florovsky, Dumitru Staniloae, Kallistos Ware, and John Zizioulas—is a tendency to identify a particular error in the West, which encompasses both Protestant and Catholic Christianities. Of interest is the fact that although the West encompasses both Protestants and Catholics, the errors of the West are usually targeted against Roman Catholics, though there are occasional references to Protestant theology. For Vladimir Lossky, the error is the introduction of rationalism into theology; for John Zizioulas, it is attempting to understand the doctrine of the Trinity within the framework of a metaphysics of substance; and, as Radu Bordieanu notes in his essay, for Staniloae it is the severing of experience from academic theology. All these Orthodox theologians share a consensus on the principle of divine-human communion in Orthodox theology. Based on this principle, one could summarize their criticism of the West, including both Protestant and Roman Catholic theologies, as a failure to ground theology in the ecclesial experience of union with God, whether that be the mystical union of the ascetic or the Eucharistic experience in the Body of Christ. Thus, these particular theologians share a self-identification of Orthodoxy against the West, but it would be difficult to accuse them of constructing an anti-Westernism, such as it is clearly evinced in the work of John Romanides and Christos Yannaras.

Both John Romanides and Christos Yannaras construct an anti-Westernism that diametrically opposes West and East in term of ethos. Both do so by extending Lossky's critique of neo-Scholasticism and extending it to Augustine. The basic mistake of the West, including both Protestants and Roman Catholics, is that it rejected salvation as *theosis* in favor of a more legalistic, merit-based understanding of salvation. Augustine sets the stage for the history of Western civilization by attempting to justify the ecclesial experience in terms of a metaphysics of substance, thus leading to the disastrous notion (according to them) of created grace. With the conquest of once-held Byzantine territories in the West by the Franks, this theological notion took shape in cultural and political forms, expanding

the difference between West and East such that it came to apply not simply to theological disagreements, but to the level of civilizations.[37] As Pantelis Kalaitzidis makes clear, the West for Yannaras is the whole of Western
European civilization, whose worldview was shaped by Augustine—a
thinker who fundamentally rejected the Greek patristic notion of *theosis*.[38]
Basilio Petrà illuminates how Yannaras's approach to the West became focused on what Yannaras coins as θρησκειοποίηση, "religionization." It is
clear, however, that what Yannaras means by this term is a mode of practicing religion that is distinct from the Orthodox ethos, which lives the relationship with God as experience. In a perversion of the apophatic tradition,
Orthodox Christianity during the twentieth century was increasingly
being defined, to varying degrees, by what the West was not. It is noteworthy that all contemporary Orthodox theologians, with the exception
of Staniloae, spent a great deal of their professional lives in the West, either living in the West, being trained in Western universities, or teaching
in Western universities. The paradoxical, if not ironic, location of self and
otherness for these authors illuminates the intricacy of naming Orthodox
identity in the twentieth century.

The "New" West

The Ottoman occupation of most of the traditional Orthodox territories
prevented the Orthodox from being forced to respond to the political
philosophical thought that emerged in Western Europe since the Enlightenment. When the goal is survival, there does not exist much luxury for
confronting questions of political theology. This situation, however, would
change in eighteenth-century Russia, when the reforms of Peter I and
Catherine II would create an open portal for the influx of Western philosophical thought. Vladimir Soloviev and Sergius Bulgakov, in particular,
would engage questions of political theology from the perspective of the
principle of divine-human communion.[39] The Soviet Communists were
more brutal to the Orthodox than the Ottomans, and they decimated
any sign of an Orthodox intellectual tradition within Russia. In perhaps
what remains as one of the greatest mysteries of twentieth-century Orthodox theology, virtually no Orthodox theologian, with the exception
of Christos Yannaras, wrote anything of substance on political theology.
Yannaras's own writings on the topic were characterized by his anti-
Westernism, criticizing the political structures in Greece as, essentially,

surrendering to the West and betraying its distinctive Byzantine-Hellenistic legacy.

Once the Iron Curtain fell, there was no escaping questions of political theology for the Orthodox. In traditional Orthodox territories, such as Russia, Romania, Serbia, Bulgaria, Georgia, and Armenia, the institutional churches found themselves with a freedom that proved as dizzying as it was liberating. Church-state relations had to be negotiated anew, and this time in the context of a West that had become fully democratized. The Orthodox churches had very few intellectual resources or models within their own tradition to confront the new political and cultural realities. What would emerge was an Orthodox ambivalence toward democracy: rhetoric that would support certain democratic principles, such as freedom of expression, freedom of conscience, and so on, but not at the expense of eclipsing what the institutional Orthodox churches argued was the privileging of the Orthodox Church, which was due to it as a result of Orthodoxy's role in the historic and cultural heritage.

As Elizabeth Prodromou's, Effie Fokas's, and Lucian Turcescu's essays indicate, at issue, ultimately, in the postcommunist period, and even in post-Ottoman Greece, is the public role of the Orthodox Church in the spaces that have been constructed into Orthodox nations. There is a general sense that something like democracy must function in traditional Orthodox nations; but there is also rhetoric that caustically criticizes the godlessness, permissiveness, extreme individualism, and immorality of Western secular societies.[40] This particular understanding of Western liberalism is especially evident in Russia, and it is often used to contrast the predominant vision of church-state relations promoted by the Russian Orthodox Church (ROC)—that is, a constitutional separation of church and state, together with a cooperation "to renew the nation's historic religious identity, which is primarily Orthodox."[41] Although constitutionally the church and state are separated, the Orthodox Church expects the Russian state to privilege it, arguing that Russian culture is inherently Orthodox. To promote and strengthen Russian cultural identity and values is simultaneously to strengthen its Orthodox foundations. Thus, although the ROC officially promotes religious pluralism and freedom of expression, it also argues that these rights cannot be practiced at the expense of the morality that is necessary for a civil society. As an example, freedom of artistic expression is fine so long as it does not blaspheme against Orthodox teachings. The ROC clearly walks a fine line here between

Western democracy and promoting a privileged public voice in the space of Russian civil society. In order to do so, it must contrast its own political vision with the godless secularism of Western liberalism, which ultimately has its foundations in heretical Protestant and Roman Catholic theologies. The "new" West is now the godless, secular liberal West, even if this West has its roots in the old, Christian West.

Postcolonial Critique as a Possible Way Forward

Given the complexity of the Eastern Christian experience and given the numerous challenges that face Eastern Christianity in the twenty-first century, we believe that it is paramount for Orthodox scholars to take a series of critical steps forward in their examination of their tradition and experience. Our hope is that the collection of papers in this volume evinces both the potential and the need for further interdisciplinary consideration. Taking a cue from the self-critical and interdisciplinary work represented in the current volume, we would like to propose more broadly that Eastern Orthodox scholars should be willing to engage and appropriate the theoretical resources provided by critical theory. Those resources are especially valuable for scholars seeking to disentangle the multi-layered, ambiguous, and ever-changing features of identity formation, religious or otherwise.

We believe that the particular sequence of historical circumstances that shapes the Orthodox present resonate in certain ways with postcolonial discourse and we would like to suggest that there is much to learn from bringing the Orthodox story into conversation with postcolonial analysis. As we will briefly describe, such an analysis illuminates the Eastern Christian constructions of self and other. What is more, bringing the Orthodox story to postcolonial studies can actually disrupt the dominant narrative of postcolonial critique of Christianity and its others.

Postcolonial critique has typically been employed to scrutinize and combat the residual effects of Western exploitation of the colonial subject, the "subaltern," in all of its cultural, political, and economic manifestations.[42] One debate within postcolonial studies has been the extent to which a subaltern community possesses the ability to speak for itself within the normative discourse of its colonizer.[43] Homi Bhabha's emphasis on "interstitial hybridity" and linguistic "negotiation" offers an especially useful framework for understanding both the inherent slippage between cultural forces that are brought into friction and dislocation by the colonial experience and the mechanisms of nonviolent subversive resistance that remain available to subaltern peoples.[44] For Bhabha, all cultural identities are hybrid, born from interstitial relationships, and marked by an unending reflexivity. Thus, from Bhabha's perspective, cultural purity is a mythical concept.[45]

With the writing of Edward Said, Homi Bhabha, and Gayatri Spivak in mind, one can quickly discern in certain Orthodox theological circles of the twentieth century a series of attitudes that reflect a search for and an attempted return to an authentic Orthodox identity in the post-Ottoman, post-Soviet world. As noted, it is mostly in this period (first in the Slavophile movement, followed by the Russian émigré scholars of Paris, and then in the theological academies of Greece), that we find sustained attempts to articulate the difference between Christian East and Christian West in a way that moves beyond the issue-specific polemics of the middle ages. Thus, for Romanides, Yannaras, and many others, the East/West divide was no longer to be narrated just in terms of specific dogmatic positions (concerning such theological controversies as *filioque* or papal authority), but, rather, in terms of a clash of civilizations—each with distinctive philosophical and cultural systems.[46] For these narrators, the purest form of Christianity had its origin in the Christianized Hellenism of antiquity.[47] Thus, we see a shift from the Byzantine theologians who had criticized their Western counterparts for specific dogmatic positions and to modern Orthodox theologians who began to differentiate themselves from the West in a new way—namely, through historicist and philosophical metanarratives. This turn to historical and philosophical explanations is, itself, proof positive that the modern Eastern intellectual tradition has been largely shaped by the Western Enlightenment: Not only is historicism, which is an Enlightenment creation, but the appeal to a past "golden age" smacks of nineteenth-century German Romanticism and Idealism.[48]

Rather than simply note the hypocrisy in the modern Orthodox attempts to self-identify vis-à-vis the West, however, we can employ postcolonial theory to understand how such ironic situations arise within a colonial context. In particular, Bhabha's concept of "mimicry" is illustrative.[49] For Bhabha, *mimicry* is intrinsic to all discourse between colonizer and colonized and is always, at least partially, disruptive of colonial rule.[50] What is so tantalizing about the possibility of bringing Bhabha's thesis of mimicry into conversation with the work of Lossky, Florovsky, Yannaras, Romanides, and others is the ironic ways in which these authors seemingly operate within the philosophical system and employ academic tools of the Western intellectual tradition for the very purpose of narrating an Eastern Christianity that was inherently free of Western pollution.[51]

Postcolonial critique, of course, could be useful for Orthodox scholars in many ways beyond simply helping them to decipher the identity constructions of self and other. For example, Dipesh Chakrabarty's provocative insights offer many possibilities for fruitful collaborative thinking. In particular, Chakrabarty's argument that colonial rule includes an insidious imposition of European models of "rational" might provide a set of tools for reflection for Orthodox intellectuals who have, historically, been more reluctant than their Western counterparts to embrace the universal or totalizing qualities of postlapsarian reason.[52] Equally promising is the possibility of following Chakrabarty's inclination to reject the European notion that religious practice can be subjected to scientific study. While Chakrabarty is certainly not the first scholar to caution about the difficulties associated with narrating religious, *nonrational*, beliefs, his insistence that reason is culturally and historically situated helps those of us who study the religious practices of premodern Christianity, especially if the foci of our studies are those expressions of premodern Christianity on the margins, or those that challenged normative theological traditions. Given that so many Orthodox scholars operate within the conceptual framework of Western European historicism, it would seem that Chakrabarty challenges us to rethink the "scientific" way that we describe the religious beliefs and practices of early Christians, Orthodox or otherwise.

What is more, the insights and experience of Eastern Christianity have the potential to disrupt the normative narrative of Christianity and its others that one finds in most postcolonial studies of Christianity. And while this is not the occasion to explore those avenues in detail, we will at least identify a few possibilities for future research.

The most obvious way that the Eastern Christian experience upends postcolonial studies is that most postcolonial analysis related to Christianity explores the impact of Christianity as a colonizing force.[53] In theological circles, postcolonial critique has typically sought to examine the ways that pre-Christian cultural considerations can disrupt, but ultimately supplement, the dominant Christian narratives.[54] But as we have already noted, Byzantine Christianity was colonized by the Franks and Venetians as early as the eleventh century. Latin outposts in the East lasted for centuries and their impact on Eastern Christianity can be discerned by the discriminating scholar to this day. What is more, during the four-hundred-year Ottoman suppression of Christianity, Orthodox Christians experienced a different form of colonization (what one might identify as "shadow colonization") through the utter reliance on a foreign and alien Christian host for the sustaining of Orthodox Christianity under Muslim domination. These experiences do far more than offer a wrinkle to the dominant understanding of Christianity as the colonizer; rather, they fundamentally challenge the presumption (championed by Robert Young and others) that colonization is primarily a modern phenomenon born in the age of European exploration.[55]

While some Orthodox scholars might be reluctant to embrace postcolonial critique simply because some of its most committed advocates would resist the truth claims of Christianity, we believe that its theoretical insights should be viewed as an opportunity for, rather than a threat to, Christian theological reflection. In general, this is because postcolonial critique, like critical theory more broadly, enables Christian theologians and historians to be more methodologically self-conscious (and honest) in their endeavor to interpret the theological thinking and records of the past. More specifically, and with respect to the questions and concerns raised in the present volume, we believe that postcolonial critique offers a unique set of intellectual resources for understanding the truly complex and inevitably ambiguous conditions that gave rise to Orthodox constructions of the West. In the end, our method, intention, and aim is to avoid an idolatrous faith based on negative projections of what is other than Orthodox. Such projections are typically about what we wish God to be rather than who God is. We consider the use of postcolonial theory as a resource for self-critique of Orthodox attitudes toward the West in the spirit of an ascetic-like noetic discipline wherein the goal is to clear a path toward communion with the living God, not the god of our projections.

The Conference and Volume

The essays collected in this volume represent an ecumenical and interdisciplinary engagement with the numerous cultural, historical, political, and theological factors that have come to comprise the multiple and often ambivalent contours of "Eastern" Christian attitudes towards an ambiguous, multiform, and ever-changing "West." As the title of the original conference and the present volume, *Orthodox Constructions of the West* was intentionally chosen to provoke our contributors and our readers into thinking critically about the very basis of identity construction for the religious self and its others with the full realization of the elusiveness and ambiguity of such an endeavor. We hope that the essays provided here will inspire further reflection and constructive ecumenical engagement.

PERCEPTIONS AND REALITIES IN ORTHODOX-CATHOLIC RELATIONS TODAY: REFLECTIONS ON THE PAST, PROSPECTS FOR THE FUTURE

Robert F. Taft, S.J.

Praenotanda

On the feast of St. Andrew, November 30, 2000, His All-Holiness Ecumenical Patriarch Bartholomew I said after Divine Liturgy at the Cathedral of St. George in the Phanar: "Revisiting the past and examining human faults must continue in all directions . . . because whoever consents to the misdeeds of another or tolerates them by his silence, shares the responsibility of their author."[1] In the same vein, in an extraordinary assembly on December 8–10, 1993, the Serbian Orthodox hierarchy formulated the following principle: "On this earth there is not nor can there be any true peace among men and nations without complete justice and the whole truth. The future cannot be built on lies and injustice."[2] It is in the same spirit of these authoritative Orthodox declarations that I shall express today my views on my own Catholic Church and on the Churches of the Orthodox tradition.

I have on more than one occasion made clear in print positions I am happy to repeat here: that I consider the Orthodox Churches the historic apostolic Christianity of the East and sister churches of the Catholic Church;[3] that I recognize and rejoice in the fact that Orthodox peoples remain Orthodox; the Catholic Church should support and collaborate with the Orthodox Churches in every way, foster the most cordial relations with them, earnestly work to restore communion with them, recognize their legitimate interests especially on their home ground, avoid all proselytism among their flocks there or elsewhere, not seek in any way to undercut them, nor rejoice in or exploit their weaknesses, nor fish in their pond, nor seek to convert their faithful to the Catholic Church. But I espouse with equal explicitness the view that it is counterproductive for the cause of Christian unity and ecumenism to roll over and play dead in the face of any Catholic or Orthodox misbehavior, misinformation, or outright lying with regard to our dolorous past or to problems that exist between us in the present.[4]

On these issues I speak from a lifetime of personal experience and proven love for Orthodoxy and its tradition, as clearly demonstrated by over half a century of study, scholarship, and innumerable publications, both scholarly and popular. On that basis I view our present relationship with mixed emotions of encouragement and disillusionment: encouragement that the Catholic-Orthodox International Ecumenical Dialogue is back on track under competent and vigorous leadership on both sides; disillusionment at our failure to bring this progress to the grass-roots level among our people, where in some places bigotry and fanaticism still reign, and, more seriously for those of us in academia, at our inability to face our difficult past with objective scholarship instead of confessional propaganda masquerading as history.

The Catholic Church, the Jesuits, and the Christian East: Perceptions

Since charity begins at home and I am a Jesuit, let me begin by examining our Catholic and Jesuit conscience, an exercise necessary because collective religious institutions like churches and religious orders have the tendency to indulge in hagiographic glorification of their own history: while they admit that individual members may be sinners, the collectivity itself is supposedly above reproach. Furthermore, a seminal aspect of the Jesuit vocation and spirituality—our "way of proceeding," as we call it—is discernment: Jesuits don't just *do* things; they also *reflect* on what they do, have done, and are going to do.

The Orthodox East views the Catholic Church and its Jesuits with deep suspicion and distrust. I cite one paradigmatic example from an article by an American-Russian Orthodox priest, Fr. David F. Abramtsov:

The Papal Eastern Rite is an invention of the Roman Curia, a creation for the purpose of deceit, subterfuge for immutable beliefs, unchanging dogmas. One enters a Uniate Church—here are the same icons, the same banners, the same vestments, the same tongue and singing, the very same services, and often the same Creed without the *filioque*. If an Orthodox émigré colony in utter destitution is found to have been cast on the cruel waves of life by a catastrophic war, one may be positive that nearby is an Eastern rite Roman Jesuit, sporting a beard and speaking the mother tongue of these unfortunates, innocently helping to educate Orthodox children (in the doctrines of the Roman faith). It would seem that nothing is changed in the Uniate "Byzantine rite" Churches. The people simply agree to commemorate the Bishop of Rome, and are lulled and soothed by the thought that the whole familiar aspect of Church life has remained unchanged.[5]

Realities

Whether or not this description is fair should not distract us from our purpose here. As Nietzsche liked to say, "There are no facts—only perceptions," by which he did not mean to deny objective reality, but only to emphasize that things exist for us only as we perceive them. The legitimacy of perceptions, however, can be ascertained only by a square look at reality. What that reality shows is the relentless proselytizing of Catholic missionaries, especially Jesuits, among Eastern Christians at a time when they had their backs to the wall, subjected to Western imperialism and/or non-Christian or non-Orthodox governments in the Ottoman Empire, India, and the Polish-Lithuanian Commonwealth. This has left a legacy of bitterness still felt today.[6]

The Catholic Church inserted itself dramatically into the life of the Christian East on two occasions: first during the Crusades and then, especially, in the sixteenth- and seventeenth-century "Age of Discovery," when it established parallel church structures in lands of already existing apostolic Christianity and created problems that exist to this day. In so doing, the Catholic Church was true to its evolving, exclusivist ecclesiology in which there was but one valid Christendom, its own, entirely under the sway of the Bishop of Rome, who thought he could use his minions to do almost anything he pleased. Can one wonder that the hierarchies of age-old apostolic Eastern Churches in places like India were more than bewildered by this sudden, uninvited intrusion into the life of their churches by a group of educated, dynamic, and foreign priests perfectly suited for the task by Jesuit founder St. Ignatius of Loyola's universalist and papalist ecclesiology, claiming to owe obedience not to the local hierarchy but to a foreign "universal bishop" thousands of miles away?[7] This invasion—in reality, if not in intention, little more than imperialism on the ecclesial level—could not but spell trouble.[8] Two paradigmatic vignettes suffice to illustrate this:

Ethiopia

Jesuit involvement with the Christian East goes right back to their founder, St. Ignatius of Loyola. In the sixteenth- and seventeenth-century "Age of Discovery," when gentlemen-explorers from Portugal and Spain spent their time discovering America and colonizing the rest of the world, Portuguese adventurer Peres de Covilham came into contact with what he thought was the mythical priest-king Prester John in the person of the Negus of Abyssinia. That legendary African potentate, who had not the slightest interest in contacting anybody, promptly interned de Covilham for life, though he had the courtesy to provide him with a wife.

Eventually, contact with the Negus was made again, and after a certain amount of skirmishing and feinting, relations were established and the Ethiopians, adherents of an ancient, pre-Chalcedonian Oriental Orthodox Church, even hinted at possible ecclesiastical union. That is how the Jesuits got into the act. On December 22, 1553, St. Ignatius's faithful Jesuit secretary Polanco[9] wrote that King John of Portugal "has this month urgently requested our Father Ignatius to nominate twelve of the Society, including a patriarch, for the lands of Prester John."[10]

After much consultation and searching about, not as much for the right men as for anyone who could be freed up for the job in those busy days, Ignatius of Loyola, a mere presbyter of the Roman Church, chose a Portuguese Jesuit as patriarch for hapless Ethiopia. On January 24, 1554, Pope Julius III confirmed the nomination of Father John Nuñez Barreto, S.J., a Portuguese nobleman, as first Catholic patriarch of Ethiopia. From today's perspective, the absurdity of the undertaking is simply breathtaking, as if President George Bush Senior had authorized Billy Graham to choose some American Baptist preacher to head the ancient, apostolic Assyrian Church of Iraq once things were cleaned up after the First Gulf War!

Fortified with instructions from his presbyter-superior, St. Ignatius, the fledgling patriarch and his coadjutor bishop, the Spanish Jesuit Andrew d'Oviedo, set sail for Ethiopia. What sort of ecclesiology puts a mere priest as boss of a patriarch still escapes me. Be that as it may, Patriarch Barreto died at Goa in 1561, but Oviedo, who succeeded him on the patriarchal throne, eventually reached Ethiopia, where Jesuits continued to labor heroically for three-quarters of a century until they got themselves kicked out.

The trouble began under the Negus Susneyios, who had already embraced Catholicism privately. At the Negus's behest, the Holy See named Jesuit Alfonso Mendez patriarch. Mendez arrived in Ethiopia in 1625, the next year the union of the Ethiopian Church with Rome was proclaimed, and the Jesuits proceeded to make the same mistakes their confrères were busily engaged in making on the Malabar coast of Southwest India. The Gregorian calendar and Latin fasts and abstinences were imposed by force of arms. Mendez even wanted to impose the Roman liturgy translated into Ge'ez. Inevitably, the people revolted, the Jesuits were expelled in 1636, and Ethiopia was closed to the Catholic Church for two hundred years.

India

Things were not much different in Malabar on the Fishery Coast of southwest India under the Portuguese "Padroãdo." In 1599, the Latins co-opted the hierarchical structure of this ancient native church and Jesuit Francis Roz became the first Latin prelate of the Syrians that same year. Portuguese archbishops of Angamali-Cranganore, all Jesuits, governed thereafter the once independent Syro-Malabar Church that had flourished in those parts for a millennium before anyone had ever heard of the Society of Jesus. The chauvinistic Jesuit missionaries allowed only Jesuits to work in Malabar, with predictable results. On January 3, 1653, the exasperated people revolted. Gathering at the cross before the church at Mattancherry, they took a solemn oath no longer to recognize the archbishop at Cranganore, and to drive out their Jesuit oppressors.

When I was a young Jesuit, our mythology gave pride of place to what we called the presuppression "Old Society,"[11] and we took justifiable pride in the remarkable cultural openness and inculturation of our famed missionaries of the sixteenth and seventeenth centuries, like Matteo Ricci and Michele Ruggieri in China, Roberto de Nobili among the

Tamils of Madurai in southeast India, Alessandro Valignano in India and Japan, all Italians. But not all Jesuit missionaries were un-chauvinistic Italians open to other cultures, so what I did was tell the other half of the story.

Uniatism

Then there is the phenomenon known today as "Uniatism,"[12] judged to be the major problem blocking fruitful dialogue and communion with the Orthodox Churches.[13] Uniatism is a pejorative term for a method of church union perceived to be politically rather than religiously motivated, and contrary to the communion ecclesiology of the Church of the first millennium.[14] In Uniatism, one church is seen as an aggressor against another church with which it is not in communion, absorbing groups of its faithful deceptively by allowing them to retain their own rite and a certain autonomy.

Today we realize that such partial reunions remove the whole ecumenical problem from its proper context. The separation between our churches resulted between the hierarchies of East and West over ecclesial questions like the primacy of Rome, and it is up to those hierarchies together, and not individuals or splinter groups of bishops, to solve these common problems. Partial reunions only divide the Eastern Churches and are seen as deceiving the simple faithful, who follow their bishops in good faith with little understanding of the issues involved. No realistic Catholic approach to the Christian East can fail to take this into account.

The Effect of Uniatism on Orthodox-Catholic Relations

Until Catholic aggression towards Greek Orthodoxy began to manifest itself in the eighteenth century, relations between our two churches were remarkably cordial in areas where Greek Orthodox and Catholic communities lived side by side. "Long after the anathemas of 1054, the sack of Constantinople in 1204, and the formal repudiation of the union of Florence in 1484, Greeks and Latins continued in practice quietly to ignore the separation and to behave as if no breach in communion had occurred. . . . Instances of *communicatio in sacris* are especially abundant in the seventeenth century,"[15] when we find that Greek Orthodox bishops invited Jesuits to catechize and preach to their people and hear their confessions, and Catholics and Orthodox participated in each other's religious festivities and services and engaged in "every sort of *communicatio in divinis*."[16]

Relations later deteriorated when Catholics attempted to foist Uniatism upon the Greeks, to say nothing of other absurdities one is embarrassed even to mention.[17] For instance, in the fallout from World War I when plans to partition Ottoman territories, including Russian designs on Constantinople and the Straits, were afoot in 1915–20 before the final settlement in the Treaty of Versailles (July 24, 1923), Vatican authorities made the madcap proposal that, because Hagia Sophia in Constantinople, the most hallowed shrine of Byzantine Orthodoxy, was built before the schism of 1054, and the Greeks were still in communion with Rome when Constantinople fell to the Turks in 1453, Hagia Sophia can be considered a "Catholic Church" and should therefore be put in Catholic hands![18]

Learning to Cope with the Problem of Uniatism

How are we to cope with the problem of Uniatism, which has become especially acute since the restoration of religious freedom in the Soviet bloc at the end of the 1980s? Only the re-establishment of communion between the Catholic and Orthodox Churches will solve our problems satisfactorily. But if, in the meantime, solutions remain provisional, interim answers to the pastoral and ecumenical problems posed by the existence of Eastern Catholic Churches must be sought with charity, objectivity, and realism. Both Catholics and Orthodox must reach the point where they can view and discuss not only Uniatism's origins, but also its past and present history—*all of it*. They must do so without gliding over the problematic nature—in some (though by no means all) instances—of its origins, its ultimate development, and its ideology, but also without the use of selective memory, double standard, and even outright slander with which Orthodox writings sometimes treat it.

Prospects for the Future: "The Healing of Memories"

What must be done to solve such problems that still divide us? I have begun with an indictment of Catholics, which is only fair, since Matthew 7:3–5 tells us to take the log out of our own eye before poking at the specks in our brother's eye. That being said, it is neither unfair nor illegitimate to put Orthodox as well as Catholics on the wish list of what must be done to resolve our common problems.

In this context, it has become customary to speak of the need for a "healing of memories." That means coming to terms with history in its entirety, not just that of others, but also our own. The uses of history are complex, as professional historians know only too well,[19] for nations and peoples live not only by their histories but by their myths as well. As one historian put it, "A nation is a group of people who hold the same mistaken view of their common history," and "every nation is a community of shared memory and of shared forgetting." So this is a problem not just of churches, but of all social groupings from churches to nations. We Americans like to think of our country as "the land of the free and the home of the brave," a beacon of liberty, justice, and democracy for all humankind—right? Well, how about the era of lynchings throughout the first half of the twentieth century, in which 4,742 black Americans were murdered by white mobs, or the fact that the Ku Klux Klan is alive and well in several states today?[20] That is America's "shared forgetting."

This healing of memories will require us to put aside our myths and confront our common past with historical objectivity and truth, own up to our responsibilities, seek forgiveness, and turn the page to move on to a hopefully better future. I would like to suggest some hermeneutical principles germane to arriving at such a balanced historical view of our common Catholic-Orthodox past. Contrary to what the non-historian might imagine, history is not the past, but a vision of the past. For ecumenism to advance, we must put aside our own limited, often hagiographical vision of our common past and try to see ourselves as others see us.

This is what I did for the Jesuits, and the Catholic Church is learning to do the same. Ecumenically-minded Catholic theologians and Church historians like Congar, Eno, Tillard, Dvornik, and others have already begun to study the origins and development of papal primacy,[21] showing thereby some problematic aspects of its evolution, especially in the ninth century under Pope St. Nicholas I (858–867).[22] This has resulted in a needed change in Catholic perception and terminology. No longer do we speak of the "Eastern" or "Byzantine Schism," as was once customary in Western writing. Today we recognize our Catholic share of responsibility for the Schism, and call it "the East-West Schism."

Furthermore, I do not know a single reputable Catholic theologian competent in East-West issues who would not agree that to foster communion with the Orthodox East, Rome will have to moderate its overly central-ized government and change substantially the way in which the "Petrine Primacy" it claims is presently exercised. The Catholic Church should have the courage to put aside the excesses of a servile Vatican curial centralism and push forward relentlessly with the renewed "sister churches" and "col-legial" ecclesiology proclaimed at Vatican II but insufficiently developed and implemented since then.

For our apostolic Eastern sister churches correctly view many aspects of Catholic Church governance as foreign to their ancient tradition. Anyone who thinks that the Orthodox East is ever going to sacrifice its age-old apostolic autonomy for this centralized Roman administration as pres-ently exercised is gravely mistaken. So, I believe that each apostolic sister church—including the Catholic Church—should now ask itself, and pro-claim publicly with supporting arguments, what it believes it must de-mand of other equally apostolic churches as the price of communion in order to remain true to its apostolic faith, and then be willing to undertake constructive, ecumenical dialogue on the topic. Meanwhile, our Ortho-dox dialogue partners might reflect honestly on the enormous benefits the Roman Primacy has brought to Catholicism in maintaining its unity in the face of all the crises posed by the present postmodern and post-Western world, and on the problems endemic to world Orthodoxy where one gets the impression that the only means available in an inter-Orthodox crisis is the rupture of communion.

Another aspect of progress towards an objective, noncontroversial, his-torical thinking as distinct from the blame-game approach to the past would be for the Orthodox to revise their attitude towards Uniatism, of which they continue to have a mythological view that ill corresponds to reality. According to that mythology, Uniatism began as the product of Je-suit machinations and Polish enforcement. The truth is somewhat different. Classical Uniatism originated during the Catholic Counter-Reformation and the struggle with Protestant denominations for the soul of Europe. In this struggle, the Orthodox Church was, in a sense, a bystander, caught in the crossfire of the main belligerents in the sixteenth-century Polish-Lithuanian Commonwealth, where on October 19, 1596, in the city of Brest (in what was then the Grand Duchy of Lithuania), five of the seven Orthodox bishops in the commonwealth entered into union with Rome.[23] This union, far from being "forced" or "imposed" on the Orthodox, as is repeatedly asserted, was the outcome not only of long negotiations, but also of a parallel religious movement tirelessly propagated for twenty years by Jesuits Peter Skarga and Anthony Possevino.

But those Jesuits, far from inventing Uniatism as they are often accused, took a dim view of Ruthenian Orthodoxy and favored conversion of the Ruthenians to the Latin rite of the Roman Church, plain and simple.[24] Possevino initially considered the retention of the Byzantine-Slavonic rite by the Ruthenians as merely a temporary expedient. In a letter from Krakow dated September 11, 1583, Possevino wrote that nothing could be accomplished among the Ruthenians unless their rite were left alone. But this was just a concession to be tolerated, Possevino said, with an anti-Semitic slur and obvious contempt for the Ruthenian Orthodox Church, "until that synagogue can be honorably buried" (*Insino che quella sinogoga si seppelisse con honore*).[25]

Thus, the idea of having the Ruthenian Orthodox enter the Catholic Church as a body, preserving their own hierarchy and rite, was not the invention of the Jesuits. Initially, at least, the union was not viewed favorably by any of the three parties—Rome, the Poles, or the Jesuits—traditionally indicted in the mythological view. Far from being the result of some preconceived Catholic strategy, Uniatism was wholly an invention of the Ruthenian Orthodox bishops themselves, and grew out of the difficult situation in which the Ruthenian hierarchy found itself, squeezed between Moscow and Poland, Protestant Reformation and Catholic Counter-Reformation. All of this has been amply demonstrated by the latest, reliable historical scholarship on the question.[26]

Prospects for the Future: What Can the Orthodox Do?

So, "purifying their historical memory" will demand that the Orthodox, too, learn the uses of history in a modern, academic climate that seeks to be fair and objective insofar as that is possible. Amid the diversity of perceptions of the past, one must eschew scapegoating, the "our-hands-are-always-clean" victimhood pretense, the use of the double standard, and must learn instead a little self-criticism and fairness. This will require that the Orthodox make their own frank examination of conscience.

Western Christianity's historic defects of imperialism, power, and domination led to the crimes for which Pope John Paul II asked pardon in Rome on the First Sunday of Lent, 2000.[27] An Orthodox response was not long in coming: Metropolitan Kallinikos of Piraeus, an official spokesman of the Orthodox Church of Greece,[28] and Russian Orthodox Bishop Pavel of Vienna,[29] responded to the pope's request for pardon and forgiveness not by forgiving and asking forgiveness in turn, as one should expect from any Christian who has ever read the New Testament, but by declaring there was nothing for which Orthodoxy had to ask pardon. More recently, an authoritative Orthodox hierarch asserted in an interview that, whereas in its history, the Catholic Church had exploited the civil authorities to achieve its aims—which is true enough—this is something the Orthodox had never done.[30] Apart from the fact that such responses make their authors the butt of sarcasm and derision from responsible, thinking people, they are also untrue. For when it had the power of the Byzantine Empire behind it, the Orthodox Church rammed itself down the throats of others without scruple (if you do not believe that, you have never talked to a Copt or an Armenian).

A short list of what the Orthodox might consider, were they to examine their historical conscience, would begin in Byzantine times with the forced conversion of Jews already from the fourth and fifth centuries but especially in the sixth and seventh;[31] with the persecution of the Syrian Jacobites, Armenians, and Copts in the aftermath of the Council of Chalcedon; and with the forced unions of the Armenians with the Byzantine Church, as in 590 AD under Emperor Maurice,[32] a clear example of Orthodox Uniatism repeated in modern times by the Russian Orthodox mission among the Assyrians[33] and the "Western-rite Orthodoxy" fostered in North America, Great Britain, and Western Europe,[34] despite the false claims that Uniatism is an exclusively Catholic phenomenon.[35]

Then, towards the middle of the eighth century, the Byzantines unilaterally and uncanonically removed the dioceses of Calabria, Sicily, Eastern Illyricum, and perhaps also Otranto—all areas historically within the patriarchate of the West from time immemorial—from the Roman obedience and placed them under the jurisdiction of the Patriarch of Constantinople.[36] This incorporation by political force, of areas that belonged by age-old right to the patriarchate of the West under Rome, included the forced imposition of Byzantine ecclesiastical authority on conquered areas of the non-Orthodox East,[37] including Catholic Southern Italy.[38]

Indeed, Southern Italy provides an interesting parallel to the Crusades, about which the Orthodox remain continually exercised, collapsing chronology and acting as if the Crusades happened yesterday.[39] By the end of the sixth century, Southern Italy was almost totally Latin except for colonies of Greeks in Reggio-Calabria and some of the coastal towns. This situation was to change rapidly from the seventh century, when the campaign of Byzantine Emperor Constans II drove the Saracens from Sicily, reviving Byzantine imperial and ecclesiastical hegemony there and in Calabria.

The Byzantine re-conquest of Southern Italy was carried out with thorough consistency across the whole socio-political horizon, including the ecclesiastical. Those who deplore the incursions of the Latin Crusaders in the East and their setting up of Latin hierarchies in competition with the already existing age-old Oriental ecclesiastical structures conveniently forget that the Byzantines did the exact same thing in Italy. Their military help against the Arab incursions in Italy was no more disinterested than the Latin help against the Turks during the Crusades, and Byzantine ecclesiastical politics in Italy also involved an imposed religious Byzantinization of the conquered areas under Byzantine political control.

The list of things the Orthodox might wish to seek pardon for would also include the anti-Latin pogrom in Constantinople in the years immediately preceding the Fourth Crusade. Latin hostility to the Greeks in the infamous Fourth Crusade was well prepared for by the Greek massacre of the Latins in Constantinople in 1182,[40] when the papal envoy, John, was beheaded and his severed head tied to a dog's tail "in contempt for the [Catholic] Church," according to the contemporary account of reliable chronicler William of Tyre.[41]

Nor is it any secret to historians that in the Fourth Crusade the Byzantine ruling class diverted the Crusaders from fighting the Muslim invaders to attacking Constantinople. Alexis IV Angelos, co-emperor with his father Isaac II Angelos, had been overthrown by his elder brother Alexis III Angelos, and sought the help of the Crusaders to regain the imperial throne for his father and himself.[42] So, the machinations of the Byzantines themselves played a key role in the resulting horrendous Fourth-Crusade disaster of 1204.[43] None of that justifies what the Crusaders did, but a dose of truth might help to re-dimension traditional Orthodox slanted views on the issue and apportion responsibilities where they belong— certainly not to the Catholic Church, in whose name Pope Innocent III bitterly condemned the Crusaders' horrific actions in no uncertain terms.

Nor was the Orthodox use of force to suppress the religious rights of others limited to the Byzantine millennium. In modern times, we have the case of Benjamin Evsevidis, a Greek Orthodox bishop who became a Catholic and in 1851 was named titular bishop of Neapolis and auxiliary to the titular of St. Nicholas of Galata, serving the small Byzantine-rite Catholic community in that quarter of Constantinople on the northern side of the Golden Horn. In 1858 the Phanar had him arrested and imprisoned in the Rila Monastery in Bulgaria, then still part of the Ottoman Empire. Released upon the intervention of the French Embassy to the Sublime Porte, Bishop Benjamin was arrested again in 1861, imprisoned first in the Phanar, and then exiled to imprisonment on Mt. Athos that same year. Released once again through the intervention of the French, he fled and sought asylum in their embassy in Constantinople, where he directed the small Byzantine-rite Greek Catholic community there until he died in 1895.[44]

But Constantinople was minor in comparison with Russia. The history of Russia is so full of the Russian Orthodox use of force against non-Orthodox Christians that a few of the more lurid examples will have to suffice.[45] In the turbulent period of the Cossack Wars and the struggle over Uniatism, two classic examples are the Polish Jesuit St. Andrew Bobola and St. Josaphat Kuntsevych, Ruthenian-Catholic Archbishop of Polotsk, who had been lynched by an Orthodox mob. The martyrdom of St. Andrew Bobola was horrendously savage: the Orthodox Cossacks tortured him, flayed him alive, and literally butchered him at Janow on May 10, 1657.[46]

In the next century, we see the persecution and martyrdom of Catholics in the Russian Empire following the partitions of Poland in 1772, 1793, and 1795, and in the wake of the Polish uprisings that Russian oppression had provoked in the second half of the nineteenth century,[47] when Latin Catholic monasteries were suppressed—two hundred of them in 1832 alone—and Catholic clergy exiled to Siberia. Rounding off that century, we see the forced conversion of Catholics—including Latin Catholics—to Orthodoxy in 1839 under Nicholas I.[48] Then, the reign of Nicholas's successor, Alexander II, witnessed the infamous slaughter of simple Greek-Catholic villagers in Drelov on January 18, 1874, and in Pratulin on January 24 of the same year, when Russian Imperial Cossack troops opened fire on the Catholic faithful gathered in front of their churches.[49]

To conclude the tale: Before the Soviet-era persecution of all believers in Russia, one of the more bizarre incidents in the well-documented history of Russian Orthodox violence against Uniatism is the saga of the Bulgarian Greek-Catholic prelate, Archbishop Josif Sokolski (1786–1879). Ordained bishop in Rome by Pius IX in 1861, Sokolski, upon his return

to Bulgaria that same year, was tricked into accompanying to Constantinople the Imperial Russian Ambassador to the Sublime Porte under pre-
text of a meeting, and was invited to visit the waiting Russian packet
Elbrus docked in the Bosphorus. As soon as the Russians had the naïve and
trusting Sokolski restrained on board, the ship weighed anchor, deporting
Sokolski to Odessa and eventual confinement in the Goloseevskaja Pus-
tin' Monastery—a dependent skete of the Kievo-Pecherskaja Lavra (Kievan Monastery of the Caves) eight versts (5.3 miles) from Kiev that St.
Peter Mohyla, Orthodox Metropolitan of Kiev from 1633–46, founded
in 1631.[50] Sokolski died on September 30, 1879, without ever seeing Bulgaria again.

Nor was Russian Orthodox use of the civil arm to suppress other Christians limited to systematic interference in the affairs of the Catholic Church
and its adherents.[51] Recall the brutal suppression of the Old-Believer schism
in seventeenth-century Russia; the forcible suppression of the Georgian
Orthodox Catholicosate in 1811 and the imposition of a Russian Metropolitan and the Church Slavonic liturgical language on the Georgian Orthodox Church that dates back to long before anyone ever heard of Russia.
So much for the claim that Orthodoxy has never exploited the civil power
to promote its cause!

Without an objective reading of the recent past, too, the present attitudes of the Orthodox and of the Eastern Catholics, and the new problems that have arisen between them in the former Soviet Empire, cannot
even begin to be understood. No fair judgment on present tensions between Orthodox and Greek Catholics in the former Soviet bloc is possible
without an objective view of the martyrdom of the Greek Catholic Churches
from the end of World War II until 1989.[52]

The Uses of History

But the uses of objective history also teach us a very important lesson
concerning such a list of horrors on both sides of the confessional divide.
One must not be anachronistic and read history backwards, basing negative judgments of the past on social structures and moral principles totally
foreign to the era in question. In premodern times, there was no idea of
our present conception of individual freedom of conscience and civil
rights for all. In earlier times, when the reigning principle was of *cuius
regio, eius et religio*, it was the group, the clan, that enjoyed certain rights,

but not its individual members. Even today, in still-existing societies without such modern principles, it is the group that counts. In the Middle East, for example, even an atheist is a Muslim or Christian atheist, just as in surveys taken in present-day, post-Soviet Russia, unbelievers will identify themselves as Orthodox.

So, did politics and coercion play a part in the establishment and protection of the majority's churches in the Catholic West as in the Byzantine East? Of course they did, just as they did in the establishment of Lutheranism and Anglicanism. Or does someone think the sixteenth-century German princelings that went over to the Reformation, taking with them into Protestantism their principalities and all the Catholics within their borders, first put the issue to a vote? Or that Henry VIII took a plebiscite to see if the English wanted to separate from Rome and be reinvented as Anglicans?

The case of present-day, eminently respectable, secular (if nominally Lutheran) Scandinavia is especially pertinent. When Denmark, which had ruled Catholic Iceland since 1380, went over to the Reformation, Lutheranism was introduced there by force between 1537–52 under King Christian III, and the last two Icelandic Catholic bishops were taken prisoner. One, the old and blind Bishop Ogmundur, died in captivity; the other, Bishop Jòn Araso of Hòlar, was beheaded in 1550, and Iceland became Lutheran by fiat. Then, there is the case of Estonia, which had been Catholic since 1227. It ceased to be so by force when, under Swedish Lutheran rule (1561–1710), the Catholic faith was forbidden, the last of the Catholic recusants were expelled in 1626, and the Catholic tradition in Estonia was extirpated.[53]

We are thus faced here with a game everyone played without exception according to the rules of the age; the refusal (or inability) of some to view things in their historical context has by now become tiresome for those with a modicum of historical sophistication.

Towards an Ecumenical Scholarship and Theology

My overall thesis has been quite simple: contrary to what one might think, the main problem we Catholics and Orthodox face in our ecumenical dialogue is not doctrine but behavior. The issue is not that Catholics and Orthodox do not know how to pray and believe and live Christianity in the right and true apostolic way. The problem is that we do not know how to behave.

Learning to do so will mean adopting what I call "ecumenical scholarship and theology."[54] Ecumenical scholarship is not content with the purely natural virtues of honesty and fairness, virtues one should be able to expect from any true scholar. Ecumenical scholarship is a new and specifically Christian way of studying Christian tradition in order to reconcile and unite, rather than to confute and dominate. Its deliberate intention is to emphasize the common tradition underlying our differences, which, though real, are usually the accidental product of history, culture, and language, rather than essential differences in the doctrine of faith.

Of course, to remain scholarly, this effort must be carried out realistically, without glossing over real differences. But even in recognizing differences, this ecumenical effort must remain a two-way street with each side judging itself and its tradition by the exact same criteria and standards with which it judges the other. Eschewing all scapegoating and the double standard, ecumenical scholarship seeks to describe the beliefs, traditions, and usages of other confessions in ways their own objective spokespersons recognize as reliable and fair.

Ecumenical scholarship seeks not confrontation but agreement and understanding. It tries to enter into the other's point of view, to understand it insofar as possible with sympathy and agreement. It takes seriously the other's critique of one's own tradition, seeking to incorporate its positive contributions into one's own thinking. It is a contest in reverse, a contest of Christian love, one in which the parties seek to understand and justify not their own point of view, but that of their interlocutor.

Such an effort and method is not baseless romanticism. Its theological foundation is our common faith that God's Holy Spirit is always with his Church, protecting the integrity of its witness, especially in the millennium of its undivided unity. Since some of the issues that divide us go right back to that first millennium, one must ineluctably conclude that these differences do not affect the substance of the apostolic faith. For if they did, then contrary to Jesus's promise in Matthew 16:18, the "gates of hell" would have indeed prevailed against his Church.

The next principle is also based on ecclesiology. The Catholic and Orthodox Churches recognize one another as historic, apostolic sister churches. Consequently, no view of Christian tradition can be considered anything but partial that does not take full account of the traditional teaching of these sister churches of East and West. Any theology must be measured not only against the common tradition of the undivided Church of the first millennium, but also against the ongoing witness of the Spirit-guided apostolic Christendom of the East and West. That does not mean that the East or West has never been wrong. It means that neither can be ignored.

Furthermore, an authentic magisterium cannot contradict itself. Therefore, without denying the legitimate development of doctrine, in the case of apparently conflicting traditions of East and West, preferential consideration must be given to the witness of the undivided Church. This is especially true with respect to later polemics resulting from unilateral departures from or narrowing of the common tradition during the second millennium of divided Christendom.

For Catholics, such an "ecumenical theology" must mean an end to declarations on the nature of the priesthood that exalt the celibate clerical state of the Latin tradition in a way that is demeaning to the thousands of legitimately married eastern clergy, Orthodox and Catholic, who are also priests of God's Holy Church—and in my not-inconsiderable personal experience, often much better priests than their celibate or monastic counterparts on both sides of the confessional divide.[55]

It might also mean Catholic theologians realizing that Latin Scholastic theology of the Eucharist is *a* theology, not *the* theology of the Eucharist—a theology that has a limited cultural context and an observable history. As recent, fully Catholic theological studies have shown, the hylomorphic theory of Eucharistic consecration—based on the Medieval Latin theology of the priest acting at the Eucharist *in persona Christi*—is a theology that became current only in the twelfth-century West,[56] and as such is a theology of the Eucharist (and a perfectly legitimate one), but by no means the only legitimate one.

To recognize that, one must learn, first of all, to distinguish between dogma and theology, and, in my view, the failure of some theologians to do so, is at the root of any real or perceived theological dissonance between East and West on this and other issues. Our common apostolic faith East and West teaches that during the celebration of the Eucharistic mysteries, the offered bread and wine become the body and blood of Christ. That is dogma. Theology is what attempts to explain how that can be, and that is historically limited and variable according to the different traditions.

The Eucharistic theology of the Latin tradition, radically Christological—the Roman Canon does not even mention the Holy Spirit except in its concluding doxology—developed, as we saw above,[57] a theology of the celebrating priest acting *in persona Christi* and explained its workings in the hylomorphic "matter" and "form" terminology of Scholastic theology: The bread and wine are the "matter," the Words of Institution are the "form." All well and good.

But other traditions, the Byzantine Orthodox, for example, ground their sacramental theology in the pneumatology so prominent in that tradition since St. Basil the Great's seminal treatise *On the Holy Spirit*[58] and the teaching of the Second Ecumenical Council Constantinople I in 381. In this theology, the priest is not the main actor in the sacramental work: "I baptize, I absolve, I consecrate *in persona Christi*." Rather, the priest calls on God to accomplish the mystery: "The servant of God N. is baptized, is absolved. . . . Come down upon these gifts, O Holy Spirit and make this bread and wine the Body and Blood of Christ, changing—i.e., consecrating—them by your Holy Spirit." Which of these two theologies is "right"? For anyone with a smattering of common sense, theological sophistication, and a knowledge of the history of theology, *they both are*, of course, since they both do what theologies are supposed to do: *explain*, explain theologically how what the faith affirms is possible.

However, according to the present teaching and liturgical discipline of the Roman Catholic Church, no minister in priestly orders is deemed to concelebrate "validly" the Eucharist unless he recites the Words of Institution ("This is my body . . . This is my blood."), regardless of what else he might do in gesture or symbol to show his clear intention to participate in—i.e., to concelebrate—the Eucharistic liturgy exercising his ministerial priesthood.[59] If this is meant as determining the sacramental practice of the Latin Church, it is acceptable; if it is meant to dogmatize and universalize Latin, Eucharistic theology, it is unacceptable.

If one were to approach the sources of the past with such presuppositions, one would be forced either to conclude that no "real" concelebration ever existed in ancient Christendom—or else to invent for the ancient Church a new form of concelebration never heard of then, "ceremonial" as opposed to "sacramental" concelebration, the latter being the only one deemed "real."[60] To maintain that verbal co-consecratory concelebration as practiced in the post–Vatican II Roman rite is the only "real" one, however, would be to question not only much of the Eastern tradition but, indeed, the whole early history of Eucharistic concelebration—a procedure patently absurd.[61] These are just some of the issues to which Catholics might apply a bit more ecumenical thinking if we really want to solve our common problems.

For the Orthodox, too, an ecumenical theology will mean distinguishing theology from dogma, and stressing what unites us, instead of using clichés as a substitute for evidence, and setting up pseudo-antitheses between our two traditions with the false polarization they cause. A few examples will have to suffice. In his Orthodox spiritual classic *The Mystical Theology of the Eastern Church*, Vladimir Lossky claimed that the spiritual "imitation of Christ" was a Western notion foreign to Orthodoxy.[62] "Oh is that so?" thought a surprised Irenée Hausherr, S.J., founder of the field of Eastern Spirituality as a scientific academic discipline,[63] who then proceeded in a famous study on the topic to cite reams of quotations from the Eastern Fathers of the Church explicitly advocating this imitation of Christ.[64] And it is fair to ask those who like to tout the famous Western spiritual classic, *The Imitation of Christ*, by Thomas à Kempis, as propagating a "typically Western" spirituality inimical to the spirit of the Christian East, how come Kempis went through some fifteen editions in Russian?[65] The cliché becomes even more ridiculous when one recalls that one of the most popular—though not the only[66]—Russian translation of *The Imitation of Christ* was the work of the arch-conservative and deeply pious Russian Orthodox jurist and university professor Konstantin Petrovich Pobedonostsev. From 1880 to 1905, he was lay procurator (*Ober-Prokurotor*) or director general of the Most Holy Synod of the Russian Orthodox Church; this was the office of the government official who effectively governed the Church for the tsarist autocracy in the synodal period of 1721 to 1917 after Peter the Great replaced the Moscow patriarchate with a Ruling Synod of bishops in an attempt to transform the Russian Church into a lapdog institution at the service of the state. Strongly opposed to all Westernizing influence on Russia and its Orthodoxy—he was nicknamed "The Grand Inquisitor" for his ultra-reactionary political and religious views—Pobedonostsev saw no problem in translating this supposedly "typically Western," devotional manual for Russian Orthodox use. His translation achieved instant popularity, and went through eight editions between 1869 and 1899.[67]

Another such shopworn cliché contrasts the "legalistic, canonical West" with a more laid-back, "mystical East." One recent instance is a press release of March 11, 2008, reporting that the Secretary for Internal Christian Affairs of the Moscow patriarchate's Department for External Church

Relations, reacting to the Vatican's updating a list of "traditional" mortal sins so as to stigmatize new types of immoral behavior such as polluting the environment, social injustice, and so on, made the following remarks: "Western Christianity is more inclined to classify even spiritual things, to file and arrange everything. Eastern Christianity is not used to a rigorous system of spiritual notions. No doubt, Orthodox religious practice names and finds proper place for each sin, but it usually relates to a concrete human soul with its various shades and transitions, so it's hardly possible to list it."[68]

The numbering and listing of sins began not with "Western Christianity" but with the Bible and its Ten Commandments (Ex 20:2–17; Dt 5:6–21), and is in no way foreign to the author's Orthodox tradition, as is obvious from the traditional penitential books of Orthodoxy, which list the number and kinds of sins in exhaustive detail.[69] This Orthodox tradition goes back to Byzantine times, as described by internationally known Byzantinist George Dennis, who informs us that "The Byzantines loved to place everything in its proper category, and so they compiled encyclopedias of heresy."[70] Like the *Panarion* of Epiphanios, bishop of Salamis, and the equally enormous *Panoplia dogmatica* of Euthymios Zigabenos.[71]

Therefore, the old maxim that the West is fixated on laws—*Ex Occidente lex*—in contrast to the *Ex Oriente lux* cliché about a supposedly unlegalistic "mystical East," is just mistaken, as is perfectly obvious to anyone who has dipped into Orthodox canonical sources like the *Pedalion*, or Orthodox anthology of canons over one thousand pages long with detailed legislation on just about everything imaginable,[72] to say nothing of the "ritual purity" restrictions still placed on women in most branches of Eastern Christianity.[73] Such pseudo-East-West antitheses have also been excoriated by well-known Orthodox "Monk of the Eastern Church" Lev Gillet,[74] as they were by Greek Orthodox theologians like Prof. Ioannis Petrou of the Theological Faculty of Thessaloniki.[75]

More importantly from a doctrinal point of view, it would be helpful if neo-Palamite Orthodox theologians stopped exaggerating their theology into a dogmatic divide between Orthodoxy and Catholicism—if for no other reason than that it is just not true.[76] Contrary to what many Orthodox seem to think, not only has St. Gregory Palamas and his theology never been condemned by the Catholic Church, but some highly respectable Catholic theologians like André de Halleux defend its orthodoxy.[77] Far from condemning Palamas, the official Vatican edition of the Greek

Anthologion of liturgical offices for the whole year includes St. Gregory's office for the Second Sunday of Lent.[78] Furthermore, St. Gregory is studied at my Pontifical Oriental Institute with the same interest and respect given him in an Orthodox theological academy, and a recent doctoral dissertation on his spiritual doctrine by one of our Catholic priest-students has just been published.[79]

Concluding Reflections: Learning from the Secular West

By way of conclusion let me say that, despite grave defects in contemporary Western society, there is also a positive side to Western values from which the East could well learn. For it is this Western culture that invented "modernity" and its traditional values: a public life that is democratic and civil; respect for individuals and their civil and religious rights; a tradition of public service and beneficence in favor of the stricken or disadvantaged both at home and abroad; an academic, intellectual, artistic, and cultural life free of political restraint or the manipulation of state-ideology, and open to all; to name but a few of its qualities. Those educated in this oft-derided "Western" culture seek to acquire habits of thought and judgment, ways of behaving and acting that, I think, we should try to instill in all those with whom we have contact.

Deliberately setting aside caricature, the virulent, one-sided, vituperative, rude, and dishonorable academic institutions and scholarly establishment in this much-berated "secularized West" try to instill the values of fairness, objectivity, dialogue, courtesy, and common human decency. This leads to openness and the desire to know the other, rather than the ghetto-like insularity and smug self-satisfaction of those who think they have nothing to learn from other traditions. Just look at the endless list of fair, objective, positive, scholarly, Western studies and publications on the Christian East, its Fathers, its spirituality, its liturgy, its monasticism, its theology, and its history. Just look at the huge list of serious journals published under Catholic auspices that deal with the culture of the Christian East objectively, sympathetically, even with admiration and love,[80] and the number of major Catholic educational institutions of higher education dedicated to the sympathetic, scholarly, objective study of the Christian East, including the one we are at today.[81]

I think that these qualities are already elemental ideals and broadly acquired realities in the Anglican-Roman Catholic ecumenical dialogue.

The point is not that Catholics and Anglicans never disagree. What it does mean is that, at the official level, disagreements can be discussed truthfully and courteously without invective, rudeness, and slander. This is a source of great hope when one recalls that not many centuries ago Catholics and Anglicans were busily engaged in killing one another; today in Great Britain, Anglicans and Catholics venerate together the martyrs from each side—Catholics martyred by Anglicans and Anglicans by Catholics—who were sacrificed for their Anglicanism or Catholicism in the horrors of their mutual past. Now *that* is real, adult ecumenism![82]

Until hearts and minds are changed, none of our other ecumenical efforts will amount to anything of substance for the unity of the Churches of God. Let us not doubt for one minute that this has repercussions for humanity that go far beyond the question of Christian unity. One thing the twentieth century, and especially the Holocaust, have taught us is that there is no such thing as ideological neutrality. One is part of the solution or part of the problem. And to be part of the solution, one must be an instrument of peace and harmony, for to be anything less is to be part of the problem.

BYZANTINES, ARMENIANS, AND LATINS: UNLEAVENED BREAD AND HERESY IN THE TENTH CENTURY

Tia Kolbaba

The study of how Byzantine Orthodox Christians in the Middle Ages define themselves in relation to the many faiths, ethnic groups, friends, and enemies who surround and live within the Byzantine Empire is as fascinating as the history of any group's self-definition and its ramifications, with some added twists.[1] Greek-speaking Christians who lived in Constantinople and called themselves Romans necessarily challenge such multivalent concepts as "the West" and "medieval Christendom." Textbooks on "Western civilization" tend to begin with the heritage of classical Greek philosophy, Roman law and government, and Christian faith, and then survey only the western and northwestern European cultures that built on this foundation. Far from being a blind spot on the part of textbook authors, this is an acknowledgement of the separate histories of the eastern and western halves of the Roman Empire. The Eastern world shared the heritage of Greece, Rome, and Jerusalem, but Eastern Christian forms of culture differ from Western forms at every turn; they would fit awkwardly, if at all, in a textbook on western Europe.[2] While much research has been focused on the not-quite-"Western" reception of Greek philosophy and Roman law in Byzantium, East-West differences in Christian religious practice have drawn the most attention, and many scholars have focused specifically on the ways that Byzantine Christians define themselves vis-à-vis the Latin-rite Christians of western Europe. This paper deals with one small piece of that religious self-definition—the history of Byzantine reactions to Latin Christianity in the tenth century.

The tenth century has played a negligible role in accounts of East-West differentiation.[3] Sandwiched between the ninth century with its "Photian Schism," and the eleventh with "the Schism of 1054," the tenth century in Byzantium is characterized by continuing struggles with the Bulgars in the northwest and victories against the Muslims in the east. There seems to be little to report about Byzantines and Latins.[4] Given, however, that the dominant Byzantine complaint about the Latins in 1054 did not exist in the ninth century, one might suspect that something happened in between.[5] In fact, several things happened. Analyzed as context for Greek-Latin relations in the eleventh century, some tenth-century events give a tantalizing glimpse of how the long history of Christian writing about heretics and heresy could be deployed by Greeks against Latins.

To understand the tenth century's importance for Orthodox-Catholic relations, one needs first to understand that notable differences between these two Christian worlds had emerged by the end of the ninth century. Four of these are particularly important for my argument here. First, there were longstanding theological differences between the Greek East and the Latin West. A precise definition or description of these differences continues to elude us, and essentialism and confessional bias have at times obscured the picture. It is nonetheless true that in the many theological controversies of the fourth through eighth centuries, differences emerged between the majority of Western, Latin theologians and Eastern, Greek ones. Already at the time of the Council of Nicea (325), Western churchmen were less likely to embrace any kind of subordination of the Son to the Father in the Trinity, and the so-called Arian controversy, which took a century to resolve in the East, plagued the Latin Western churches far less in the fourth century.[6] The language of Trinitarian theology was a vexed issue, and whether the differences between the mostly Cappadocian formulations of Trinitarian theology in the East and the largely Augustinian Western ones were merely semantic or profoundly theological, they did exist.[7] The disputes about Christ's one or two natures that preceded and followed the Council of Chalcedon (451) also saw a number of Roman-Constantinopolitan schisms.[8] That said, however, conflicts that could have arisen from these theological definitions are rare in the ninth and tenth centuries—in part because neither side could read the other side's theologians and engage with them in significant ways.[9] Ignorance, in this case, was bliss—or at least ignorance led to a conviction that all was well between Rome and Constantinople because they agreed on the formulae of the first six ecumenical councils.

The second crucial context for Byzantine-Latin relations in the tenth century is the conversion of the Germanic peoples north of the Alps— some from polytheist traditional religions, others from Arian Christianity. Their conversion to a Christian doctrine and practice centered on Rome, and profoundly reverential towards St. Peter and his successors, changed the Western Church in ways that were to be recognized only gradually in Byzantium. This is not surprising given that the implications of the Germanic conversions became evident only over a period of centuries in Rome itself.[10] Both the pope and the patriarch, for example, saw no need to include Frankish bishops or the Frankish king in the preparations for and meeting of the Council of Nicea (787)—an oversight that caused another set of problems. Misled by a bad translation of the *Acta* of that council, the Franks rejected the veneration of icons—at least as they understood the decisions of Nicea (787).[11] Also as a result of these *Acta*, the Franks discovered that the Byzantine Church's Creed was lacking (as they saw it) the crucial belief in the procession of the Holy Spirit from the Son as well as from the Father.[12] When they complained to the pope about this latter issue, however, the pope reprimanded them, saying that indeed the Creed should not have the *filioque* added to it.[13] This disagreement between Frankish theologians and the pope had not yet reached Byzantine ears in the eighth century, but it would reach them in the ninth, when the third important factor developed.

In the ninth century, both Western Christianity and Eastern Christianity were expanding through missionary work. Since some of the western expansion was eastwards and some of the eastern expansion was westwards, the two sets of missionaries met: in Moravia and in Bulgaria. When they met, they became aware of their differences, which were mostly not theological in nature; as mentioned above, neither side had the language skills and other tools to engage deeply with the other's theology. Instead, from texts such as the so-called Encyclical Letter to the Eastern Patriarchs of Patriarch Photios of Constantinople (858–67, 877–86), we know that ritual and disciplinary differences were the issues of concern. Photios, for example, complained about differences in fasting practices, the requirement in the Roman Church that priests be celibate, the Roman insistence that confirmation must be performed by a bishop, and the addition to the Creed.[14] Such differences, observed in the context of Byzantine-Frankish competition in central and eastern Europe, led to the conviction in some quarters that the other side's practices were not just different, but wrong.

The final crucial feature of the ninth century is the effort of the Byzantine emperor to re-establish Byzantine hegemony in parts of southern Italy and shore up Byzantine defenses there.[15] Any such effort was going to involve the patriarch as well as the emperor, for the restoration of imperial hegemony meant the restoration of a Greek church hierarchy, and vice versa. At least that was the ideal. So the ninth-century patriarchs wrote to and dealt with bishops, popes, and other Western church officials with some regularity throughout this century.[16]

Indeed, there were flurries of interaction between the two churches in the ninth century, and we have many texts with which to study that interaction. It is all the more striking, then, that the tenth century mostly lacks such texts. In the tenth century, the Western Church seemed hardly to be on the minds of the Byzantines. The exceptions to this general rule almost all stemmed from southern and central Italy. From that region came such famous examples as the Greek-rite, Greek-speaking Neilos of Rossano (c. 910–1005) and his monks, who lived for fifteen years in a monastic house belonging to the monastery of Montecassino, birthplace of Benedictine monasticism.[17] From the same region—in fact from Montecassino itself— came Latin monks who traveled throughout the East and spent time on Mt. Athos. From that region came the Amalfitan monks who established a monastery on Mt. Athos.[18] Late in the tenth century, the Byzantine Empire managed to regain control of large areas in southern and central Italy, driving out Islamic raiders and subjugating Lombard kings and princes. Interactions between Byzantine officials and such Italian institutions as the Monastery of Montecassino—to give just the best-documented example— increased.[19] All of this contact also meant that awareness of differences in practice surfaced in this region. According to Neilos of Rossano's biographer, for example, there was no question of actually integrating the Greek and Latin monastic communities, and Neilos had conversations with the Latin monks about differences between Greek and Latin fasting practices.

Outside of this Italian zone of interaction, however, the tenth century has no surviving treatises on the *filioque*; no criticism of Latin use of unleavened bread in the Eucharist; no complaints about the Latin Church enforcing clerical celibacy; no notes about different fasting practices—

weekly and during Lent; and no criticism of the Latin sacrament of confirmation. Each of these issues—and sometimes all of these issues together—had been raised in the ninth century, but they nearly disappeared in the tenth. So, too, power struggles between the churches of Rome and Constantinople were notable only for their absence. Perhaps because the papacy was wrapped up in intramural Roman disputes and relatively unconcerned with the empire in the East,[20] relations between Rome and Constantinople were cordial. There was nothing remotely like the "Photian Schism," in which Pope Nicholas I's (858–867) ambition for his office was a significant factor in conflict with the patriarchate in Constantinople and Byzantine missionaries in eastern Europe.[21] Eastern churchmen could even admire the popes and acknowledge their past leadership of the Church, for the papacy had withstood all the blandishments and threats of iconoclast emperors, opposing iconoclasm to the end and protecting iconodule refugees from the East. Besides, the West had not been the source of the heresies that occupied the Greek polemicists of this period. All of the most threatening heretics—especially the non-Chalcedonian Armenians and Syrians—were in the east or in western regions of the empire to which easterners had been transplanted.

Then why look at the tenth century? For a number of reasons. First, as a historian, I may be incapable of skipping a whole century; I cannot conceive of a hundred years in which nothing happens. Second, it is even more difficult to conceive of such a prolonged period of inactivity when it comes between two centuries of more or less continual argument, debate, and negotiation. Third, the issue that most concerned many of the Greek combatants in the eleventh century—the Latin use of unleavened bread in the Eucharist—did not emerge in the ninth. We must seek its origins in the tenth.

A significant part of the story of what happened in Greek-Latin relations in the tenth century took place in the West. Out of a period of conflict, corruption, and decline in the papacy came new levels of German involvement in Rome and a reform movement with new ideas and ideals. The papal reformers of the late tenth and early eleventh centuries stressed a number of issues that were anathema in Constantinople: the primacy of the pope within the universal church; the absolute independence of the church from secular rulers; and the need for all priests to be celibate. Each of these concerns had its historical logic in the Western context, but to the Eastern Christian world they were alien. The Eastern Churches objected to radically new ideas about the nature of the pope's authority, accepted a symbiosis of empire and church that was incomprehensible in the West, and allowed clerical marriage. We could ascribe the open conflict of the eleventh century to these Western developments alone, but this would also be facile. While these changes in the West are much stressed in Orthodox historiography,[22] and are indeed crucial, they are not the whole background of the eleventh-century crises; there is a background of change and anxiety in the Greek East as well.

One could become aware of changes in the Greek East in a number of ways. I happen to have come to that awareness because of another puzzling feature of the eleventh century: the rise of the question of the Eucharistic bread. Greek Eastern Christians use leavened bread in the Eucharist; Latins use unleavened. By the tenth century, this was a difference of long standing that seems to have troubled neither side. We hear little of it—in fact, almost nothing, and literally nothing that argues for its importance. But in the middle of the eleventh century (before, during, and after the infamous events of 1054), this issue of Latins being "azymites"—that is, users of bread without leaven—obsessed writers both East and West. There is no doubt that Greeks first raised the issue and first argued that that the difference was significant; Latins, in this case, merely reacted to Greek polemic.

Since this question of the Eucharistic bread had no roots in the ninth-century disagreements between Constantinople and Rome, or between Greek and Latin missionaries in eastern Europe, we seek its roots in the tenth or early eleventh century. At least forty years ago, Mahlon Smith made the necessary connection in a little-known book: treatises against the use of unleavened bread in the Eucharist begin not with attacks on the Latins, but on the Armenians.[23] To understand the new importance of Armenian Christians to eleventh-century Byzantines we need yet another piece of historical background.

The tenth century saw remarkable gains for the Byzantine Empire on its eastern frontier. What had been a frontier of defense-in-depth against Islamic attack from the late seventh century on became a region in which Byzantium made substantial gains against the Islamic caliphate. In the process, the empire became the ruler of Syria and a force to be reckoned with in Armenia. From 915 on, Byzantium was the strongest power active in the Transcaucasus. In 944, Byzantine forces besieging Edessa acquired Edessa's most famous relic, the Mandylion, and transported it to Constantinople. Under the emperors Nikephoros II Phokas (963–969) and John I Tzimiskes (969–976), much of Syria was returned to Byzantine rule, including Antioch (969). By 1022 most of the warrior nobility of Armenia had put themselves under the protection of the Byzantine Empire. These victories in the east were accompanied by a policy of resettlement that peaked in the first decades of the eleventh century. Both to remove Armenian elites from their centers of power, where they might regroup and rebel, and to resettle areas of Anatolia that had been depopulated in the previous centuries, the Byzantines partly compelled and partly persuaded Armenians to move westward. Gérard Dédéyan has detailed how this process worked during the reign of the emperor Basil II (976–1025). He summarizes it as a policy of "deportation of [military, civil, and ecclesiastical] elites combined with fiscal flexibility and religious tolerance."[24] Basil II was not a gentle man, but he seems to have seen the benefits of keeping the Armenians quiescent. If that required tolerance of their religious differences, so be it. His reputation among the Armenian chroniclers is good: he is said even to have stopped the Greek clergy in the region of Sebaste from harassing the Armenian clergy there.[25]

The Syrian migration into and settlement in the empire proceeded a bit differently, but it also involved a level of imperial toleration for churches that the ecclesiastical authorities in Constantinople considered heretical.[26] Michael the Syrian reports that Nikephoros II Phokas promised the non-Chalcedonian Patriarch of Antioch John VI that he would prevent Chalcedonian church authorities—that is, Phokas's own church, including the patriarch and synod in Constantinople—from bothering Syrian Christians if they migrated to the area around Melitene, a region devastated by Nikephoros's wars. John agreed to oversee and lead this migration, in part because his people and clergy were being harassed by the Chalcedonian patriarch in Antioch. Ironically, the latter had been strengthened by the return of Antioch to Byzantine rule in 969. Thus, imperial reconquest reinforced Chalcedonian Christians in Antioch but allowed considerable autonomy for non-Chalcedonians in devastated areas that needed to be revitalized.[27]

In these moments of religious tolerance, we must see the interest of the emperors. As often happened in Byzantium, the emperors' concern for peace, prosperity, tax revenues, and a reliable source of soldiers overcame any scruples they might have had about religious difference.[28] Both the Syrian and the Armenian sources report on such emperors with approval.

In fact, Gilbert Dagron has noted that the non-Chalcedonian sources see a clear connection between imperial toleration of their communities and imperial victory: Emperors who allowed the heterodox communities to live in peace and even prosper were victorious in war; those who persecuted them were defeated.[29] Such imperial policy had its limits, of course, especially for emperors who were particularly dependent upon the support of the church in Constantinople. Still, it is clear that for Nikephoros II or Basil II the question of Syrian or Armenian heterodoxy was relatively unimportant when weighed against other imperial needs: separating Armenian and Syrian elites from their traditional power-bases; encouraging settlers to revitalize lands that had been devastated by centuries of intermittent warfare and raiding; and ensuring a reliable source of revenue and soldiers. In this context, refusal to accept the decisions of the Council of Chalcedon (451) was a minor issue.

On the other hand, while emperors were often ready to compromise in these ways, and some churchmen were willing to go along with the compromise, there were always those who found such tolerance intolerable. Writing about the twelfth century, Paul Magdalino memorably describes a group he calls "the guardians of orthodoxy"—an intellectual and bureaucratic elite, primarily clerical and monastic but with a significant contingent of lay intellectuals—who defended the existing political, ecclesiastical, and social structures of Byzantium against all comers. Depending on their own profession, interests, and pursuits, these guardians might have stressed theological, ritual, ethnic, linguistic, or even legal purity. Regardless, at the heart of their defense was a conviction that God's Roman Empire was superior to all governments, its church was God's church, and its maintenance a matter of continuing to be pure before their God.[30] Obviously, some of these concerns would have manifested themselves differently in the twelfth century than they did in the ninth, but there were also significant similarities. Magdalino notes, for example, that the guardians of orthodoxy were likely to make the most noise when they felt threatened—not merely by outsiders such as Muslims, but also by those who may have challenged the system more intimately, from within. He writes that in the twelfth century,

> The crisis was more one of confidence in the cultural superiority of Orthodoxy. Its guardians had seen their space invaded literally and metaphorically, and they were putting up more and higher barriers

to keep insiders in and outsiders out. But what did these barriers actually signify or achieve? I would contend that they were being erected across the main thoroughfares, and at the heart of the built-up area, of Byzantine culture. In other words, they were going up at precisely those points where insiders and outsiders mingled and were therefore liable to become indistinguishable—points where forbidden zones look very accessible, familiar and safe.[31]

Compare this descriptive passage from Magdalino's work on the twelfth century to Mark Whittow's description of tenth-century Byzantium:

From the late ninth century onwards, by which time any real threat of conquest had disappeared, the political and cultural structure which had preserved Byzantium through its Dark Age began to face new difficulties, paradoxically, brought on by success. Firstly, the advances in the east and the new security these obtained for the rest of Asia Minor created alternative sources of wealth and status that could counter-balance the authority of Constantinople. . . . Secondly, the conquest after 957 of wide areas of the northern Fertile Crescent not only further threatened Constantinople's role as sole source of wealth, but possibly more significant threatened the ideological coherence of the empire. Muslims were the least of the problem. . . . The difficulty lay with the large Christian populations. Armenians and Syrians had their own strong cultural traditions and a sense of identity bound up in their languages, churches, and literature. . . . For the Constantinopolitan elite the identity at stake was that of the orthodox empire, and the fear existed that an alliance between disaffected soldiers in the eastern armies and the non-orthodox peoples of the east would endanger the unity of the empire and the relationship with God that had so far preserved the state from destruction.[32]

In other words, as it did in the eighth and twelfth centuries, Byzantine society in the tenth and early eleventh centuries confronted a changing world order. After the Restoration of Orthodoxy in 843, Byzantines had rewritten their history to explain the Islamic invasions, the eruption of iconoclasm, and the newly diminished territory that was their empire. For the Constantinopolitan elite, the guardians of orthodoxy, who emerged from these struggles to rule the empire in the later ninth and first half of the tenth centuries, it was above all Orthodoxy without blemish that had preserved their polity. Like their military brothers, they had opted for a sort of defense-in-depth of their cultural superiority. Living in Constantinople, the center of culture and an impregnable fortress, they had little interest in what happened on the eastern frontier. They did not like the military families of the east who had profited from the eastward expansion of the empire and who represented a different vision of what made Byzantium strong—Orthodoxy, certainly, but also soldiers. The famous dialogue between Nikephoros II Phokas, a scion of the military aristocracy, and the synod in the capital illustrates this. When Phokas asked that his soldiers who died in battle be granted the status of martyrs for the faith, the synod refused his request with horror, citing Basil the Great who had said that soldiers who kill in battle must do penance for their deeds.[33]

Similarly, when the synod in Constantinople became aware of the level of religious tolerance that was being extended to Armenian and Syrian non-Chalcedonian populations in the east, it perceived a threat.[34] Those who emphasized the need to distinguish between Armenians and themselves, the "pious Romans," were not fabricating differences between the two groups. Instead, they were marking certain preexisting differences as too significant to be overlooked, disagreeing with the position of those who tolerated non-Chalcedonians, presumably on the grounds that they were not *that* different.[35] It is notable that the synod particularly objected to rumors that priests in Anatolia were allowing Orthodox people to marry non-Chalcedonian "heretical" Syrians.[36] The threat came from religious impurity, which could rupture the special relationship of God to his chosen people, the Christian Romans, and nothing threatens purity—be it national, racial, or religious—more than miscegenation. If priests were allowing Orthodox men to marry Armenian or Syrian women and many people saw nothing wrong with this, then it was the obligation of the guardians to describe the impurity of these heretics and make it obvious to their compatriots. The Armenians, they argued, were guilty not only of rejecting the two-nature Formula of Chalcedon but also of a number of other faults, some of which had been enumerated at the Council in Trullo (692).[37] The canons of Trullo condemned Armenians for offering the Eucharistic wine unmixed with water (Canon 32) and for an insufficiently rigorous Lenten fast (Canon 56), but more importantly for such "Judaizing" practices as ordaining only men who had descended from priestly families (Canon 33) and cooking and distributing meat to the priests within the sanctuary (Canon 99).[38] Most strikingly, for our purposes, the

Byzantines who wrote treatises against Armenian teaching and practices emphasized the Armenian use of unleavened bread in the Eucharist. For the Orthodox writers, this usage became a sign of Armenian Judaizing. The canons of the Council in Trullo had accused Armenians of Judaizing in various ways, and such accusations had become commonplaces of heresiology written against Armenians. Moreover, accusations of Judaizing had gained force in Byzantium during the iconoclast era when the defenders of icons consistently accused the iconoclasts of being influenced by Jews.[39]

In the decades from the late tenth century to the middle of the eleventh, a number of developments both regarding Jews alone, and connecting (in the Byzantine mind) Jews to Armenians, further reinforced the sense of the guardians of orthodoxy that they were under attack from Jews and Judaizing Armenians. Jewish immigration from Islamic lands to Byzantine ones increased. Andrew Sharf speculates that this was a result of the tenth-century Byzantine victories in the east and the end of Byzantine persecution of Jews.[40] Jews may have been integrated, in fact, to an extent that bothered some Byzantine Christians; their unease would explain the renewal of laws against Jews holding imperial office, for example.[41] Additionally, there were riots in Constantinople in relation to an imperial succession crisis in 1042, where, as the Jewish chronicler known as bar-Hebraeus reports, "many aliens—Armenians, Arabs, and Jews participated." These aliens, he adds, had migrated to Constantinople within the last thirty years.[42] Meanwhile, on the fringes of the empire, Bari, then under Byzantine control, had a Jewish revolt in 1051 that ended in the burning of the Jewish quarter.[43] As Smith puts it, "While not many of these incidents can themselves be shown to have even an indirect influence on the development of this azyme controversy, together they indicate that there was considerable religious unrest during the mid-eleventh century in precisely those Byzantine centers that became involved in the dispute with the Latins."[44] In other words, in Antioch, Constantinople, and southern Italy, Jews were believed to be involved (whether they were or not) in incidents of civil unrest; in the same regions, Latins were also perceived as a problem.

The association of Jews with Armenians and with Latins may not stand up to twenty-first-century scrutiny, but it made perfect sense in the eleventh century for two reasons. First, the Byzantines had adopted, from Justin Martyr (103–65) to Epiphanios of Salamis (c. 320–403) and then through centuries of tradition after that, the idea that heresy is unoriginal, that it is a family tree with different branches, and that what can be said of one group of heretics can usually be said of many. Thus, they had a readymade system for defining all kinds of differences between themselves and others as "heresy."[45] In this great heresiological tradition, if a group behaved in ways similar to heretics who had already been defined and described, then everything about those defined heretics could now be applied to the contemporary group. If Armenians used unleavened bread, were Judaizers, and denied the Formula of Chalcedon regarding the two natures of Jesus Christ; and if Latins also used unleavened bread, then the Latins were also Judaizers and Monophysites. There is clearly very little—if any—value to such conclusions for the history of theology. Western European Christians do not use unleavened bread to symbolize that Christ had only one nature, or no human nature, or no human soul (all accusations of later Greek commentators), nor in imitation of Jews except in the broadest possible sense of believing that the Last Supper was a Passover meal.[46] Latin support of the Formula of the Council of Chalcedon, based as it was on a papal statement of doctrine, was unwavering. To the heresiologist, though, superficial similarity mattered more than what the "heretics" themselves would say they believe.

The second reason that the link from Jews to Judaizing to Armenians to Latins made sense to tenth- and eleventh-century Byzantines was a slippage between doctrinal or theological traits, on the one hand, and ethnic ones on the other. In the eleventh century, for example, the writers of anti-heretical polemic increasingly identified their opponents not by a label related to their doctrine or their mythical arch-heretical founder—that is, "Monophysite," "Nestorian," "Jacobite," and the like—but rather by their ethnic origin: "the heresy of the Armenians," "the heresy of the Syrians," "the heresy of the Latins."[47] As has been the case throughout Christian history, some Greek-rite, Greek-speaking Christians could accept that cultural variations among ethnicities were unrelated to Orthodoxy or un-Orthodoxy. Others, however, feared that ethnic diversity meant doctrinal diversity—that is, heresy—and began to equate Greek language and culture with Orthodoxy, but anything different with heresy.[48]

On the other hand, the eagerness with which the Byzantines applied the label "heresy" to any threatening difference—and even to some that are not particularly threatening—suggests that there is something to be found in and something to be learned from a careful reading of their heresiology. We are clearly not going to learn about heresy or heretics, but we will learn about the heresiologists. I am still not sure what we are going to learn, nor have I yet had that crucial moment of insight that might make me think I profoundly understand the heresiologists and can explain their thinking. Yet somehow I am sure that we are missing something essential in Byzantine culture until and unless we understand their reasoning. As Averil Cameron puts it, "Whether we like it or not as historians, writing heresy, in all its various forms, did occupy a major place in Byzantium—so much so indeed that a full treatment would in its way constitute a new history of Byzantium. This is far from having been written. But meanwhile, at the very least, I suggest that one ought to read these compositions, so strange to our minds, as part of Byzantine pedagogy and the Byzantine sociology of knowledge, self-perpetuating constructions that helped to formulate thought and underpin social norms."[49]

This brief survey of the connections between Armenians and Latins in the Byzantine heresiological literature is only a small piece of that new history, but it reveals how heresiologists might mark a certain difference as significant while ignoring many others. This process of distinguishing significant from insignificant difference is often a mystery. It has, for example, often been remarked that the emphasis on the Latin use of unleavened bread seems strange in light of what most of us would consider more important variations between the liturgies of East and West: for example, marked differences in church form and decoration, in the movements of the clergy throughout the Eucharist, and in the recitation of the Creed. I suggest that the heresiologists' concern can be understood only in the context of heresiology: that is, it is not some wider anxiety about the real presence in the Eucharist; it is not a Eucharistic controversy in any theological context that explains this concern. The connection exists only in the oddly constructed world of heresiologists. In that world, the weapons used against one group of heretics can be sharpened and reused against another, because no matter what heretics say, we know that they are all alike. Latins may deny it, but by their use of the same bread as the Armenians, they are also implicated in whatever other heresies Armenians teach. The structure and coherence attributed to heresy and heretics exists only in the mind of the heresiologist; it is nonetheless a fascinating structure.

"LIGHT FROM THE WEST": BYZANTINE READINGS OF AQUINAS

Marcus Plested

It is a truth universally acknowledged that East and West possess fundamentally opposing theological bases, presuppositions, and methodologies. But the assumption that East and West are meaningful and clearly delineated theological categories is of relatively recent provenance. It is the burden of this paper to demonstrate that this assumption of opposition was by no means prevalent in the last century of the Roman (or Byzantine) Empire. I propose to make this point through an examination of a range of Byzantine responses to the work of Thomas Aquinas.

The title of this essay, "Light from the West," deliberately invokes and reverses the "orientale lumen" lauded in the *Golden Epistle* of William of St-Thierry. Writing to a Carthusian monastery in the Ardennes in 1144, William famously praised its monks for their shining example of asceticism that made "the light of the East and the ancient fervor in religion of Egypt" shine amidst the "darknesses of the West and the cold regions of Gaul."[1] William's happy phraseology was taken up by Pope John Paul II as the *incipit* of his much-heralded Apostolic Letter of 1995, *Orientale lumen*. In that letter, the Roman Catholic Church is bidden to give heed to the wisdom and distinctive charisms of the Christian East. It must be said that the reverse process is all too rarely undertaken in the Christian East itself: few are the voices who would counsel the Orthodox to seek wisdom in the traditions of the Christian West. The certainty of eternal opposition can be comforting: it is far easier to expatiate on the follies and errors of the West than to come to terms with the problems and failings of our own tradition, let alone seriously consider what might actually be learnt from the Christian West.

With such musings in mind, I was delighted to come across a fifteenth-century Byzantine canon in honor of Thomas Aquinas, hailing him as a light or star from the West. The canon is the work of Joseph, Bishop of Methone (John Plousiadenos) and praises Thomas in the best and most florid tradition of Byzantine hymnography. Here is a brief extract:

> As a light from the west he has illumined
> the Church of Christ
> the musical swan
> and subtle teacher,
> Thomas the all-blessed,
> Aquinas by name,
> to whom we, gathered together, cry:
> Hail, universal teacher![2]

One particularly ingenious feature of this verse is the rendering of Aquinas not by the more usual ἐξ Ἀκινάτου or similar, but by Ἀγχίνους, a choice of term that conveys a sense of shrewdness, sagacity, and quickness of mind. This composition is not, of course, in liturgical use in the Orthodox Church and, as the work of a unionist bishop, carries no credence in Orthodox circles. It stands, nonetheless, as a poignant witness to the possibility of a creative interaction between Latin and Byzantine cultural and theological traditions.

We can be very precise about the date and even the hour at which Thomas emerged fully onto the Byzantine scene. It was at three o'clock in the afternoon of December 24, 1354, that the high imperial official Demetrios Kydones put the final touch to his translation of the *Summa contra gentiles*—a task that had taken a year to complete amid his many other pressing concerns.[3] Why he felt compelled to be quite so precise in the timing he gives in his manuscript is something of a mystery: Perhaps he was indicating on the eve of the Nativity that this translation was itself a kind of incarnation; or perhaps he was simply practicing or showing off his Latin. But whatever the solution to that particular conundrum, it is clear that Thomas enjoyed a certain vogue in the last century of Byzantium, down to and beyond the cataclysmic fall of the City in 1453. Thomas's popularity was, however, emphatically not confined to a literary elite of anti-Palamite pro-unionists. What is perhaps most fascinating about the

Byzantine reception of Aquinas is the sheer diversity of those who took him seriously: both to learn from him and to critique him. Among his admirers we find unionists and anti-unionists, Palamites and anti-Palamites (and, indeed, any combination of those categories).

All this runs somewhat counter to the deeply ingrained scholarly supposition that theological method lies at the heart, or at least close to the center, of the theological estrangement between East and West. In the twentieth century, theologians on both sides of the gulf have urged this position of methodological incompatibility. Martin Jugie and Gerhard Podskalsky pursue this line from a Western standpoint, both taking St. Gregory Palamas and his supporters as archetypal of the philosophical incoherence and theological muddle of the Christian East.[4] We also find shades of this approach in Rowan Williams's early critique of Palamas.[5] Virtually all Orthodox theologians of the twentieth century have been content to accept the methodological gap between East and West, but with the sympathies reversed. Thus, the philosophical rationalism of the West is routinely contrasted with the experiential and mystical theology of the Christian East. This is true across the board, pertaining both to the so-called neopatristic and Russian religious schools of Orthodox thought.[6]

In the latter category, Sergius Bulgakov takes the rationalism of the Latin West to be encapsulated in Aquinas's doctrine of transubstantiation. This doctrine he sees as accomplishing the enslavement of theology by philosophy. It is a "rationalistic, groundless determination." Such unwonted probing of the mystery of transmutation is taken to be typical of medieval Western Scholasticism, in whose recesses lurked the "rationalism that was just beginning to raise its head and would lead to the humanistic Renaissance." The only way out of the stifling confines of such earthbound rationalism is a return to the Fathers: "By relying on the patristic doctrine, we can exit the scholastic labyrinth and go out into the open air."[7]

Almost identical sentiments are expressed in the work of Vladimir Lossky, a theologian associated with the neopatristic revival of modern Orthodox theology and conventionally treated as something of an opposite to Bulgakov. For Lossky, it is not transubstantiation but rather the *filioque* that most aptly represents the ills of Western theology with Aquinas, again, its principal proponent. The *filioque* represents an unwarranted rationalization of the mystery of the Trinity, a rationalization that leads inexorably to secularism.[8] For Lossky, mystery and the experience of deification are the hallmarks of Orthodox theology, whereas Scholasticism has been fatally flawed in its elevation of reason and consequent loss of any real apophaticism or truly participatory theology. Indeed, he doubts that between the positive rationalizing approach of the West and the negative mystical approach of the East there is really any common ground at all: "The difference between the two conceptions of the Trinity determines, on both sides, the whole character of theological thought. This is so to such an extent that it becomes difficult to apply, without equivocation, the same name of theology to these two different ways of dealing with divine realities."[9] For Lossky, as for Bulgakov, only a creative return to the Fathers offers a real alternative to the sorry Western saga of decline and fall. This is also the position of Georges Florovsky and John Meyendorff, and has become virtually standard within modern Orthodox theology.

Aquinas features prominently in these juxtapositions of East and West as the foremost exponent and champion of the Scholastic method, a method that is presented in modern Orthodox theology as antithetical to the approach of Gregory Palamas. In practice, Palamas has become for many Orthodox a kind of anti-Thomas or "our answer to Aquinas." This process is certainly to be seen not only as a rejoinder to Jugie but also as a response to the success achieved by the creative retrieval of Thomas led by figures such as Étienne Gilson and Jacques Maritain.

But it has not always been thus. When we turn back to the last years of the Byzantine Empire, we see that the situation is far more complex than such comforting dichotomies would allow. It is difficult not to read these years as one might a Greek tragedy. The recapture of the Queen of Cities in 1261 and diplomatic triumphs such as the Sicilian Vespers were bright spots in an otherwise relentless story of political decline and fall, exacerbated by civil wars and bitter theological disputes. The empire was reduced to client status before the ever-growing might of the Ottomans. It is one of those extraordinary historical conjunctions that 1354—the year of Kydones's translation—was also the date of the Ottoman capture of Gallipoli, which gave the Turks their first permanent foothold in Europe and thereby effectively sealed the fate of the embattled empire.[10] For Christos Yannaras, Kydones's translation was quite as catastrophic in consequence as the loss of Gallipoli. The translation marked the beginning of the extinction of "real Hellenism," the process whereby the living tradition of the Gospel and the Greek Fathers was made subservient to and eventually subsumed by the West. Yannaras notes: "The great historical cycle which started motion in 1354 with Demetrios Kydones as its symbolic marker seems to be coming to a conclusion in the shape of Greece's consumption by Europe—the final triumph of the pro-unionists."[11]

The problem, for Yannaras, is that Scholastic methodology sets a boundary between humanity and God. God becomes an object subjected to the individual intellect and treated as a syllogistically defined entity knowable in his essence. A brief look at questions 2–26 of the *Prima pars* of the *Summa theologiae* will, claims Yannaras, suffice to confirm this impression.[12] In Aquinas, there is no notion of participation. Theology is a rational exercise:

> Man in the Western scholastic tradition does not participate personally in the truth of the cosmos. He does not seek to bring out the meaning, the logos of things, the disclosure of the personal activity of God in the cosmos, but seeks with his individualistic intellect to dominate the reality of the physical world. This stance truly forms the foundation of the entire phenomenon of modern technology.[13]

This estimation is broadly Losskian in inspiration and also conforms closely to the grand narrative articulated by Philip Sherrard in his *Greek East and Latin West*.[14]

There is much of value in Yannaras's work and more subtlety than such snippets would suggest. His critique of neo-Palamite theology, by which term he encompasses the theology of the whole Russian diaspora, is especially salutary. For Yannaras, neo-Palamite theology has too little purchase in historical reality, whether of the fourteenth or the twentieth century. More worrying for Yannaras is that neo-Palamite theology is "certainly and perhaps exclusively a theology of dialogue," structured and determined by its relationship with the West. This oppositional mode of theologizing vis-à-vis the West represents an immense danger:

> If we continue to theologize dialectically with the West, we shall perhaps come in a short time to represent no more than an interesting, somewhat exotic, aspect of the Western theoretical worldview, or a narrowly confessional doctrine which belongs to the sphere of 'archaeology of ideas.' This is, I believe, where the ecumenical dialogue is inevitably leading us; all of us have, I think, personal experience, at conferences and encounters, of the fact that Orthodox views ring out beautifully as poetical notes, deeply moving but completely utopian, having no actual reality within our own Churches today.[15]

This is a warning that deserves the most serious attention, particularly in light of the fact that Yannaras recognizes that many of his strictures against the West apply equally to himself and to his homeland.[16] One might perhaps wish that Yannaras had heeded his own precepts more consistently in his work, which remains, it must be said, unduly dialectical and unwontedly oppositional. Yannaras is a brilliant thinker whose penetrating and urgent vision is not best served by the sweeping historical judgments and impossibly simple dichotomies with which he cloaks his grand narrative. He is, for instance, certainly mistaken when it comes to the Byzantine admirers of Thomas. In particular, he assumes that such admirers were completely in thrall to Thomas and quite incapable of critical reception. Moreover, Latin sympathies, for Yannaras, are always and without exception tantamount to unionism. This is, in fact, far from being the case. But rather than belaboring the work of Yannaras still further, let us turn now to some of the key *dramatis personae*, beginning with Demetrios Kydones himself.

In an elaborate *Apology*, written against his many detractors in his own homeland, Kydones recounts the sense of revelation he felt on encountering Thomas for the first time. Like many of his compatriots, Demetrios had not expected much from the Latins. The Latins were generally encountered as merchants and mercenaries, or perhaps as innkeepers. But through his study of Latin and of Thomas in particular, it became apparent to him that the Latins too had people of the highest intellectual caliber. Demetrios was deeply impressed by the sheer discipline and limpidity of Latin theological method, its elegant use of reason and philosophy to articulate the truths revealed in Scripture. What above all seems to have impressed Demetrios was the sheer extent of classical philosophical learning in Thomas and his fellows.[17]

In all this, Demetrios is not welcoming an alien culture to which he feels inferior but rather recognizing the fundamental congruity between Romans (Byzantines) and Latins. Fed by the same philosophical springs, and heirs to a common tradition of patristic theology formed by Scripture, both Roman and Latin traditions are deeply united at source. While he acknowledges the estrangement that has built up between these traditions, he understands the divide to be largely a cultural—and especially a linguistic—matter, coupled with a good deal of plain old-fashioned prejudice. He pours scorn on the apparently common assumption of Roman superiority, especially the enduring belief that the world is divided between

Greeks and barbarians, that is, between the Romans and the rest. In this scenario, the Romans are the heirs of Plato and Aristotle, while the Latins barely recognizable as human, fit only for menial activities.[18] Such an attitude has led, inter alia, to a widespread rejection of the testimony of the Fathers of the West and a willingness to accept only that of those who hail from the East. Here he quite explicitly states that this is to make of the geographical distance between East and West a theological divide that is, in essence, non-existent.[19] This absurd conflation of geography and identity represents a manifest betrayal of the truth, truth being neither the property of those of Asia nor of those of Europe.[20] Demetrios is certainly aware of a tendency to make the geographical West into a uniform theological category but he resists any such notion with all the forces at his disposal.

Demetrios went on to translate many works of Aquinas, including most of the *Summa theologiae*, in which task he was joined by his brother, Prochoros. Demetrios's translations themselves are done with a good deal of care, most notably in his frequent correction of Thomas's citations of Aristotle against the original Greek.[21] But in matters theological he finds little, if anything, to critique. Indeed, he came to accept Thomas's teaching on papal primacy and the *filioque*, and was in due course received into communion with the church of the elder Rome. Demetrios's interest in Latin theology was very much bound up with his broader political project of opposing accommodation with the Ottomans and seeking help from the West in order to shore up the embattled empire.[22] Demetrios was, of course, largely disappointed in such hopes and had always to contend against the deeply ingrained hostility to the Latins in Byzantium itself. Few were prepared to accept the commonality of Old and New Rome and to heed his plaintive rhetorical question: "What closer allies have the Romans than the Romans?"[23]

Demetrios had little sympathy with official Palamite theology. While he wisely kept his own counsel during the key phases of the controversy, the condemnation in 1368 of his brother and fellow-translator of Thomas, Prochoros, prompted him to condemn what he characterized as a verbose and nonsensical revival of polytheism. Prochoros was certainly more theologically astute than his brother, if less gifted in diplomacy. A devout Athonite hieromonk, Prochoros had become the de facto leader of the anti-Palamite party on the death of Nikephoros Gregoras in 1360, and assembled a refutation of Palamite theology largely based on Thomas: on grounds of divine simplicity, the inadmissibility of potentiality in the wholly actual deity, and the impossibility of direct participation in uncreated grace.[24] But while Prochoros never felt impelled by his Thomist sympathies to leave the Orthodox Church, he was unwise enough to join the fray only after Palamite theology had been definitively vindicated—not a good tactical move. Demetrios fell into disfavor as a result of his protestations on his brother's behalf—a disfavor his various apologies labored vainly to dispel. Prochoros himself died excommunicated.

But for all his personal trials and tribulations, Demetrios had unleashed something of great power onto the Byzantine world. There were many from across the theological spectrum who found much to admire and emulate in the angelic doctor. Thomas's impact was certainly not to be restricted to anti-Palamite pro-unionists such as Demetrios Kydones.[25] In fact, in what follows I shall focus largely on the Palamite and anti-unionist reception of Thomas (not that these two categories always coincide). In other words, I shall be looking at the least obvious areas in which one might expect to find positive estimation of Western theology.

The Palamite party itself betrayed no particular animosity to Western theology per se. Palamas himself was impressed by Augustine, drawing directly on Maximos Planoudes's translation of the *De Trinitate*, and making intriguing use of some Augustinian themes and concepts.[26] As heir to a long tradition of Byzantine Scholasticism, he vigorously defended in Aristotelian terms the proper use of reasoned argumentation against the theological agnosticism of Barlaam, even going so far as to defend the Latin use of the syllogism.[27] The Emperor John VI Kantakuzene, under whom Palamite theology received canonical status, patronized Demetrios's translation of Thomas and facilitated its wide circulation. He also drew directly on another of Demetrios's translations, the *Refutatio alcorani* of Ricoldo da Monte Croce, for his own anti-Islamic treatises.[28] And while Kantakuzene composed a laborious refutation of Prochoros's critique of Palamite theology, he made no criticism of the Scholastic method in general, nor of Thomas in particular, but objected only to the anti-Palamite conclusions reached.[29] He even cited Thomas, in Demetrios's translation, with approval, taking the methodological considerations of *Summa contra gentiles* 1.9 as programmatic for his own demolition of Prochoros.[30] The sole sure foundation of his refutation was to be Scripture, but with arguments demonstrative and probable drawn from philosophers and holy men to convey the truths revealed in Scripture. Given that

Prochoros's work is solidly based on Thomas (often doing little more than stringing citations together), the use of Thomas to refute Prochoros is not without a certain irony, but it does serve to underline further the willingness of Palamites to embrace much of what they found in Aquinas, especially in terms of methodology.

Neilos Kabasilas, Archbishop of Thessaloniki, is another intriguing example of a Palamite willing to make limited use of Thomas. Neilos had initially welcomed Thomas with unreserved enthusiasm, praising Demetrios's translation and reckoning Thomas an exceptionally valuable teacher. Demetrios himself records that Neilos was at first madly in love with Thomas (μανικὸς ἦν ἐραστὴς) and with Latin wisdom in general.[31] But he goes on in his *Apology* to bemoan the fact that Neilos was pressured to go back on his initial stance of unqualified praise under anti-unionist pressure. Nonetheless, even in the treatise on the procession of the Holy Spirit—a piece that attacks Thomas in detailed and vigorous terms—Neilos frequently draws on Thomas's more apophatic declarations in support of his strictures against the untrammeled use of reason in theological discourse.[32] By doing so, he is attempting to expose the inherent contradictions in Thomas, contrasting his protestations of the inadequacy of human reason with his evident reliance on reason. Neilos also adopts a Scholastic methodology, including use of the formula of proposition and objection. John Meyendorff observes that Neilos was consciously trying to "overcome the dilemma" between Palamism and Thomism.[33]

To nuance the situation further, it is worth noting that in his attacks on the illegitimacy of syllogisms, Neilos depends greatly on similar arguments put forward by Barlaam the Calabrian, the first major enemy of the hesychasts. Here we have an anti-unionist Palamite drawing on Thomas in his critique of Thomas while making use of an anti-Palamite source. This underscores, once again, just how complex the situation really was. There simply are no party lines in the Byzantine reception of Thomas, and certainly no default setting of anti-Scholasticism among either Palamites or anti-unionists.

A similar complexity is evident in the work of Theophanes of Nicaea—a critique of Thomas that nonetheless seems to draw significant inspiration from the angelic doctor. Like Neilos, Theophanes was both a Palamite and an anti-unionist. Ioannis Polemis has made a strong case that Theophanes borrowed some key ideas from Thomas, such as the threefold pattern of divine knowledge and the identity of God's essence and his intellect.

Theophanes organized his refutation around a series of *aporiae* or difficulties requiring solution—a sure sign of his affinities with Scholastic methodology.[34]

We have another interesting case in point in Nicholas Kabasilas, nephew to Neilos. Nicholas betrays no sense of animosity towards the West and, indeed, is distinctly irenic in his discussions, for example, of divergent Latin liturgical practices. He remained technically a Palamite, but shows no trace of Palamite theology in his writings. Indeed, he composed a treatise explicitly defending the use of reason in theological discourse, a work that has plausible connections with Aquinas and has even been interpreted as anti-Palamite.[35] And even the most fervently committed of anti-unionists found it perfectly admissible to make use of Aquinas: witness Joseph Bryennios's and Makarios Makres's adoption of arguments (for example, on the incarnation and consecrated virginity) from the *Summa contra gentiles* in their anti-Islamic works.[36]

All this does not amount to a wholesale approval of Thomas, still less to a school of "Byzantine Thomism," but it indicates that the supposition of methodological incompatibility between East and West is deeply flawed. The considerable enthusiasm for Aquinas across party lines—Palamite and anti-Palamite, unionist and anti-unionist—shows that the situation is far more subtle and complex than such a supposition would imply. Indeed, I know of only one Byzantine critique of Thomas that asserts methodological incompatibility in wholly unambiguous terms: the refutation of the *Summa contra gentiles* composed by Kallistos Angelikoudes.[37] In this bitter and unrelenting polemic, Thomas is characterized as heretical not only in his theological conclusions but also in his very approach to the matter of theology—his use of natural reason and excessive reliance upon Aristotle leading him into the errors of, among others, Arius and Mohammed. For Angelikoudes, human reason has nothing of real value to contribute to theology. Angelikoudes's strategy, if one can call it that, is to pile insult upon insult, calumny upon calumny, with very little clarity of argument or structure. It is not an edifying piece and serves as a painful reminder of the depths of hostility to the Latin world felt in some quarters of Byzantium.

Such instinctive hostility to the Scholastic method is, to repeat, relatively rare on the level of sustained theological discourse. It remained perfectly possible in the Byzantine world to receive Western theology sympathetically without compromising one's Orthodoxy. George (later Patriarch

Gennadios) Scholarios is a particularly intriguing example in this respect.[38] Scholarios has the distinction of being both an exceptionally fervent Thomist and the leader of the anti-unionist party the period following the reunion council of Ferrara-Florence (1438–39). Scholarios himself doubted whether Thomas had any more devoted disciple than him: "I do not think that any one of his followers has honored Thomas Aquinas more than I; nor does anyone who becomes his follower need any other muse."[39] He regarded his master as quite simply "the most excellent expositor and interpreter of Christian theology," valuing especially his impeccable grasp of philosophy (especially of Aristotle) and his foundation in the universal patristic tradition. As was the case with Demetrios Kydones, Scholarios was not welcoming a foreign import but recognizing essentially "one of us"—albeit in unfamiliar Latin garb.

Scholarios was certainly no uncritical reader of Thomas. He was quite prepared to disagree with him on any matter on which he departed from the teachings of the Orthodox Church. But he was ready to take on board new doctrines to which the Orthodox Church had no definite objection, for example the doctrine of transubstantiation. He was also prepared to adopt Scholastic positions not embraced by Thomas: for instance, the notion of the immaculate conception as developed by Duns Scotus.

The fact that Thomas was plain wrong on a number of counts—the *filioque*, the papal claims, the essence-energies distinction—in no way detracted, for Scholarios, from his overall value. As Gennadios famously laments: "If only, most excellent Thomas, you had not been born in the West! Then you would not have been obliged to justify the errors of that Church concerning, for instance, the procession of the Spirit and the distinction between the divine essence and operation. Then you would have been as infallible in theological matters as you are in this treatise on ethics."[40] Thomas ought, in short, to have been born a Byzantine.[41] In a similar vein, Gennadios observes: "This Thomas, although he was Latin by race and faith, and so differs from us in those things in which the Roman Church has in recent times innovated, is, in other respects, wise and profitable for those who read him."[42] In this passage, he is defending himself against the ever-deadly charge of Latin-mindedness, but at the same time refuting any notion of fundamental opposition between East and West. The deviations of the Church of Rome are unfortunate aberrations that must not be allowed to obscure the essential congruity of East and West.

Turning now towards a summary conclusion, I would emphasize that positive reception of Thomas often revolves around his methodology and anti-Islamic potential. Acceptance of particular conclusions, especially on contentious theological issues, is less prevalent. Similarly, we must not neglect the substantial anti-Latin prejudice in Byzantine society at large that made sympathy for Western theology always a risky pursuit. But the examples I have given, albeit necessarily by way of an *Überblick*, show that the supposition of a methodological gap between Scholasticism and Orthodoxy simply does not hold. There was no default setting of antipathy to Thomas among either Palamites or anti-unionists. Aquinas found admirers among unionists and anti-unionists, Palamites and anti-Palamites alike.

The Byzantines who welcomed Thomas did so in a critical fashion. They were quite capable of a sophisticated mode of reception that did not necessarily lead to any form of doctrinal compromise. They also welcomed him not as an alien import from a superior culture but as one of their own, as an exceptionally able exponent of traditional Christian Aristotelianism rooted in Scripture and in the Fathers. It is by no means far-fetched to see in this reception the recognition of the common tradition of Greek East and Latin West, a Christian universalism that was certainly disintegrating but was by no means dead in the water even in the fourteenth century.

Modern theologians, Orthodox and Catholic alike, have tended to take this disintegration of Christian universalism as a given, reading back into the last years of Byzantium a theological gulf that is simply not in evidence at the time. The Byzantine reception of Thomas must prompt us to seriously reconsider the whole issue of theological incompatibility between East and West.

Georges Florovsky may be of some use here. Florovsky was distinctly and deeply allergic to Scholasticism when it came to what he saw as its wholly baneful influence on Russian theology: This is the *leitmotif* of his masterwork *Ways of Russian Theology*. In this respect, he conforms exactly to the supposition of eternal opposition I have discussed. But Florovsky was also able to see potential in "high Scholasticism" for a revival of Orthodox theology as part of what he called a "new creative act."[43] He took Lossky to task for his exaggerated and un-nuanced depiction of Thomas, observing that he "probably exaggerates the tension between East and West even in the patristic tradition."[44] But Lossky, too, could be remarkably positive when dealing with Western theology in its own terms, away from the question of its influence on the Christian East. He pays warm tribute to Étienne Gilson's "existentialist" retrieval of the "authentic Thomism of St. Thomas and his immediate predecessors," and sought in his own thesis to discern a continuing apophaticism in the medieval West in the shape of Meister Eckhart.[45] Such sentiments in Florovsky and Lossky are no more than hints, but they do serve as a cheering indicator of the potential for an Orthodox reappropriation of Thomas.

If we are indeed to move beyond the dialectical theologizing that has characterized Orthodox theology in the twentieth century, then the Byzantine reception of Aquinas may serve as a useful starting-point. The reception history I have outlined offers a paradigm for the recovery of the capacity for critical but sympathetic reception of Western sources within the context of a Christian universalism. It means, in short, regaining the ability to recognize orthodoxy in unfamiliar garb and eschewing any hermetic and reactive form of self-definition. Eastern Orthodoxy is of little value so long as it remains merely Eastern. If Orthodoxy is to have any real purchase in the twenty-first century it is going to have to be both oriental and occidental. Light from the East indeed, but also light from the West.[46]

FROM THE "SHIELD OF ORTHODOXY" TO THE "TOME OF JOY": THE ANTI-WESTERN STANCE OF DOSITHEOS II OF JERUSALEM (1641–1707)

Norman Russell

The ambivalence of Orthodoxy's attitude to the West is reflected in the contrasting approaches of contemporary Orthodox thinkers. For some, Western culture embodies spiritual values that have the potentiality to enrich Orthodoxy.[1] For others, the West represents an alien ideology dominated by individualism and consumerism that threatens to overwhelm the Orthodox understanding of life as relational.[2] The latter perspective is based on the conviction that the West is the home of a distorted version of Christianity, whether Catholic or Protestant, characterized by a preoccupation with authority and the exercise of power. The origins of this perspective may be traced back, via the Russian Slavophiles, to the fifteenth-century pro-hesychast opponents of the Council of Florence. It was in the late seventeenth century, however, in the letters and publications of Dositheos of Jerusalem, that it received one of its most important narrations. By his retrieval of late hesychast ecclesiological teaching, Dositheos laid the foundations for the intellectual anti-Westernism dominant in some Orthodox circles today. An examination of the stages by which Dositheos formed his ideas can help us understand the background of this important and enduring current of Orthodox thinking.

Around 1907, on the occasion of the second centenary of the death of Dositheos, there was a spate of publications on him underlining his controversial status.[3] For Chrysostomos Papadopoulos, who became archbishop of Athens in 1923, he was a champion of Orthodoxy at a critical period of the Tourkokratia.[4] However, for Aurelio Palmieri, the author of the first scholarly monograph on Dositheos, he simply perpetuated a sterile struggle against the Latins, leaving works that "only render the hatred of the Greek theologians against the Latin Church more tenacious."[5]

Subsequent studies, although more moderate in tone, have tended to confirm these partisan positions. In a standard Greek work of reference, the *Thrēskeutikē Enkyklopaideia*, Ioannis Karmiris praises Dositheos—in terms that would not, however, have commended themselves to Dositheos himself—as the defender of "the middle way between Roman Catholicism and Protestantism."[6] A Romanian student of Dositheos, writing in the 1970s, describes him as "a teacher and guide of Orthodoxy [who] had done much in many different fields for the good of Orthodoxy and Hellenism."[7] Gerhard Podskalsky sums up the prevalent Western view: Dositheos, he says, is remembered chiefly as "a Church politician of a high order and an organizer and patron of Orthodox apologetics against the West."[8] What I wish to suggest in this paper is that Dositheos was not merely an accomplished apologist bound by the confessional mentality that characterized so many of his contemporaries, but a man whose anti-Westernism was the product of a profound conviction in Orthodoxy's ecumenicity.[9]

There is no doubt that Dositheos was very able. He was born in 1641 at Arachova, a village in the Peloponnesus now called Rizon.[10] We do not know his baptismal name, but his family name was Scarpetis.[11] His father died when he was eight years old and he was taken under the wing of the metropolitan of Corinth, Gregorios Goulanos, who had baptized him. Metropolitan Gregorios admitted him to the Monastery of the Holy Apostles at Corinth under the name of Dositheos, and ordained him deacon at the age of eleven.[12] His education was entirely monastic. Unlike many of his contemporaries, he did not study at an Italian university, and to the end of his life preferred to write in a straightforward vernacular Greek.[13] In 1657, a stroke of good fortune changed his life. On a visit to Constantinople in that year he caught the attention of the Patriarch Paisios of Jerusalem (1645–60) and was taken into his service. For the next three years he accompanied Paisios on fund-raising trips in the Balkans and along the Black Sea coast. In 1660 he was lucky again. On the island of Kastellorizon, en route to Jerusalem, Paisios died, "breathing his last," Dositheos tells us, "with his head on my knees."[14] Dositheos was nineteen years old. He was alone on a small island with a large sum of money that the local Turks were eager to plunder. Somehow he managed to escape (with the money) and return to Constantinople. At a meeting of the Holy Synod in

January 1661 a learned monk, Nektarios, was chosen to succeed Paisios.[15] Not surprisingly, Nektarios kept Dositheos on the patriarchal staff and made him his archdeacon. After another fund-raising tour, Nektarios left for Jerusalem, taking Dositheos with him. In 1666, he made him metropolitan of Caesarea, thereby signaling his fitness for the patriarchate. Three years later Nektarios resigned on grounds of infirmity as a result of advanced age. A synod convoked by Methodios III of Constantinople elected Dositheos to succeed him.[16] Although he was only twenty-eight years old, he was judged, rightly, to have already acquired sufficient experience to take on the burdens of patriarchal office.[17]

The burdens with regard to Jerusalem were twofold: the state of the patriarchal finances and the ambition of the Latins to control the Holy Places. The first thing Dositheos did was to visit Moldavia and Wallachia to solicit donations. As a result of the generosity of the Romanians, he raised the very considerable sum of twenty thousand piastres.[18] He also approached a rich Greek benefactor who lived in Constantinople, Manolakis of Castoria, who agreed to pay for the restoration of the Church of the Nativity at Bethlehem, which was in imminent danger of collapse.[19] The work began in 1670 and, with the Orthodox villagers of the surrounding area giving their labor free of charge, the work proceeded rapidly. The Franciscans, however, opposed the project and persuaded the governor of Jerusalem to give orders for the new work to be destroyed. Dositheos immediately went to Adrianople, where the imperial court was in residence, and, through the influence of Grand Dragoman Panayiotis Nikousios, was able to have instructions sent to the governor to allow the work to continue.[20] The renovated church was reconsecrated with great pomp in 1672.

Two years later there was another contretemps with the Latins. The new French ambassador, the Marquis de Nointel, had been instructed by Louis XIV to secure the Holy Places for the Franciscans.[21] He obtained permission from the Porte in 1674 to go to Jerusalem to assess the situation for himself. Unfortunately, his arrival in Jerusalem coincided with the Sunday of Cheesefare, the beginning of Orthodox Lent. When the Franciscans started to deck out the Church of the Holy Sepulchre in festal fashion for the reception of the ambassador the Orthodox objected, and in the ensuing fracas a stone flung by one of the friars killed an Orthodox monk. Dositheos made a formal protest through Nikousios to the grand vizier, Fazil Ahmed Köprülü, and in 1675 an *iradé* was issued confirming the Greeks to be in possession of the Holy Places.[22]

Theological issues were not so easy to resolve. When the Church of the Nativity was reconsecrated, Dositheos took the opportunity of the presence of so many bishops to hold a synod. Known as the Council of Bethlehem (or Jerusalem), this synod considered a matter that had been troubling the Orthodox for several decades: the Calvinist *Confession of Faith* of Ecumenical Patriarch Cyril I Loukaris. This *Confession* had been published first in Latin in Constantinople in 1629 and then in Greek in Geneva in 1633, and although it had been condemned by synods held at Constantinople (1638) and Jassy (1641), Protestants were still claiming a patriarch of Constantinople as one of their own.[23] At the Council of Jerusalem in 1672, Dositheos undertook to prove that the *Confession* was not by Cyril at all but a forgery.[24] The resulting acts, together with an Orthodox confession of faith, were published in Paris in 1676 under the title *Shield of Orthodoxy*.

The text, sent to Paris by the Marquis de Nointel, was edited and furnished with a Latin translation by the learned Maurist, Michel Foucqueret.[25] The French found it useful to be able to claim Orthodox support against Protestantism, and indeed the *Shield of Orthodoxy* is not overtly anti-Latin. The villains of the piece are the Protestants, supreme heretics who, in Dositheos's words, no longer "partake of the Church in any way" because they have been rejected by Rome.[26] The appended Confession of Faith, drawn up by Dositheos himself, maintains the Latin doctrines of transubstantiation and purgatory (although Dositheos was to retract the latter—*hēmartēmenōs eipōn*—in his own publication of the Acts in 1690).[27] The Protestants were enraged and eventually published a refutation of the *Shield* by the Calvinist Jean Aymon, entitled *Monumens authentiques de la religion des grecs*.[28]

The Protestants, however, were wrong in assuming that Dositheos was leaning towards the Catholics. The very title of his work, *Aspis orthodoxias*, had been framed as a response to the *Romanae fidei scutum*, the notorious *Targa*, which had been publicly burned in the Ottoman Empire in 1658 at the request of Ecumenical Patriarch Parthenios IV.[29] The *Targa* was the work of a French Jesuit, François Richard, written "against the errors of the Greek schismatics" in order to promote the triumph of the Roman faith, "without which it is impossible to please God."[30] If this book had been written in French or Latin, it would not have provoked any great reaction from the Orthodox hierarchy. But it was written in the Greek vernacular, an early sign of the more aggressive approach to proselytization that was to be characteristic of the Ottoman Empire's Jesuit mission in the latter part of the seventeenth century.[31]

The events surrounding the publication of the *Shield of Orthodoxy* made it clear to Dositheos that he needed his own press. The setting up of a press in the Ottoman Empire was not an easy matter. In 1515, Selim I had made any attempt at printing punishable by death, for the *ulema* considered printing dangerous to Islam.[32] Indeed, a Turkish press was not established until 1729. The prohibition did not extend to non-Muslims—the first Hebrew press in Constantinople dates from 1493, and the Armenians set up a press in 1567—but the position of the ecumenical patriarch as the head of the Orthodox millet (perhaps a quarter of the population of the empire) made a Greek printing press highly sensitive politically. Patriarch Cyril I had set up a press in 1627 but it had been destroyed by the Ottoman authorities in less than a year.[33] The solution lay in a press on Ottoman territory but not under the nose of the government, ideally in one of the two Danubian principalities.

Dositheos had first visited Moldavia, the more northerly principality, in 1662 with Patriarch Nektarios. Although a province of the Ottoman Empire, it had its own independent administration under a ruling prince (the voivode), supplied since the mid-seventeenth century by one or another of the Greek Phanariot families.[34] Dositheos tells how in 1680 he gave six hundred piastres to a Vlach monk called Metrophanes to make him a Greek fount.[35] So began the printing of a series of books, first at Jassy and then later also at Bucharest and Rimnic, that was designed to bolster the position of the Orthodox in the Ottoman Empire.

The first book to issue from the press was an act of piety, but nevertheless on a topic that fitted perfectly with Dositheos's program: Nektarios of Jerusalem's *On the Papal Primacy* (Jassy, 1682), written after Nektarios had resigned the patriarchate.[36] It caused quite a stir. A Latin translation by Pierre Allix appeared in London in 1702, provoking a refutation, published in Paris in 1718, by the distinguished Dominican patristic scholar, Michel le Quien.[37]

The second book, which came out in the following year, was a volume containing the editiones principes of two late Byzantine works, *Against Heresies* by Symeon of Thessaloniki (d. 1429), and a *Commentary on the Liturgical Office* by Mark of Ephesus (c. 1392–1445) (Jassy, 1683).[38] Both works share a common theme: the mystical interpretation of the Divine Liturgy. Dositheos's intention in this case was not to attack the West directly but to help Orthodox Christians resist Latin influence by deepening their experience of liturgical life.

There was then a gap of seven years. Dositheos's second book had come out in October 1683, only a month after the catastrophic defeat of the Turks at Vienna. The Ottoman Empire was immediately plunged into turmoil. In December, the grand vizier was executed. Later, Moldavia was invaded by the Poles. During this period Dositheos did not remain idle. When it became possible to resume printing again in 1690 (now in Bucharest), he issued three works in quick succession. In January came *Against the Schism* by Maximos Peloponnesios (1565/70–1621/30),[39] and in September *Against Loukaris* by Meletios Syrigos (1585–1663)[40] together with the reissue of the *Shield of Orthodoxy* under a new title: *Manual Refuting the Calvinist Madness Slandering the Eastern Holy Catholic and Apostolic Church*.[41]

This new version of the *Shield of Orthodoxy* gave Dositheos the opportunity to make some amendments. In a second preface he explains the genesis of the work, tracing first the progress of the Reformation up to Calvin and then describing the impact in the Orthodox world of the Calvinistic *Confession* attributed to Cyril. This *Confession*, he insists, was a forgery brought to Constantinople by Calvinists from Geneva and "put out in the name of the patriarch Cyril as if he were the author."[42] The book was very disturbing to the general public. Cyril, however, in Dositheos's opinion, never deviated from the Orthodox faith. He always taught Orthodoxy from the pulpit. But he did live for six years without repudiating the *Confession*, which understandably gave rise to suspicion. He was, therefore, deposed, mainly as a result of Western pressure. The Spirit then moved the voivode Basil Lupul to call a council at Jassy in 1641, resulting in Meletios Syrigos's compilation, *Orthodox Confession of Faith of the Eastern Church*. Then "in around 1670 the ambassador in Constantinople of the king of France sought from some bishops and the patriarchs their written opinion on the teaching of the Eastern Church on matters of faith. Many have done this, including the Holy Synod in Constantinople. Whereupon we too have drawn up a refutation of the Calvinist madness."[43] The "Celts" wanted documents and they duly got them.

The doctrinal modifications Dositheos made in this new edition of his *Confession* are interesting. The article on the Eucharist remains unchanged. He uses the term "transubstantiation" (*metousiōsis*) and makes the Scholastic distinction between substance and accidents in a moderately Westernizing manner that goes back to George Gennadios Scholarios, the first patriarch of Constantinople under the Ottomans.[44] The article on purgatory, however, has been corrected and expanded in an anti–Roman Catholic spirit.[45] The idea of expiatory suffering has been retained but the theory of purgatorial fire has been rejected. It is only after the resurrection, when souls will be reunited with bodies, that they can be punished by fire. As Timothy Ware points out, this is a view that had been put forward by the Greeks at the Council of Florence in 1439.[46] The change between the editions of 1676 and 1690 is an indication of how, in the interval, Dositheos was beginning to recover the theological traditions of late Byzantium.

Todt calls the *Manual Refuting the Calvinist Madness* Dositheos's *theologische Hauptwerk*.[47] But perhaps the most important of the works, historically, to issue from Dositheos's press are three vast compilations: the *Tome of Reconciliation*, the *Tome of Love*, and the *Tome of Joy*. These form a veritable trilogy encapsulating Dositheos's vision of Christian order and unity. Even the progression of titles from reconciliation to joy is significant—the Latin Church is portrayed as the prodigal younger son who will one day see the error of his ways and be received back with joy into his father's house.

The first work in the trilogy is called *Tome of Reconciliation* because it is not only a refutation of Latin theology, but also an appeal to the Westerners to return to Orthodoxy. "My Latin brothers," cries Dositheos in the preface, "I urge you on behalf of Christ to be reconciled with God; return to the orthodox, catholic and apostolic Church, from which you have wrongly strayed, that from now on we may be one Church, a single flock with a single shepherd."[48] The ways in which the Latins had strayed are made clear in the texts assembled in the body of the book: (1) an anonymous treatise *Against the Latins*, dating from the first decade of the fifteenth century; (2) *Antirrhetics against the Council of Florence* by John Eugenikos, the brother of Mark of Ephesus; (3) a *Manual on the Procession of the Holy Spirit* by George Koressios of Chios, a contemporary of Dositheos's; (4) an opusculum on the *filioque*, *Against the Latins*, by Makarios Makres; (5) an *Apologia* of the bishops and clergy of Constantinople to the Emperor John VIII against the decisions of the Council of Florence; (6) an anthology of texts made by Theodore Agallianos, archivist of the Great Church under the last emperor, Constantine XII; (7) an anonymous tract against the *filioque*; and (8) a treatise *Against the Latins* by the fourteenth-century controversialist Matthew Vlastares.

All these are late works. They were assembled by Dositheos (from either the Patriarchal Library of Jerusalem or that of the Metochion of the Holy Sepulchre in Constantinople) specifically to counter the increasing number of pro-Latin books that were coming into the Ottoman Empire.[49] In his preface, Dositheos singles out Leo Allatius in particular (a great scholar of Chiot origin and, until his death in 1669, librarian of the Vatican) as one who had uttered extreme blasphemies and slandered the Eastern Church.[50] He says that the *Tome* is a response to Allatius's *Enchiridion de Processione Spiritus Sancti*, which had been reprinted in Rome four years previously.[51]

Dositheos's large folio volume cannot have circulated as easily as the pocket edition of Allatius's work, but he was sufficiently encouraged by its reception to issue a sequel six years later. The *Tome of Love* (1698)—Dositheos claims that unlike the Latins he conducts his own polemics "with love and gentleness," hence the title—is also conceived as a response to Latin works aimed at proselytization. The volume, he says, is directed specifically against Baronius, Bellarmine, and "the atheist *Targa*."[52] The *Targa* we have already met. Baronius (1538–1607) is mentioned for his *Annales Ecclesiastici*, which since Dositheos's time have also been criticized by Western scholars for their bias against the Greeks. Bellarmine (1542–1621) completes the trio because of his *Dottrina Christiana Breve*, which had just been reprinted in Rome in 1695 with a vernacular Greek version in Greek and Latin character "at the order of the Supreme Pontiff and at the instance of George Perpiniano, bishop of Tinos and Mykonos [. . .] in order to teach country people and children the facts of our most holy faith."[53]

One of the most interesting features of the *Tome of Love* is the defense it mounts of hesychasm. Richard, in the *Targa*, had accused Gregory Palamas and Philotheos Kokkinos of heresy. Moreover, hesychasm had become a matter of debate again in the Greek-speaking world with attacks on it by Paisios Ligarides, the controversial archbishop of Gaza, and the Greek Catholic Ioannes Matthaios Karyophylles, both of whom came under the lash of Dositheos, the *Latinomastix*.[54] The *Tome of Love* prints a number of Palamite texts for the first time, preceded by a long introductory essay on hesychasm.[55]

With the publication of the *Tome of Joy*, the hostility towards Rome increases. The symbolic significance of the title is explained by Dositheos as expressing the joy Orthodox feel "when with a few crumbs of doctrine they confound all the novelties and blasphemies of the papists, as if destroying a spider's web."[56] A new militancy is evident as Dositheos "blows the sacred trumpet" to alert the faithful against Latin aggression. The Jesuit-sponsored Uniat movement in the Ukraine is singled out as a supreme danger for the Orthodox, for it is "nothing other than separation from the true God."[57]

To understand the change of tone, we need to recall the critical political situation at the time Dositheos was beginning his program of publications. After the defeat of the Turks outside Vienna in 1683 the complete collapse of the Ottoman Empire was only narrowly averted. The situation was eventually stabilized by the Peace of Karlowitz in 1699. This treaty (negotiated on the Ottoman side by the grand dragoman, Alexander Mavrokordatos, who had succeeded Panayiotis Nikousios in 1673) recognized, among other things, the loss of Transylvania to Austria, thereby allowing the Habsburgs to push on with their conversion of the Orthodox to Uniatism.[58] At the same time the condition of Orthodox Christians in the Ottoman Empire saw a marked improvement. Taxes were lowered and restrictions on church building were eased.[59] From the Ottoman perspective, the loyalty of the sultan's Orthodox subjects was clearly worth encouraging.

For the Orthodox ecclesiastical authorities there were three possible responses to these developments: to confine themselves to the affairs of the Ottoman Empire, to seek support from the West, or to look for a closer relationship with Russia. The first option was not practicable. The Rum millet's commercial and ecclesiastical networks extended throughout Europe with an Orthodox exarch stationed in Venice from the end of the sixteenth century.[60] Contacts were frequently sought by both sides, by Westerners for confessional advantage and by Easterners for the financial benefits that accrued from them.[61] Finally there was always the pressure exerted in Constantinople by the European ambassadors.

The second option had its supporters, but Dositheos was not one of them.[62] He could only see Western policies towards the Ottoman Empire as deeply injurious to Orthodoxy. The progress of the Unia Transylvania and Ruthenia, with its forced conversions, horrified him. In a letter to Peter the Great on June 2, 1702, Dositheos refers to the Austrian emperor as "that false, pope-crowned Caesar [. . .] a worse persecutor of the Orthodox Church than Diocletian."[63] The French were no better. In 1690, profiting from the Ottoman need for their support against the Austrians, they had obtained an *iradé* restoring Franciscan privileges in the Holy Places. In protest, Dositheos never set foot in Jerusalem again.

The remaining option was a closer relationship with Russia. Here there seemed to be real opportunities. In 1696, Peter the Great became sole ruler. In the same year, the Turkish garrison of Azov, at the mouth of the Don, surrendered to the Russians after a two-year siege. There were scenes of jubilation in Moscow. Patriarch Adrian "wept at Peter's news of the first Russian victory in a generation over the enemies of Christ."[64] Russia's new military prowess also impressed the Greeks, encouraging secret dreams of the restoration of the Byzantine Empire. Dositheos, however, was very cautious in this respect[65]—and was no Caesaropapist. He disapproved of Peter's ecclesiastical policy even before the radical religious reform that was to be imposed on the Russian Church in 1721, fourteen years after his death.

Nevertheless, Dositheos took the greatest interest in Russian affairs, and from the 1680s was in close touch with Moscow.[66] In 1683, Patriarch Joachim had appealed to him for teachers of Greek for a new academy to be founded in Moscow. Dositheos had sent two brothers, Ioannikios and Sophronios Likhoudes, who had impressed him with their learning, but in spite of their anti-Latin and anti-Protestant writings they proved a bitter disappointment to him.[67] It is not entirely clear why, but is possibly connected with the role of Ioannikios in negotiating an anti-Turkish alliance between Moscow and Venice in 1689. Dositheos became increasingly suspicious of Greeks like the Likhoudes brothers who had had a Western education. When Peter the Great appealed to him in 1696 for suitable Greeks to be appointed to Azov and other episcopal sees, he wrote back insisting that "Your Majesty is never to make a Greek, Serb or Ukrainian metropolitan or patriarch, but only Muscovites [. . .] however many faults they may have, however uneducated they may be [. . .]. It is important, most pious lord," he goes on to say, "that a foreigner should not be brought to your great episcopal throne and that Your Majesty should not send a Greek to Azov."[68] Instead, he suggests that the tsar should send young Muscovites to him and he would train them for office himself. He had no confidence in the products of the Academy of Kiev or the Italian universities. Peter did not take Dositheos's advice, entrusting the affairs of the patriarchate after Adrian's death to a former Uniat, Stefan Iavorskii.[69] Dositheos was dismayed at the promotion of such a notorious Westernizer. He had even heard reports that Iavorskii had introduced statues into Moscow's churches,[70] and wrote a long letter to him in November 1703, in which he admonished him for destroying the Greek Academy at Kiev and encouraging Latin studies instead.[71] He nevertheless continued until his death to support the cause of authentic Greek learning in Russia, sending many Greek manuscripts to what was to become the Moscow Synodal Library.

Dositheos died in Constantinople at the Metochion of the Holy Sepulchre on the night of February 6/7, 1707, and was buried in the church of Ayia Paraskevi at Hasköy, across the Golden Horn from the Phanar. Eight years later, his remains were transferred to Jerusalem by his nephew and successor, Chrysanthos Notaras, and reinterred in the Church of the Forty Martyrs.[72] Todt describes Dositheos as "without doubt the most important Greek Orthodox Patriarch of Jerusalem in the entire second millennium of the Church's history,"[73] and rightly so. No patriarch since Sophronius, who had played a leading role in the early seventh-century Christological controversies and had surrendered Jerusalem to the Arabs in 638, had made a more significant contribution to Orthodox self-understanding. In the circumstances of the seventeenth century, such self-understanding was necessarily defined in relation to the doctrines and ecclesiastical politics of post-Reformation Europe. Dositheos's approach stands out from that of many of his contemporaries. He neither accepts the Western theological approach *tout court*, nor does he simply display an inherited visceral hostility. His criticism of the West is the product of his experience of the Franciscans in Jerusalem and of the Jesuits in Eastern Europe. In 1671, for example, he was happy to have the friars come to the patriarchate to debate theological questions.[74] But by 1704 he was praising Grand Prince Alexander, who had replied to a delegation of cardinals sent from Old Rome in 1237, with the words: "As the Apostles taught, as the Fathers commented, as the Synods defined and confirmed, that is what we believe and we do not accept any other discussions on the faith."[75] Dositheos was fully aware of the vulnerability of Orthodox theologians who thought they could engage in debate with the Society of Jesus.

For all his hostility towards the Jesuits, however, for Dositheos "the West," in an important sense, was fellow Greeks who had adopted different criteria of self-identity from those he regarded as properly Orthodox. Hence his bitter polemics against Leo Allatius and Ioannes Matthaios Karyophylles, and the measures he took against Paisios Ligarides and the Likhoudes brothers. True Orthodoxy, in his view, was defined by the hesychasts and anti-unionists of late Byzantium.

Dositheos was not anti-Western because he wanted to further Greek ecclesio-political aims. He did not deify Greek culture or seek to extend the jurisdiction of the ecumenical patriarchate. He was an Ottoman Christian with a vision of a universal Orthodoxy that he hoped, like many after him, the Russian tsar might be able to promote. The Western missionaries aroused his fury because they promoted a doctrine of the Church of Rome as the sole vehicle of salvation, thereby undermining popular confidence in Orthodoxy. His response was not to claim a mirror-like exclusivity for the Eastern patriarchates, but rather to make the traditional Byzantine appeal for Rome to return to the status quo ante, that is to say, to the situation before the adoption of the *filioque* and the rise of the papal claim to universal jurisdiction. The books he published, he said, were meant as "a sign to be believed, that is for reformation of [the Westerners'] innovations and for their return to the Catholic and Apostolic Church, in which their forefathers were of old."[76] This view, reflecting Dositheos's deepest convictions, is still widely held today.

The Burdens of Tradition: Orthodox Constructions of the West in Russia (Late 19th–Early 20th cc.)

Vera Shevzov

The nineteenth century was pivotal in the history of both Russian intellectual and modern Orthodox thought. In the first half of the century, following Russia's defeat of Napoleon in 1814 and the Decembrist uprising in 1825, many of Russia's educated elite, who later would be identified as the first generation of Slavophiles and Westernizers, fervently debated the future of Russia vis-à-vis the West.[1] Passionately addressing what would eventually be called "the Russian idea"—the idea of Russia's distinctiveness with respect to Europe—these debates had long-lasting consequences not only for Russian self-identity, but also for Orthodox conceptualizations of the West. As historian Peggy Heller has recently argued in an essay on the emergence of the concept of the West in Russia, alongside their striving to articulate a Russian identity, Russia's intellectuals also "constructed a conception of the West as a single and unified cultural entity."[2]

Indeed, the topic "Russian constructions of the West," or even more generally speaking, "Orthodoxy and the West" in nineteenth-century Russia, could comfortably rest on the examination of the nineteenth-century debates between Slavophiles and Westernizers, as Orthodox Christianity played a formidable role in them. The more nuanced topic of "Orthodox constructions of the West," however, is somewhat different. While the early Slavophiles—Aleksei Khomiakov, Ivan Kireevskii (1806–56), and Konstantin Aksakov (1817–60)—were devout believers, it could be argued that their profoundly influential philosophical ideas as a whole were concerned not immediately with Orthodox Christianity or with the fate of the Christian Church as such, but primarily with Russia and its future with respect to the West.[3] For this reason, their legacy is often presented as part of a broader literary-philosophical tradition that is traced from the writings of Petr Chaadaev (1794–1856) to Nikolai Berdiaev (1874–1948).[4] Moreover, though they were Orthodox laymen, they were speaking as members of educated society. In their day, they were not considered official voices of Orthodoxy but voices of secular society, whose relevance specifically to Orthodox thought and theology at that time was not at all clear.

To examine *Orthodox* constructions of the West, therefore, this essay turns to Russia's Orthodox professional academics—theologians, historians, and philosophers—who were graduates of and professors in Russia's theological academies, located in St. Petersburg, Moscow, Kazan, and Kiev. While less well known than Russia's secular intellectuals, the voices of these academics, a large number of whom were also laymen, are no less significant. As one-time students and teachers in these institutions, and sometimes in universities, and as active scholars who published in Russia's often spirited Orthodox theological and devotional journals, they in many ways represented the Orthodox establishment during this period.[5] In contrast to the Slavophiles and Westernizers whose main intellectual work took place in urban salons, these men were steeped in a particular ecclesial milieu in which preoccupation with the West had its own distinct historical and theological parameters.

Insofar as it was of religious, spiritual, and confessional concern, the West in the Church's academic and clerical circles was an ancient preoccupation. If the history of the Russian idea and its correlative concept of the West is usually traced to early nineteenth-century Russia, the history in Russia of what we might refer to as the "Orthodox idea"—namely, the belief in Orthodoxy's distinctiveness from its Western Christian counterparts—is much older, and in Russia can be traced back at least to the thirteenth century, if not earlier to Russia's Byzantine inheritance.[6] Eventually expressed in the prevalent narrative that asserted that since the Western Church had fallen away from universal Christian unity, the Christian East had the responsibility and special task of safeguarding the authentic Christian faith, the Orthodox idea can already be found in Russia's *Primary Chronicle*. In this well-known twelfth-century account of Prince Vladimir's baptism, we find that the priest reminded the prince of the main tenets of the Christian faith, recounting for him the Nicene-Constantinopolitan Creed and the teachings of the Ecumenical Councils. Notably, he completed his recitation of the tradition with the following: "Do not accept the teaching of the Latins, whose instruction is vicious. . . . avoid their doctrine. . . . God guard you from this evil, oh Prince!"[7]

Such stories were not lost on posterity, even almost a millennium later. In 1906, commenting on the Byzantine legacy of Russian Orthodoxy, the Russian religious thinker, Vasilii Rozanov, wrote that it was as if "decaying and dying, Byzantium whispered to Russia all of its vexations . . . and bequeathed Russia to guard them. Russia, at the bedside of the departing one . . . gave its word: mortal enmity toward the western tribes."[8] Two years later, in 1908, Constantine Shebatinskii, a graduate of the Kiev Theological Academy, expressed a similar view. The Greeks, he wrote, provided guidance to Russia's entry and immersion into Christian culture and civilization. While the West might have served this function, argued Shebatinskii, the Greeks discredited the Latins in the eyes of Russians and therefore left little room for them in this process.[9]

Yet, even while bearing this perceived nonnegotiable heritage within a universal Christian mindset that included its own understanding of history, Russia's Orthodox academics in the late nineteenth century were also part of the modern world where the West symbolized much more. Primarily living in urban areas, they were part of a society which was not only extraordinarily open to the West, but in the prior century and a half had made every effort to incorporate European culture so as to solidify Russia's place in the European world. Many Russians considered Russia to be a part of Europe, even if only as an outlying "province"; others spoke of Europe as their second home.[10] Some of Russia's academic theologians believed Russia had been too successful in its imitative efforts, maintaining that "our [contemporary] culture is not of our own native creation . . . it has been transplanted from the West."[11]

The West also figured prominently in the Orthodox Church's ecclesial life. Since even before the time of Peter the Great, Western Christian influences had been making themselves felt in Russia by means of the Ukraine and Belarus. Theological schools in Russia came under the influence of Western Christian ideas especially following the ascension to the throne of Peter the Great, when Protestant influences increased and when many of the more educated clergy from Kiev were invited to teach in schools in the more central and northern regions of Russia. Indeed, Orthodox seminarians received their education predominantly in Latin until the early nineteenth century.[12] Similarly telling is the fact that even remote peasant icon workshops during this period often had Western reproductions of images by Michelangelo and Leonardo da Vinci alongside Orthodox iconographic manuals.[13] Consequently, however these Orthodox academics might have imagined it, their church world, along with their social, political, and broader cultural worlds, over the preceding century in particular had become soundly intertwined with the West.

Because of strong Western influences in their own midst, the Church's academics could not help but become caught up in a parallel set of questions plaguing educated society. If, for secular society, the current questions had to do with *Russia's* identity, originality, and future with respect to the West, for Orthodox academics the most pressing issues concerned the nature of Orthodoxy, its uniqueness (*samobytnost'*) and its relationship to the Christian West.[14] In part, according to Alexander Lopukhin, historian, theologian, and graduate of St. Petersburg Theological Academy, this need in Orthodoxy stemmed from the impact of Protestant and Catholic thought on Orthodoxy in the eighteenth century: "We have not yet worked out in relation to them the originality and independence which we theoretically consider inherent to Orthodoxy."[15] The repetition of doctrinal definitions, often arbitrary lists of differences, and weathered historical arguments were no longer effective. Neither was the common practice of assuming a Protestant persona when debating with Catholics or a Catholic one when debating with Protestants.[16]

Yet, when speaking of Orthodoxy, the issue of originality posed its own set of dilemmas. If, as the Slavophiles had claimed, the essential difference between Russia and the West was one of kind and not degree; if, indeed, as Vasilii Zenkovskii maintained, "the orientation of Slavophiles was not anti-Western, but external to that of the West"[17]—what might be the effect of analogous thinking regarding Orthodoxy and Western forms of Christianity? Given the historically broader framework of the idea of the universality of the Christian faith, their non-negotiable commitment to the Orthodox idea of safeguarding Christianity's "primordial completeness,"[18] and the history of division with the Western churches, how, we might ask, did Russia's academic theologians conceptualize the West during these critical decades before Russia's 1917 Bolshevik Revolution?

Orthodoxy, Modernity, and the West

Whereas Russia's intellectuals began their debates about Russia and the West in the early nineteenth century, Russia's academic theologians began considering these issues in print later, during the reign of Emperor Alexander II (1855–81). Encouraged by a period of "glasnost," many Orthodox academics embarked on a conscious mission to make Orthodoxy relevant in the modern world. Until this time, by their own admission, the theological academies had tended to be "deaf to all practical demands of life" and, hence, relatively removed from society.[19] Orthodox thought—be it theology, ethics, history, philosophy—was carried out within the academies and for fellow academics.[20] In order to sustain Orthodoxy's relevance in a rapidly changing society, many of these academics advocated taking theology "out into the streets," as it were, and proactively engaging modernity (*sovremennost'*)—a metonym for the West—on Orthodox terms.

Very much aware that members of Russia's educated society "nourished themselves on the fruits" of the West, the academics' enterprise involved engaging the West and the related notion of modernity in a new way.[21] They were aware that they had to develop a new understanding of their own vocations, a new style and language of discourse, as well as a new approach to the meaning and purpose of Orthodox scholarship, knowledge, and science (*nauka*).[22] On the immediate practical level, the more progressive of the academics believed they and their colleagues had to shed their perennial suspicion of philosophical ideas and cultural currents emerging from the modern West and instead find inspiration in the phrase from St. Paul's first letter to the Thessalonians (5:21): "Test everything, hold fast to what is good."[23] Alexander Ivantsov-Platonov, a proto-presbyter and professor of Church history at Moscow University, insisted that "those who extend their hand to contemporary civilization were not cowards or renegades or traitors to Orthodoxy."[24]

One of the most well-known advocates of this approach was Archimandrite Feodor Bukharev (1824–71), whose often complex ideas have been recently examined by Paul Valliere.[25] In his 1860 essay, "On the Relation of Orthodoxy to Modernity," Bukharev maintained that awareness of one's contemporary environment was a biblical mandate; a lack of such awareness posed its own set of dangers to faith. As guidance in his relation to the West and its ideas, Bukharev sought not so much the dogmatic teachings of the ecumenical councils, but the *spirit* of those councils, with which, he maintained, their participants took up the challenges of their times.[26] In this vein, he and other like-minded academics encouraged mastering Western treasures of knowledge and wisdom in order to discern their "applicability" to Orthodoxy, and even advocated passing through the "Western school" in order to learn as much as possible.[27] Only in this way, he argued, could Orthodoxy remain a vital force in the modern world.

As long as the West was conceived in terms of modernity, some Orthodox academic theologians consciously took a more neutral or even fraternal stance toward the Christian West. Journals like *Pravoslavnoe obozrenie* (*The Orthodox Review*), for instance, published Russian translations of modern Western Christian apologetic writings against modernity's culture of unbelief without accompanying critical commentaries, thereby signaling that their content, for all intents and purposes, was "Orthodox."[28] In light of the common challenges that modernity posed to the Christian faith, it was not difficult for many Orthodox theologians to overlook confessional divisions. Maintaining, as one author did, that "all Christian societies, despite confessional differences, enjoy points of contiguity," they oriented themselves to the Christian West accordingly.[29]

The Christian West: Polemics in a New Key

The influence of the West was not merely the subject of pastoral concern with respect to the quality of Orthodox sensibilities within educated society or a theological concern involving Orthodox understandings of "the world." At the same time, Orthodox academics were preoccupied specifically with the *Christian* West because of growing support for Christian unity in both Europe and Russia, and because of a related concern regarding what they felt were inaccurate Roman Catholic and Protestant perceptions of Orthodoxy.[30] Despite the hope on the part of some that the perceived new era in the history of Orthodox thought would be "postpolemical," focusing on such positive endeavors as anthropology and ecclesiology, it was evident from Orthodox publications that traditional polemical literature remained paramount.[31]

Certain academic theologians, however, began to question the effectiveness of traditional polemics. The Church historian Evgenii Smirnov, for instance, reminded readers in 1877 that the Patriarch of Constantinople, Gregory, had declined a papal invitation to the First Vatican Council because he had not wanted to engage in age-old accusations and refutations that would only "re-spark animosities that had subsided . . . and would end in strife and enmity."[32] As theologian and church historian Nikolai Barsov wrote in 1870 regarding the Christian West, "we need to look not only at differences in faiths, but to understand what lies at their foundations, what gives them strength, vitality, and their character."[33]

In part because of their desire to move beyond doctrinal debates and examine what they felt were the more essential differences in ecclesial experiences between Christian East and West, some of the more progressive academic theologians turned their attention to the theological writings of Aleksei Khomiakov.[34] In the 1860s, two graduates of the Moscow Theological Academy, Nikita Giliarov-Platonov (d. 1887) and Alexander Ivantsov-Platonov (d. 1894), contributed to translating Khomiakov's essays on the Western confessions of faith from their original French and to publishing them in the journal *Pravoslavnoe obozrenie*. By publishing his essays, the journal officially, though posthumously, introduced Khomiakov as a potential peer into modern Orthodox academic discourse on this issue.[35]

Despite considering him a "theological dilettante," some of Russia's more progressive Orthodox academics were attracted to Khomiakov because "he had shed the usual polemical tactics" and offered what they considered a fresh approach to the Christian West (and to Orthodoxy). In this context, whether they agreed with him or not, Orthodox academics generally credited Khomiakov for at least having initiated this discussion in new terms.[36] Others went so far as to maintain that his formulations on both the nature of the Christian West and of Orthodoxy were so successful as to remain the last word on the subject in modern Orthodoxy.[37]

In contrast to the conventional wisdom of his day, Khomiakov conceived of the Christian West not in terms of two separate and opposed confessions of faith—Roman Catholicism and Protestantism—but as a single phenomenon that culturally and historically could be traced from the civilization of the Roman Empire and the rise of the Roman Church, through the Germanic tribes and the appearance of the Protestants, and beyond to the emergence of a modern culture of unbelief. Similarly, in contrast to conventional polemics of his day, Khomiakov maintained that the main factors separating the Christian West and East were not essentially doctrinal, but relational, dispositional, and, ultimately, experiential.

Khomiakov traced the essential differences between Orthodoxy and the Christian West to sensibilities regarding the fundamentally communal nature of the mystical union in Christ, the Church. "Romanism began," wrote Khomiakov, "at the moment when Christians in the West placed personal independence and regional opinions over and above a universal unity of faith."[38] By its act of unilaterally changing the Creed, the Roman world, he argued, "implicitly declared that in its eyes the entire East was nothing other than a world of helots in matters of faith and teachings. With it, ecclesial life ended for an entire half of the Church."[39] The act of the insertion of the *filioque* into the Creed, for Khomiakov, therefore, was more significant than the meaning of that clause: Its insertion, in his estimation, was no less than an act of "moral fratricide" in the life of the Church.[40]

Since the life of the Church, according to Khomiakov, is grounded in "a living tradition of unity, based in mutual love," its essence lay "in the agreement and unity of spirit and life of all the members who acknowledge it."[41] Consequently, any individual or local appropriation of the right to decide universal ecclesial matters, such as doctrinal teachings, institutionalizes what he calls "Protestantism."[42] Protestantism thus symbolized "the freedom of inquiry ripped from living tradition . . . based on mutual love."[43] As long as Rome was in union with the universal Church, its local practices and teachings, just as those of other local churches, were legitimately part of a universal Christian culture.[44] The sacred balance between the human and divine that in Khomiakov's estimation is maintained in the communal life of the Church was broken when the Western Church, even before the Reformation, propagated its individual and local ways as universal.

The propensity toward unilateral thinking and action—be it individual or local—without due regard for what Khomiakov understood as the communal body of the universal church, did not merely result in schism, but also in the unavoidable decline of faith in the West. By its very nature, argued Khomiakov, such a propensity "deprived faith of its moral foundation," thereby making authentic faith impossible.[45] Having negated the moral foundation of religious knowledge and having broken its bonds with the communal body of the Church, the medieval West fell back on sheer rationalism in its exercise of spiritual cognition.[46] Consequently, while Khomiakov honored the West for its contributions to human civilization, the arts and sciences, its strivings in charitable work and jurisprudence, he nevertheless maintained that since its "fateful crime against the holy law of Christian brotherhood," as a Christian culture, it entered upon an epoch of spiritual decline.[47]

According to Khomiakov, therefore, Orthodoxy and the West were separated by different principles of relationality within what he understood as the sacred body of the Church. The West, in his view, was characterized by another set of values concerning the relationship between the individual and the communal, the local and the universal, and ultimately, between humans and God. The result was three forms of unity—Roman, Protestant, and Orthodox, which were "decisively contradictory in principle."[48] Since the differences, in his view, were so foundational, he had little confidence that any institutional measures—such as the calling of a council—could bridge them.[49]

Khomiakov's opposition between Orthodoxy and the West—in which the former maintained its "incorrupt wholeness"[50] and the latter was the source of its own demise—was based in large part on his historiosophical views that were inspired by German Romanticism.[51] As recent scholarship has shown, Khomiakov and the Slavophiles were far from "conservative dreamers" with regard to their views of Russia and the West.[52] Whereas in the eighteenth century, many of Russia's intellectuals measured Russia's progress in terms of its imitation of European culture, by the nineteenth century, they shifted their views in accordance with those of their European counterparts. German Romantic thinkers at this time spoke of nations in terms of organisms that, like individuals, enjoyed certain unique, personal features that should be developed if a nation or people were to live most fully.[53] In this view, originality mattered more than imitation in terms of a nation's development, significance, and contribution to universal human progress.[54]

The emphasis on originality among peoples as a positive feature in universal history offered a convenient context for accommodating the notion of the "Orthodox idea." According to Khomiakov and his colleagues, the universal Christian message was affected in the process of its appropriation by various peoples; by "passing through the filters of consciousness of different peoples and nations," Christianity manifested itself in different forms among different peoples.[55] Accordingly, Khomiakov traced the schism between the Latin West and the Byzantine East not to the papacy but to Roman culture and civilization, to "the free expression of the Western world view in general."[56] As a result, Orthodox Christianity's uniqueness stemmed more from historical and cultural factors than from doctrinal matters.

Because Christianity in the West had been so closely intertwined with the cultures in which it had taken root, the differences between the Christianity of the West and that of the East were, in theory, as great as the differences between their respective civilizations. For this reason, Khomiakov did not fear that interaction with the West might in any way jeopardize the relational ideals he attributed to Orthodoxy. Russia and the West's differing foundations, in his view, made it virtually impossible for the "protestant principle," as he defined it, to be generated within Orthodoxy.[57]

In the end, Khomiakov's views were the result of an interaction between modern German philosophy, a deep knowledge of Orthodox patristic tradition, and his own Orthodox experience—precisely the type of work advocated by more progressive Orthodox academics. By publishing Khomiakov's writings regarding the Western confessions of faith in a progressive Orthodox academic theological journal, Orthodox academics introduced his theological ideas into an institutional church context. The appeal of Khomiakov's ideas rested in part on their language and narrative. Characteristic features of Slavophile discourse—including reference to social bodies as organisms, the uniqueness of nations and civilizations, and the notion of the decline of the West—dovetailed with aspects of the Christian narrative of salvation history as Russia's Orthodox Christians often understood it, thereby offering new ways of thinking about old issues.

Khomiakov and the West: The Academic Theological Critique

Not all Orthodox academics at the time, however, agreed that Khomiakov's presentation was successful. Criticism fell along two lines. First, some Orthodox academics found fault with his views of Orthodoxy and of the Church. Maintaining that Khomiakov himself had fallen under Western influence, the historian Peter Kazanskii (1819–78) stated, "We would need to reject entirely our understanding of the Church in order to accept his point of view."[58] The dean of Moscow Theological Academy, Alexander Gorskii (1812–75), felt that the Slavophiles' view of Orthodoxy was not "Orthodoxy" as he understood it.[59]

Second, and more significantly, Orthodox academic theologians often criticized Khomiakov and other Slavophiles for their identification of

Christianity with nations or cultural types. The professor of homiletics, Vasilii Pevnitskii (b. 1832), for instance, argued against assuming that particular national traits overcame or compromised religious sensibilities in the formation of Christian churches. Whatever institutional or practical differences arose because of particular cultural differences, they paled before the all-embracing revelation of the Christian faith.[60]

Similarly, historian Filipp Ternovskii argued against drawing sharp divisions between the spiritual dispositions of Russia and "the West." Commenting on Ivan Kireevskii's view that the evolution of Russia and the West resulted in two different spiritual types—a holistic and a fragmented one—Ternovskii argued that such a sharp differentiation between Russia's and the West's "spiritual dispositions" was historically unfounded.[61] It would not be difficult to find events and traits in European history that testified to an integral Western "spirit"; likewise, from Russia's history could be culled evidence that supported a fragmented spiritual type.

Ternovskii also questioned Kireevskii's understanding of historical development. However valid Kireevskii's characterization of Russia and "the West" might have been for a distant past—late antiquity and the Middle Ages—it did not take into account the character of modern times. "The [current] spirit of the times," maintained Ternovskii, "is a powerful force that is capable of transforming peoples and placing them on new, completely unexpected paths of human development."[62] Because, in Ternovskii's view, Russia and the West shared a common historical context, such strict divisions according to cultural and spiritual types were obsolete.

Finally, Ternovskii challenged Kireevskii's evaluation of the holistic type as superior to the fragmented one, drawing on the sentiments of his academic colleagues who did not agree with the Slavophile elevation of the Russian people at the expense of others. If, indeed, the Russian spiritual type was superior, why did Russia not exert more of an influence on Western development? Why, as a spiritually lower "type," would Europe be so successful historically?

Even Alexander Ivantsov-Platonov, who helped to facilitate the translation of Khomiakov's theological works, disagreed with the Slavophiles' generally negative views of the Christian West, chiding them for holding such views while at the same time partaking of the West's intellectual fruits.[63] As one author summarized, "we are far from regarding [Khomiakov's thought] slavishly and from accepting each of his propositions uncritically."[64]

Khomiakov and the West: The Orthodox
Assimilation of a Narrative

Despite such caution, many Orthodox academics in the late nineteenth and early twentieth centuries incorporated many of Khomiakov's views into their own characterizations of the West, though often with modifications. Many shared Ternovskii's assessment that Russia, or, in other cases, Orthodoxy, and the modern West, could not be thought of in such independent, geographically confined terms. For instance, in the course of his support of Orthodoxy's engagement of modernity, Archimandrite Bukharev distilled the "spirit" of Roman Catholicism and of Protestantism that he felt could internally affect Orthodoxy.[65] Other academics dispelled the geographical associations altogether. One essay published in 1905, for example, characterized "practical papism" and "practical Protestantism" as "universal psychological phenomena." According to the anonymous author of this essay, "practical papism" referred to the routine conflation of the spirit of monastic obedience with hierarchical subjugation, while its counterpoint—"practical Protestantism"—signified the disregard for authentic hierarchical ordering and the meaning of that ordering in the life of the Church.[66]

Some Orthodox academics retained Khomiakov's conceptualization of the relational order of the Christian West but connected it to doctrinal concerns. Archimandrite Feodor Bukharev, for instance, wrote of a "papal" force—which he did not identify with Catholicism as a whole—that signified a particular ecclesial disposition that grew from a misunderstanding of the person and work of the Holy Spirit, as testified by the Western appropriation of the *filioque*.[67] The *filioque* clause, from Bukharev's perspective, essentially altered the perceived relational dynamic of the Holy Trinity and did not allow for a full and authentic understanding or experience of the power of the Holy Spirit. In so doing, it altered the patterns of relations within the ecclesial body and the experience of the Spirit in it. Instead of being transparent to Christ, in whom the Spirit of God, the Father, rested, and who in turn directed the relational disposition of the faithful to God, the Papacy distracted believers' gaze on to itself. By doing so, and by redirecting the focus of their faith to an institutional hierarchical figure, the papal spiritual type, maintained Bukharev, "stops the flow and movement of the life of the spirit" in the ecclesial body.[68] It redirects love of God toward a pseudo-authority figure within the institutional church, who then gains independent importance for believers and "shackles minds and hearts through subordination."[69] While admiring the Protestant West for having liberated the human spirit from this subjugation, Bukharev nevertheless maintained that as a spiritual type, Protestantism took a form that was no less relationally wayward. In its case, however, this disposition was driven by doctrinal teachings concerning Scripture.[70]

Similarly, in 1885, in a series of public lectures on the religious and moral state of the West, Alexander Lopukhin developed Khomiakov's notion of the West's "one-sidedness" in terms of soteriological types: the Petrine type, which he associated with Roman Catholicism; the Pauline type, which he associated with Protestantism; and the Johannine type, which he associated with the Orthodox East. Looking to early Christian times, Lopukhin argued that the Petrine and Pauline types fell short of understanding the full meaning of the Incarnation, which only the evangelist John was able to capture. Limited predominantly to their respective one-sided approaches, neither Catholics nor Protestants, in his view, grasped the full essence of Christianity. Since Christianity was "the basis of our civilization," he maintained the view that the Christian West was contributing to the general weakening of that civilization.[71]

The debate between Slavophiles and Westernizers largely concerned the cultural role that Russia was to play with respect to the West, especially in light of what the Slavophiles saw as the latter's demise. Orthodox academics shared this concern in somewhat modified form. Their concern lay specifically with the role of Orthodoxy with respect to the Christian West in light of the future of Christianity. In 1875, the professor of dogmatic theology, Alexander Katanskii, published an essay on the characteristics of Orthodoxy, Roman Catholicism, and Protestantism. In that essay, he considered the meaning and consequences of the "Orthodox idea" with respect to Christian unity and relations among Christians in theological terms. Basing his argument on the assumption that the laws of divine activity are everywhere the same, how can one account, he asked, for the apparent fact that among Christian peoples, some seemed called to be carriers of the "pure Christian truth" and others not?[72]

According to Katanskii, such collective vocational callings did not involve a notion of divine chosenness. Instead, he turned to teachings on grace and free will, and the cooperation between divine and human will, and applied them to nations. While Katanskii agreed with other Christian thinkers that through the acceptance of Christianity many characteristic features of a given people may have been elevated, these characteristic features were not eliminated. Cultural particularities could either facilitate or obstruct people in their efforts to appropriate Christianity in its authentic forms and spirit, though they did not predetermine the result.

While reaching the predictable conclusion that the cultural particularities of the Greek peoples had historically made it easier for them to grasp more fully the implication and meaning of the Incarnation, Katanskii's conclusions regarding the relationship between Orthodoxy and the modern West were more nuanced. In his view, the Christian West historically had excelled with respect to the development of its inner potential. Both Catholicism and Protestantism had been living forces quick to respond to contemporary needs. The developmental trajectory of the Eastern Orthodox faith, however, came to a premature halt because of political circumstances. The Byzantines became obsolete and their successors, the Slavs, had barely yet begun to live a conscious historical life, especially in the Christian sense. Because the Christian East had "paused" in its sociohistorical development, it chose to focus on the past and on the preservation of its ancient tradition. Hence, the "Orthodox idea" was born from a position of its political weakness, not strength.

In the end, Katanskii compared Orthodox Christianity to a healthy, though not yet fully developed, organism. "Undeniably," he wrote, "its sluggishness and lack of energy is a shortcoming."[73] He depicted the Christian West, in both its Roman Catholic and Protestant forms, as fully developed organisms which had challenged themselves on their mutual paths and lived intensively, but now were entering upon a period of collective developmental decline. Yet, in this decline, Katanskii held out hope for future Christian unity. He imagined that the Christian West, out of self-preservation, would pass through a period of self-reflection in which it would have to identify those principles within its historical development that had proven unsound; it would turn to the Christian past in search of other principles. In this search, Katanskii concluded, the Christian West would discover an undeniable resemblance between that past and Orthodoxy, and the paths toward unity on both sides would be cleared.

Alexander Lopukhin also had a nuanced view of Orthodoxy's role with respect to the West. Lopukhin agreed with much of Khomiakov's narrative of the West's historical development. He also agreed that the West's developmental path had led to a distorted view of Christianity, which, in turn, had resulted in the modern West's turning elsewhere for knowledge and direction, and to a perception of Christianity as harmful. Yet, despite their different paths of historical evolution, Lopukhin held out hope for unity between the Christian East and West. In his estimation, unity would be achieved by means of the Orthodox "living remnant" that remained in the West's "unconscious" tradition. This remnant, in his view, could be identified historically in the great saints of the West, as well as in the voices of those like Jan Huss. Similarly, Lopukhin maintained, in more recent times theologians had surfaced from within Roman Catholicism and Protestantism who were like "wandering will o' the wisps of Orthodoxy in the darkness of the non-Orthodox West," testifying that Orthodoxy still survived. Similar to other academics who believed that active proselytizing was foreign to Orthodoxy, Lopukhin pointed out that Orthodox Christians had not sought out these "elements" but instead remained on the sidelines, responding only when approached.[74] According to Lopukhin, the future of universal Christianity lay with a new reformation movement from within the West itself, led by "remnant beacons of Orthodoxy."[75]

However one imagined Orthodoxy's precise role with respect to the fate of Christianity in the modern world, Khomiakov's views made it difficult, if not impossible, to envisage the ground upon which reconciliation would take place. Indeed, if among Russia's secular intellectuals, the issue for many was how Russia would best participate in and contribute to European civilization and universal history, among Orthodox theologians the order of integration was reversed: How could Western Christians join the universal Church, which they firmly insisted was embodied by the Christian East? The difficulties were noted by one commentator on Khomiakov's views, who maintained that Khomiakov's picture of the historical development of Christianity made reconciliation with the Christian East "a virtual impossibility." because he so tied West and East with "the psychologies of peoples."[76] Khomiakov's conceptualization of the relationship between Orthodoxy and the West left little room for those who envisioned less rigid ecclesial boundaries between the two.

The influence of Khomiakov's ideas, for instance, can be seen in a 1917 correspondence between professor of theology, Archimandrite Ilarion Troitskii, and Robert Gardiner, secretary for the commission charged with the organization of a World Conference of Christian Communities. In his letter to Gardiner, Troitskii discussed the widespread modern view, held even by some of his Orthodox academic colleagues, that acknowledged that all believers, both in East and West, who identified themselves as Christians constituted the universal Christian Church.[77] The unity of the universal Church, in this modern view, might have been significantly weakened because of historical circumstances and disagreements, but differences among the churches nevertheless remained ones only of degree.

Troitskii found this approach problematic. For him, as for Khomiakov, the perceived act of the West's separation from what was once a unified Christian body held deeper repercussions for notions of belonging to the universal Church than had any perceived dogmatic differences. "I cannot understand," he wrote Gardiner, "how the East and West [can be seen as having] remained one Church following 1054. What then does the fact of 'separation of churches' mean?" Basing his views on the image of the Church as an organism, he maintained that after the breach of 1054—whether West separated from East or visa versa—the difference between the Churches became one of kind and not merely of degree. Reminding Gardiner of the long list of conflicts between West and East over the past several hundred years, Troitskii rhetorically asked, "Is it possible that they were all worthless trivialities, mundane details, bearing no witness to any ruptures in the mystical depths of the body of Christ?"[78]

Finally, faced with growing challenges from political nationalisms which threatened ecclesial unity on the one hand, and from intellectuals such as Vladimir Soloviev and Leo Tolstoy, whose views promoted a universalism that tended to eclipse local cultural identities on the other, Orthodox academics considered the relationship between Christian unity and national identity.[79] In a 1901 essay on Christian unity and the integrity of nations, a graduate of Moscow Theological Academy, Dmitrii Vvedenskii, maintained that, given appropriate understanding, national identities and local particularities were not a threat to Christian unity. He maintained that as "psychophysical beings," whose physical and spiritual constitutions allowed for the coordination of seemingly disparate sensibilities, humans were capable of understanding the qualitative difference between local national identities and the universality of a Christian identity. According to Vvedenskii, the human constitution enables people to live simultaneously attuned to a higher, supernatural order, which involves mostly what he terms "the inner person," and to a lower, natural order. The moral unity presupposed by Christian universalism, maintained Vvedenskii, belonged to the higher order of human life; national unity belonged to the lower order. From the Christian point of view, Vvedenskii argued, Christian and national identities were not mutually exclusive but involved a proper ordering.[80] Genuine Christian sensibilities neither suppress national identities nor allow them to grow into nationalism.

In his vision of the relationship between nations and Christian unity, Sergei Levitskii, a seminary graduate and son of a professor of psychology at Moscow Theological Academy, utilized the Slavophile and Romantic nationalist understanding of nations as collective "persons." Since, in his estimation, people will act on their national sensibilities even if they are not aware of them, Levitskii advocated cultivating national self-awareness in order to promote a more conscious, "developed," collective nationality. As with individuals, nations' respect for other nations grows proportionately to their self-awareness. Since all humans are members of the single organism—humanity—as nations, they are all "called to serve the common idea of humanity."

When speaking of confessional identities in light of nations, Levitskii agreed with the common premise that different peoples appropriate Christian truths in their own way. Religious truths might be one and unchanging, argued Levitskii, but they manifest themselves in "countless configurations when refracted through the prism of the human mind." Consequently, he maintained, the universal body of the Church consists of a multitude of diverse subjective views, not one of which from its limited perspective can claim to possess the fullness of Truth. "Truth" belongs only to the universal Church, the body of Christ, in the fullness of all its members. From this multiplicity of views, some of which might appear to be in discord with one another, Levitskii proposed that unity among Christians could be imagined not in terms of forced conformity—or a single-toned unison—but in terms of polyphony, whereby the seemingly discordant individual tones are correlated into a "single, well-balanced harmony."[81]

Concluding Remarks

No brief essay can do justice to the depth and breadth with which Russia's academic theologians actively engaged the West during the late nineteenth and early twentieth centuries or to the resulting wide-ranging array of notions regarding the West that such engagement produced. Even a cursory review of the table of contents of the numerous theological journals that began their publication during this dynamic period in the history of Orthodoxy in Russia reveals a remarkable level of interest in the West—theologically, philosophically, historically, and polemically. The interest in Aleksei Khomiakov and the Slavophiles is just one aspect of this involved preoccupation, though, as far as our topic is concerned, arguably one of the most significant and long-lasting.

At first, many academic theologians embraced Khomiakov's theological views as providing a progressive new approach to an old topic. Indeed, one academic even suggested that Khomiakov and the early Slavophiles may have helped to inspire the modernist movement in Catholic Europe and thereby helped to cultivate a basis for ecclesial unity.[82] By the early twentieth century, many of Khomiakov's views were becoming virtually normative and were gradually entering into the annals of tradition. In 1915, the professor of philosophy Fedor Andreev published an essay that linked the Slavophiles to the Moscow Theological Academy.[83] More significantly, in 1911, the future bishop Ilarion Troitskii (1886–1929), who later corresponded with Robert Gardiner and who eventually met his death in a Soviet prison camp, published an essay that affirmed that Khomiakov's polemical writings belonged in the line of tradition of Ignatius of Antioch, Irenaeus of Lyon, Tertullian, Cyprian of Carthage, and Augustine.[84] Whether one considers Khomiakov authentically "traditional" in his views or not, he provided a tempting narrative regarding the Christian West, many aspects of which fit well with age-old Orthodox sensibilities in Russia regarding the "authenticity" and "fullness" of the Orthodox faith. Moreover, he did so in a way that many Orthodox academics in the late nineteenth century felt most effectively explained the originality of Orthodoxy to audiences at home and abroad. Some Orthodox academics actually felt that such a cultural narrative was more ecumenically beneficial than conventional polemics. As Nikolai Barsov argued, when given such a narrative context, any perceived "errors" would not appear as "willful" and could therefore "be more easily excused as a product of Western history."[85]

By turning to Khomiakov, however, Russia's academic theologians introduced a historico-ecclesiological narrative into Orthodox thought that at times seems inseparably intertwined with that of nations and peoples, a topic which in turn posed its own set of challenges for Orthodox theologians. Such a narrative spawned a proliferation of proposed "types" and stereotypes of the Western Christian Other that could also easily be adopted by Orthodox Christians in other lands and recast to fit their own self-perceived national traits. The long-term political, ecumenical, ecclesiological, and even spiritual consequences of this narrative are yet to be fully appreciated. Accordingly, the last word in the late nineteenth and early twentieth centuries (and perhaps the first word in the twenty-first) on the subject belongs to Fr. Pavel Florensky, professor of philosophy at Moscow Theological Academy. In 1916, he published a lengthy and controversial review of a two-volume work on Khomiakov by a fellow academician, historian V. Z. Zavitnevich, who taught at the Kiev Theological Academy.[86] In that critical essay, Fr. Florensky found that the tight familial nature of the early Slavophile circle, combined with Khomiakov's sociological reductionism of fundamental theological issues, resulted in a questionable conceptualization of ecclesial boundaries. For these and other reasons, Florensky shed light on the challenges that "Khomiakov and Khomiakovism" posed not only for Khomiakov's own contemporaries in the nineteenth century, but for Florensky's own times: "They have not only not stopped being a problem for us," he reflected, "but have revealed a new series of problems that need investigation."[87] A century later, especially in light of the resurgence of Orthodox Christianity in postcommunist lands, Fr. Florensky's words still resonate.

Florovsky's Neopatristic Synthesis and the Future Ways of Orthodox Theology

Paul L. Gavrilyuk

Archpriest Georgii Vasil'evich Florovsky (1893–1979) is commonly credited with initiating a return to the Fathers in twentieth-century Orthodox theology. For Florovsky, Christian Hellenism was the norm by which all modern theological proposals were to be judged. He believed that Western influences upon modern Russian theology led to dangerous distortions and to the "Babylonian captivity" of Orthodox life and thought. Consequently, he offered his neopatristic synthesis as a reform program for Russian émigré theology. In his writings, the neopatristic synthesis emerged as an inspired vision intended to chart the only authentic direction of Orthodox theology.

Though neopatristic synthesis was the guiding vision connecting all aspects of his scholarship, from Russian studies to ecumenical work, Florovsky never developed this vision into a comprehensive theological system.[1] He did not produce anything comparable in scope to Sergii Bulgakov's major trilogy *On Godmanhood* or Vladimir Lossky's *The Mystical Theology of the Eastern Church*. He was too much of a historian of ideas to complete a systematic theology. Most of Florovsky's theological works are historically structured; his historical expositions, in turn, are theologically driven.

In this paper, I discuss the polemical motivations and the constructive aspirations of Florovsky's retrieval of the Fathers. To throw the neopatristic synthesis into a sharp relief, I consider Florovsky's program against the background of the major social, intellectual, and ecclesial currents of his time. I also discuss how his engagement with the Eurasian movement influenced his thinking about the ways of Russian theology. I argue that there are considerable methodological parallels between Adolf von Harnack's account of the Hellenization of early Christian theology and Florovsky's account of the Westernization of Russian theology, and, I identify the limitations of Florovsky's appeal to the normativity of Christian Hellenism. I conclude by suggesting two directions in which Florovsky's vision takes Orthodox theology today.

Florovsky's Participation in the Eurasian Movement

Florovsky was born in 1893 in the southern Ukrainian city of Elizavetgrad (modern Kirovograd), which then was a part of the Russian Empire.[2] His family was both clerical and well educated. His father combined his priestly duties with seminary teaching and administration. At the age of eighteen, Georges Florovsky had plans to enter the Moscow Theological Academy in Sergiev Posad, and even corresponded with Fr. Pavel Florensky (1882–1937), who then was assistant professor at the Academy, seeking his advice and assistance in the matter. Unfortunately, for health reasons Florovsky had to abandon these plans and pursue his undergraduate education closer to home, at the University of Odessa. Florovsky's well-rounded college education included natural sciences, law, history of philosophy, psychology, physiology, and languages, but not religion. In theological subjects Florovsky was entirely self-educated. It should be noted that Nikolai Berdiaev and Sergii Bulgakov, the two leading minds of the older generation, were equally unspoiled by the formal theological education imparted in the prerevolutionary Russian Orthodox seminaries.

Young Florovsky was both conversant with, and yet felt an outsider to, the main currents of the Russian Silver Age. At the age of sixteen Florovsky fell under the spell of Vladimir Soloviev (1853–1900), whose religious philosophy and poetry had been a major inspiration for the generation of Bulgakov and Berdiaev.[3] Soloviev cast many of his philosophical arguments in the form of the history of ideas. Florovsky found this approach to be quite congenial: The history of ideas, be it patristic thought or Russian intellectual history, was both his first love and his scholarly forte. In the spirit of Soloviev and German Idealism, Florovsky would come to describe his own project as a synthesis.[4] While the spell of the father of Russian sophiology did not last very long—Florovsky's first bibliographic essay already shows a fairly critical assessment of Soloviev's religious philosophy—it is clear that Soloviev provided a major impetus for Florovsky's further studies in Russian intellectual history.[5]

In 1920, during the Red Army's occupation of Crimea, Florovsky's family decided to leave Russia, never to return to the country again. Florovsky would spend the second third of his life in Western Europe and the last third in the United States. He shared the experience of dislocation with religious thinkers of an older generation, including Berdiaev, Bulgakov, S. Frank, and numerous others who were forced to leave Russia in the early 1920s. In the first issue of an influential émigré journal *Put'* (*The Way*) its editor Berdiaev described this experience succinctly and aphoristically: "Russian dispersion is a unique phenomenon. In its scope it can only be compared to the Jewish Diaspora."[6]

Berdiaev's apt analogy could be extended further. For the ancient Israelites, the profound historical trauma of the Babylonian exile provided an impetus for the recording, selection, and preservation of the Torah and prophetic writings. The exile and its aftermath forced the Jewish people to articulate their beliefs and practices into a canon of scripture and become especially concerned with the preservation of their religious identity. Similarly, the relocation to Western Europe, a different kind of exile, prompted the leaders of the Russian emigration to spend much of their energies reflecting on the Russian émigré community's distinct role and identity in the West. The meaning of the Russian past had acquired a greater existential significance now that Bolshevik Russia was building a future from which the Russian exiles had been excluded.

Florovsky began one of his first published essays with an observation that "The history of Russian thought had not been written yet."[7] For the next quarter of a century, Florovsky was engaged in interpreting this history. His articles on Russian religious figures that appeared from 1912 to 1937 were the building blocks of his magnum opus, *The Ways of Russian Theology*, published in Paris on the eve of the Second World War. Florovsky's work followed a larger trend in Russian intellectual history, for it appeared in the same year with Berdiaev's *Roots of Russian Communism*, and a year after Fiodor Stepun's *The Russian Soul and Revolution*.[8] This period was marked by several catastrophic events: the First World War, two Russian revolutions—the second of which brought the Bolsheviks to power—the subsequent banishment of a significant part of the Russian religious intelligentsia to Western Europe, and the emergence of Hitler's National Socialist Party in Germany. Along with many of his European contemporaries, Florovsky shared a keen sense of living through a time of crisis. This sense would not leave him in the postwar years.[9]

The relocation to Western Europe also meant that the West was no longer a geographically distant reality. On the contrary, the West, its social institutions, its expressions of Christianity, and its modes of life, were now encountered as the unavoidable "Other." In these new circumstances, many leaders of the emigration turned for inspiration to the paradigmatic debate in nineteenth-century Russia between the Westernizers and the Slavophiles. The Westernizers welcomed Russia's integration with Europe, whereas the Slavophiles accentuated Russia's unique destiny, distinct from that of the West. Upon his arrival to Europe, Florovsky joined the Eurasians, who to some extent followed the Slavophile trajectory in the new historical circumstances. The original Eurasian group included four young scholars: linguist and geographer prince Nikolai Trubetskoy (b. 1890, Moscow, d. 1938, Vienna), geographer and economist Petr Savitsky (b. 1895, Chernigov, d. 1968, Prague), musicologist, pianist, literary critic, and philosopher Count Petr Suvchinsky (b. 1892, St. Petersburg, d. 1985, Paris), and Florovsky himself. The Eurasian movement became public after the publication of the programmatic collection of essays, *Exodus to the East*.[10] Florovsky contributed to this and the next two volumes published by the Eurasians, *On the Ways* and *Russia and Latinity*.[11]

The Eurasian movement aimed at becoming the future ideology of Russia-Eurasia. Its leaders hoped that in due course their political platform would replace the ideology of Marxism-Leninism. The Eurasians emphasized the historical and cultural uniqueness of Russia-Eurasia and decried Russia's Westernization.[12] The Eurasians positioned themselves as relentless critics of the "rotten," or decaying, West, an expression borrowed from Nikolai Danilevsky and the Slavophiles.[13] Oswald Spengler's *The Decline of the West*, the first volume of which appeared in 1918 and was widely read in émigré circles, also had an influence upon the Eurasian conception of the future of Western Europe.[14] Spengler's notion of cultural "pseudomorphosis" would play a major explanatory role in Florovsky's analysis of Russian religious thought.

The polemics against "Latinity," that is, Roman Catholicism, were a prominent feature of the Eurasian ideology. The Eurasians emphasized the differences between Eastern Orthodoxy and Roman Catholicism. They insisted on the unity of the Orthodox Christians with the Asian peoples, in particular, with the Tartars. Their strongest attack against Roman

Catholicism was launched in the third Eurasian collection of essays, entitled, *Russia and Latinity* (1923). The introductory article of this volume advanced a claim that for the Orthodox believer in France to be converted to Roman Catholicism was worse than to be killed by the Bolsheviks in Communist Russia, on the grounds that the former led to the eternal perdition of the soul, whereas the latter caused merely a temporal destruction of the body.[15] When this astonishing idea was criticized by Prince G. N. Trubetskoy on the pages of *Put'*, the Eurasians promptly responded with an open letter in defense of their moral comparison of the repressive character of Bolshevism and Catholicism. Florovsky, who was one of the contributors to the Eurasian volume *Russia and Latinity*, had signed the open letter in question. In the same issue of *Put'*, Florovsky also felt compelled to defend the Eurasian position against Berdiaev in a separate article.[16] Hence, in the early 1920s, Florovsky must have shared, at least to some extent, the staunchly anti-Western and anti-Catholic views of his fellow Eurasians.

The Waywardness of Russian Theology and the True Way of the Church Fathers

During the Eurasian meeting in Berlin in 1926, Florovsky began to distance himself from the other leaders of the movement. The final break with the Eurasians was marked by Florovsky's article, "The Eurasian Temptation" (*Evraziiskii Soblazn*), published in 1928. Retrospectively, Florovsky was inclined to emphasize that he had never completely agreed with the Eurasian agenda, especially its political side, even at the time of the movement's inception. It is not clear, however, whether Florovsky's memory served him well. Whatever the vagaries of Florovsky's relationship with the Eurasian movement, Andrew Blaine's conclusion seems to be essentially on target: "Although Florovsky's involvement with Eurasianism lasted little more than the two years he lived in Bulgaria, he remained under its shadow for several years to come."[17] Indeed, there is a connection between the anti-Western impulse of Eurasianism and the fundamental methodological assumption of *The Ways of Russian Theology*. The Eurasians claimed that the preservation of the unique national identity of Russia-Eurasia depended on Russia's faithfulness to Eastern Orthodoxy. In contrast, they held that any rapprochement with the West would in the end distort Russia's historical identity.

In his preface to *The Ways of Russian Theology*, Florovsky writes: "The study of the Russian past has convinced me that an Orthodox theologian today can find the true norm and the living spring of creative inspiration only in the heritage of the Holy Fathers. I am convinced that the intellectual separation from patristics and Byzantinism was the main cause of all interruptions and spiritual failures in Russian development. A history of these failures is narrated in this book."[18]

For Florovsky, the history of Russian religious thought is a drama in three main acts, with a drawn-out and largely silent prelude as well as a brief interlude. In the prelude, appropriately named "The Crisis of Russian Byzantinism," medieval Russia makes a historically fateful decision to embrace Byzantine Orthodox Christianity, but then fails to engage its theology and remains theologically inarticulate for more than a half millennium. In "The Problem of Old Russian Culture," Florovsky explains that the reason Byzantine theology did not "awaken [the] Russian soul" was because "Byzantium had offered too much at once—an enormous richness of cultural material that simply could not be absorbed at once . . . The heritage was too heavy and too perfect."[19] While Russia was able to appropriate Byzantine piety, asceticism, and iconography, it failed to draw creatively upon Byzantium's theological heritage.

In the first act, which takes place in seventeenth-century Kiev, Russian thought experiences the first major pseudomorphosis consisting in "acute Latinization" of its theological education. Florovsky describes the impact of the Kievan metropolitan Peter Mohyla, the founder of the first theological school in Ukraine, in the following way:

> Under Mohyla, the Western Russian Church comes out of its disarray and disorganization from which it suffered from the time of the Union of Brest. Yet everything is suffused with a foreign, Latin spirit . . . This was an acute Romanization of Orthodoxy, a Latin pseudomorphosis of Orthodoxy. A Latinizing school system was built on an empty spot; not only ritual and language, but also theology, worldview, and religious psychology became Latinized. The very soul of the people was Latinized.[20]

This passage resounds with the harsh rhetorical condemnations of Latinity reminiscent of the Eurasian pamphlets. The inspiration here is precisely Eurasian, rather than Slavophile, since it is free from the Slavophile tendency to idealize Russian Orthodox folk piety as it existed in Russia before Peter the Great.[21] Spengler's notion of "pseudomorphosis" is here applied to the ethos of the Orthodox Church to emphasize that the new development was a distortion, a profound disruption of the ages-old modes of piety and patterns of theological thought.

In the second act, ushered in by the Petrine reforms of the early eighteenth century, Russia experiences a "Protestant pseudomorphosis of ecclesiastical life."[22] Among the indicators of such a pseudomorphosis is Peter's abrogation of the office of the patriarch of Moscow and the justification of government absolutism in the writings of Bishop Theophan Prokopovich. The Westernization of education in Russia's theological schools now takes the form of Protestant influences.

A decade later, in his address at the formal opening of St. Vladimir's Orthodox Theological Seminary in New York, Florovsky summarizes the story of the first two pseudomorphoses thus:

> The first theological schools in Russia, in the seventeenth century, were Latin by language and rather Romanizing in spirit—Aquinas and Cardinal Bellarmine were for a time regarded as one supreme authority. Later on came a sudden change and for the whole of the eighteenth century the theological teaching in Russian seminaries and academies was based on Protestant authorities [. . .] It was an abnormal "pseudomorphosis" of the Orthodox theology. But we have to keep in mind that it was the school theology that went astray—the worshipping Church kept close to the patristic tradition. A certain tension, divorce, and opposition between piety and teaching was the most unhappy outcome of this historical adventure. This tension and divorce were overcome to a great extent in the heroic struggles of the nineteenth century.[23]

During a brief interlude, which Florovsky dates to the first part of the nineteenth century, Russian theological education in the person of Metropolitan Filaret of Moscow attempts to recover its Eastern identity by shaking off the Western theological approaches. Unfortunately, this period is short-lived. In the final act, ushered in by Vladimir Soloviev and continued by the promoters of the "new religious consciousness," Orthodox theology was turned into a system of speculative metaphysics under the damaging influence of German Idealism.[24] While admitting that Soloviev's religious philosophy had stimulated a religious ferment in Russia, Florovsky emphasized that theological creativity was achieved at the expense of even greater estrangement from patristic and Byzantine theological tradition.

The assumption of the normativity of patristic theology appears fairly early in Florovsky's writings, beginning with his review article of the literature on Vladimir Soloviev. As one would expect, Florovsky came to formulate this assumption with greater clarity in the course of his more sustained study of the Fathers. While continuing his work on *The Ways of Russian Theology*, Florovsky was also reading lectures in patristics at the newly founded St. Sergius's Theological Institute in Paris.

The invitation to teach at St. Serge came from the school's first dean, Sergii Bulgakov, who saw Florovsky as a promising young historian and, for a brief period, as his "spiritual son." To accept Bulgakov's offer, Florovsky, recently married, had to relocate with his wife from Prague to Paris. Florovsky hesitated: He was worried that his conservative theological views would not be well received by his senior colleagues at St. Serge; he also felt underprepared to teach patristics, since his previous academic work was in other areas (in Prague he defended a master's thesis on Alexander Herzen's historical philosophy and subsequently taught the philosophy of law[25]). In the end, Bulgakov convinced Florovsky to come to St. Serge, assuring him that with his talent and command of languages he would soon gain the requisite expertise in Church history.[26] Florovsky proved a remarkably quick learner; the first volume of his patristics lectures, *The Eastern Fathers of the Fourth Century*, was published in Paris in 1931, about five years after he had assumed his post at St. Serge.

In the introduction to the volume, Florovsky states: "I believe and know that only patristic theology opens the right and sure way to the new Christian synthesis, which is being craved and desired so much in our time."[27] Florovsky's lectures on patristic theology were not merely a historical study but also a theological manifesto. When he studied the Fathers, he thought of the waywardness of Russian theology.[28] In turn, when he read Russian authors, he put them on trial, measuring them constantly against the (rarely articulated) patristic norm. It is as if his patristics lectures and his *Ways of Russian Theology* were engaged in a constant dialogue with each other.

The titles of the two communications that Florovsky delivered at the First Congress of Orthodox Theologians in Athens in 1936 are especially telling in this regard. The first communication, entitled "Western Influences in Russian Theology," presents the negative conclusions of *The Ways of*

Russian Theology in a condensed form, while the second communication, entitled "Patristics and Modern Theology," is an impassioned appeal to go "back to the Fathers" in order to liberate modern Orthodox theology from its Western captivity.[29] It is ironic that a Russian theologian, born in the southern Ukraine and residing in France, would come to Greece to deliver his first communication in German and his second communication in English in order to protest the "Western captivity" of Orthodox theology. One might be inclined to think that such a theologian "doth protest too much."

Florovsky's two volumes of patristic lectures and *The Ways of Russian Theology* constitute a trilogy of sorts: the "right and sure" way is charted in the first two volumes; the ways of errors and failures, the ways of interruptions and distortions, are criticized in the last volume. It is telling that Florovsky's exposition of Byzantine theology breaks off in the eighth century, right at the point when the story of Russia's conversion to Christianity is about to begin.

Florovsky's Westernization and Harnack's Hellenization

Methodologically, but not in content, Florovsky's account of the Westernization of Orthodox theology bears a rather unexpected similarity to Adolf von Harnack's (1851–1930) approach to the process of early Christianity's Hellenization. According to Harnack's *Dogmengeschichte*, Hellenization amounts to a corruption of the original message of the gospel by Greek metaphysics. Jesus preached the simple message of the Fatherhood of God and the brotherhood of men.[30] The Church had distorted this message by attempting to fit it into an alien philosophical framework, resulting in the especially pernicious doctrines of incarnation and deification. Gnosticism was a product of what Harnack called "acute Hellenization." The theology of the Church Fathers did not fare much better in comparison, since it, too, was the result of a more gradual, but equally damaging, impact of Hellenization. The original message of the gospel was obfuscated, corrupted, and distorted. The task of a Church historian was to "overcome dogma by history." The study of the history of dogma spelled the end of dogma. One studied doctrinal history in order to intervene in the course of history by purging biblical Christianity of the alien accretions of metaphysical Hellenism.

Florovsky's appeal to the normative character of Christian Hellenism was a polemic against Harnack's grand narrative of Hellenization. In a programmatic essay "Christianity and Civilization," published in the first volume of a newly founded journal, *St. Vladimir's Seminary Quarterly* (as it was originally called),[31] Florovsky expounds his notion of Christian Hellenism and points out his fundamental disagreement with Harnack in no uncertain terms:

> It was a "New Hellenism," but a Hellenism drastically christened and, as it were, "churchified." It is still usual to suspect the Christian quality of this new synthesis. Was it not just an "acute Helleniza-tion" of the "Biblical Christianity," in which the whole novelty of the Revelation had been diluted and dissolved? Was not this new synthesis simply a disguised Paganism? This was precisely the con-sidered opinion of Adolf Harnack. Now, in the light of an unbiased historical study, we can protest most strongly against this simplifica-tion. Was not that which the nineteenth-century historians used to describe as an "Hellenization of Christianity" rather a *Conversion of Hellenism*? And why should Hellenism not have been converted? The Christian reception of Hellenism was not just a se[r]vile absorp-tion of an undigested heathen heritage. It was rather a conversion of the Hellenic mind and heart.[32]

Florovsky's Christian Hellenism was hardly a product of "unbiased historical study." Clearly, Florovsky offers a highly selective and idealized exposition of Christian Hellenism in response to Harnack's equally un-compromising denunciation of Hellenized Christianity. If Harnack advo-cated a de-Hellenization of Protestant theology, Florovsky, on the contrary, proposes a re-Hellenization of Orthodoxy.[33] Considered from this vantage point, Florovsky is Harnack's theological antipode.

However, methodologically, the two historians had much in common: Westernization in Florovsky's equally devastating criticism of Russian re-ligious thought played an explanatory function akin to that which Har-nack accorded to Hellenization. Both German and Russian historians saw the theology of a specific period as a timeless criterion by means of which all later theologies were to be judged. Harnack restricted such a period to the time of "primitive" or "biblical" Christianity. Florovsky's much broader historical horizon includes the theology of the Greek Church Fa-thers up to the time of Gregory Palamas. For Florovsky, "the teaching of the Fathers is a permanent category of Christian faith, a constant and ul-timate measure or criterion of right belief."[34]

Harnack interpreted the development of Christian doctrine in the post-apostolic period as a corruption of the original gospel. Florovsky makes a similar interpretative move by condemning the history of Russian religious thought as a story of interruptions and failures, indeed a story of pseudomorphosis and corruption of the Byzantine theology by various Western influences. Like Harnack, who distinguished between acute and gradual Hellenization, Florovsky speaks of an acute and less severe "Latinization" of Russian theology.

Harnack's theological purpose in writing *Dogmengeschichte* was to purify German Lutheran theology at the turn of the twentieth century from non-biblical accretions. Harnack fought the Lutheran confessional Scholasticism of his time. The historian, on his view, was a heroic and prophetic figure, someone who announced a new theological paradigm, the liberation from dogma. As I showed earlier, Florovsky turned to the Fathers in order to rescue contemporary Orthodox theology from its Western captivity, to overcome the Western pseudomorphosis of Russian Orthodoxy.

As noted by John Meyendorff, and well documented by Alexis Klimoff, the background of Florovsky's work in patristics is his tireless polemic against the sophiological trend in modern Russian theology.[35] If Harnack was a consistent anti-Hellenist, Florovsky is an unbending anti-sophiologist. Florovsky is convinced that the advocates of a "new religious consciousness," who counted among themselves Nikolai Berdiaev, Sergii Bulgakov, Semen Frank, Georgii Ivanov, and Dmitrii Merezhkovskii, were profoundly misled by their Western sources. To return to my comparison, both Harnack and Florovsky wrote their respective histories with a view of reforming the theology of their contemporaries.

According Harnack, any mixture of Christianity with Hellenism led to the aberration of the gospel. Harnack discounted even the possibility that Christianized Hellenism could retain continuity with the original message of Jesus. The inevitable implication of Harnack's position was that Hellenism simply could not be Christianized. Similar to Harnack, Florovsky holds that the encounter between Russian Orthodoxy and the West had led to a slavish imitation of Western patterns of thought and dangerous distortions of Byzantine Christianity. An encounter with the West in which Eastern Orthodoxy would not be subject to pseudomorphosis, while possible in principle, was yet to occur.

The concluding chapter of *The Ways of Russian Theology* addresses this matter with the following promissory note:

The future polemical [*oblichitel'noe*][36] theology must offer a historio-sophic explanation of Western religious tragedy. This tragedy must be experienced as our own, in order to manifest its possible catharsis in the fullness of ecclesial experience, in the fullness of patristic heri-tage. In this new, sought-after Orthodox synthesis, ages-old experi-ence of the Catholic West must be accounted for with greater diligence and sympathy than has been done in our theology before. This does not mean that we should borrow or accept Roman doctrines, or oth-erwise imitate Romanism.[37]

If there was to be a new encounter with the West, such an encounter had to happen on an equal footing and without slavish imitation.

In practice, however, Florovsky continues to maintain a guarded atti-tude towards Western thought and shows little interest in undertaking the program of "the possible catharsis of Western theology in the fullness of Orthodox ecclesial experience." A decade later, Florovsky, now an in-fluential voice in the ecumenical movement, notes with satisfaction the success of his program at the formal rededication of St. Vladimir's Ortho-dox Theological Seminary:

The Orthodox theology has, in recent decades, been speedily recov-ering from the unhappy "pseudomorphosis," by which it was para-lyzed for rather too long. But to regain once more its own Eastern style and temper must mean for the Orthodox theology no detach-ment from the rest of the Christian world. What is to be rejected and repudiated in the Westernizing school of Orthodox theology is its blind subservience to the foreign traditions of the school, and not its response to the challenge of other traditions, and not the fraternal appreciation of what has been achieved by the others. All riches of the Orthodox tradition can be disclosed and consum-mated only in a standing intercourse with the whole of the Chris-tian world. The East must face and meet the challenge of the West, and the West perhaps has to pay more attention to the legacy of the East, which after all was always meant to be an ecumenical and catholic message.[38]

In this speech, Florovsky offers a captivating and prophetic vision of the meeting of the East and the West as equal partners in theological dialogue.

The Limitations of Christian Hellenism

Despite this glorious vision, which encompassed "fraternal appreciation of what has been achieved by others," Florovsky's own theological attention is largely focused on the heritage of the Greek Fathers. In his writings, he repeatedly stresses that it is this heritage, not any other, that possesses a lasting significance. In 1936, he provokes much discussion among the Orthodox theologians gathered at the Congress in Athens by issuing the following appeal:

> In a sense *the Church itself is Hellenistic*, is a Hellenistic formation,—or in other words, *Hellenism is a standing category of the Christian existence* . . . And thus any theologian must pass an experience of a spiritual hellenisation (or re-hellenisation). . . . Many shortcomings in the modern developments of Orthodox Churches depend greatly upon the loss of this hellenistic spirit. And the creative postulate for the next future would be like this: *let us be more Greek to be truly catholic, to be truly Orthodox*.[39]

Florovsky was not inclined to nuance his position over time. About twenty years later, in 1957, Florovsky addresses the Greek-American readers of *The Orthodox Observer* with a passionate appeal that sounds like a variation on the same theme: "The task of our time, in the Orthodox world, is to rebuild the Christian-Hellenic culture, not of the relics and memories of the past, but out of the perennial spirit of our Church, in which the values of culture were truly 'christened.' Let us be more 'Hellenic' in order that we may be truly Christian."[40]

Christian Hellenism is here offered as a universal, transcultural norm of authentic Christian identity in all times and places. Incited by the slogan "let us be more Greek in order to be truly Orthodox," the minds lacking Florovsky's cosmopolitan upbringing would be tempted to conflate ethnic and religious identity. Taken out of its context, such a slogan may be misread as an invitation to ecclesial triumphalism, ethnic isolationism, and a certain phobia of the religious "Other"—mental attitudes that the ecumenically engaged Florovsky would have been the first to criticize.

One could ask, if Christian Hellenism is the only form of authentic Christianity, what is one to make of the existence of other cultural expressions of Christianity, for example, the one represented by the Latin Fathers? Florovsky gives a baffling answer: "What is the difference [between East and West]? Here I, first of all, offer one of my 'heresies.' I believe that the early period of Christian theology, sometimes described as patristic, was purely and thoroughly Hellenic, Hellenistic, Greek, and that Latin patristics [had] never existed."[41] The astonishing claim that "Latin patristics [had] never existed" is bound to raise questions even among the most ardent Hellenophiles. Making a generous allowance for rhetorical exaggeration, we may interpret what Florovsky here calls his "heresy" in light of what he says in the already mentioned address at the rededication of St. Vladimir's Seminary:

> For several centuries Christendom has been united in theology, under the uncontested lead of the Greek Fathers and masters. Western theology up to St. Augustine was basically Greek, though in Latin dress: St. Hilary, St. Ambrose, St. Jerome, all of them were but interpreters of the Greek tradition, and even St. Augustine himself was deeply Hellenistic in mind. Tertullian also fits easily into the same Hellenistic frame.[42]

The predilection for sweeping generalizations, the tendency to reduce the contributions of recognized thinkers to "influences," which was so prominent in *The Ways of Russian Theology*, also finds expression in Florovsky's attempt to fit the Latin Fathers "into the same Hellenistic frame." It appears that it is precisely on this assumption that Florovsky draws upon the theological insights of Tertullian, Cyprian, Jerome, Augustine, Vincent of Lérins, and other Latin patristic authors.

We should stress the asymmetry in Florovsky's evaluation of the theological contributions of the East and the West. Arnold Toynbee argued that the Christian West was a separate "intelligible world" which could be understood independently from the Christian East.[43] Against Toynbee, Florovsky maintains that the theology of the Eastern (read: "Greek") Fathers was a common foundation both for the East and for the West. On this reading, the Christian patristic East possessed a degree of self-sufficiency and comprehensiveness that could not be claimed by the West.[44] Florovsky believes that the theology of the Latin Fathers, in the final analysis, derived from that of the Greek Fathers. In contrast, all forms of Western theology after the Great Schism of 1054 represented various deviations from the Greek patristic norm. It followed that all Western theologies were culture bound; Christian Hellenism alone had a universal value.[45]

Given Florovsky's peculiar contention that the Latin patristic tradition (up to Augustine) is a species of Christian Hellenism, it is understandable why his St. Serge lectures on patristics do not contain separate chapters discussing the distinctive contributions of the Latin Fathers. To remind the reader, the two volumes of his lectures were published under the titles *The Eastern Fathers of the Fourth Century* and *The Byzantine Fathers of the Fifth–Eighth Centuries*. Actually, the titles could just as well be *The Greek Fathers of the Fourth Century* and *The Greek Fathers of the Fifth–Eighth Centuries*, since the non-Greek Eastern theologians did not fare much better than their Latin counterparts. For example, his discussion of the Syriac Fathers, relegated to the last and shortest chapter of the first volume, is hurried and dismissive.[46]

We have solid grounds for believing that these rather eccentric views remained dear to Florovsky till the end of his life. In his "Theological Will," recently published by Andrew Blane, Florovsky sums up one of his guiding convictions thus:

> Salvation has come "from the Jews," and has been propagated in the world in Greek idiom. Indeed, to be Christian means to be Greek, since our basic authority is forever a Greek book, the New Testament. [The] Christian message has been forever formulated in Greek categories. This was in no sense a blunt reception of Hellenism as such, but a dissection of Hellenism. The old had to die, but the new was still Greek—the Christian Hellenism of our dogmatics, from the New Testament to St. Gregory Palamas, nay, to our own time. I am personally resolved to defend this thesis, and on two different fronts: against the belated revival of Hebraism and against all attempts to reformulate dogmas in categories of modern philosophies, whether German, Danish, or French (Hegel, Heidegger, Kierkegaard, Bergson, Teilhard de Chardin) and of alleged Slavic mentality.[47]

What is one to make of the claim that "to be Christian means to be Greek," which Florovsky repeats with troubling persistence? How should we interpret this surprising conflation of cultural and religious identity? Is Christian Hellenism a historical reality or a utopian reconstruction of a much more complicated past? In particular, should the Orthodox biblical scholars simply shrug their shoulders at the rediscovery of the Jewishness of Jesus? The proclamation of cultural hegemony of the properly converted Hellenism left Florovsky deaf to the ways in which revelation could become incarnate in other cultures, including that of the ancient Hebrews. Are we meant to hide under the "sacred canopy" of Christian Hellenism from the philosophical problems raised this side of modernity? Should the Orthodox theologians simply ignore Hegel, Kierkegaard, Heidegger, and others, on the grounds that these philosophers were not interested in the restoration of Christian Hellenism? It should be admitted that among the Orthodox, Florovsky's rhetoric has at times provoked affirmative responses to these questions. When such responses are used to make curricular changes at the Orthodox seminaries, the consequences become dire.

The Enduring Value of the Neopatristic Synthesis

Yet it is also possible and, I would think, desirable, to take Florovsky's vision in a quite different direction. I suggest that there is a second, alternative way of completing Florovsky's neopatristic synthesis. At the heart of the neopatristic synthesis is not a mindless glorification of Hellas's past, but the Church's ongoing experience and proclamation of Christ. Christian Hellenism, as Florovsky uses the expression, is a paradigm for a comprehensive conversion of intellectual culture. Such a conversion is nothing less than a "dissection of Hellenism by the sword of the Word, of the Christian Revelation."[48]

Florovsky argues that in the process of undertaking such a conversion, the Church Fathers created a "new philosophy" which was quite distinct from anything that pagan Hellenistic philosophers had to offer.[49] The ahistorical cosmism of the Greeks gave way to the mighty acts of God in history; the conception of a divinized eternal cosmos was replaced with the intuition of creaturehood, i.e., of the creature's contingency and dependence upon God; the metaphysical primacy of the universal over the individual was challenged by Christianity's emphasis on the uniqueness of persons; the determinist accounts of divine and human agency were rejected in order to safeguard God's radical freedom in creation and redemption, as well as the human freedom to cooperate with the divine grace.[50]

Florovsky takes this new philosophy to be a Christian *philosophia perennis*, a perennial philosophy, which incidentally was the title accorded to Aristotle's system in Scholasticism.[51] In contrast, Florovsky sees Western Scholastic theology as a species of insufficiently Christianized Hellenism (largely due to its overindulgence in the philosophy of Aristotle).

The same charge applied, mutatis mutandis, to German Idealism, in this case for the failure to sufficiently Christianize Plato.[52] Hence, the deeper problem with modern Russian theology was not its Westernization per se. The problem was that, by adopting Western philosophies, Russian religious thinkers accepted a historical development of Hellenism that was inadequately Christianized, that is, did not do justice to the historical divine revelation received by the mind of the Church. In fact, the alleged flaws of pagan Hellenism—cosmism, panentheism, impersonalism, and determinism—are also, in Florovsky's interpretation, the gravest errors of Russian sophiology.[53]

Admittedly, the historical value of these sweeping generalizations is rather dubious. Florovsky might be a relentless critic of German Idealism, but he surely shares the Idealists' predilection for grand historical narratives. Florovsky might be a persecutor of Romanticism in Russian thought, but he himself indulges, despite his protestations to the contrary, in romanticizing Hellenism. He theologizes history and historicizes theology. While engaging patristic thought he is constantly reaching after "a new synthesis," a constructive vision that would enable contemporary Orthodox theology to properly reconnect with its patristic and Byzantine roots. He frequently emphasizes that merely repeating old patristic formulae is not enough. It is more important to capture the spirit than the letter of patristic writings. It is vital to share in what Florovsky calls "ecclesial experience."

In an early essay, "The Father's House," Florovsky maintains that "Christianity is experience."[54] For Florovsky, "ecclesial experience" is a broad category referring to the appropriation of the historical divine revelation by the mind of the Church. Similarly to Lossky, Florovsky contrasts ecclesial or catholic (*sobornyi*) experience with the experience of divine reality found in the individualistic forms of Western mysticism. To participate in ecclesial experience is to overcome the subjectivity of private religious experience. Florovsky does not elaborate on how, precisely, this is to be accomplished. I should note that his appeal to the category of "ecclesial experience" as something self-authenticating is not immune from the charge of circularity.

According to Florovsky, the earliest ecclesial experience is prior to Scripture, inasmuch as Scripture is a fruit of the Church's reception of the divine revelation. The Bible may be authentically interpreted as Scripture only within the Church. Florovsky is especially fond of repeating Tertullian's claim, in *De Praescriptione Hereticorum*, that outside of the Church there could be no Scripture, properly speaking.[55] By receiving and interiorizing the rule of faith within the Church, the believer is able to grasp the *skopos*, that is, the overarching plan and intent of Scripture.

For Florovsky, ecclesial experience includes a liturgical dimension,[56] a matter that will be developed with great force by Alexander Schmemann. The "enchurching" (*votserkovlenie*) of the self is intended to bring about a cognitive transformation necessary to enter into the mind of the Fathers or the "common mind of the Church."[57] Florovsky understands this cognitive act to be akin to intellectual intuition rather than discursive reasoning, on the basis of authoritative premises supplied in patristic tradition.[58] He questions the notion of the "development of doctrine," especially the models of such a development that were proposed by German Idealist philosophers as well as the Russian followers of Soloviev.[59] The Fathers made their theological terminology more precise not in order to "develop a doctrine," but rather to defend the ecclesial consciousness against the distorting impact of the heresies, in order to guide minds to the knowledge of God.

In his religious epistemology, Vladimir Lossky places an equally high cognitive premium on experiential knowledge culminating in the "vision of God."[60] For Lossky, the apophatic purification of religious language functions as a spiritual discipline preparing the mind for the contemplation of God. Less concerned with apophasis, Florovsky stresses to a greater extent than does Lossky the definitive character of dogmas and the Christocentricity of the divine revelation. Florovsky's theology begins and ends with Christ. For him, the doctrine of the Church is "a chapter of Christology."[61] Both his ecclesiology and his eschatology are robustly Christocentric. He places comparably little emphasis on the work of the Holy Spirit.[62]

In his writings, Florovsky decries the loss of the Christological focus in Russian sophiology, especially in Soloviev and Florensky.[63] He insists that contemporary Russian Orthodox theology needs to be firmly grounded in the central dogmas of the historical revelation, especially the Trinitarian vision of the Nicene Creed and the Chalcedonian definition, and only then be concerned with speculative metaphysics and disputed doctrinal questions. According to Florovsky, Russian sophiologists did precisely the opposite: they were preoccupied with abstract metaphysical questions and made debatable *theologoumena* (e.g., the multiple identities of Sophia, the metaphysical principle of Godmanhood) foundational for their theological systems. Florovsky insists that it is by entering into the mystery of

Christ first that one can properly survey the rest of the mysteries of faith, including the Trinity and the Church.

Florovsky proposes that the Chalcedonian Christology, properly understood, is asymmetrical. Whereas the divine nature of Christ eternally possesses its own divine hypostasis, the human nature of Christ is enhypostasized in the incarnation.[64] Here Florovsky draws on Leontius of Byzantium's development of Chalcedonian Christology in order to counter Bulgakov's claim that Christ's humanity is eternally, rather than only contingently, rooted in the divine. As a polemicist, Florovsky practices a peculiar *reductio ad heresim* of modern Christologies that deviate, in one way or another, from the patristic norm. Thus he speaks of the Gnostic character of Russian sophiology, of the "Monophysite" tendencies in Protestant neo-Orthodoxy, as well as of the "Nestorianism" of Protestant liberalism.[65]

As a historian, Florovsky stands on the shoulders of the Russian prerevolutionary patristic scholars, especially Vasily Bolotov, Nikolai Glubokovsky, Aleksandr Gorsky, Aleksei Lebedev, Viktor Nesmelov, and Anatoly Spassky, as well as his contemporaries Lev Karsavin, Mikhail Posnov, and others. Florovsky was equally well acquainted with the European patristic scholarship of the late nineteenth and early twentieth centuries. He finds particularly congenial the work of the German theologian and church historian Johann Adam Möhler (1796–1838), who issued an appeal to return to the Fathers, which went largely unheeded in the Catholic Church of the early nineteenth century.[66]

It is also significant that the publication of his patristics lectures and *The Ways of Russian Theology* coincided with the first stirrings of the *ressourcement* movement in French Catholic theology, represented by such figures as Gustave Bardy, Louis Bouyer, Henri de Lubac, Jean Daniélou, Hans Urs von Balthasar, Yves Congar, and Marie-Dominique Chenu. There was much in *la nouvelle théologie* that resonated with Florovsky's new synthesis of the Fathers. The *ressourcement* theologians announced a return to the patristic sources in order to challenge the intellectual hegemony of neo-Scholastic rationalism in Catholic theology.[67] Chenu insisted on the primacy of the historical revelation over speculative metaphysics and emphasized the centrality of the history of salvation for theology. Balthasar spoke of the need to reappropriate "the fundamental and secret intuition which directs the entire expression of [patristic] thought."[68] According to Daniélou, the publication of the patristic series *Sources Chré-*

tiennes, begun in 1941, had a theological, rather than a merely historical, purpose. For Daniélou, the Fathers were "not only the truthful witnesses of a bygone era; they are also the most contemporary nourishment of men and women today, because we find there a certain number of categories which are those of contemporary thought and which Scholastic theology had lost."[69] While Florovsky's reform program has Russian sophiology, rather than Scholastic theology, as its primary target of criticism, his appreciation of the contemporary value of the Fathers agrees with the theological agenda of the *ressourcement* movement. Like Florovsky, the *ressourcement* theologians saw a great ecumenical potential in the retrieval of the Greek Fathers.

Thus Florovsky's promotion of the neopatristic synthesis, despite its anti-Western orientation, is much facilitated by the revival of patristic studies in the West. We should also note that Florovsky takes part in and writes a euphoric review of the first two international conferences on patristic studies that took place at Oxford in 1951 and 1955. He describes the spirit of these gatherings in terms reminiscent of his own theological program:

> There is a vigorous revival of interest and study in the field of Christian Antiquity, and of the theology of the Fathers in particular, in all countries throughout the world. The most distinctive feature of this modern study is probably that "Antiquity" is no longer regarded as something "antiquated," or as a burdensome "survival" of an outlived past which can be assessed simply by a sympathetic archeological curiosity, but rather as an integral constituent of the contemporary mind, and a living spring of inspiration.[70]

One might recall how, twenty years earlier in the preface to *The Ways of Russian Theology*, Florovsky speaks of the need to return to patristic theology in order to find "the living spring of creative inspiration."[71] Allowing for Florovsky's tendency to assess the intellectual currents of his time through the prism of his own theological agenda, it cannot be doubted that the theology of the *ressourcement* movement gave a significant impetus to the Oxford patristics conferences. For at these meetings, Florovsky rubbed shoulders with Jean Daniélou, Henry Chadwick, and other world-class patristic scholars and theologians. Florovsky always stayed *au courant* of early Christian and Byzantine studies, as his numerous reviews of books in several European languages attest. The fact that so many

Orthodox theologians today wear the hat of a patristic scholar owes at least as much to the revival of patristics in the West as it does to Florovsky's vision.

A Generation after Florovsky: Two Ways Forward

Florovsky's retrieval of Christian Hellenism can be taken in two principal directions. On the one hand, Florovsky's program can encourage among the Orthodox an all-too-familiar ecclesial triumphalism and self-satisfaction: an idealization of the past resulting in a tendency to belittle the work of the Holy Spirit in the Church's present; a posture of spiritual superiority vis-à-vis the Western "Other" and a concomitant spiritual and intellectual isolationism; a deep-seated phobia of all things non-Orthodox; a siege mentality which, from time to time, especially in the monastic circles, finds its outlet in misguided apocalypticism; a fixation upon ethnicity, be it Greek or Slavic, verging on idolatry; a reluctance to confront massive intellectual, social, and moral dilemmas of our times; a heresy-hunting zeal encouraged by what one might call "patristic fundamentalism"—that is, an attitude of holding on to the patristic letter and denying the spirit thereof; a "theology of repetition" which still paralyzes Orthodox efforts in the areas of biblical studies, political theology, moral theology, as well as science and religion, to name only a few examples. Such is the first direction that finds its support among a vocal minority of Orthodox leaders and faithful.[72]

On the other hand, properly understood, Florovsky's vision can lead Orthodox theology in an entirely different direction. Far from sanctioning triumphalism, Florovsky's searching criticism of Russian religious thought invites an intense self-examination, a *metanoia* of ecclesial consciousness, which is so needed in the age of chronic failures of episcopal leadership and obsession with the jurisdictional disputes in local Orthodox churches. Florovsky calls on us to acquire the mind of the Fathers, to be emboldened by their example as we join in the arduous work of planting the seeds of the Gospel in our increasingly pluralistic cultures. In this process, the Fathers are not our infallible teachers, but rather our spiritual guides to Christ. In this context, Christian Hellenism stands for a theological vision that refuses to subordinate the historical divine revelation to any philosophy that compromises the centrality of the divine incarnation. Despite Florovsky's misleading rhetoric, it is not the cultural hegemony of "sacred Hellenism," but the Christ of the Gospels, the Christ of the Seven Ecumenical Councils, the Christ of the Church, that is at the center of his neopatristic synthesis.

Orthodox theology is a house of many mansions. There will always be room in it for those who wish to dedicate themselves entirely to the study of the Fathers. But neopatristics also requires that we go beyond such archeological explorations. Having regained its patristic foundations in the last fifty years, Orthodox theology today is poised to take on issues of contemporary relevance with greater confidence and determination than before. In the spirit of Florovsky's motto "forward, to the Fathers," we need a new Origen in the Orthodox biblical scholarship. We need a new John Chrysostom to tackle moral and prophetic theology. We need a new Augustine to pursue anthropology, gender problems, and sexuality. We need a new pseudo-Dionysius the Areopagite to address postmodern theories of religious language. We need new Cappadocians, a new Athanasius and Maximus the Confessor, to help us navigate the metaphysical and epistemological options on offer in our time. We need a new Symeon the New Theologian to recover the charismatic dimension of our faith. We need a new Palamas to continue translating the experience of deification into the categories of modern church life.

In addition, in the spirit of Florovsky's ecumenical work, a new creative encounter between the East and the West must occur in the twenty-first century, an encounter transcending geopolitics and manipulation, an encounter in which both traditions would speak as partners rather than adversaries. The East must make an effort to attend to the wounds of the West. Orthodox theologians should embark on this work without the fear of somehow drowning in the theological ocean of the West. It would be a sign of our theological maturity when we begin to treat the iconic figures of the Western theological tradition—Augustine, Anselm, Aquinas, Luther, Calvin, Barth, and others—neither as convenient straw men, nor as untouchable "Others," but as partners worthy of serious engagement. Unfortunately, this day has not arrived yet; dare one hope that it arrives in this century?

Nevertheless, there are some encouraging signs that the task of engaging the West is being undertaken by the Orthodox scholars of my own and younger generations.[73] Much further work needs to be done in this largely uncharted territory. For example, it would be a good idea to publish a new series of books offering the distinctly "Eastern" readings of the most significant expressions of the Western theological tradition. Beyond this, we need to begin a discussion about curricular changes in our theological schools. The manner in which the Orthodox seminarians are presently introduced to Western theological sources, especially in the traditionally Orthodox lands, leaves much to be desired. I realize that much discernment is required in this arena and we need to proceed with due caution.

We need to reconsider the familiar juxtaposition of the faithful East and the misguided West in our thinking. The difference between the theological "grammars" of the East and the West is not a sufficient ground for forever guarding our theology against all Western influences. The distinctly Western theological beliefs are often assumed to be false, merely on the grounds that they are Western. This genetic fallacy has poisoned our theological thinking for too long. If we reject the Western "Other" without making an effort to understand the "Other," paradoxically, we are letting ourselves be more dependent on that "Other." It is precisely the staunchly anti-Western Orthodox thinkers who end up being utterly dependent upon the West, even if this dependence takes the form of unreflective rejection. The search for truth cannot be limited by geography. It is not the cultural uniqueness of Eastern Christianity, but the divine revelation appropriated by the Church, that should serve as the main criterion of Orthodoxy. We need to overcome the limitations of Florovsky's historiography in order to fulfill his extraordinary vision.

Eastern "Mystical Theology" or Western "Nouvelle Théologie"?: On the Comparative Reception of Dionysius the Areopagite in Lossky and de Lubac

Sarah Coakley

This volume is devoted to the intriguing topic of Orthodox constructions of the West. The very term "construction," of course, suggests a certain hermeneutics of suspicion: What Orthodoxy "constructs" could turn out, on inspection, seriously to mislead. But caution must be exercised, equally, in not overreacting into an opposite danger: that of presuming all Eastern characterizations of the Latin tradition to be straightforwardly one-way, stereotypical projections. Perhaps especially in the modern period, mutual and complex interactions and dependencies between so-called Eastern and Western authors have been more common than is generally allowed, even as supposedly unbridgeable disjunctions have been rhetorically announced between them. This has been the case precisely because Orthodox constructions have been forged in very close contact with the West, and indeed often within the West itself.

It will thus be the central thesis of this paper that there is no such modern "Orthodox construction of the West" that is not also, and simultaneously, an implicit *responsive* conversation with Catholic or Protestant interlocutors, often animated by underlying strands of Western critique and renewal that the two sides ironically share. Only such a commonality provides the attractive matrix for a so-called Orthodox construction of richness and insight. And conversely, only such a commonality makes an Orthodox construction memorable and illuminating to Westerners themselves.

To test this point, I shall in this paper focus on one moment of crucial significance in the twentieth-century forging of such an Orthodox construction, in the form of Vladimir Lossky's elevation of the "mystical" work of Dionysius the Areopagite over and against Western Scholastic theology.[1] The new receptions of Pseudo-Dionysius in France of the 1930s through the 1960s will, in fact, form the unifying theme in this account.[2] I shall start with a succinct restatement of Lossky's position on this Eastern mystical theology, so-called, and his strikingly attractive, but frankly quite manipulative, use of Dionysius in constructing it. His work on this theme has of course already been given scholarly attention and analysis of some detail.[3] But I want to suggest that there remain certain hidden *Catholic* dimensions to Lossky's attendant, and negative, construction of the West in this regard that deserve closer historical analysis than they have previously received in these earlier treatments of Lossky's own work. In particular, in situating Lossky in the Paris of the late 1920s up to the late 1950s, in recalling that Étienne Gilson was his ongoing mentor and doctoral advisor, and in reflecting on the near-simultaneous growth of the influence of de Lubac and his Jesuit circle on what would later come to be called *la nouvelle théologie*,[4] we are brought up against the paradoxes of a parallel and *shared* Eastern and Western renegotiation of Dionysian tradition at this important juncture in the modern development of French Christian thought. Key to this renegotiation from the Catholic side was, of course, a new reading of the revelatory theology of Thomas Aquinas, and especially a reconsideration of Thomas's relation to the negative theology of the Dionysian corpus. To put it boldly: What Lossky and the burgeoning proponents of the Catholic *nouvelle théologie* shared was—despite Lossky's distractingly polemical anti-Western and anti-Thomist rhetoric—arguably more than what divided them.

To lay my cards on the table at the outset, then, I can think of *four* common propulsions between Lossky and his reforming Catholic contemporaries, which I will trace throughout this paper. First, there was a shared loathing of the rigid and rationalistic rendition of Thomas in the Catholic seminary textbooks of the post–*Aeterni Patris* era;[5] second, there was a shared reconsideration of the importance of the Greek patristic, and especially negative, theology traditions for a renewal of thinking about the metaphysics of revelation;[6] third, there was a shared concern for the renewal of spiritual practice and its relation to some form of vibrant modern experientialism (which it was difficult to divorce from the new stirrings of existentialism at the time[7]); fourth—and perhaps most interestingly—there was a shared agreement that any new engagement with the work of Dionysius, specifically in relation to these moves, must sternly head off a reduction of Christianity to Platonic or Neoplatonic philosophy, or indeed even any straightforward alliance with it. That Lossky was to present a profoundly different *assessment* of Dionysius on this last point from that of, say, Gilson, Chenu, or de Lubac should not, as it has tended to do heretofore, distract us from these other underlying commonalities. What we shall conclude by the end of this paper is that, some time after Lossky's untimely death in 1958, the anti-Western polemics of his most famous works seemed, not least to his own son and to his former *Doktorvater*, something of a shadow-boxing, albeit a creative one. Those polemics had both been partly *induced* by contemporary French Catholic concerns, and had in turn issued in an implied ecumenical agreement between them that was greatly to affect the course of Vatican II. In short, here was an Orthodox construction of the West—one of the most polemical and memorable of the modern period—that had ironically assisted in a certain intra-Western theological purgation.

In what follows, I shall divide my exposition of this central thesis into three unequal parts. I shall attempt, in my first and most substantial section, a new account of Lossky's assessment of the Dionysian corpus and its importance for his construction of the West, noting any covert absorption of Western themes within it, and also putting it into relation with Lossky's crucial interactions with the work of his doctoral advisor, Étienne Gilson. Second, I shall then place this account against the backdrop of what was happening in the theology of de Lubac and his circle at roughly the same time: a markedly different initial assessment of the Dionysian corpus, but one which was to transmute, in due course, into something more positive under certain political and theological pressures. Thirdly, I shall substantiate again, in closing my core thesis, that the West and the East, at this crucial moment in the modern development of French Christian thought, shared much more than one could guess from their initially different assessments of the Dionysian heritage. The "Dionysian paroxysm," as we might call it, of these crucial mid-century decades in France was ultimately to produce a certain muted ecumenical accord.

Lossky's Rendition of the Dionysian Corpus

Lossky arrived in Paris in 1924 not as an émigré but as an exile, as his son Nicholas Lossky was later concerned to stress.[8] He was fleeing not only

from the persecution of his church in the new Soviet Union (he was, and
faithfully remained, a member of the Moscow patriarchate and had witnessed, as a very young man, the trial and execution of Metropolitan Benjamin of St. Petersburg, led out before his people to his death),[9] but he was
also fleeing from the philosophical agendas of Bulgakov, which his father,
the elder Nicholas Lossky, shared.[10] The younger Lossky enrolled in
courses in the Sorbonne from 1927, and started his study of patristic and
(Western) Scholastic theology under the agnostic Ferdinand Lot and the
brilliant younger Catholic scholar, Étienne Gilson, who was in due course
to become his supervisor in a doctoral thesis on Meister Eckhart. It is impossible, therefore, to underestimate the extent to which Lossky's patristic
study in France was influenced by scholarly developments in Catholic Europe at the time: even his assimilation of the importance of the thought of
Gregory of Nyssa, for instance, was to be mediated through Puech (whom
he constantly cites) and later by interaction with Daniélou;[11] and it is hard
to see how his reading of Dionysius, which was to become the centerpiece
of his new, polemical account of Eastern thought, was not equally affected
by the new French editions and translations of Dionyius's work that appeared in Paris in the 1930s.[12] This was an exciting time in the new Catholic impetus towards patristic *ressourcement*, and Lossky was not to escape
its impetus.

Lossky's first publication[13] was in fact on Dionysius himself, and already announced many of the distinctive anti-Western accusations of the
slightly later *Mystical Theology of the Eastern Church* (orig. French, 1944):
indeed, some parts of this article are directly reproduced in Chapter 2
("The Divine Darkness") in that volume. I propose here to enumerate some
of the central themes of this neopatristic (but more truly for Lossky, neo-
Dionysian) theology in a way that draws attention to the Western provenance of Lossky's distinctively *anti*-Western posture.

First, as is emphasized immediately in this first published article,[14] and
again in *The Mystical Theology*,[15] the Dionysian corpus for Lossky represents not an assimilation to Neoplatonic emanationism, but an achievement
that transcends not only Neoplatonism but any possible reduction of Christian revelation to philosophic or rational explication in human terms. This
is Lossky's first and boldest pronouncement, and it animates his whole
project. It is also, frankly, one of his least defensible claims in historical
and textual terms. Conveniently omitted here in these first published discussions of Dionysius is any reference to Proclus and his possible connec-

tion to the Dionysian corpus—an issue which, if tackled directly, would surely have had to lead to an acknowledgement of strong textual closeness, if not actual dependency. Instead, it is Plotinus who, for the meantime, becomes Lossky's acceptable whipping boy;[16] and Lossky makes the claim that whereas Plotinus "reaches out" for the One, beyond the multiplicity of beings (and thus it is for him a noetic union with the One that constitutes the philosophic goal), Dionysius, in contrast, insists on the *absolute* unknowability of God, and thus on the ecstatic going forth of the mind *beyond* itself to meet God: "The God of Plotinus is not incomprehensible by nature," writes Lossky, for "The ecstasy of Dionysius is a going forth from being as such. That of Plotinus is rather a reduction of being to absolute simplicity."[17] Whatever we make of this claimed disjunction—which even Lossky is forced to admit comes with some "striking resemblances" between the two authors[18]—the rhetorical disjunction it enshrines is crucial for his central claim that Dionysius represents a distinctive and Eastern vision of Christian revelation and Christian anthropology that reaches back to the Cappadocians and then on to the eventual Palamite synthesis. "*The God of revelation is not the God of the philosophers*," Lossky concludes, and "it is this recognition of His fundamental unknowability which marks the boundary between the two conceptions [between Platonic philosophy and Christianity]." Any resemblances between Platonism and Christianity are "outward" ones, then, which "do not go to the root of [the Fathers'] teaching, and relate only to a vocabulary which was common to the age."[19] Just superficial semantics, it seems, have deceived us into assuming a philosophic collusion on the part of Dionysius.

For the meantime, let us set aside the misleading historical and textual judgments enunciated here,[20] although we shall return to them later. What I want, rather more irenically, to draw attention to for my present purposes is the specifically Western, and Parisian, context in which Lossky is announcing them. Not only is he using established, and revered, Western scholarship on Neoplatonism and Dionysius as his point of *resistance*, but his whole animus is against the possibility of Platonic philosophy—or indeed any philosophy—inappropriately *intersecting* with authentic Christian revelation. He does not here even consider the possibility that equally for—say—an Origen (whom he trenchantly criticizes) or a ps.-Dionysius (whom he reveres), such an intersection might have been regarded as both axiomatic and wholly unproblematic. For in the background we must assume various interconnected forms of revulsion against such a potential for philosophy's positive entanglement with revelation.

What animates this critique? Several explanations come to mind, and it may be that all of them are playing some part in Lossky's reflections at this time. First, Lossky's rejection of the Bulgakov School's mingling of post-Kantian Western philosophy and Orthodoxy theology is one important and personal factor, as we have already noted, and it was what caused the intellectual break with his father. But I do not think we can also rule out the significance of two other aspects of the Western European theological scene closer to Paris, which may have been equally, if not more, significant for Lossky's thinking at this time. One can only speculate. On the one hand, Gilson's teaching and writing—as we shall examine more closely shortly—was carefully turning a critical, historically enunciated, spotlight on the supposition of the Roman textbooks that a form of modern, rational philosophy could supply a *foundation* for revelation in Thomas's thought.[21] Here too, then, although in a different way from the question of Bulgakov's use of the Western Romantic tradition, the unproblematic alliance of revelation with a modern philosophical base was being called into question, as it was to be more forcibly in the writing of de Lubac not long after. On the other hand, Karl Barth (whom Lossky certainly knew about from his friend Florovsky[22]) had of course been announcing for some time an even more ardent resistance to the idea that secular philosophy could in any sense *ground* revelation. In short, this first, and crucial, plank of Lossky's "construction" of Eastern theology (its insistence on the strict incompatibility of Neoplatonic philosophy and authentic Christian revelation) can, I think, only, and best, be understood against this particular Western intellectual backdrop. Whether for reasons of Protestant neo-Orthodoxy, or of Catholic reassessment of neo-Tridentine rationalist Scholasticism, any collusion between non-Christian philosophy and revelation was to be treated with grave suspicion. It is also "constructed" by Lossky—if I may put it thus—with a certain hyperbolic self-deception: "The question of the relations between theology and philosophy has never [even] arisen in the East," he avers in his concluding climax to Chapter 2 of *The Mystical Theology*.[23]

But secondly, and no less importantly, the notion of the West that Lossky then puts forth as the unacceptable alternative to his Eastern view, is—I would suggest—equally revealing of his own Western, Parisian context of the 1930s and '40s. For it is hard, again, to read this anti-Western

polemic without at least some echoes of the emerging *Catholic* resistance
in France to rigidly rationalistic readings of Thomas and to the myth of a
pure nature that could exercise itself in the prerevelatory building of
philosophical foundations for faith.[24] We might therefore say that Lossky's
critique represents the reverse side of his elevation of Dionysius to the status of Eastern archetype. The fatal flaw of Western Christian thought, for
Lossky, is always in some measure the submission of its theology to *philosophical* categories: of substance and of relation most notoriously, where
Western Trinitarianism is concerned, such that "Latin philosophy first considers the nature in itself and [only then] proceeds to the agent."[25] The
connected problem of the *filioque* is then, from here, merely one more
outworking for Lossky of this mistake in starting point for the West. Its
supposed preference for substance and unity over and against person
means that the Father, the Son, and the Holy Spirit are no more than
"three modalities of a unique substance."[26]

But Lossky also has to face the manifest evidences of Dionysian influence precisely in the West itself. How could these manifestations have become so besmirched by the supposed mistakes of Western essentialism?
The answer (as Lossky later put it succinctly in *The Vision of God*) is that
"the influence of Dionysius [in the West] is indeed *more striking*, it draws
more attention to itself."[27] But because it fails to make the proper Eastern
distinction between incomprehensible essence (*ousia*) and divine pro-
cessions (*energeia*, or *proodoi*), it falls back into its own trap of philosophical essentialism: "If in the East the tradition of Dionysius marks a definite
triumph over Platonic Hellenism, in the West, on the contrary, the work of
Dionysius, *poorly assimilated*, will often become the vehicle for Neoplatonic influences."[28] Note the subtle paradox that is enunciated here: According to Lossky, one approaches close to the truth only at the risk of the
worst perversions of it. The same critique (of mistaken Western Dionysianism) pervades Lossky's otherwise sympathetic reading of Eckhart in his
long-delayed and posthumously published doctoral thesis.[29] Again, Eckhart, for all his closeness to the Dionysian tradition and his clear use of
Dionysius's *Divine Names* and *Mystical Theology*, has, according to Lossky,
been fatally misled by Thomas's rendition of Being: the divine *esse* becomes
the "foundation" of divine unknowability for Eckhart, rather than divine
unknowability radically destabilizing *esse*.[30] The One, rather than the
Good, becomes the highest principle for Eckhart, says Lossky, and so Neoplatonism again triumphs over authentic "mystical" Christianity.[31]

A third and further way in which Lossky's construction of the West is, in my view, actively but implicitly affected by his own Western context, is in his insistence that Dionysian apophaticism is superior to Western forms of negative theology because it moves above and beyond a dialectics of positive and negative statements about God (as Lossky interprets Thomas's position) to a form of unknowing that is beyond understanding, but experientially "theophanic." Lossky is quite right here to refer to Dionysius's insistence in the *Mystical Theology* that even negations about God must be transcended by a further negation.[32] But at least at the stage of writing *The Mystical Theology of the Eastern Church*, the way Lossky expresses what he sees here as the distinctive superiority of Eastern apophaticism to anything to be found in Thomas is as something "existential" or "experiential"—beyond thought and even beyond negations of thought. This is, as he puts it, a "radical apophaticism";[33] it is (for Dionysius) "a refusal to accept being as such, in so far as it conceals the divine non-being: it is a renunciation of the realm of created things in order to gain access to that of the uncreated: a more existential liberation involving the whole being of him who would know God."[34] It is both an experience and not an experience, it seems—*not* a "mystical experience" in the Western or modern sense, which supposedly involves "a purely intellectual exercise," but "an experience which surpasses all understanding."[35] The account of Dionysius *over against* Thomas here surely remains a contentious one;[36] but for our purposes the interesting attendant language in Lossky of "existentialism" and "experience," along with the demand to rise "beyond being," cannot but summon associations of the Heideggerian project of *Sein und Zeit* (1927), only recently published at the time of Lossky's first studies in Paris. While there is no evidence that Lossky himself read Heidegger, he certainly knew people in Paris (such as the Jewish philosopher Jean Wahl, in the *Dieu Vivant* circle[37]) who did. And it is hard now to read his language of "existential liberation" and of a God "beyond being" without sensing some sort of familiarity with a new, Heideggerian, or possibly Sartrian, philosophical fashion.[38] It is also difficult for the Westerner to read his insistence on the paradoxes of Dionysian thought, between absolute unknowing and contentful, incarnational revelation, without detecting, perhaps behind that, an unwitting echo of Kierkegaard.[39]

Fourthly, and finally, we should underscore how significant to Lossky's construction of an Eastern theological superiority is the notion of antinomies in the tradition, on the one hand,[40] and of corresponding dialectical propulsions in the early development of Eastern Christian thought and its final outworkings towards mature Palamism, on the other. "Antinomy," first, is of course a distinctively Kantian technical notion, although Lossky nowhere, as far as I know, remarks on that obvious terminological fact. Instead, he borrows the term to express what he sees as the irresolvable paradox at the heart of Dionysian theology: of simultaneously denying knowledge of God, and affirming a contemplative and ecstatic intimacy with that God—of insisting on the radical unknowability of the divine "essence" and on the equally radical and effusive revelatory presence of the "energies."[41] While this Kantian antinomic tension is held within the very life of God itself ontologically, along the timeline of the church's chronology there is a *dialectical* passage of development towards the truth; here we might say we detect a more Hegelian touch of influence. Interestingly, Clement of Alexandria and Origen, respectively, represent for Lossky the dialectically related misfires which must be sublated by Dionysius, who in turn anticipates the full Palamite synthesis; whereas John Meyendorff (who had a very different assessment of Dionysius[42]) would later represent Evagrius and Macarius as parallel polar tendencies in need of such Palamite correction and completion. Neo-Hegelian dialectical historiographies of this sort were of course the stock-in-trade of doctrinal textbooks from the nineteenth century, even until very recently, but the pattern and the convention of such we may also name as culturally Western in provenance and origin.

By highlighting so far these four central dimensions of Lossky's creative early reception of Dionysius for the purposes of his construction of the West (his setting of Dionysius over against Neoplatonism, *tout court*; his elevation of Dionysian revelatory darkness over Western essentialism; his claims for an apophatic Dionysian experientialism beyond Western positive and negative theologies; and his defense of an antinomic ontological distinction between essence and energies in God), I have by no means attempted a full account of Lossky's rich and creative theological program. I have concentrated here only on those features of Lossky's writing that specifically suggest an important, if veiled, connection with his immediate Western location, with its exciting new philosophical and theological stirrings. If my analysis seems largely critical, it is not really that tone which I intend to dominate here: Lossky does indeed massage his patristic texts in remarkably willful ways at times, and the result is simultaneously electrifying and disturbing to the Western reader who is under fire. But it is, frankly, that *electrification* that caught Lossky's audience, not least because it was so generative of responsive theological reaction.

But we should not presume that Lossky himself was immune from criticism or dogmatically incapable of receiving it, and here we move to a brief reflection on how he may all along have been in interactive conversation with Gilson and with some of his other French Catholic interlocutors. In fact, Lossky was later to admit an explicit change of mind on at least some of what he had earlier enunciated about Dionysian theology in *The Mystical Theology* (I am not sure how much this has been remarked upon in the secondary literature to date).[43] For instance, by the time of writing the late essays he was gathering a few months before his death (to be published posthumously as *In the Image and Likeness of God*[44]), he made at least two important concessions to critics and reviewers. First, he recanted—in the face of stern criticism from Gandillac and others[45]—on his earlier insistence that a great and unbridgeable gulf is fixed between the apophaticism of Plotinus and that of Dionysius; but he still insisted that the Eastern discipline of what he now calls "the non-opposition of opposites" is a negative way superior to that of reducing the Trinity of persons to a "transpersonal Unity," as he found in Neoplatonism.[46] Secondly, he now also acknowledged that he should not have spoken so unguardedly in his earlier writings of Dionysian apophaticism as involving a positive "experience." "In Dionysius," he writes, we are "concerned less with mystical experience of ecstasy than with dogmatic speculation"; but immediately he turns this concession into another critical dart: It is only the modern West, after all, that is seduced towards a distracting mysticism of *experience*. More properly, the East, with Dionysius, states the rules for the blanking out even of that expectation: God is beyond being, and therefore beyond any expectation of an ecstatic sense of control.[47]

At the end of his life, then, we see Lossky responsive to the critique and reception that his earlier work had engendered. But one is bound to ask: Where, earlier on, do we see the expected influence of Lossky's *Doktorvater* and long-term mentor and friend, Étienne Gilson, in the extraordinary trajectory of Lossky's anti-Western polemic and his elevation of Dionysian superiority? And was Lossky himself, contrariwise, not to leave any mark on Gilson's own thought in this area? Apart from Gilson's affectionate and somewhat pietistic remarks on the recently deceased Lossky in the introduction to the thesis on Eckhart,[48] we are left speculating on this matter, reliant on "hints half guessed." But it cannot be that the two men did not over the years intensively discuss this central matter of how the Dionysian trajectory, and its reception, should be read in its impact on both Byzantine and Scholastic traditions. And it is hard to see how Gilson, at least initially, could have done anything but disagree with Lossky's strikingly negative "construction of the West" on this point. Maybe this was part of the reason why the completion of the doctoral dissertation was so long delayed?

Yet a close reading of Gilson's own work on Thomas in the crucial years from the late 1920s to the '50s (exactly the period of his interactions with Lossky), indicate that he, too, was gradually changing and refining his mind about the significance of the Dionysian heritage for Thomas, for Bernard, and for others in the West. In the fifth edition of *Le Thomisme* (1944), for instance (the same year as the appearance of Lossky's *The Mystical Theology*, and perhaps more significantly, just two years before the appearance of de Lubac's controversial *Surnaturel*—on which more in a moment), Gilson feels obliged to add a new expanded section on Dionysius's influence on Thomas, one that replaces only scanty remarks in earlier editions.[49] Without mentioning his pupil Lossky, he insists here that the God of Dionysius *is* the "One" of Neoplatonism (contra Lossky's emphatic insistence on the opposite in his early work); but in Thomas's hands—says Gilson—Dionysius's influence becomes fully compatible with Thomas's robust and positive notion of Being.[50] Do we catch an echo here of responsive discussions with Lossky? Lossky, in turn, in his own thesis on Eckhart, was to go on to refer precisely to this new passage in the fifth edition of *Le Thomisme*, and to acknowledge that Gilson is correct in his careful interpretation of Dionysius's and Thomas's notions of God's Being and of Thomas's particular rendition of Dionysius on this point.[51] It is hard to resist the conclusion that lengthy negotiations had not lain behind this at least partial burying-of-the-hatchet, along with Lossky's late admission, already noted, that he had earlier overplayed the disjunction between Neoplatonism and the Dionysian corpus. At the same time, it is equally hard to resist the conclusion that the effect of having Lossky as a somewhat intransigent pupil would have forced Gilson into a new appreciation of the complexities of the different histories of reception of Dionysius, East and West! Perhaps this also shows somewhat earlier, we might note, in his nuanced assessment of Dionysian influence on Bernard's theology, in lectures originally delivered in 1933 and later published in 1940 as *The Mystical Theology of St. Bernard*.[52] Is it not tempting to see Lossky's

1944 monograph, *The Mystical Theology of the Eastern Church*, as an implied riposte to his own doctoral advisor?

But since, frustratingly, we have no actual correspondence between Lossky and Gilson, we are left to do such detective work as we have essayed here in our hypotheses about mutual influence. Still, as late as the early 1960s, Gilson could remark, and somewhat unrepentantly, that there was really no need for all this fashionable recourse to the Greek patristic heritage when Thomas himself contained all the best bits from the Greek fathers, such as Gregory of Nyssa, and from Dionysius, already nicely digested in the right way![53] He also expressed only belated and mixed indications of his acknowledgement of Heidegger's new philosophical critique of Being, emanating from Freiburg. Yet his much later, and charmingly affectionate, correspondence with de Lubac,[54] mostly from the later 1960s and '70s, shows a growing retrospective allegiance, post–Vatican II, with the central goals of *la nouvelle théologie*, and an acknowledgement that he had earlier underestimated the importance of Eastern patristic *ressourcement*. It is therefore to the crucial figure of de Lubac, and to *his* own reception of the Dionysian heritage, seemingly so different from Lossky's, which we must now turn for a brief contrapuntal reflection. If I am right, de Lubac and Lossky shared many goals, although initially they may have seemed to be set on quite divergent paths of Dionysian reception. It was Gilson who formed the bridge between them.

De Lubac's Assimilation of the Dionysian Corpus

There is no evidence that Lossky ever corresponded with de Lubac (this I checked quite recently with Fr. Chantraine, the biographer of de Lubac, who has sadly since died[55]); and whether the two men even met also remains strangely unclear: de Lubac was, after all, mostly in Lyons and the Jesuit house at Fourvière there, from 1929 on, except when he went on the run in the Resistance during the war, whereas his younger Jesuit colleague Daniélou, definitely well known to Lossky, was closer to hand in Paris. Yet, given the public furor occasioned over the publication of de Lubac's controversial monograph *Surnaturel* in 1946, his subsequent banning from 1950 until 1961 by his Jesuit superiors and by Rome (largely for his questioning of the regnant hegemony of the sort of neo-Scholasticism which Lossky also abominated), and given also his deepening friendship with Gilson, it surely cannot be that de Lubac's work entirely escaped

Lossky's notice. And we do know that both men were involved in the Parisian *Dieu Vivant* circle and its journal.[56] Yet nothing in Lossky's footnotes would ever suggest such a recognition. This is one of the many mysteries of omission I have had to acknowledge in my research for this project. Yet, as we shall note again at the end of this paper, Lossky's son was later to regard de Lubac as one of his father's friends.[57]

Given this lack of explicit communication between the men, I wish only to draw attention here to two, somewhat paradoxically related, dimensions of de Lubac's own assimilation of the Dionysian mystical heritage at the same time as Lossky's interpretation was being published. Like Gilson, de Lubac seems to have changed and developed his views on this heritage over some decades, and one cannot help but wonder whether, via Gilson, some greater appreciation of Dionysius may have gradually emerged as a handmaid to de Lubac's initially Augustinian impetus to theological reform.

The first point to underscore is that, in the original heady years of Greek patristic *ressourcement* in France from the early 1930s on, leading to the founding in 1940 (with Daniélou), of the *Sources Chrétiennes*, it was Origen who was for de Lubac the prime recovered hero, and along with him Gregory of Nyssa and then, among a few others in the Greek pantheon, Maximus the Confessor: These were the writers who were regarded as the key Eastern authors in need of retrieval by the West, according to the de Lubac circle. Von Balthasar, who was formed under de Lubac in the Jesuit house at Fourvière in the early 1930s, tells us, charmingly, that while other young Jesuits were letting off steam on the soccer field of an afternoon, he, Daniélou, and Bouillard, among others, studied the texts of these particular Greek authors in their original Greek form under the generous tutelage of de Lubac, who "referred us beyond Scholasticism to the Church Fathers, generously making his notes and excerpts available to us."[58] Von Balthasar, of course, was to write a monograph on each of these hallowed three: Origen, Gregory of Nyssa, and Maximus.[59] Dionysius, in contrast, was treated for a very long time with some reserve by de Lubac—and ironically for the very same underlying reasons that Lossky wholeheartedly embraced him. For what both men could agree on was that any sellout to Neoplatonism in a Christian author was a mark of decadence and danger. While Lossky exonerated Dionysius from the Neoplatonist taint, then, de Lubac—following the more standard scholarly presumptions of the time—made precisely the opposite assessment. We see this point still

expressed with force in an essay de Lubac wrote much later, in 1965, entitled "Mysticism and Mystery," and dedicated to a Jesuit confrère, Fr.
Ravier, for his Festschrift volume.[60] Here, de Lubac acknowledges that
mysticism is *not* a latecomer to Christianity, having been present in the
tradition well before ps.-Dionysius; but in its generic modern (Jamesian)
sense, just as in its late antique Neoplatonist variety, it holds great spiritual
dangers, he says, as well as the possibility of great good: "Mysticism is the
best of things, and it can become the worst,"[61] a view that—as we have
seen—could equally well have been expressed by Lossky at a slightly earlier period. It *becomes* the worst, according to de Lubac, when it gets dis-
sociated from the true mysteries of the Gospel, which are to be received as
a supernatural gift from God and *in Christ*. If ever it becomes dislocated
from the incarnation, then, and from meditation on holy Scripture, it
tends to a perverse course.[62] This judgment, too, might just as well have
been written by Lossky, but whereas Lossky chides Origen for selling out
to philosophy and elevates Dionysius to the true status of archetypal
"mystical theology," de Lubac notably reverses the preference in authors.
Origen is to be retrieved for his spiritual insight, his pervasive Christological seriousness, and the figural depths of his Scriptural analysis; Dionysius is to be suspected for his collusion with Neoplatonism and his
inadequate Christology.[63] .

In a similar vein, when de Lubac devoted the years of his banishment
from teaching to his four-volume study, *Medieval Exegesis*, significant notes
of criticism of Dionysius and his influence in the West again creep in: that
he sold out to Neoplatonism; that he was insufficiently Scriptural; that he
was too "metaphysical" in emphasis; and that, from the mid-twelfth century on, his influence in the West resulted in what Marie-Dominique
Chenu—whom de Lubac follows on this point—called a "spiritual trauma"
as "mystical understanding" transmuted into false "speculative mysticism."[64] The irony in this analysis, of course, is that it precisely mirrors
Lossky's own assault on the corruption of Dionysianism in its Western
medieval variants. What initially appears to be a straight contradiction
between Lossky and de Lubac on the assessment of Dionysianism, turns
out, on closer inspection, to be more like an ironic convergence. Even more
interesting, perhaps, is the further little "ecumenical" irony that Chenu's
critique of Dionysian metaphysics over against Biblical seriousness, a critique explicitly followed by de Lubac at this point, draws appreciatively on
Anders Nygren's influential *Agape and Eros*.[65] Again, we must not presume

that influential Protestant thought was not also a factor in the particular intellectual fashions of this time.

But criticism of Dionysius was not to be de Lubac's only, or consistent, response to his corpus. His most controversial book, *Surnaturel* (1946), did not make Dionsyianism into any conscious focus, since the insistent novelty of the book was its recalling of a deadened neo-Scholasticism to a liberative Augustinianism, and to a new sense of the participatory gift of grace available to all.[66] Any explicit *ontology* of desire, such as is characteristic of the Dionysian corpus, was thus not to be found in de Lubac's theological armory at this time; indeed—as John Milbank has recently underscored—there is an overall coyness in *Surnaturel* about the expression of any clear ontology at all: de Lubac's position at this period, says Milbank, is a sort of "non-ontology," suspended paradoxically between "the field of pure immanent being proper to philosophy on the one hand, and the field of the revelatory event proper to theology on the other."[67] Hence the ease with which his position could be misunderstood by his detractors, for it "concerned the paradoxical definition of human nature as intrinsically raised above itself to the 'super-nature' of divinity."[68] Even to speak thus, however, is already strongly to evoke themes from the Dionysian *Mystical Theology*; and for de Lubac's later *Le Mystère du Surnaturel* (which pushed forward the issues in the latter part of *Surnaturel*), it is striking that he now chose a citation from Dionysius's *Divine Names* (Chapter 3.3) as his eye-catching title page, with Dionysius's vision therein of "superabundant" Life, Wisdom, and Goodness, flowing out in an "excess of being" to the whole of creation and inviting that creation to participate in it.[69]

Had de Lubac definitively changed his mind, then? This brings us to a final, and perhaps unexpected, reason why de Lubac ultimately shifted his earlier critical views about the apophatic traditions in Christianity in general, and implicitly therefore about Dionysius as well. Like Gilson and Chenu, he was initially suspicious, and that residual suspicion of Dionysius himself probably never completely lifted; but like Gilson also, over the years, and in response to critics of *Surnaturel* who had misunderstood him as taking up a purely immanentist approach, de Lubac gradually began to evidence a new sympathy to apophatic sensibilities more generally as a means of loosening a falsely reified, or immanentist, concept of revelation. As David Grumett shows in his recent book on de Lubac,[70] it is in de Lubac's books of the late 1950s and '60s, *The Discovery of God* (in the section on "The Ineffable God") and *The Christian Faith* (the chapter on "The Unity of Faith") that a new apophatic sensibility begins to emerge in de Lubac's approach to supernaturalism, and to pervade it with a strong sense of transcendent divine mystery. " 'He who is' cannot be designated and is beyond our reach, a secret at once disturbing and inviolable," he writes in *The Discovery of God*;[71] or again, in *The Christian Faith*, "Whatever is understood through knowledge is delimited by the understanding of the one who knows. So, if you have understood, it is not God."[72] Strikingly, however, de Lubac does not directly appeal to Dionysius himself when he makes these new claims; instead, it is to one of Dionysius's Western inheritors, now given new credence. For de Lubac, the necessary apophaticism does not have to be sought, then, in the "mystical" East; it is every bit as much available in Anselm, in Thomas, in Cusanus. What had begun as a project to reacquaint himself with the Eastern fathers, and then with the Augustinian traditions of prevenient grace, thus ended for de Lubac with a new appreciation of the divine ineffability already encoded in the Western assimilations of Dionysius.

Conclusions: East and West and the Dionysian Paroxysm

Let me conclude. I have in this paper been intent on placing Vladimir Lossky's Orthodox construction of the West firmly into its original French Catholic context. While we have seen that Lossky's elevation of Dionysianism to the status of the essential core of Eastern theology was in some ways highly manipulative in its exegesis of Dionysius himself, its production was strangely congruent, underlyingly, with the simultaneous impetus to the critique and reform of neo-Scholastic thinking being undertaken by Gilson, de Lubac, and others. Had someone remarked in 1944, however, on the first appearance in Paris of *The Mystical Theology of the Eastern Church*, that its author would one day be regarded as a close ally of the leading *periti* of a coming liberative Catholic Church Council, he might have been met with a look of incomprehension. Yet the polemics against the West in this pioneering book were set, as we have now amply demonstrated, against the same enemies whom Gilson and de Lubac also resisted. Moreover, the place of the Dionysian heritage and its interpretation, both East and West, proved to be the hermeneutical lynchpin that both united and divided the two sides, as I hope I have also shown. I said at the beginning of this paper that there is no modern Orthodox construction of the

West that is not also, and simultaneously, "an implicit *responsive* conversation with the West, often animated by underlying strands of 'Western' critique and renewal which the two sides ironically share." Perhaps this explains why John Meyendorff can talk of a remarkable softening that Lossky displayed towards those around him in his last years;[73] perhaps, too, it can indicate why Nicholas Lossky, Lossky's son, can insist that his father was after all a great Westernist himself, and can conclude his survey article on the "Theology and Spirituality" of his father with these remarkable words: "Frs. Congar, Daniélou, de Lubac, Dumont and many others were [my father's] friends, after theological jousts conducted in the purest spirit of the medieval tournaments, where the 'adversaries' profoundly respected one another and always displayed perfect intellectual honesty."[74] As a polemical Orthodox constructor of the West, Lossky was in many respects a remarkable product of it.[75]

The Image of the West in Contemporary Greek Theology

Pantelis Kalaitzidis

The relationship between Greek theology[1] and the West has nearly always been one of ambivalence: On the one hand, the Greek side has shown a pronounced rejection and a radical critique of its Western counterpart, which has lately been justified in the name of authenticity and faithfulness to Orthodoxy, and is usually accompanied by an attitude of triumphalism against Western heresies; on the other hand, Greek theology is fairly replete with observable and tangible influences and borrowings from the West, which sometimes border on a secret admiration for the accomplishments, dynamism, and high scholarly and academic standards of Western theology. Vis-à-vis the West, Greek theology was destined to travel a long trajectory: From the wars between the pro-unionists and the anti-unionists, or between the Thomists and the anti-Thomists in the last centuries of Byzantium, it would enter a phase of almost total Westernization during the Turkish occupation, followed by a period of dry academic Scholasticism throughout the first hundred years of its liberation (after the 1830s), including a strong pietistic and moralistic trend imported from Europe and exemplified in the Christian fellowships such as Zoe. Following the legendary "return to the Fathers" that was propagated by the First Congress of Orthodox Schools of Theology held in Athens, in 1936—but which was to become the dominant theological paradigm in Greece after the 1960s—Greek theology rediscovered its Orthodox identity and tradition in the form of a total reimmersion in Orthodox patristic and ascetic literature; all this on the *sine qua non* condition of its liberation from all Western traces, a move that has come to be known as libera-tion from "Orthodoxy's Babylonian captivity."

Our reference to anti-Westernism by no means should be taken as a rejection of the legitimate Orthodox critiques of the West; nor does it signify a disagreement with moderate assessments of the fundamental dif-ferences between the two branches of Christianity and/or the intrinsic problems and impasses plaguing the West. What we are referring to, rather, is the simplistic ideological construction, the one-sided, inaccurate, and condemnatory critique that sees in the West nothing but errors and here-sies (while praising the Eastern Church for its doctrinal purity and up-rightness), and which continues to see East-West relations in terms of unabated confrontation and division, often in flagrant disregard for his-torical accuracy, thus discounting ten centuries of common Christian life and ecclesiastical communion. Such voices are suspiciously oblivious to the fact that for there to be ecclesial catholicity, both traditions are needed, since they jointly constitute Christianity's "twofold lungs" or "Siamese sisters," in Fr. Florovsky's own terms.[2]

Even so, it would be unfair to chide the theologians of the 1960s for anti-Westernism in broad strokes: First, because the generation as a whole was influenced theologically not just by the Russian theologians of the Dias-pora, but by major works coming from Western theological scholarship as well, as represented by O. Cullmann, J. Danielou, Y. Congar, H. de Lubac, L. Boyer, Th. de Chardin, D. Bonhoeffer, H. von Balthasar, K. Barth, R. Bultmann, K. Rahner, P. Tillich, and others. Of course, it is a matter of debate whether the 1960s theologians did in fact converse with these grand Western figures and their successors (J. Moltmann, W. Pannenberg, H Kung, J-M Tillard, etc.) openly and sincerely. Secondly, though, it would be unfair because not all of the Greek theologians of the 1960s share this strong anti-Western sentiment. Indeed, we would be seriously remiss if we blurred the subtle and important differences among the main representa-tives of this theological generation vis-à-vis their attitude towards the West. Their views on this matter run across a wide spectrum, ranging as they do from the near absence of an East-West polarity and the critical or even friendly dialogue with the West (usually accompanied by the adop-tion of its theological agenda and its academic/critical methods), down to the radical denunciation and demonization of the entire Western tradition, an identity-centered entrenchment, and the promotion of an anti-Western and anti-ecumenical spirit.

The so-called "theological generation of the 1960s," however, which treads along the path of the call to return to the Fathers, has been hugely instrumental, in regards both to the agenda and structure of contemporary Greek theology, and with respect to the latter's current image of the West. With the exception of Biblical studies (an underdeveloped and rather marginalized discipline in Greek Orthodox circles, at any rate), this trend has been the dominant theological paradigm in Greece. The now legendary "return to the Fathers" was initially espoused by the vast majority of the theologians of the 1960s, such as Nikos Nissiotis, John Zizioulas, Demetrios Koutroumbis, Christos Yannaras, Fr. John Romanides, Panagiotis Nellas, Nikos Matsoukas, and Fr. Vassilios Gontikakis, and in the process ended up becoming a commonplace reference, indeed an Archimedean point for the theological schools, the Church, the average sermon, ecclesiastical and theological literature, and so on. But as we have indicated elsewhere, the fact remains that despite Fr. Florovsky's own intentions when he coined it, one of the inevitable consequences of this movement to "return to the Fathers" was the acute polarization of the East-West divide and the cultivation of an anti-Western, anti-ecumenical sentiment.[3] This paper will focus on the two most influential anti-Western theologians of the "theological generation of the 1960s," Fr. John Romanides and Christos Yannaras.

Fr. John S. Romanides and the Rivalry between Romiosyne and Francosyne

The theology and overall mindset of Fr. John S. Romanides (d. 2001) makes for an apt illustration of Greek Orthodox, anti-Western triumphalism. Born in Piraeus, Greece, in 1927, to a family of Greek refugees from Cappadocia and raised in the United States, where his family eventually emigrated, Fr. Romanides studied with Fr. Georges Florovsky and was graced with a promising academic career beginning at Holy Cross Greek Orthodox School of Theology in Boston. He first made an impact in Greek Orthodox scholarship with the 1957 publication of his book, *The Ancestral Sin*,[4] which had been approved as a doctoral dissertation (not without some controversy) by the Faculty of Theology of the University of Athens. In this highly acclaimed work, Romanides reminded Greek theologians that "the ethos of the ancient Church, which is preserved in the Eastern tradition, is not legalistic but healing and compassionate in nature."[5]

Thanks to this work, therefore, in addition to his professorship at the Aristotle University of Thessaloniki's School of Theology from 1970 to 1984, his lectureship for well over a decade as visiting professor at Balamand Orthodox Institute of Theology in Lebanon, his lectures in the United States and elsewhere, as well as his frequent participation in official theological dialogues as a representative of the Church of Greece, Romanides has put a lasting seal over Orthodox theology, Greek and non-Greek alike. He did this to such an extent, in fact, that some, like Fr. George Metallinos of the National and Kapodistrian School of Theology of Athens, have gone so far as to talk about pre- and post-Romanidian theology.[6] Others, notably the French Orthodox priest and scholar Patric Ranson, whose work borders on zealotry, called Romanides "the greatest living Orthodox theologian, whose work constitutes a critical reading of Augustine's corpus in light of patristic theology."[7]

Here we would be remiss in failing to mention that Romanides had already proven himself a capable and pioneering theologian long before this period, following a series of important papers in English published primarily in the *Greek Orthodox Theological Review* between 1956 and 1965 (for example, on Ignatian ecclesiology, the ecclesiology of Aleksei Khomiakov, Justin Martyr and the Fourth Gospel, Palamism and the Christology of Theodore of Mopsuestia, St. Cyril of Alexandria, and St. John of Damascus). What is clear in this early, American period of his scholarly career, which coincides with the 1960s and the turmoil associated with it, is that Romanides's theological interests are wide and broad-minded, as can be seen from his involvement in the ecumenical movement, which he assessed positively,[8] and his concern for religious freedom,[9] and even such far-flung topics as Islam.[10]

Nonetheless, Romanides's broadmindedness suffered a dramatic retreat after 1975, when his book *Romiosyne* was published.[11] In this work, the notorious divide of Greek (Orthodox) East versus Latin (Roman Catholic) West gives way to the radical and absolute chasm between so-called Orthodox "Romiosyne" Greek and Latin-speaking, on the one hand, and a heretical "Francosyne," on the other.[12] From the appearance of *Romiosyne* onward, Romanides's discourse has nothing in common with the moderate and carefully qualified prose of *The Ancestral Sin* and other early theological writings. Hereafter, the West is wholly demonized and proclaimed responsible for all the misfortunes of the Orthodox, both theological and historical/national.

The ideas expressed in the first publication of *Romiosyne* is further explicated in two briefer papers. The first of these is entitled "Costis Palamas and *Romiosyne*," originally published in the Greek language, ultraconservative ecclesiastical newspaper *Orthodoxos Typos*[13] and independently by Romiosyne Press, Athens, 1976; the latter paper, entitled "The Romiosyne of 1821 and the Great Powers," was again published in the *Orthodoxos Typos*.[14] Romanides's project is later supplemented by a historical/theological essay, published in English in 1981, under the title *Francs, Romans, Feudalism, and Doctrine: An Interplay between Theology and Society*, offering a panoramic overview of his theologico-political ideas.[15]

From that time on, Romanides's texts would be structured as inextricable mixtures of theology, national history, culture, and politics. The reason behind this blend, according to his distinguished pupils, was that it provided the "hermeneutical keys" required for a thorough comprehension of theology and history, thereby probing more deeply and more successfully, where others before him had failed, such as Fr. Georges Florovsky, whom Romanides supposedly follows in that respect.[16] In this spirit, Romanides adds a new prologue to his second Greek edition of *The Ancestral Sin*,[17] where in a frenzied tone, strongly reminiscent of conspiracy theories, he accuses the Francs of conniving against Romiosyne and Orthodoxy. The opening lines of this prologue are highly enlightening as to Romanides's ulterior motive of incorporating a historical-political manifesto into the body of an otherwise theological work:

> The present study dates from a time when efforts were made to isolate heterodox influences on Orthodox theology, and digressions from patristic tradition were all too evident. Nowadays, we are in a position to account for the political and theological circles which launched heterodox initiatives for the annihilation of *Romiosyne* and the westernization of Orthodoxy.

Elaborating somewhat on his reference to these "political circles," Romanides further stipulates:

> Back when this work was written, no one yet realized that foreign think tanks had designed not only the annihilation of *Romiosyne* but the distortion of Orthodoxy as well, according to western principles. Today, research leads curiously to Napoleon and his associates as the chief architect of this policy.[18]

Napoleon is further accused of aiming for more than merely seizing authority by impersonating the revolutionary. In Romanides's view, Napoleon, as a Franc, sought to undercut the force of the French Revolution of 1789, which on Romanides's account was nothing but an uprising of "the enslaved Gallo-Romans against the Francs, France's nobility." Or, as he indicates a few lines later, "the majority of Franc officers abandoned the revolution, which developed into a war of Romans versus the Francs," while for their part, "the French revolutionaries of 1789 were proud of their lineage from Rome and the Peloponnese."

Even purely theological texts, such as Gregory Palamas's *In Defense of the Holy Hesychasts*, published by Romanides in a series of patristic works characteristically entitled "Roman or Romioi Church Fathers," would be read from this selfsame and indivisible ethno-religious, historico-theological, and theological-political perspective, as seen in its introduction.[19] From the earliest pages, Koraes (a Greek scholar of the Enlightenment) is already chided as responsible for the transformation of Romiosyne into "Hellenism," effected through trading hesychasm (the very heart of the nation) for metaphysical and social philosophy. In the same vein, his introduction ends with a fierce assault on Europeans, Russians, and so-called "Latin Greeks" or "neo-Franco Greeks," who are held responsible for the destruction of Romiosyne and the undoing of its spiritual context. The introduction then closes with a call addressed to all genuine Romans to reclaim their leadership and unfetter Romiosyne from its alien spiritual bonds.

The above historical-theological hermeneutic (Greek- and Latin-speaking Romans versus heretical Frankish invaders, Romanity versus the Franks), combined with the "three stages" theory (purification, enlightenment, deification/theosis), hailed by Romanides as the distinctive hallmark of Orthodoxy—i.e., what sets it apart from all other religions and traditions[20]—will henceforth assume dominance in Romanides's scholarship. It will color and undergird all of his remaining texts, regardless of topic (ecclesiological, dogmatic, or ecumenical, the relationship between faith and culture, national issues and territorial disputes with Greece's neighbors, even the relationship between religion and Orthodoxy, and between science and Orthodoxy): The unbridgeable rivalry between Romanity and the Francs, the rancorous common struggle of Greek- and Latin-speaking Romanity against the Frankish usurpers of Rome's throne and the Teutonic distorters of the true spiritual experience (purification, enlightenment,

deification/theosis), was bound to be Romanides's permanent theme after the 1970s, his hermeneutical key for understanding and explaining
all kinds of problems, concerns, and challenges (theological, ecclesiological, etc.).

With the exception of Christos Yannaras, who will adopt it only gradually and selectively, this hermeneutic has become popular among notable
Greek theologians and even secular scholars (such as Metropolitan Hierotheos Vlahos of Nafpaktos, Fr. George Metallinos, Anastasios Fillipidis, Kostas Zouraris, etc.), as well as Orthodox clerical and lay theologians
in Lebanon, Syria, Jerusalem, and also converts from North American
Orthodoxy, who popularized and further developed Fr. Romanides's
analyses and ideas.[21] In fact, one of Romanides's early theses concerning
Romanity would be quoted verbatim by the former metropolitan of Demetrias and the late archbishop of Athens, Christodoulos.[22]

From the preceding brief analysis, it should become clear that Romanides's theology has dominated the Greek theological and broader ecclesiastical scene. It has had a decisive impact on the thought not only of
bishops, priests, and especially monks, but also lay theologians and numerous religious groups as well, inasmuch as it furnished a convenient
and comforting conspiratorial explanation for the historical woes of Orthodoxy and Romiosyne. As an explanation, of course, it is devoid of the
slightest traces of self-criticism, since blame is always placed upon others:
the heretics, the Franco-Latins, the Pope, Westerners, Napoleon Bonaparte,
the Slavs, and so on.

Small wonder, then, that Romanides's theology has won such a large
and widespread following among conservative circles in the Church as well
as the Far Right. In truth, he flattered the repressed frustrations, prejudices, and psychological complexes of the historically defeated modern
Greeks to the effect of cultivating theological self-sufficiency, cultural introversion, aggression, and an intemperate sense of superiority. His theories
on Romiosyne have never been resisted or challenged by a robust counter-
theology, nor has his selfsame titled book been subjected to serious critical
commentary, even thirty-five years after its first appearance.[23] What interests us here, with regard to Romanides's texts and teaching, is the total
demonizing of the West, the chiliastic conflation of Orthodoxy and spirituality with Romanity/Romiosyne, and last but by no means least, the
reductive geographical identification of all those graced with the vision of
God and the uncreated light with the so-called citizens of Romanity/

Romiosyne. In the characteristic words of Metropolitan Hierotheos of Nafpaktos and St. Vlassios, one of Fr. John Romanides's most faithful followers, "Fr. Romanides had devoted himself entirely to the cause of *Romiosyne*, which to him was the quintessence of all genuine spirituality, the kind that frees us from self-love, material lust, and every other expression of fallen humankind."[24]

Beyond the terrain of Romiosyne—Greek or Latin—Romanides sees no possibility for such things as repentance, spiritual struggle, holiness, sanctification, or even salvation. It seems as if he delimits all these to a certain cultural domain. Therefore, based upon his own definition of Romiosyne and the "Roman," we can assume that, in the eyes of this Greek-American theologian, holiness, the vision of God, and Orthodoxy in its pure form, is intrinsically intertwined with a certain empire: i.e., the Roman Empire and its citizens. Thus, even Orthodox peoples who formed no part of this empire, by chance or choice, such as the Slavs, for instance, are either ignored by Romanides or openly denounced as collaborators with the Francs and traitors of Romiosyne. It is certainly not accidental that, so far as I am aware, nowhere does Romanides make reference to Slavic or Russian saints or ascetics. Likewise, in his ambitious and grandiose plans for the (political) rebirth of Romanity/Romiosyne, he includes—based on culture, language, and national symbols—the present countries of Greece, Albania, Romania, and Cyprus, while also including at the heart of "Rum" or "Roman Identity," the Orthodox populations of Syria, Lebanon, Palestine, and the descendents of the Latin-speaking Romans of Western Europe, respectively.[25]

This is not the place to elaborate on Romanides's notorious theological and ecclesiological ideas of the Church as a sort of "spiritual hospital" and of Orthodoxy as the supreme method of psychotherapy and medical (spiritual) rehabilitation,[26] all known for their powerful appeal to many distinguished clerics and theologians. It will have to suffice to indicate here, for our present purposes, the existence of a deeper, underlying link between Romanides's peculiar ecclesiological oligarchy (i.e., his demand for a proven and objectified vision of God as a prerequisite for doing theology, and the restriction of this possibility to "Romans") and the peculiar racism and anti-Westernism that his theology has promulgated.

It should be added that Romanides's political involvement as a candidate for the Far Right in the 1977 parliamentary elections in Greece, a mere three years after the fall of the Greek junta, is in line with the overall ideas and stereotypes that his corpus conveyed in its entirety. The moment we recollect his unwavering position toward the "Other," especially the heterodox "Other" (Westerners, Francs, etc.), or even toward the Orthodox "Other" (Slavs, Russians, etc.), we are forced to admit that his involvement in Far Right politics could hardly have been an unfortunate accident, as some of his supporters have claimed in his defense.[27]

In sum, let us briefly add that Fr. Romanides's overall theory concerning Romiosyne may well serve as a perfect, but not unique, illustration of two powerful tendencies in twentieth-century Orthodoxy: On the one hand, it embodies the pernicious slide from the theological per se to the cultural and historical; on the other, it exemplifies the romantic tendency and perennial temptation of many Orthodox to long for premodern social patterns and structures, which found a voice and inspiration in Romanides's anti-Western mania that so savagely damaged his own theology, and beyond that, the presence and work of the Orthodox Church in Greece and in the broader postmodern world scene.[28]

Structural Anti-Westernism in the Corpus of Christos Yannaras

For all of its popularity in the marginalized setting of the Greek far right and in conservative Church circles, Fr. John S. Romanides's worldview never gained an audience beyond its own microcosm. It never managed to draw significant public attention to it, nor did it resonate with intellectuals, artists, or the educated classes in Greece. While still enjoying some considerable appreciation among certain religious groups, it is readily dismissed by the Greek secular intelligentsia as a ludicrous, or at best, a romantic version of Hellenism, a refined and ideological form of collective overcompensation. Such is not the case, however, with respect to Christos Yannaras, whose presence in Greek academia goes back to the 1960s.

The immensely diverse work of Greek theologian and philosopher Christos Yannaras has been decisively influential in the development of theological and Church affairs in Greece since the 1970s, and more intensely so from the 1980s onward, a turning point in Yannaras's literary career during which he became probably the most widely read theologian in Greece.[29] Beginning in the 1980s, his work gradually became something of a must-read for a wide circle of Greek intellectuals and artists, who are one way or another related to the so-called "neo-Orthodox" movement. Yannaras's output gained more popularity throughout the 1990s, in the wake of the geopolitical fluidity of that decade and the resultant rise of nationalism and the identity crisis that went with it; nevertheless, the nationwide popularity of his work would be in reverse proportion to its theological robustness, which suffered a progressive diminution as Yannaras's theological criteria became increasingly blurred. In spite of that, Yannaras's intellectual labors have been received with enthusiasm not only in Greece but throughout the wider Orthodox world as well, as his books gradually became available in European, Slavic, and Balkan languages. Yannaras's thought has been described as "a creative theology of international range," to recall the words of French Orthodox theologian Olivier Clément[30] on his first-rate scholarly work, which could be attributed as much to the fact that it effected a huge paradigm shift, theologically as well as culturally, as to the fact that it appeared in the form of a radically challenging theology.

Yannaras's theology, like the theology of the 1960s as a whole, is indeed one of disputes and reversals. It has mainly sought to overcome two formerly mainstream paradigms that dominated the Greek theological and ecclesiastical establishment in the pre-Yannaras era: dry and sterile academic Scholasticism, and the Western-style pietism of the religious fellowships in Greece.

Obviously, therefore, Yannaras's radical theology sought from the very outset, among other things, to rid the Orthodox ethos from alien Western influences, to effect its liberation from the "Babylonian captivity" to Western theology, and to thus reconnect Orthodoxy with its indigenous roots— the patristic sources. At the same time, Yannaras's initiative aimed at making Orthodoxy conversant with the challenges and impasses of modern consumer culture. In his post-1972 writings in particular, as soon as he gained access to the public sphere as an essayist and columnist, beginning with the Greek daily *To Vima* and from 1994 onward in *Kathimerini*, Yannaras, as a natural extension of his theological and philosophical agenda, has increasingly pressed for the emancipation of Hellenism from the alienating influences of the West, while exploring the possibility of an authentic modern Greek identity structured along the lines of its Byzantine Orthodox origins. An integral aspect of this proposal is the understanding of the history of Hellenism in terms of a culture, of a mode of being, as opposed to a geographic or state narrative. These ideas, along with his strong suggestion for a Greek "reading" of Plato and Aristotle, the related urging for the formation of a Greek mode of philosophizing (marked by the rubric of a single, unitary Greek approach to philosophical questions),[31] and especially his peculiar hermeneutic advocating an unbreakable continuity of the Greek logos, throughout the centuries, in its conception of truth as an event of communion and participation in it, all assume an absolute priority in Yannaras's later thought, to the extent even of overshadowing his theology proper.[32]

Here we must point out that, although Yannaras often appears to be the anti-Western theologian par excellence in Greece, and while the twin demand for the liberation of Orthodoxy from the Western Scholastic and pietistic influences, no less than the rediscovery of true Orthodox tradition, still remains the hallmark and backbone of his theology, we should refrain from reaching oversimplified assessments of his agenda; by the same token, we would be just as remiss to assume that Yannaras's thought is unaffected by major developments in modern Western theology. In his early scholarly period, at least, not only does he steer absolutely clear of nationalism and similar tendencies, but he seems more amenable to ecumenical dialogue and productive conversations with Western theologians.[33] Yannaras's early, but—as we shall see—discontinuous, openness to contemporary Western Christian thought accords, to a degree, with his positive references in his early works to contributions made by Western theologians such as Jean Daniélou, Henri de Lubac, Hans Urs von Balthasar, Yves Congar, Endre von Ivanka, Olivier Rousseau, Roger Schutz, Louis Boyer, Thomas Merton, and others.[34]

But already by the late 1970s, culture (and in particular, Greek culture) had become so central to Yannaras's thought that it had ascended to an Archimedean requirement and criterion of ecclesiastical integrity and catholicity. By the same token, Greek culture became a basis for exclusion from the ecclesiastical event, as in the case of Western medieval civilization and culture, which in Yannaras's view was decisively shaped by the invasion of barbaric tribes and races in the Western Roman Empire between the fourth and sixth centuries AD, an event that led him to view the West in terms of barbarism and cultural inferiority. For Yannaras, it is not spiritual self-sufficiency, selfishness, lack of repentance, or conformity to the spirit and logic of "this world" (see Romans 12:2; 1 Peter 1:14), or "another law at war with the law of my mind," as Paul says (Romans 7:23), that excludes us from the Church, but rather the level of our given culture, indeed our cultural preconditions, for which we are nonetheless not personally responsible, in view of the national and cultural contingency of human birth. Nor does one's personal response to Jesus Christ's call, according to Yannaras, appear to be a matter of personal choice, free of necessity and the confines instituted by gender, race, and social or *cultural* preconceptions. In his view, even so personal a decision as one's response to Christ's call is inextricably intertwined with the cultural progress of our biological or spiritual forefathers and their traditions.

Here we cannot help wondering whether we would be remiss if we described Yannaras's glorification of culture as a "totalizing cultural predestinationism" from a soberly theological point of view. Are critics like the former editor-in-chief of *Synaxis*, Sotiris Gounelas, off the mark when chiding Yannaras's beliefs as comprising a "cultural totalitarianism," a tendency toward a Greek-centered cultural requirement that consigns the mystery of the Church (and the Incarnation) to a secondary status, for the sake of Hellenizing the Church?[35]

Hellenism's presumed cultural sovereignty over the Church, as Yannaras propounds it, cuts across the problem of anti-Westernism that concerns us in the present paper. For Yannaras's analyses, more elaborately presented in his 1992 classic *Orthodoxy and the West: Hellenic Self-Identity in the Modern Age*,[36] and more recently summarized in a brief paper in the journal *Synaxis* (issue 88, 2003) about "the hordes of primitive races that swarmed the western territories of the Roman Empire from the end of the 4th century till the 6th century AD, and which rushed to convert en masse to Christianity," are at the heart of his anti-Western attitude, which is simply another aspect of his Hellenocentrism, forming as they do its core justification. Yannaras believes, and states quite explicitly, that the primitiveness of these northern barbarian invaders prevented them, even after their Christianization, from becoming actual sharers in the ecclesial event.

The structural anti-Westernism running throughout Yannaras's entire thought as its internal necessity is in a real sense a "construction," a contrived new version of Church history and theology, wherein the continuous confrontation between Orthodoxy and the West, Eastern and Western Christianity, Greek and Western European tradition, is now placed at the center of the unfolding drama. Though initially presented as a theological affair, the said confrontation is soon transformed into cultural identity warfare, for such was really its starting point: not so much theology, but a historical and cultural identity-formation process. Yannaras's systematic and structural anti-Westernism will even go so far as to portray leading Thomists and medieval scholars such as Marie-Dominique Chenu, Étienne

Gilson, art historian Erwin Panofsky, and historian Georges Duby, unbeknownst to them and despite their own intentions, as providing in their own works all the historical and theoretical material needed for a radical, nearly destructive criticism, and ultimately the rejection of the medieval and modern West. There is hardly a single column or essay penned by Yannaras after 1970, once he had acquainted himself with these writers, that fails to quote them in support of his basic thesis, i.e., that the theoretical preconditions for the impasses of modern Western culture (a culture of gross consumerism) must be traced back to Western medieval theology and philosophy. As Yannaras himself points out in his autobiographical book *On Himself*, in the process of highlighting the significance of his discovery:

> There are, nonetheless, certain books which give readers a permanent pause. You cite them over and over again in your writings, as if your bibliographical information has stopped with these. They become keys to interpreting an entire era or a civilization across the centuries. Perhaps every scholar can single out such books that opened up his or her mind's eyes, as if they were written just for them. Such books may have been widely read, but it was up to an individual's sensibilities to bring to the fore their radical, overarching vision. Occasionally you may even feel that the very author of such a revealing book was unaware of the true magnitude of his or her text. For if they did, they would have certainly reached radical conclusions. I ran across three such key books in Paris: the small, rigorous study of art historian Erwin Panofsky, entitled *Architecture gothique et pensée scolastique*;[37] M.-D. Chenu's solid and impeccably qualified work *La théologie comme science au XIIIe siècle*;[38] and Étienne Gilson's classic *La philosophie au moyen âge*.[39] Shortly before I departed from Paris, I added to my roster of key works Georges Duby's three volume series *Adolescence de la chrétienté occidentale — L'Europe des cathédrales — Fondements d'un nouvel humanisme*.[40]

At the bottom of this systematic misreading of the aforementioned scholars (who were obviously read outside their proper context), and Yannaras's overall critique of the West, there lies the ideological hermeneutic of a radical contrast between Orthodoxy and the West and the kindred construction of a view of the modern world as a product of the Western Middle Ages. To be sure, Yannaras is not the creator of this irreconcilable divide between East and West. It was he, however, who turned it into a system and endowed it with a theoretical background; he who attempted to ground it in Western/non-Orthodox sources (Gilson, Chenu, Panofsky, Duby); it was he, finally, who felt perfectly entitled to construe not just the Western Middle Ages but Western civilization as a monolithic cultural space, down to its tiniest and most contingent details, and who still claims in his assorted writings (whether monographs or weekly columns) that many of the world's modern ailments—including instrumentalized reason, totalitarianism and the atrocities of the two world wars, the ecological crisis, the advertising deceit, consumerism and ideological brainwashing, as well as utilitarianism and the objectification of human personhood—must all be traced down to the theological texts and ecclesiastical and social structures of the West's Middle Ages. But Yannaras's anti-Westernism is merely the flipside to his Hellenocentrism—it is its *sine qua non* prerequisite.

If the absence of all eschatological perspective in Yannaras's corpus, on top of his protological reading of history and theology, have resulted in an inevitable idealization of the Orthodox past and the consequent injunction for a return to roots and tradition, his misreading of history and personal lack of an ecumenical sensibility have in turn led him to adopt a strategy that still enjoys widespread popularity among the Orthodox: juxtaposing the most infamous and tired picture of the West with the shiniest and most progressive version of Orthodoxy. The West that Yannaras has in mind and denounces is often a mocking caricature of the real West. In any case, his negative assessment of it largely depends on references to medieval sources, particularly those of Thomas Aquinas, Anselm, and Augustine, but never to any important contemporary Western theologian, notwithstanding the fact that many Western theologians are keenly familiar with both patristic theology and the fundamentals of the Russian theology of the Diaspora, and are nowadays aptly versed in Eucharistic theology and ecclesiology, including the theology of personhood. Thus, while references to Aquinas, Anselm, Abelard, Augustine, and others abound in Yannaras's works, references to the fruitful challenges posed by Protestant or Roman Catholic theologians of the twentieth century are flagrantly absent. Indeed, it is extremely rare in Yannaras's entire corpus (comprised of thousands of pages) to find references to contemporary Western theologians (e.g., Oscar Cullmann, Jean Daniélou, Yves Congar, Henri de Lubac, Hans von Balthasar, Rudolf Bultmann, Karl Rahner, Paul Tillich, Jürgen Moltmann, Wolfhart Pannenberg, Hans Küng, Jean-Marie

Tilliard, André de Halleux, Hervé Legrand, etc.) or, more importantly, instances of a substantial interaction with their core ideas. Even as regards the problem of Christianity's "religionization" (*thrēskeiopoiēsē*), the radical differentiation of the Church from religion, of the ecclesial from the religious way of life, which has dominated Yannaras's agenda over the past twenty-five years, and which he has hitherto (at least until the publication of his *Contra Religion*[41]), attributed solely to the West, inasmuch as he believed that it pertained exclusively to Western Christianity—or to the East only insofar as it had become Westernized—Yannaras does not find it appropriate or useful to make a single mention of Karl Barth and his seminal distinction between religion and revelation. He also ignores Dietrich Bonhoeffer and his deeply original analysis of the possibility of a nonreligious Christianity, made in his prison cell just prior to his execution by the Nazis.

Yannaras is deeply convinced that the Western Middle Ages have put a permanent dent in the overall development of Western societies, including their philosophical and theological course; so much so, in fact, that he elects to focus his energies on and to dialogue with the distant medieval theological past at the expense of the present dynamic of Western theology, where a series of tumultuous and very important changes, revisions, reinterpretations, and disputes have long been taking place.

Indeed, contemporary Western theology can rightfully boast a progress that Yannaras (and those among the Greek theologians of the 1960s sharing his overwhelming anti-Westernism) simply does not follow. For one thing, neo-Scholasticism and neo-Thomism have both ceased to command any attention in Roman Catholic scholarship as living theological options. Accordingly, few Western scholars are still looking for answers to current problems and challenges in medieval theology as a reservoir of perennial wisdom. That does not mean that historical research in medieval schools and trends is currently at a low ebb; on the contrary, medieval studies have bloomed since the late 1980s, especially in French-speaking academia, Catholic and secular alike, where a renewed interest in medieval philosophy and theology has been manifest. But interest in that field is almost exclusively academic, a matter of concern for the history of philosophy, not in the sense of an effort to revitalize a long-defunct tradition as a spiritual guide for the present age. Few, if any, scholars nowadays would dream of delving into Scholasticism the way Yannaras does— especially in the aftermath of the Second Vatican Council, the widespread renaissance of Biblical and patristic studies, and the Catholic endorsement of modern hermeneutical methods. Much less would anyone attribute to medieval theology the heightened role assigned to it in Yannaras's worldview. It is fairly obvious that Yannaras opposes a straw man, a long-defunct entity that has ceased to exert a material influence in contemporary societies, thereby making a mockery out of his implacable resolve to base his conclusions on medieval thought with almost complete disregard for current trends in Western theology, and true to his conviction that the modern world is simply the result of the Middle Ages and cannot be adequately construed unless this is first thoroughly studied and understood for the purpose of characterizing and defining the identity and self-consciousness of Western Christianity.

In light, then, of Yannaras's problematic premises, such as those just outlined, it is to be expected that his analyses of East-West relations would be hopelessly biased and one-sided: For example, the distortion and progressive "religionization" (*thrēskeiopoiēsē*) of Christianity (with all the modern negative connotations attached to this term) are wholly attributed to the West, while the Greek East is cleared of all blame, except for the occasional historic (as opposed to doctrinal/theological) failures to measure up to its own fine standards. Accordingly, the Schism of 1054 AD, which severed Christian unity, is seen as the historical analogue of the Gospel's antithesis between the fallen "world" and the "Kingdom of Heaven," as the radical differentiation between the Church and the "religionization" of its Gospel, which became identical (in the case of the West and its church) to the fallen world and even death.[42] Accordingly, "the grand, and only surviving heresy" (Christianity's disfiguring "religionization"),[43] the sum total of all existing heresies according to Yannaras, is exclusively attributed to the West.

Interestingly, Yannaras has mitigated somewhat his sweeping anti-Western conviction in his 2006 work *Contra Religion*, where he acknowledges signs of "religionization" even in pre-fourteenth-century Eastern Orthodoxy, down to the very core of the Orthodox tradition: He sees these in patristic writings, in the synodal canons, in hymnology and worship, in asceticism, popular piety, and certain aspects of Church administration. Chief among these instances are, for example, the beginnings of an individualistic understanding of the Eucharist, the demonization of sexuality, the insistence on the postnatal virginity of the Theotokos, the establishment of Christianity as the "official religion" of the Roman Empire, the "religionization" of ecclesiastical Orthodoxy as illustrated par excellence in the literary genre of the *Philokalia*, and so on.[44]

But in spite of this small yet important recantation, Yannaras still adamantly holds the barbaric invasion of northern tribes largely responsible
for the "religionization" of Christianity in the West and eventually for the
Schism itself, which he attributes to the cultural inferiority of these tribes.
In his view, the barbaric races that swarmed the western part of the Roman Empire simply lacked the level of sophistication needed to compre-
hend and appreciate the Greek mode of being and the fundamentals of
the Christian good news of salvation, and instead turned it into a "religionized" version of individual ownership of the truth, a self-centered certainty, and a juridical objective morality. This hermeneutic is repeated with
astonishing frequency in Yannaras's works,[45] but more so in the Greek
original of his work *Orthodoxy and the West: Hellenic Self-Identity in the
Modern Age*,[46] in which he claims Greek cultural superiority over the West
on the basis of his interpretation of the latter's origins in barbarism, sav-
agery, and cultural backwardness.

Such an overall, sweeping rejection of the West (where the West is still
seen by many Orthodox as the source of all evil, while being just as coveted
by the same quarters as a secret object of desire) runs throughout Yannaras's
work. It fits in perfectly with his well-known ideas about the uniqueness
and cultural supremacy of the aristocratic race of the Greeks, the adoption
and further modification of historian Constantine Paparigopoulos's ideological construction of the unbreakable continuity of Hellenism from antiquity and Byzantium through modern Greece, the romantic idealization of
the political, cultural, and social conditions of the Turkish occupation period, the "sermon" on the return to the authentic tradition, which in many
ways is reminiscent of the call to "return to the fundamentals of the faith,"
and especially the rejection of modernity's accomplishments. It was this
body of theses which led some to place Yannaras's work, along with the
broader neo-Orthodox movement—of which he is the most eminent
figure—in the roster of fundamentalist doctrines, and even to compare it to
similar trends in Islamic and Jewish/Zionist fundamentalisms. As these critics would have it, Yannaras's views (no less than those of the "neo-Orthodox"
intellectuals) have been forged under the influence of German Romanticism,
particularly its vision of the nation, which came to the attention of the Greek
intelligentsia via the thought of the Russian theologians of the Diaspora,[47]
and raised the question of the sources of his anti-Westernism.[48]

The Slavophile movement of the nineteenth century and the recently
documented intellectual debts of its representative figures (Khomiakov,

Kireevskii) to German Romanticism, which infiltrated Yannaras's thought mostly via Russian religious philosophy and the theology of the Diaspora, and partly from Dostoevsky, must have been highly instrumental in shaping his anti-Westernism. Yannaras shares with the Slavophiles the same populist disdain for the West: the metaphysical, almost messianic, import that is bestowed upon the common folk and their alleged mission, the return to the land and to indigenous traditions, the classic polarizations of East-West, Western rationalism versus Eastern Orthodox mysticism, Western individualism versus Eastern communitarianism, Western Scholasticism versus Eastern patristic tradition, and so on, are as abundant in Yannaras as they are in the Slavophiles, whose ideological core comes from Friedrich Wilhelm Schelling and other German philosophers of the eighteenth and nineteenth centuries. The Slavophiles' critique of the West is combined in Yannaras's thought with Martin Heidegger's critique of Western metaphysics and technology and his nostalgic longing for the primeval truth alluded to in the texts of the pre-Socratics. Yannaras sees in Heidegger, the last great metaphysical philosopher of the West, a potential conversation partner with patristic thought and especially with the apophatic theology of the Eastern Christian tradition ("the Greek philosophy of the early and middle Christian period," as Yannaras calls it in his later works). He sees Heidegger, moreover, as someone who understands the reasons why Western medieval theology and philosophy can lead directly to European nihilism (this rationale is more elaborately stated in *Heidegger and the Areopagite*, but is frequently summarized in other works of his, including his weekly essays). Despite being itself free of anti-Western assumptions, Heidegger's criticism provided Yannaras with the framework, as well as the irrefutable arguments and authoritative references, with which to construct his own vision, in which a strong anti-Western sentiment is evident from the very beginning[49]—both in terms of a simplified portrayal of the West and in the form of its subsequent popularization. Vladimir Lossky, for his part, with his emphasis on mystical theology and apophaticism, his reappreciation of the Areopagitic writings (hailed by Lossky as the premier authoritative text of the Eastern Christian tradition), and his overemphasis on the *filioque* as a theological indicator of East-West differences, seems to have served as an extra source of inspiration for Yannaras, despite the fact that this great Russian theologian of the Diaspora never really drifted into any form of cultural anti-Westernism.

Any attempt to understand Yannaras's anti-Westernism will only go so far unless the historical tragedies of Orthodoxy and Hellenism (events such as the Fourth Crusade of 1204, the Frankish Rule, the fall of Constantinople in 1453, the Turkish occupation, the infiltration of missionaries in Greece, the Asia Minor disaster in 1922, the occupation of northern Cyprus by Turkish forces since 1974, NATO's bombardment of Serbia, and the Macedonian dispute) are seriously taken into account. Given his regular weekly columns in prestigious Greek newspapers (originally in *Vima* and since 1994 in *Kathimerini*), the widespread circulation of his ideas and comments, as much promoted by the frequent broadcasting of his views in the media as by the natural charm and force of his thought, and, of course, the prodigious sales of his books, there is no question as to the impact of his Hellenocentric and anti-Western discourse on a massive segment of Greek society willing to lend an ear to such "sermons" in its desperate search for self-assurance. Even so, the range of Yannaras's ideas goes further than that, as his views have been espoused and individually adjusted by clergymen, theologians, and intellectuals, in their own ways themselves influential in Greek society and in the Church (including the late archbishop of Athens, Christodoulos, Fr. George Metallinos, Kostas Zouraris, Theodoros Ziakas, Fr. Theodoros Zisis, etc.), thereby adding fuel to a growing anti-Westernism that intensifies polarization, resentfulness, and negative historical memories, but worse than that, perhaps, it diminishes every prospect for reconciliation, strengthening as it does the anti-ecumenical sentiment already rampant in Greece and throughout the Orthodox world.[50]

Translated from Modern Greek by
Haralambos Ventis; edited by Fr. Gregory Edwards

CHRISTOS YANNARAS AND THE IDEA OF "DYSIS"

Basilio Petrà

I do not intend in this to deal with every aspect of the idea of *Dysis* in the thinking of Christos Yannaras, for in Yannaras's vast oeuvre the theme of the West comes up in many different contexts and plays a variety of roles.[1] I shall look at his thinking *statu nascenti*, or in the early years of his reflection—that is to say, from 1964 to 1967, from his leaving the Zoe Brotherhood to the publication of his first theologico-philosophical work, *On the Absence and Unknowability of God*.

The distance that Yannaras covered in these years may be described in the following way: from a moral/spiritual criticism of the West according to Dostoevsky to an ontological criticism of the West according to Heidegger; from Orthodox (Greek) responsibility in relation to the salvation of the West to Greek (Orthodox) responsibility in relation to the ontological truth and salvation of humanity as a whole. The word "distance" indicates here not a succession of phases but rather a journey in which his initial ideas were deepened and radicalized by his discovery of the ontological hermeneutics of the West through his encounter with Heidegger and by a conviction that Western nihilism could be overcome only through Eastern apophaticism and personalist ontology.

The interpretative model of the West that emerges in these years, under the decisive influence of Heidegger's *Holzwege* (especially of Heidegger's interpretation of Nietzsche's proclamation of the death of God), will remain constantly present and active in Yannaras's subsequent reflection; it will constitute his permanent horizon. Within this model, the idea of the

West is constructed as a loss of being and of the true mode of existence, a loss that is capable of transforming even the Christ event by making it heretical and transforming it into a religion—a dominant institutional-ization of ethics.

This rigorous reading of the West offers Yannaras the possibility of a new vision of Hellenism, always on the heels of Heidegger. Indeed, Hel-lenism, *from the time of its historical emergence*, becomes for him the trustee of the authentic mode of existence, of the authentic mode of the knowl-edge of truth (a truth that is participative and communitarian). This is because it became capable of an authentic reception of the proclamation of the Gospel and of the ecclesial event. It tried to oppose the predomi-nance of the West, but without success. In spite of the Schism, Hellenism has long been under Western domination—but not totally. The Orthodox people, and to a certain extent the monastic tradition, have conserved the authentic Orthodox ethos and its living sources: the liturgy, the icon, the parish. For this reason, Hellenism, so long as it is reaffirmed in its (Ortho-dox) truth, preserves the authentic ethos of the Gospels and serves as a way to salvation for a West that is suffering a mortal crisis.

Nevertheless, in the course of time, and especially in Yannaras's most recent works, one notices a change of perspective: The dualism between the West and Orthodox Hellenism flows, as it were, into a dualism be-tween religion and the Gospel proclamation or ecclesial event.

In light of this overview, my treatment of Yannaras will proceed ac-cordingly: In the first section, I shall examine the criticism of the West according to Dostoevsky and the responsibility of the Orthodox towards the West. The second section will address the criticism of the West ac-cording to Heidegger—namely, how Yannaras believed that it was possi-ble to move beyond Western nihilism through Eastern apophaticism and a personalist ontology. Given the decisive relevance of the encounter/con-frontation with Heidegger, the third section seeks to illumine how Hei-deggerian thought exerted its influence upon Yannaras's ontological understanding of West and Greekness. In the fourth section, I shall then go on to study—on the basis of the framework delineated by the encoun-ter with Heidegger—a term that emerges progressively in Yannaras's thinking and that is revelatory of the essential ontological alienation of Western Christianity—namely, θρησκειοποίηση, "religionization." This will enable us to observe very clearly Yannaras's change of perspective in the way I have already mentioned. The West tends to become an ontological category rooted in a more radical anthropological category, one that is indicated as "the natural religious need," the need of (fallen) humanity to place under objective control—precisely through *religion*—the unknown forces to which its existence is subject. From this point of view, the West becomes one of the forms of *religionization*, or even at times a synonym for the *religionization* of the ecclesial event. My concluding remarks will touch briefly on a question that arises inevitably from the trajectory of Yannaras's ontological hermeneutics of the West—that is to say, the question of the relation between a personalist ontology and Orthodoxy.

Criticism of the West According to Dostoevsky: Orthodox Responsibility in Relation to the West

What Yannaras knew of Russian diaspora theology were ideas forged largely from the literary work of Fyodor Dostoevsky (1821–1881).[2] The young Yannaras had drawn on those ideas in order to rebel against a Christianity that had been reduced to a system of ethics. One of the Karamazov brothers, Alyosha, proved most helpful in this respect, and accordingly, Yannaras dedicated to him the earliest of the texts assembled in *Honest to Orthodoxy*, an essay entitled "Models of Morality."[3]

For Dostoevsky, Europe is not Christian. Catholicism has betrayed Christianity, and transformed it into a worldly social finality. It has succumbed to Christ's third temptation, the temptation of worldly power. The story of the Grand Inquisitor is a most searching criticism of Catholicism, the revelation of the religious dominion of Antichrist, and the West has not responded to this challenge. Even Protestantism, for Dostoevsky, has denied Christianity, having reduced it to a system of ethics. Christ is merely an ethical model and, as such, it is unimportant if he is a man or both man and God. In Protestantism, there is also room for the denial of the Incarnation of the Word. Thus, for Dostoevsky, only Russia remains. Russia has Orthodoxy; it has the criteria for the awareness of truth, and therefore, only in Russia can there be critical judgment. Europe does not have the possibility of assuming a consciousness of judgment. It lacks the appropriate criteria and rests in an illusory Christianity, believing itself to be Christian without really being so.[4]

Inspired by the *Lecture on Pushkin* that Dostoevsky gave on June 8, 1880,[5] and in particular by some prophetic words contained in it, Yannaras speaks of the duty of the Orthodox to save "old Europe,"[6] to give it new life. In doing this, he feels himself in harmony with the vision of Georges Florovsky and his presentation of the first Slavophiles: "The older Russian Slavophiles saw their task in terms of European requirements, the unresolved or insoluble questions raised by the other half of the Christian World. The great truth and moral power of early Slavophilism is found in this sense of Christian responsibility."[7]

Russian Orthodoxy, for Yannaras, has in some measure already realized Dostoevsky's prophecy:

> A series of philosophers and theologians, who subsequently played a central role in European life, is the vital succession that this first group of Slavophiles has bequeathed: Bulgakov, Florensky, Khomiakov, Berdyaev, and the contemporary Russian theology of the diaspora—Lossky, Florovsky, Evdokimov, Zander, Meyendorff, and Schmemann, are spiritual presences immediately noticeable in European life. The second group makes available today the responses of Orthodox theology to the questions of contemporary Western man. Through the same first perception of the central core of life that exists in the Russian Orthodox tradition, these men have in a wonderful way realized Dostoevsky's prophecy about the capacity of the Russian nation to effect a substantial reconciliation with the Western world.[8]

Yannaras insists, it should be noted, that nothing of this sort could have been achieved if the lived experience of popular Orthodoxy (the place of the preservation of Orthodox truth) had not been embodied in the spiritual renewal of nineteenth-century Russia (St. Seraphim of Sarov).[9] Moreover, the heirs of the first Slavophiles deliberately drew back from Slavophile exaggerations: the excessive emphasis on the popular element, as if the people could be substituted for the Fathers of the Church, "the nationalism of Russian Orthodoxy that has nourished the dreams and forces of Panslavism."[10]

An extraordinary symbol of this realization of Dostoevsky's prophecy, for Yannaras, is Camus's drawing near to *The Possessed* and to the great Russian author in general, whose prophetic character he acknowledges. It is therefore with deep feeling that Yannaras draws from Camus's prologue to the dramatization of *The Possessed* as a French play:

> For a long time Marx has been regarded as the prophet of the twentieth century. Today we know that what he prophesied is no longer

expected. And we know very well that Dostoevsky was the true prophet. He prophesied the rule of the Grand Inquisitor and the triumph of force over justice . . . . For me, he is above all the writer who well before Nietzsche was aware of contemporary nihilism, who grasped and foresaw its bestial and insane consequences and sought to establish the message of salvation.[11]

But there is something here that is more than symbolic. Camus's intellectual journey brought him near to Orthodoxy: first of all, because he perceived the crisis of the West and wanted to go beyond the West's illusions; second, because he was an atheist and had therefore rejected the epistemological-rational schemes of Western metaphysics (Aquinas, Descartes, the Enlightenment) in order to seek existential truth.[12] In Camus, Yannaras saw an example of how a European, conscious of the death of God and affected by the resulting experience of perdition, could be ready for the Orthodox message of salvation, exactly as Dostoevsky had prophesied.[13] Yannaras recalls in this connection a fact communicated to him by Olivier Clément that struck him very deeply: "Shortly before his death, Camus read Lossky's book, *The Mystical Theology of the Eastern Church*. For Camus, this theology was an unexpected surprise. 'This really is something I can discuss,' he said. And he began his dialogue by dramatizing Dostoevsky's *The Possessed*. But he had no time to continue with it."[14]

The true sign, however—an epoch-making sign—that announced the arrival of Orthodoxy's time in the West was seen by Yannaras in the events of May 1968, and the spirit of confrontation that spread over the West at the end of the 1960s. He said so, formally, in the pages that introduced the first Greek edition of *The Freedom of Morality*: "It seems to be the hour of opportunity for the word of the Eastern Orthodox tradition. We are living at a privileged time, perhaps, of a preliminary exit from the scheme of the conventional morality that has been enshrined within the cultural boundaries of Europe ever since the Western deformation of Christianity—the morality that is based on the legal conception of sin, on the idea of individual transgression or individual merit, on the forensic conception of the relation of humanity with God."[15]

Where does Greek Orthodoxy stand in relation to this? For the young Yannaras, Greek Orthodoxy is at a standstill; it is still in a situation like that experienced by Russian Orthodoxy at the beginning of the nineteenth century. On the one hand, there is the institutional and cultural influence of the West, the forced Europeanization that has aimed and still aims at eradicating Greekness from the Orthodox life of the people, from "popular truth"[16] reduced to an anthropological exhibit. On the other, there is the rootedness in the people of a few prophetic voices, the Greek Dostoevskys: "Makriyannis, Solomos, Papadiamantis—they at least—have clearly measured the depth of the nation and not just its breadth, right down to the roots. And these roots—that they have uttered prophetically like Dostoevsky—can nourish not only Greece but also the West, which has grown old 'in the sins' of rationalist systems."[17] Arrested in this moment, Greek Orthodoxy continues to live in a deep dream, while "a true and veritable earthquake" is taking place—namely, the rediscovery in the West of the Greek Fathers, of Byzantium, of Orthodoxy, and even of the *Philokalia*.[18] Western theologians are editing Eastern texts and studying them with passion. The Greeks limit themselves to drawing some benefit from tourism and feeling a certain pride in Orthodoxy—nothing more.

For that which happened in Russia in the nineteenth century is happening in Greece. And the same miracle is needed to create the spiritual presuppositions: behind the Russian intellectuals was Seraphim of Sarov. It is also necessary that in Greece "a handful of people" should dare "the silence of action," or should put down roots in "the land of the Orthodox East," and offer today a prophetic testimony to God, giving flesh to the Logos "by silence, humility, abnegation and asceticism."[19]

But where can these people be found, and how can they avoid the temptation simply to identify Greek Orthodoxy with popular Greek culture and/or Greek nationalism? For Yannaras, the prophetic role is represented historically by two figures: the monk and the martyr.[20] By 1964, however, we are speaking of martyrs capable of taking up the cross of technology,[21] and of monks who can recover from oblivion an Orthodox sense of their proper mission.[22]

The prophetic role calls for the rejection of heretical Orthodoxy, an Orthodoxy that has in some way accommodated two specific characteristics—heresies—of the West: the founding of faith on rationalism and its reduction to an ethical pietism.[23] It calls for the rejection of an *anerastos* Orthodoxy that is incapable of demonstrating the erotic substance of the Christian experience,[24] the rejection of an iconoclast Orthodoxy (iconoclasm always accompanies a conservative pietism).[25]

The prophetic role, then, calls for a Greek Orthodoxy that is capable of recovering its proper ecumenical mission and presenting the universality of Orthodoxy,[26] without reducing it to nationalism, which is a considerable problem not only for Greek Orthodoxy but also for Orthodoxy in general.[27] Is a renewal of this kind possible? While writing the preface to *Honest to Orthodoxy* in Bonn in March 1967, Yannaras was pessimistic. He speaks of the end of Greek Orthodoxy, not of its end as an institution but of its end as a salvific presence:

> A historical end does not always imply historical disappearance as well. It may simply signify historical aphasia. Orthodoxy in Greece does not show signs of presence in the historical present. It constitutes, rather, an absence both as theological self-awareness— in dialogical relation with the present—and as renewed worship, ecclesiastical art, monasticism, and contemporary pastoral practice. The preservation of a museum-like tradition and identification with the destiny of national life are also objectively elements of survival; they do not negate the fact of a historical end.[28]

Before concluding my account of this period, it may be useful to make two observations. The first is this: The ecumenical aphasia of Greek Orthodoxy that Yannaras laments is already attributed to Western influence, even if—for the time being—it is seen principally as beginning with the Bavarian monarchy imposed on Greece in 1832, and is identified especially with the reduction of Christianity to pietism and ethics. This means that even from that time Greek Orthodoxy was aphasic because it was not really Greek, because it had betrayed its proper Greek identity. The very discourse on ecumenicity as a vocation of Greek Orthodoxy cannot but appear ambiguous. On the one hand, according to Yannaras, it is true that authentic Greek Orthodoxy is that which opens itself up to ecumenicity (there are such indications in Yannaras's texts of this period).[29] On the other, it may also be true that Greek Orthodoxy is truly ecumenical if it becomes more Greek, more rooted in the Orthodox authenticity of the Greek Fathers, of Palamite hesychasm, of the Orthodox life of the people, of the Greek Dostoevskys. The first route leads one to judge Hellenism in the light of ecumenicity and, therefore, to value the elements that it has in common with the West. The second, by contrast, leads one to identify ecumenicity with the *via aurea* of Orthodox Hellenism, in the measure in which it is Orthodox—that is, in the measure in which it is not Western. The risk of the latter route is that it transforms anti-Westernism into a necessary part of the structure of Yannaras's Orthodox thinking, as is emphasized by Pantelis Kalaitzidis, for whom the risk has become reality. In fact, this second route seems not only to predominate but also to be radicalized and to become much stronger as a result of what might be called the *Heideggerian shift* in Yannaras's thinking.

And here I would make my second observation. In 1966, clear signs began to emerge that Yannaras had been reading Heidegger's *Holzwege* (*Off the Beaten Track*).[30] His intuition is that Heidegger's interpretation of nihilism, in the footsteps of Nietzsche and beyond him, offers elements that go further than Dostoevsky. It is not simply a matter of rejecting the institutional deformation of Christianity (the Grand Inquisitor), and registering nihilism as the crisis of the West, as the experience of perdition that opens up the West to "Orthodox" salvation.[31] Beneath nihilism there is something further, something more radical that affects the very manner in which humanity confronts the fact of being. Towards the end of 1966, Yannaras's ontological vision was taking shape, as he says himself in the Prologue of *Person and Eros: Theological Essay of Ontology*.[32]

Criticism of the West According to Heidegger. Beyond Nihilism: Eastern Apophaticism and Personalist Ontology

The Criticism of the West According to Heidegger

"In Germany I learned a lot. How Western I was, how differently Western."[33] Yannaras not only learned a lot of things in Germany, but something happened to him there—almost casually—as he later recalls.[34] He discovered Heidegger. And from Heidegger, Yannaras soon developed his style of writing: "The marriage of poetical language with philosophy: this is what struck me in Heidegger. Particularly that which his suspicious Catholic critics mocked him about. *Denken als Kunst, Mystik, Romantik*? An ontology that refused to identify reality with its intellectual meaning was impossible for them. Their mocking suspicion justified his criticism, a criticism that demolished Western metaphysics."[35] From that moment, Heidegger accompanied him on his path: "Always close to Heidegger, the challenge of an ontological realism."[36] The encounter with Heidegger determined the ontological thrust of Yannaras's thinking, or *the discovery of the ontology* (and the connected ontological understanding) of the West as well as of Orthodoxy.

One may justly say—in my opinion—that from 1966 onwards, the comparison with the thought of Heidegger remains the explicit/implicit horizon of Yannaras's reflection in such a way that Heidegger's interpretation of the West becomes for him *canonical* or *normative*. For the whole of 1966, Yannaras engaged reflectively with Heidegger, assimilating deeply his ontological approach to reality and to culture. He recalls that he wrote *On the Absence and Unknowability of God: Heidegger and the Areopagite* at Bonn between January 1966 and February 1967, publishing it later the same year in Athens.[37]

The fundamental idea that dominates this first work is consistently Heideggerian: Western metaphysics, as developed from Plato onwards, through the prevalence of the ontic interpretation of being, has generated a historical process that, in relation to being—both in its affirmative form (natural theology, rationalism) and in its negative form (Western apophaticism, irrationalism)—leads by way of Kant to the Hegelian metaphysics of absolute subjectivism, which in the end "transforms metaphysics into an axiology." In this light, "the reality of beings is no longer a logical necessity but an empirical or historical necessity," and "the empirical or historical validity of beings is tied to their utility, not to their truth."[38] Practical value becomes the criterion of the value of beings themselves qua beings. Yannaras underlines Heidegger's words in *Holzwege* where it is said that the coup de grâce given to God, when he was raised/reduced to the rank of supreme value, was not delivered by the atheists, but by the faithful and their theologians.[39] Nietzsche, with his proclamation of the death of God, has only made explicit the sense and the internal necessity of the development of the West's mode of behavior towards being.[40]

Beyond Nihilism? Eastern Apophaticism and the Ontology of the Person

What particularly interested Yannaras was the fact that, for Heidegger, the proclamation "God is dead" did not at all signify the triumph of atheism, but only that the place of God would remain always empty, because nothing could be said about this place by human reason without falling again into ontological and axiological determinations.[41] Heidegger, therefore, recognizes that there is a space for apophaticism. But it is a closed space, according to Yannaras, for Western apophaticism, because in it, negation is simply a moment of discursive or critical reasoning.[42] Thus, Yannaras concludes that Western apophaticism always remains within the domain of reason.

There is, however, a different apophaticism—a non-Western kind that has remained outside the nihilistic necessity of Western metaphysics. This is the Eastern kind, the apophaticism of Dionysius the Areopagite, which was taken up by Vladimir Lossky—and, in some measure, by Nikos Nissiotis—and which is based "on the distinction between the essence and the energies of God."[43] This is an apophaticism of *renunciation* or abandonment.[44] Eastern apophaticism is a path of knowledge that passes by personal existence: it is participation in the imparticipable Godhead;[45] it is an ecstatic communion of love between God and humanity.[46]

Eastern apophaticism, therefore, goes beyond Heidegger by opening up to an ontology of the person. If in 1967 Yannaras had not yet arrived at saying this in a formal way, he was to say it clearly twenty years later when he republished the book:

> The nihilism of Heidegger, as respect for the unrestricted limits of questioning thought—as refusal to subject God and Being to conceptual constructs—seems provisionally to fit in with what we have here called, in reliance on the Areopagitical writings, apophatic *abandonment*. It differs crucially from the apophaticism of the Areopagite both in its presuppositions and in its consequences, presuppositions and consequences that make up the *ontology of the person*, the linking of apophaticism to the existential principle of freedom and otherness.[47]

The Discovery of the Ontological Hermeneutics of the West: (Greek) Orthodox Responsibility in Relation to the Ontological Truth/Salvation of Humanity

The approach of the 1967 essay demonstrates the decisive importance of the discovery of Heidegger for the young Yannaras. It shows a kind of *conversion to ontology*. I use this term because it seems to me the most appropriate for indicating the depth and seriousness of what is happening to Yannaras: He takes up the ontological approach as his normal method for addressing questions regarding humanity and its existence; in a particular manner, he takes the ontological hermeneutics that Heidegger applies to the history of the West and makes it his own, sensing in it a fascinating route to the possibility of rethinking the history of the Orthodox East itself, especially the history of (Orthodox) Hellenism. I am referring to a decisive passage. This is a page in Yannaras's autobiographical writings that expresses very lucidly the significance that this discovery of Heidegger's ontology had in his life, and shows how it generated in him—precisely as a *Greek intellectual*—a vocation, a call to a true work of his own that, in the years to follow, would be pursued in a consistent way:

> The study of ontology illuminated the development of Western culture, the necessary conclusion of nihilism—a development and a conclusion that Nietzsche had opportunely deciphered and Heidegger had turned to account. Moreover, for a Greek scholar, the illumination of the historical process is the greatest stimulus to self-awareness that he could receive [on these points]: how and why the ancient Greek theory of knowledge—the identification of *alithein* (to say the truth) with *koinonein* (to make something together with)—saves an ontology centered on the *ousia* of the ancient Greeks from ending up in nihilism; how and why the new ontology of Christian experience unites with the flesh of Greek reason (*logos*) and remains the same theory of knowledge, despite the ontological renewal, demonstrating the organic continuity of the Greek philosophical struggle with the ontological question; how, when, and why medieval Europe's break with the Greek tradition, the radical inversion of the terms of Greek culture both on the level of the theory of knowledge and on the level of ontology, occurred and what it involved; how and why, beginning with a theory of knowledge based on the need for an individual-centered intellectual certainty, the phenomenon of dogmatic ideology appeared that led to a phenomenon never before seen in history, the monstrous configuration of totalitarianism; in what measure the ontological person-centered realism of the Byzantines could function today as a proposal for leaving the dead-end of nihilism, how one may express oneself in contemporary language, how one may enter into dialogue with Heidegger and Sartre, with the theater of the absurd, with the surrealism of painting and poetry, with the principles of the political economy or with the technical language of quantum mechanics.[48]

This page is probably the clearest and most probing exposition of the truth of a fact just noted: all of Yannaras's intellectual research issues strictly from the encounter with Heidegger (i.e., with ontology), and from the intuition that right away there are possibilities of thinking and reflecting that are offered to a *Greek Orthodox intellectual* by the perspectives Heidegger opens up. The ontological encounter with Heidegger, considerably more profound than that which in certain respects Yannaras had with Sartre, was to remain a sort of permanent leitmotif in his thinking. Even some of his recent writings demonstrate that, for him, Heidegger's nihilistic ontology is the final word of Western ontology: only Greek personalist ontology offers a true alternative.[49]

For anyone who has even a slight acquaintance with Yannaras's work, the page I have just cited in full is revealing. In it, Yannaras himself interprets all his activity after 1967 in a unitary fashion, beginning with his discovery of Heidegger's ontological hermeneutics. The plan of research drawn up in this page of text is all but complete. Here I can give only a taste of it by mentioning some of the lines of thought Yannaras indicates, so far as is relevant to my exposition.

First is the claim that there is a Greek continuity on the level of gnoseology, a continuity that persists despite the passage from antiquity to Christianity with the ontological overturning that it entails. The claim carries with it the necessity of a *Greek* rereading of ancient Greek philosophy, an idea also based on Heidegger.[50] What seems to Yannaras to be especially needful is a rereading of Aristotelian philosophy, which had been distorted in the Scholastic and the Western European approach, generally.[51] The Christian overturning of ontology, well expressed by the theology of the Cappadocians in its affirmation of the identity of person (*prosōpon*) and *hypostasis*,[52] does not affect the essential aspects of this continuity,[53] according to John Zizioulas's interpretation.[54] Yannaras repeats this in many texts, often in a provocative manner,[55] and arrives at speaking in this sense of a *Greek metaphysics*.[56]

Yannaras sees in this continuity the permanent source of Greek cultural identity, of the universal mission of Hellenism: He says so in a very dense passage welcoming the appearance of the essay by Zizioulas already mentioned.[57] It may be noted here *en passant* that Yannaras sees in Zizioulas's theses a substantial confirmation of his own ontological perspectives that from the beginning establish an essential connection between personal existence, relation, freedom, love, and truth.[58]

There emerges clearly here the quasi-inevitability of a second line of thought: the claim that Greek (Byzantine) ontology—personalist and apophatic, with the category of relation (*schesē*) at the center[59]—is the "way out" from the West's nihilist approach. Yannaras seems enflamed by the conviction of a historic mission: to manifest the salvific and veritable fecundity of Greek (Orthodox) ontology. Consequently, his task is to demonstrate this truth, on the one hand, by criticizing in contemporary terms the signs of the Western ontological distortion in various spheres of existence and human culture; and, on the other, by submitting this same truth to the test of modern knowledge. Although the encounter begins with Heidegger, Sartre, political economy, and quantum mechanics, it continues with linguistics, law, postmodernism, psychology, and neurobiology, reaching an engagement with Karl Marx, Max Weber, Karl Popper, Jacques Lacan, Ludwig Wittgenstein, and others, in an attempt to respond in an *ontologically consistent* manner to fundamental questions: the truth of God, eros, beauty, evil, and death.

A critique of the Western ontological distortion is necessary; indeed, it is the first necessity. Without this mode of Western existence, which also altered the reception of Greek philosophy, and began *the path towards nihilism*, the Greek (i.e., Orthodox) reception of the Christian message would have maintained the path of authenticity. But it did not happen that way. The West created a Christianity in accordance with its own ontological approach: the Schism of 1054 is not simply a dogmatic and disciplinary separation, it is an ontological schism;[60] the excommunication of the West on the part of the Eastern Church was an act of love in hope of the salvation of humanity.[61] As early as 1970, Yannaras listed the Western errors that lie behind the Western mode of thinking and living the Christian faith. He did this in a lecture delivered in Boston under the title "Orthodoxy and the West".[62] "Let us summarize the basic elements of the stance of Western man in face of the world and history. These are the following: the priority of the conceptual explication of revealed truth—the dividing boundary between the transcendent and the world—the will to dominate nature and history; the banishment of God to an empirically unreachable realm; the separation of religion from life and the reduction of religion to symbols; the elimination of ontology, that is to say, dogma, and its substitution by Ethics."[63] The list was to be lengthened and the centrality of certain accusations was to emerge ever more clearly: rationalism, individualism, moralism, legalism, authoritarianism, utilitarianism, totalitarianism.

The critique of the West, as is said a number of times and as is apparent here, is, therefore, an ontological critique. Certainly, it has a reference that is also geographical, but only in the sense that the geographic West is the place exemplarily and originally marked by a mode of existence—an ethos—that has precise ontological connotations, which leads to a distorted reception of the Christian event. Thus, the critique of the West can become a critique of that which is "Western" wherever it manifests itself. Yannaras believes that what is vitally pressing is a critique of the West hidden in Orthodoxy par excellence—namely, in Greek Orthodoxy. His fierce attacks on the Western elements in Greece are well known: he spares neither academic theology, nor the pietism of the theological brotherhoods, nor Athonite monasticism (in particular Nicodemos the Hagiorite), nor even the Holy Canons.[64] At the heart of this critique, one notes the emergence and imposition of a term that summarizes and defines, for Yannaras, the essential distortion to which the Western approach to ontology has subjected the message of the Gospel and the ecclesial event: "religionization," the term to which we now turn.

The Western Modality of the Ontological Deformation of Christianity: *Thrēskeiopoiēsē*—a Significant Modification of the Notion of the West

The term *thrēskeiopoiēsē* is not easily translated even if its sense is clear enough: it indicates a process by which a reality (here Christianity) becomes an institutional religion. This term does not appear in Yannaras's early writings. So far as I know, it is not found in any text before the middle of the 1980s. If we carefully examine the texts with a strongly anti-Western content such as *Truth and Unity of the Church* of 1977, or *The Freedom of Morality* in both its 1970 and 1979 editions, we will not come across this term. The terms with which Yannaras describes his understanding of the Western alteration of Christianity are heresy, *ekkosmikeusē* (secularization), and *thesmopoiēsē* (institutionalization). The West is an ontological heresy, which reifies that which it touches and transforms it into a secular reality, an objective structure and an institution, to the extent of altering the truth of the Church and its sense of liturgy and revelation.[65] The expression perhaps nearest to the sense of "religionization" is the one we find in *The Freedom of Morality*, where, in speaking of art, he refers to the "'religious' alienation of ecclesial truth."[66] To my knowledge, the first place we encounter this word is in a text published in 1986, in which Yannaras offers a diary of the days he spent in Moscow and Leningrad in May 1982. He describes a concert of the Moscow State Symphony Orchestra, in which some Russian religious music was performed that felt religious but not "ecclesial."[67] He also sees this heresy expressed especially in religious art of the Western type.[68]

It should be emphasized that Yannaras makes these reflections on the basis of observing the presence of the West in the religious art of Russia, because this presence leads him to think that there is a strange accord between the West and Orthodox Russia, in particular: Both of them, albeit in different ways, have sought to distance themselves from the Greek original, to differentiate themselves from it.

> All these differences have the common characteristic that they tend towards the pompous and the Baroque, towards that which suggests feeling or sentiment. This has to do not with a local style but with a different ethos, an ethos, I would say, that is intensely "religious." An estrangement from the Early Christian Greek prototype has led imperceptibly to a Western religionization. From what I know of history, it was the same need for differentiation—dictated by an anti-Greek political goal—that moved the Franks to bring about the schism in the eleventh century.[69]

If these words were really written in 1982, they constitute the first instance where the idea of Western Christianity's manipulation of the original Christian fact is articulated in terms of religionization. As we have already seen, this is an idea to which Yannaras arrived through Heidegger's *Holzwege*. What I now add should therefore not surprise us.

1986 was not only the year in which Yannaras published his Russian diary of 1982. It was also the year in which he signed the preface of the second revised edition of *On the Absence and Unknowability of God*.[70] This is an interesting edition from our point of view, for the term "religionization" now appears. And it appears to be precisely a comment on the texts of Heidegger's *Holzwege*, which I have already mentioned. "The way in which Heidegger," writes Yannaras, "understands the Nietzschean proclamation of the 'death of God' presupposes a fundamental historical testimony: the differentiation of the *thrēskeipoimenou* (religionized) Christianity of the Western European tradition from the primordial fact of the experience and witness of the Church."[71] According to this reading,

> Nietzsche's proclamation points out, indirectly but quite clearly, the fundamental "heresy"—the deviation from the original fact of the Church—which constitutes the historical temptation of Western Christianity: the quest to impose itself rationally and socially, finally the Church's religionization, its transformation into a religion

that satisfies individual needs for emotional and intellectual security, while also sustaining the practical moral interests of society.[72]

From 1986, then, the word "religionization" seems to be certainly present
in Yannaras's texts. It becomes the compendious expression for defining
the ontological and existential heresy of the West, the distortion of the
original Christ event. This means that every trace of religionization—
whatever it may be and wherever it may be found (theology, ecclesiology,
ethics, sacramental theology, various forms of art)—becomes a sign of
Westernization or of Western influence.

In the 1990s, Yannaras publishes a very dense work in which he uses
this term in an organic fashion—with the cultural ideas and schema that
it entails—to present a rereading of the whole of modern Hellenism's cultural history. This is *Orthodoxy and the West in Modern Greece,*[73] a work
that has been much discussed, not least for its many provocative aspects.

"The West's innovations," writes Yannaras, "resulted in what we may
call a religionization of the church." Christianity is an ecclesial and Eucharistic *mode of existence*: what has actually happened is that this *mode*
has been lost in the West, where "Christianity became an individualistic
religion dominated by private convictions, the acquisition of individual
merit, and the institutional control of faith and morals."[74] Yannaras goes
on to say:

> Western Christianity in fact represents in history the radical over-
> turning and inversion of the terms of the Christian Gospel. . . . The
> axis and recapitulation of these changes is the religionization of the
> ecclesial event; the West rejected (or failed to understand) the prior-
> ity of the truth of the *person*, returning to the abstract conception of
> God as supreme Essence.[75]

It would be an easy matter to demonstrate the significant presence of the
term in successive works of the 1990s and the first years of the new millennium.[76] Nevertheless, it seems to me more important to underline a
significant modification of Yannaras's notion of the West that is associated with this term.

Yannaras gradually gives increasing attention to the fact that religionization constitutes the victory of natural religion over the experience of
salvation in the Church—namely, over the ecclesial event: natural religion is the system of collective convictions, of rites and moral rules that

spring from the need of human beings to protect themselves and guard themselves against transcendent forces.[77] As a consequence, there is a shift in the East-West dualism Yannaras had previously perceived; or rather, this dualism comes to be grafted on to a broader and more radical one: that between religionization and the ecclesial event, indeed between religion and the ecclesial event, as emerges very clearly in *Against Religion*.[78]

This does not at all imply the loss of the primacy of ontological Hellenism, nor does it change the ontological interpretation of the Schism, but it does imply that the Western religionization (in its twin forms of Catholicism and Protestantism) is only one version of religionization. There is also the Eastern version (Orthodoxism), in part determined by Western influence after the Schism (Scholastic and confessional theology, art, etc.), in part derived directly from the imperial Church (certain canons, for example, and the role of the Sacred Canons in general), and in part generated by internal forces: Yannaras criticizes Philokalic hesychasm very strongly, reflecting particularly on the success of the *Philokalia* in the West.[79] Nevertheless, "the final stage of religionization, even of the so-called Orthodox Churches"[80] lies not in these aspects, but in the fact that these Churches continue to give credence to a mythological cosmology and anthropology (the myth of the prelapsarian world) that is incompatible with the data of modern science, without such a dualism being considered problematic in any way. For Yannaras, the Orthodox Churches thus seem to be content to offer a space of psychological refuge—a mythical world—corresponding to humanity's desires and instinctual needs, and in some sense, being a projection of them. This last point should be noted especially, because not only does Yannaras *not* accuse the West of this,[81] but he states clearly that such mythological cosmology/anthropology has to be rethought on the basis of the findings of modern science (which is a part of Western modernity).

This modification of the meaning of "religionization" has a particular effect: The ontological difference between East and West comes to be based on a more primitive difference that is anthropological rather than ontological—namely, the difference between a person who tries to enclose the Gospel proclamation within the limits of natural religion, and one who accepts the evangelical (ecclesial) transformation of the mode of existence; the latter is a new mode of existence that nevertheless maintains elements of continuity with the *Greek* mode of existence that found exemplary realization in the first Christian centuries.

This is not just a difference between one person and another; it is also an internal difference within a single human being and within the community: Religionization is the constant temptation that accompanies the very proclamation of the Gospel and its acceptance. Like the wheat and the tares, the proclamation of the Gospel and religionization grow together until harvest time.[82] This reformulation of the term "religionization" does not abolish the ontological significance of Hellenism, nor diminishes Yannaras's conviction that Hellenism has tried heroically to oppose the religious transformation of Christianity, but without success.[83]

One can, therefore, say that the term "West" in Yannaras's recent thinking acquires a more general sense, which is the surrender of the Christian to the temptation to transform the Gospel proclamation into a natural religion instead of assuming and transforming the natural religious need into a Eucharistic experience, into an ecclesial mode of existence. This temptation has met with particular and profound success in the historic West, but it has also been active everywhere and at all times, including in the Orthodox Churches.

Thus, it appears clear that, for Yannaras, natural religion cannot simply be denied; it must be assumed and transformed. Just as the sacrament of matrimony assumes and transforms the natural sexual need by engrafting it into the *ecclesial mode* of existence, and just as the Eucharist engrafts the need for self-preservation into the same *mode*, so humanity's natural religious need can be assumed and transformed in the very fact of the Church, in the sacrament that the Church itself is, insofar as it is the "realization and manifestation of the Trinitarian *mode* of existence." This is a mode "that the *synaxis* of the 'body' of the Church realizes and manifests in every particular sacramental action, but preeminently in the Eucharistic meal, where the realization and manifestation of the body is accomplished by active participation in eating and drinking of the one bread and the one cup."[84] The human person in this perspective can break out of the circle of the imprisonment of natural religion by welcoming the ontological call to Trinitarian existence.

Concluding Reflections

This essay has emphasized the dominant role of certain intellectual figures in Yannaras's comprehension of the West,[85] especially Fyodor Dostoevsky and Martin Heidegger. From a moral view of the West (the Western betrayal of Christ and the primacy of the logic of power), Yannaras broadens his understanding to take in the ontological error that lies at the bottom of Western history, with all the potentialities that a Heideggerian reading offers to an intellectual who feels himself to be Greek, and to stand in the uninterrupted continuity of Hellenism. A personalist ontology that is both relational and apophatic becomes the *via regia* along which Yannaras travels: It allows him to view the truth of Orthodoxy as a unity, as the true (ecclesio-Eucharistic) mode of human existence (in terms of freedom-communion-love), and as the authentic interpretation of the various spheres of existence and human knowledge. It is a path that seems to open up for Orthodoxy, and for Greek Orthodoxy in particular, the possibility of a message that is both universal and liberating in the face of the nihilistic, objectivist, utilitarian culture of the West with its totalitarian tendencies. Yannaras pursues this line of thinking programmatically by developing personalist critiques of ethics, law, political economy, quantum mechanics, and so on, and by seeking a dialogical encounter with great thinkers, among whom (after Heidegger), we find Jean-Paul Sartre, Ludwig Wittgenstein, and Jacques Lacan.

At a certain point in his journey, Yannaras begins to use the compendious term "religionization" to indicate the Western deviation of Christianity and, even more, of the *ecclesial event* so as to point to the salvifico-existential, primordial, and orthodox truth of Christianity. This leads to certain modifications of the sense of the very term "West," which, viewed as religionization, becomes the typical expression of the continual temptation to subordinate the Gospel proclamation to humanity's natural religious need.

In connection with this point, one can say that in Yannaras, we no longer have before us simply the (geographical) dualism of West and East. This dualism is included, but then modified, into another dualism, that between a Christianity that has been "naturalized" (present everywhere but exemplified principally in the West) and a natural religion that has been "saved or assumed" (conserved principally in the living experience of Orthodoxy but certainly not in Orthodoxism, which is one of the forms of religionization).

I cannot, however, conclude these pages without posing a last question, which is one that accompanies the whole of Yannaras's journey right from his youthful discovery of ontology. The question could perhaps be formulated in the following way: Even if the limits of language with regard to reality are admitted (a constant theme in Yannaras), it is nevertheless true that, for him, personalist ontology (apophatic and relational) in the Greek and non-Western tradition does manage to safeguard the authenticity of Orthodox experience and deliver it, at least linguistically, from the risk of heresy. Consequently, one might ask: What is the connection between the language of personalist ontology and the concrete reality of Orthodoxy (Orthodoxy according to the Sacred Canons and tinged with Orthodoxism)—that is, the concrete practice of Orthodox magisterium? Is it ontological personalism that defines linguistically what is Orthodox and who is to be considered Orthodox? And which ontological personalism are we referring to? Of which religious philosopher or of which theologian?

Furthermore, is ontological personalism only *one* of the linguistic possibilities of expressing being-as-saved, or is it the *only* authentic possibility? Is it perhaps to be considered the *philosophia perennis*, the definitive philosophy that is written in the heavens? But if that were the case, is there not the risk that ultimately it would only be another mode of succumbing to the temptation of the religionization of the ecclesial event?

I pose these questions without any replies, for at this point there begins another, rather difficult, discourse, which, as one can easily imagine, is eminently intra-Orthodox.

RELIGION IN THE GREEK PUBLIC SPHERE: DEBATING EUROPE'S INFLUENCE

Effie Fokas

I n 1999, Peter Berger, renowned sociologist of religion, did something scholars rarely do. A leading figure in the development of the theory of secularization—the theory that predicted that modernization would necessarily lead to the decline of religion—Berger professed that he had been wrong: "The world today," he wrote, "is massively religious, is *anything but* the secularized world that had been predicted (whether joyfully or despondently) by so many analysts of modernity."[1] Berger's revised position reflected a series of events taking place globally that significantly challenged the theory of secularization, including the Iranian Revolution in 1979; the rise of the Solidarity movement in Poland and the Catholic Church's role in the eventual fall of communism there; the role of Catholicism in political conflicts throughout Latin America; and the public re-emergence of Protestant fundamentalism as a force in American politics.

Alongside that famous retraction statement, Berger listed two debatable but commonly cited exceptions to what he describes as the "desecularization" of the world: first, Western Europe (there, he argued, secularization has continued to thrive), and second, a global, secularized elite. But he also made a new bold statement, one bearing particular relevance for our topic today: Berger suggested that Eastern European (including Orthodox) countries would also secularize to the degree that they are integrated into the European Union.[2] In other words, his expectation is that European secularization is contagious and will spread eastwards with European enlargement.

Against the backdrop of Berger's prediction, the central question I wish to address here is whether Europe, and specifically the EU, may be exercising a secularizing influence over Orthodox Greece. In other words, is European secularization contagious, and is Greece vulnerable to this contagion? A related question, which speaks more directly to the theme of this essay, is, what are the Greek Orthodox reactions to this European—often conflated with Western—influence?

In addressing these questions, first I will make reference to opposing perspectives to that of Peter Berger, drawing on the ideas of a range of scholars whose view it is that Orthodoxy entails an exception to the secularization thesis. I will then assess the validity of both perspectives, drawing on illustrations from the Greek case. Finally, through an examination of Greek Orthodox reactions to two particular instances of influence from Europe (perceived or real), I will draw insights about Europe's influence on Orthodox secularization.

Questioning Orthodox Secularization

Far more prevalent among scholars than Peter Berger's perspective on Orthodox secularization is one that points instead to Orthodox specificities rendering the faith resistant to secularization, or at least to secularization as we know it in Western Europe. Indeed, a number of scholars bear a critical attitude to Berger's perspective, along a spectrum of difference. David Martin, who with Peter Berger was one of the leading sociologists writing about secularization in the 1960s and '70s, is a prominent voice in the latter category, differing from Berger on the main point of whether Orthodoxy resists or adapts to secularization coming from Western Europe and, specifically, from the European Union.[3]

Martin speaks in terms of differing degrees and kinds of secularization in the Orthodox world and considers whether there might be a distinctive Eastern European version of secularization, and one particular to Orthodoxy.[4] Martin contends that there are significant differences between types of secularization, and that these differences hinge on the historical experience in particular countries, and especially on whether or not religion was positively associated with the origins and myth of the nation; on the relation of religion to class structure, to power, and to the state; and on the type of religion (with Protestantism faring radically differently from Orthodoxy, for example).

On the basis of the above, Martin traces what he calls a "common Eastern European pattern" of secularization, with the operative link being an ethno-religiosity that is stimulated by subjugation to an alien empire of a different religion—in the Greek case, the (Muslim) Ottoman Empire; in other Orthodox cases, the (atheist) communist Soviet Union. Martin posits that "there are more countries where religion was strengthened rather than weakened" by subjugation, "thus giving the impression that persecution is good for religion, and creating what looks like a common Eastern European pattern."[5]

In what could be described as a "multiple secularizations" perspective, he invokes the multiple modernities approach in support of his argument. Considering individualization as a prerequisite to modernization and to secularization, Martin reasons that "it is perfectly possible many countries will not proceed from a rather organic kind of collectivism to individualization, and thus neither to democracy nor to secularization."[6] He raises the Greek example explicitly and wonders:

> whether there is an Orthodox cultural bloc resisting assimilation to the kind of secularity represented by Western Europe, and more explicitly by the EU. Greece has been in the EU for some time, but it remains resistant to the kind of secularity explicitly promoted by the EU. One aspect of that secular thrust would be the full acceptance of religious pluralism, and in most Orthodox countries there is a powerful current of opinion by no means restricted to the ecclesiastical hierarchy, and including non-believers, that defines pluralism as a form of cultural invasion.[7]

Key to the entire equation for Martin is the "unproblematic and undifferentiated" nature of the relation of Orthodoxy to national identity: "Culture and religion, in Greece and Orthodox Eastern Europe generally, are woven without seam throughout."[8]

It is worth noting that Martin recognizes the elements of this perspective reminiscent of Samuel Huntington's "clash of civilizations" thesis, but he argues that "One does not need to take on board all the geographical implications of this map to explore the possibility of a different mode of modernity in the sphere of Eastern Orthodoxy. Nor does one have to assume an adamant resistance to democracy, since most Balkan states are to this or that degree democratic."[9]

Even defenders of secularization theory entertain the idea that Orthodoxy might entail an exception to the theory inasmuch as the latter predicts a decline in the social significance of religion. For example, Loek Halman and Veerle Draulans, writing on the basis of European Values Survey results, also draw the conclusion that the social significance of religion will not decline in cases where religion provides the resources for defending the national, local, or ethnic culture, and that churches may remain in a strong position due to historical-political factors such as if a church "provided a central focus of cultural identity in opposition to an imperialistic neighbor which sought to impose an alien set of cultural values and identities" or because religion "serves as a carrier of nationalism."[10]

Further along the spectrum of difference from Peter Berger's perspective, the possibility of an Orthodox exception is also echoed by Slavica Jakelić, who argues that in "collectivistic Christianities," as in Orthodox contexts, religion is a constitutive element in people's collective memory. The belonging of these individuals is "shaped by religious identification that is ascribed to individuals rather than chosen by them, and experienced as fixed rather than as changeable."[11] Thus from this perspective, she contends that Europe should brace itself for a significant wind of change as encounters increase between secular Europeans and collectivistic Christians.

In fact, this argument echoes the core thesis of the Byrnes and Katzenstein text, *Religion in an Expanding Europe*. As described by Peter Katzenstein in the book's introduction, eastward EU enlargement is "infusing renewed religious vitality into Europe's political and social life, thus chipping away at its exceptional secularism."[12]

We have, then, a range of perspectives whereby Orthodoxy is resistant to secularization and may, in fact, bear the potential to inspire a European *de*secularization. Indeed, academic literature on Orthodoxy is often characterized by an explicit focus on such "exceptional" characteristics. However, even further along the aforementioned spectrum of difference, in many cases such literature suggests an inevitability and *inability* of Orthodoxy to conform to Western European norms, including secularization. For example, one scholar in *Religion in an Expanding Europe* writes:

Orthodoxy, thus, is a religion which—to quote Shakespeare—"looks on tempests and is never shaken"—not even when it should be. Whatever changes may impact the world, the Orthodox Church refuses, for the most part, to accommodate itself to change, standing fixed in time, its bishops' gaze riveted on an "idyllic past" which serves as their beacon.[13]

The article makes the broader argument that Orthodoxy generally carries a mistrust of liberalism, cosmopolitanism, universalism, and democracy. Elsewhere in the same volume, T. Bynes suggests that the ties between religion and nation are "much more pronounced and organic in the Orthodox tradition."[14]

Such conceptions of Orthodoxy as seamless and timeless, and with "organic" links between religion and national identity, are often taken for granted and embedded in both media and academic representations of Orthodoxy as incompatible with Western or European norms. For example, one author suggests that "the centrality and unchanging nature of Orthodox dogma promote anti-intellectualism and racist and xenophobic attitudes."[15] Focusing on the Greek case, another author argues that "Greece's organic conception of society embodied in the nation-state and the centrality of Orthodoxy makes accommodation to Europe difficult at best," because Greece is a society "in which the ethnos, religion and the state constitute an organic whole."[16] And Orthodoxy's relation to pluralism, if we are to judge from the above descriptions, is, as Elizabeth Prodromou has put it, "ambivalent" at best.[17]

Contesting and Nuancing the Accounts

Which perspective, if either, is correct: the view of Orthodoxy as an outlier in its resistance to secularization, or the view that Orthodoxy will catch the Western European contagion of secularization?

Clearly, before attempting to address this question, it is important that we make two careful distinctions. The first, harkening back to the spectrum of difference, is between perspectives highlighting Orthodoxy's differences from Western Europe, on one side of the spectrum, and those emphasizing organicity and noncontingency, on the other. This range of perspectives should not be merged into a single category. Below I limit my attention to that of David Martin, which lies at the former end of the spectrum.

Second, we must distinguish between three different meanings of the term "secularization": secularization as decline of religious belief and practice; secularization as privatization of religious belief and practice; and secularization as institutional differentiation.[18]

Bearing these distinctions in mind, I have certain reservations with regard to both perspectives on Orthodox secularization presented here. I will draw on illustrations from the Greek case specifically, but my arguments have broader resonance for other Orthodox contexts as well. First, regarding David Martin's arguments, they may be read to *suggest* at least a certain immovability in the relationship between religion and national identity.[19] The relationship between religion and national identity is certainly powerful and deep-rooted, but it is not organic: As many scholars have argued,[20] this relationship has been painstakingly and calculatingly maintained through "the production and reproduction of collective memory managed and maintained by clergy, theologians and academics, propagated through official speeches, commemorative acts and other media and then duplicated through the school curriculum and holidays."[21] The link between religion and national identity is also maintained by politicians yielding to Church pressure, particularly around election time.[22] Such trends have served precisely to inhibit secularization as institutional differentiation—e.g., full separation of church and state.[23] They have also served to keep religion public and the Church very visible. And most importantly, they are conspicuously contingent factors. The extent to which we can generalize about the effects of collective memory cultivation on secularization as religious belief and practice is difficult to measure.[24]

Second, Martin describes the relationship between religion and national identity as "unproblematic" among the population in question, but certainly in the Greek case it can be described as highly problematic, and it problematizes a very large number of scholars,[25] but also certain politicians, clerics, and theologians.[26] In fact, a particular issue worthy of serious consideration is the ways in which the relationship between religion and national identity serves to perpetuate a close relationship between church and state, and in fact vice versa—in other words, the particular relationship *between* these two relationships: of religion and national identity, on the one hand, and of church and state, on the other. It is the specific mechanisms governing the latter that are, in my view, where we need to look to understand specificities in Orthodox secularization(s)—for example, agency (both political and religious), party politics and church politics, education systems, and legal systems. And certainly these mechanisms, too, are highly contingent and thus complicate notions of staticity, organicity, and the like.

Finally, with reference to Martin's observations on Orthodox attitudes to pluralism, the Greek case is rife with supporting illustrations, from resistance to the establishment of a mosque in Athens to the Greek state's poor standing vis-à-vis the European Court of Human Rights (ECtHR) regarding religious freedom.[27] However, lest this fact be raised as a marker of Orthodox exceptionalism from Western Europe, we should at least examine it alongside resistances to pluralism elsewhere in Europe, not least in response to Islam in several countries that, in their earlier lives, have been hubs of pluralism and tolerance but whose status as such today might be questioned.

Regarding Peter Berger's prediction that Western European secularization would spread eastwards, if by secularization he implies the decline of religious belief or practice or the privatization of religion, then this is a question to be addressed through longitudinal quantitative and qualitative research, ideally spanning the length of participation in the European unification project (for Greece, from 1981); such data is unfortunately unavailable for Greece but will be for newer Orthodox member states.[28]

However, if the secularization contagion refers to institutional differentiation, then I expect that Berger is correct. One, perhaps banal, example is the fact that the European Union directive on the protection of personal data served as a much-needed excuse for the removal of religious affiliation from Greek national identity cards in 2000. In other words, it was an EU directive that helped make politically feasible an action that would otherwise have been difficult for Greek politicians to take, given the staunch resistance posed by the Church. Another example is the potential influence on Greece of the *Lautsi* decision of the European Court of Human Rights, where the Court ruled that the display of the crucifix in Italian classrooms is in violation of the European Convention on Human Rights, *should* that decision hold following the results of the Grand Chamber hearing.[29]

In the Greek case, the presence of religious symbols (namely, icons) in school classrooms is not regulated by Greek legislation but is widespread by popular will. Again, the *Lautsi* verdict is still subject to appeal, but should it stand, Greek Justice Minister Haris Kastanidis has declared that Greece will have to comply by removing religious symbols from public spaces.[30] Accordingly, Western European legal and political norms can and do influence secularization as differentiation in Orthodox Greece.

Greek Orthodox Reactions to Europe's Influence

I would now like to address briefly reactions within the Church to these two influences (potential, perceived, or real) from "Europe": the identity-card issue and the religious symbols issue. I should note that by "Church" I mean an institution represented by its hierarchy rather than as a body of believers. For each case, I have consulted press coverage in the six weeks immediately after these issues arose.[31]

The Identity Card Issue

The details of the identity-card issue have been much discussed, and published and republished in a long list of texts.[32] For my purposes, it will suffice to draw on just a few major characteristics of the Church's reaction to the state's decision to remove reference to religious affiliation from the national-identity cards.

The government's argument for the decision was that Greece needed to conform to the European Union Directive on the protection of personal data, in accordance with which reference to religious affiliation on public documents (such as identity cards) violates the individual's right to privacy. The Church, in response, and especially Archbishop Christodoulos, presented the issue as a threat to national identity, given that reference to Orthodoxy (for the ninety-some percent of the cases) would disappear from the national identity cards. Christodoulos argued that if religious affiliation were removed from the identity cards, "then the people will be disconnected from Orthodoxy . . . which especially for us Greeks entails a fundamental element of our identity."[33] "We will not become grave-diggers of our ethnos," he declared. "We are more than they who want to destroy the country. The People endorses [sic] what I say. Let there then be a referendum."[34] In spite of insistence by the president of the Republic that a referendum could not be called on such a basis, the Church still gathered signatures from the public to petition a referendum. The repeated argument for a national referendum was that "the minority cannot force its terms on the majority."[35] In addition to gathering some three million signatures, the Church also held two mass rallies, one in Athens and one in Thessaloniki.

Clearly, another motivating factor for the Church's efforts was a sense that the whole situation represented a threat to church-state relations; this sense was heightened by the fact that the decision was taken by the government without first consulting the Church. Christodoulos complained about this specifically, stating that the prime minister practiced back-door policymaking in making the decision while the archbishop was away from Athens. Besides the government though, the main target of the Church's and—especially—Christodoulos's indignation was Europe, or the EU. In fact, the Church leadership wavered between blaming Europe, the government, and Greek intellectuals who, according to one cleric, are "more European than the Europeans." Characteristic of this "wavering" was Christodoulos's statement during one of the mass rallies when, speaking against the backdrop of a massive EU flag behind the stage, he declared that "Europe may fill our pockets, but it can empty our souls." Also characteristic of an ambivalent approach to Europe was the fact that a number of individuals (arguably, informally on behalf of the Church) took the case to the European Court of Human Rights in hopes of "support from Europe," which, however, dismissed the case in favor of the Greek state.[36] In the decision's aftermath, Fr. George Metallinos referred caustically to the European Court as "Our Master's voice." But even when the critique was directed against the government for using the EU directive as an excuse to alter the balance in church-state relations (because Church leaders did their homework and found that the EU directive was non-binding), still, the fact that it was an EU directive on which the government leaned for its decision was reason enough for many clerics to complain about "Europe's" secularizing influence on Greece.

The Religious Symbols Issue

In November of 2009, a new potentially secularizing influence arose from Western Europe in the form of the *Lautsi v. Italy* case. Though the two issues are not strictly comparable (and the *Lautsi* case was, at least until the time of writing, still open), the "religious symbols" issue offers an interesting parallel with the identity-card issue, one under the rule of Ieronymos rather than Christodoulos, who of course had a very well-entrenched reputation as a populist leader with a penchant for undertaking national-identity causes and for struggling to maintain close church-state ties.

Under Ieronymos, a very different character from Christodoulos, one might expect a somewhat different handling of such issues. When he was first elected, the media coverage heralded a new era for the place of religion in the Greek public sphere.[37] The change introduced by Ieronymos was a recurrent theme in the newspaper coverage, where the term "new page" factored prominently. One journalist wrote that "the new page in the book of the Church of Greece seems that it will differ greatly from the previous one."[38] Another indicated that "the Church, for ten years, lived the dynamic but also exuberance of Christodoulos. Now, the hierarchy judged that the Church had to move from the 'I' to the 'we' and to return to its synodal course, with a prudent, low-key (meaningfully so) archbishop at its head."[39] "This is how we want the church," suggested one member of parliament.[40]

How, then, was the *Lautsi* case received in the Ieronymos era? The most conspicuous characteristic of the Church response—especially in comparison with the response to the identity cards—was its muted character: The Church hierarchy was relatively calm and measured in its statements. To a large degree, this was due to a plan to *not* take the case seriously, indicating an expectation that the decision would not hold up in the long run. So, a central characteristic of the response was dismissal. For example, Ieronymos described the discussions on the issue as "ludicrous" and stated that "rights are not only for minorities but also for the majorities."[41] Another characteristic of the response was defensiveness, with reference to Greek national identity: Ieronymos criticized as "provocative the stance of certain people who struggle for the disappearance from our lives of faith, holy symbols and the ethos with which our nation followed its path."[42] "These things are unacceptable in Greek tradition and will, of course, not happen."[43] And, Ieronymos emphasized, "All Greeks will need to recognize that others [e.g., a European court] cannot decide for us."[44] Finally, when asked directly by a journalist what his reaction is to the notion that Greece will implement the *Lautsi* decision if it is upheld in the end, Ieronymos responded that:

The Church, or rather the faithful, have many ways of rejecting this. Certainly, the Church is opposed, but we should note that in Europe the presence of religious symbols was ensured by law—the Concordats and such. In Greece, it emerges from everyday life and practice. The question is what is more important—the ruling, or the national right to our tradition and history? As we pursued our European [Union] course, they often told us that the identity and traditions of peoples will be respected. Is the ruling stronger than the identity of a people? The people can express their will through a referendum.[45]

As with the identity-card issue, on this case, too, the Church has done its homework and is acutely aware of the fact that if something can be interpreted primarily as a symbol of national identity (as was argued, though unconvincingly, by the Italian state with regard to the crucifix), then that symbol will, as one Greek bishop put it, be "protected" from "European harm."[46]

Again, the verdict is still out (at the time of writing), both with regard to the ECtHR Grand Chamber decision and to whether, in the end, the decision would actually be implemented in Greece. But if the decision holds (regardless of the wisdom or lack thereof of that decision), and if the Greek Justice Minister's words are to be taken seriously, then the *Lautsi* decision would indeed represent another case of a secularizing influence from Europe in terms of institutional differentiation. Notably though, the Justice Minister's statement on the necessary implementation of the final verdict included the following words: "always in communication with the Church," representing perhaps lessons learned from the intense Church-state struggle over the identity cards (a decision taken *without* consultation of the Church), and the feared political costs of another church-state confrontation.[47]

However muted the response on the *Lautsi* case, a disapproval both of the decision and of the potential influence from Europe is still clear in the Church response. The Church's reaction to secularization as represented in both issues (identity cards and religious symbols) is, as David Martin describes, resistant, and this applies not only among the Church hierarchs but also within the broader population. And in both cases, there is a heavy emphasis on the threat to national identity posed by the particular measure at hand.[48] Other striking similarities in the Church's handling of the two cases are the reference to the rights of the majority versus those of the minority; the perceived threat to church-state relations; and the warning/invocation of a referendum should the state insist on implementing the European-driven change.

For all their differences then, the positions of Christodoulos and Ieronymos on matters of the religion–national identity link are notably similar: There is resistance to such European secularizing influences. But this does not mean that the secularizing influence (as in institutional differentiation) cannot and will not take root: It did in the identity-card case and, for better or for worse, it might in the religious symbols case. And in both cases, this is clearly a matter of political will in relation to Church pressures, party politics, the timing of elections, and other such variables, rendering the Orthodox factor a dependent rather than an independent variable.[49]

From all of the above, we can conclude that even if an Eastern Orthodox pattern of secularization can be identified based on historical trends in Orthodox countries, we should certainly question its utility as a map to explain the present and future. Rather, instead of general statements on Orthodox secularization, I would suggest a focus on case-by-case examinations of those mechanisms influencing how the links between religion and national identity impact church-state relations, and vice-versa, and the extent to which both the latter, in turn, influence the state of secularization in various Orthodox contexts.

Concluding Remarks: Situations in Flux

Finally, it is important that we place the discussion of Orthodox secularization within the wider frame of discussions and debates on European secularization. The situation is very much in flux, both in real and normative terms. In relation to the real, we have a vibrancy of Islamic faith and practice alongside new religious movements and new expressions of spirituality, on the one hand, and on the other we have political and legislative moves towards the limitation of religion in the public sphere—such as the *Lautsi* ruling and bans on the burka—either implemented or under discussion in European states. At the normative level, we have the juxtaposition of the very diverse writings (both in terms of content and scholarly quality) of Jürgen Habermas, José Casanova, Charles Taylor, Talal Asad, Bikhu Parekh, John Gray, Marcel Gauchet, Christopher Hitchens, and Richard Dawkins, *all* engaged in intense debates on whether we are or should be moving towards a postsecular Europe. It is therefore exceedingly difficult to determine in what direction the winds are blowing regarding European secularization. Accordingly, thinking in terms of a general theory of European secularization at this juncture is of questionable validity; doubly so are efforts to develop a general theory of Orthodox secularization in relation to European secularization.

Shaking the Comfortable Conceits of Otherness: Political Science and the Study of "Orthodox Constructions of the West"

Elizabeth H. Prodromou

Orthodoxy and Western Culture have had more to do with each other than is usually supposed, even by learned academics, but there is much to be gained on all sides by more communication.

The invitation to contribute to the conference that eventuated in this volume afforded a much-welcome opportunity to engage in cross-disciplinary inquiry into the subject of Orthodox constructions of the West. As a political scientist, I am especially enthusiastic about the possibility for such cross-disciplinary excavation of an intellectually complex and practically urgent problematic, given the renewed salience of the binary/antinomy "Orthodoxy-and-West" in the disciplinary sub-fields of international relations and comparative politics. Two events have generated a renewed, intense interest in and deployment of Orthodoxy and West as putative, mutually exclusive, "Others" in political science—the eastern and southern enlargement of the European Union, enabled by the events proceeding from the collapse of the Berlin Wall and the dissolution of the Soviet Union; and the articulation and consolidation of the War on Terror as the core security strategy of the Transatlantic Alliance in the wake of terrorist attacks by self-proclaimed Islamic jihadists against targets such as the United States, Spain, and the United Kingdom.

For political scientists, the aforementioned historical events and processes have provoked a relatively rich—if ideologically charged—scholarly rush to re-examine the historical bases for explaining, and eventually justifying, the emergence of a conceptual apparatus that, for the most part, has positioned Orthodox Christianity as the religious epicenter of a cultural and political space whose essential differences form an alternative to the Western cultural and political space determined by Roman Catholic and Protestant Christianity. According to this dominant narrative, the West is the unmarked category and Orthodoxy is the marked category, whereby "unmarked categories retain power as the standard against which" [1] marked categories are positioned and evaluated. In this regard, political science scholarship in the late twentieth- and early twenty-first centuries has relied on historicized, hegemonic Western constructions of Orthodoxy, whereby the conceptual category, as Jose Casanova precisely sums up, "is not a neutral descriptive category but rather an evaluative, normative and highly emotive category that emerges from within the [foundational] ideological epistemic conflicts between secularism and religious worldviews"[2] as related to the notion of 'modernity.'[3]

Contemporary political science arguments built on and endorsing the West-Orthodoxy binary are problematic for their tendency to be under-researched and lacking in theoretical elaboration, especially when compared to the effort that has gone into theorizing and empirically investigating the causalities and correlations between Western Christianity and democratic regimes and human rights (including foundational questions about the legal-formal relationship between church and state, social and political ideas and practices related to war and peace, and universal norms and practices associated with liberal democracy, pluralism, and tolerance). Social science studies that reiterate the West-Orthodoxy antinomy are consequential because they neglect, in theoretical terms, the rich body of Orthodox Christian thought on the ontology and anthropology of freedom, thereby leading to distortions in our understanding of how Orthodox theology has shaped political ideas about national self-determination and ideological debates about liberal democracy; equally consequential is the neglect, in substantive terms, of the history of Orthodox Christianity in the political and cultural forms associated with Christendom, Europe, and Eurasia.

In short, whether unexamined or, more often, deliberate, the deployment of the West-Orthodoxy antinomy has been a commonplace in political science research on religion in international relations and comparative politics, reinforcing the hegemony of a binary whose intellectual and operational consequences have been profoundly negative *for understanding and affecting* the political, social, and cultural consolidation of democracy in Orthodox-majority countries; for preventing the eradication of Orthodox minority populations in nondemocratic polities; for elucidating and utilizing specifically Orthodox concepts that may have value for resolving contemporary problems of social justice and economic inequity; and, for avoiding the imperialistic dimensions and unintended consequences of militarized approaches to humanitarian intervention.[4]

The fact that the operative logic for political science studies of Orthodox Christianity and modern politics and international affairs has been based on "Western constructions of Orthodoxy" is inextricably linked to, and amplifies the need for, critical analysis of the formulation that drives the inquiries in this volume—namely, "Orthodox constructions of the West," or a reversal of the West-Orthodoxy binary to Orthodoxy-West. In framing this volume, the editors, Aristotle Papanikolaou and George Demacopoulos, asked "whether the Orthodox recovery of identity would take the form of opposition to that which is seemingly the religious, cultural and political 'Other.' "[5]

From the vantage point of political science, the editors' query is most significant for the reflexivity that it reveals. Specifically, my chapter turns on the assumption that Orthodox intellectual, political, and social leaders must be unflinching in their commitment to a principled self-critique of Orthodox constructions of the West; such self-examination is as much a matter of intellectual interest as it is practical urgency, given the questions posed by "anti-democracy and anti-human rights rhetoric coming from traditional Orthodox countries that have recently been liberated from communism . . . and [which] often associates liberal forms of democracy and the notion of human rights in general as 'Western' and, therefore, not Orthodox."[6] Thus, I propose that a critical study of the Orthodoxy-West antinomy is inextricably related to, and optimally undertaken in conversation with, a robust analysis of the West-Orthodoxy antinomy. My working proposition involves two related premises: First, Orthodox constructions of the West are, to some degree, the result of Orthodox thinkers having unconsciously adopted and internalized the hegemonic logic of Western views of Orthodox alterity; and second, Orthodox leaders, in some cases, have opportunistically and self-servingly manipulated Western constructions of Orthodoxy in order to instrumentalize the Orthodoxy-West alternative as the basis for their own domestic and foreign policies.

In order to build a case for the plausibility of my proposition and premises, the chapter proceeds as follows. I begin with a selection of representative thinkers whose scholarship (and, in some cases, activism) has shaped the narrative of Orthodox constructions of the West in the twentieth century, offering a stylized review of the grammar and rhetoric on which the Orthodoxy-West antinomy has been built. I also suggest that there is a distinctive feature that identifies twentieth century Orthodox constructions of the West—namely, defensive triumphalism[7]—and what differentiates these contemporary articulations from similar formulations associated with the deeper-historical past. Such defensive triumphalism is optimally understood in terms of the organizing structures and logics of the Westphalian international order.[8] The defensive triumphalism that is the defining salient in twentieth-century Orthodox constructions of the West is both a reaction to and guard against the cultural and material power struggles rooted in the logic of the sovereign state system based in the seventeenth-century Peace of Westphalia.

Part 2 explicates my proposition regarding the reflexive connections between Orthodox constructions of the West and Western constructions of Orthodoxy by providing a synopsis of the dominant voices in political science scholarship whose arguments have perpetuated and reproduced the historically rooted narration of Orthodoxy as intrinsically alien to the ontology of the West. Particularly significant is the fact that Western constructions of Orthodoxy have created a knowledge regime whose dissemination and perpetuation has depended upon material factors of power. As the twentieth century concluded, the reiteration of the main features of the knowledge regime by which the West constructed the alterity of Orthodoxy was intrinsic to establishing Transatlantic geostrategic hegemony in the post-bipolar international order.

Part 3 concludes with reflections on the methodological lessons drawn from this effort to co-investigate the Orthodoxy-West binary in dialogue with the West-Orthodoxy binary. A deconstruction of the Orthodoxy-West opposition from the vantage point of political science reveals a remarkable convergence of theoretical and empirical research with theology, history, and the broad social sciences, hinting at an emergent consensus over the need for a move beyond the intellectually sterile and operationally malignant oppositions of the Orthodoxy-West/West-Orthodoxy formulations; instead of reflexive antinomies, recent scholarship has begun to reconceptualize the categories of Orthodoxy and West in terms of elasticity, porousness, and hybridity. In short, political science scholarship, and more broadly, multi-disciplinary research across the social sciences, demonstrates an active skepticism about, if not outright rejection of, the conceptual categories and valorization that have made the comfortable conceits of Otherness by which both Orthodox constructions of the West and Western constructions of Orthodoxy have been iteratively produced. To paraphrase Jaroslav Pelikan—whose oeuvre rejects the comfortable conceits of Otherness on which the antinomies are built and is recognized as magisterial by "Orthodoxy" and "West" alike[9]—the project of dissecting Orthodox constructions of the West turns on the need for theologians, historians, and political scientists to "read their way into each other's disciplines"[10] on a symbolic and geostrategic map that is both pre- and post-Westphalian in its geography.[11]

Orthodox Constructions of the West: Contemporary Variations and Defensive Triumphalism

A genealogy of Orthodox constructions of the West necessarily begins far earlier than the twentieth-century focus of this volume. Some scholars posit that the deep historical footprint of what Vasilios Makrides and Dirk Ulfmann characterize as "anti-Westernism"[12] in Orthodox thought can be traced as far back as the fifth century, with the barbarian invasions in the western portions of the Roman Empire, seen from Constantinople in the east as a sign of the effects of the institutional corruption and decay over which Rome presided. The growing estrangement between "the Greek East and the Latin West"[13] was an empirical fact, whether relying on geographic or quantitative metrics, but there is also incontrovertible evidence that Byzantine Christian Emperors invested enormous blood and treasure in trying to liberate Rome and the western provinces from barbarian control and, therefore, in restoring unity to the Christian *oecumene*.[14]

The aforementioned gradual estrangement did not begin to assume definitive features in the form of Orthodox constructions of the West as a hostile, alien, monolithic Other until the twin events of the Great Schism of Christianity into the (Eastern) Orthodox Church and the (Roman) Catholic Church,[15] and the Western Church's attack on Constantinople in the name of providing assistance against the steady Islamic military expansion and conquest over the Christian populations in Asia Minor and the Near East.[16]

While contemporary Orthodox standard-bearers who construct the West as an essentialist marker of alterity may draw from the theological[17] taproot of earlier formulators of the Orthodoxy-West dyad, it is within the historical context of the twentieth century that the distinctiveness of Orthodox constructions of the West emerges. Taking into account the plural form of the noun "constructions," and recognizing that there are myriad permutations[18] of the categories of Orthodox and West (depending on disciplinary vantage and interpretive position), there is a cohesion that emerges from the paradigmatic works[19] on Orthodox constructions of the West during the past century. Emblematic works in the discourse of Orthodox constructions of the West are those by the Greek philosopher-theologian Christos Yannaras and the Russian theologian Vladimir Lossky.

Yannaras develops an anthropology of personhood that proposes the irreconcilability of Orthodoxy and the West, defined in specifically theological terms centered in the doctrine of the Holy Trinity,[20] so that Orthodoxy and West are conceived as doctrinal constructs with institutional (i.e., ecclesiological) implications. His scholarship, as well as his stature as a highly controversial public intellectual, ranges as far as Platonic and Heideggerian philosophical interpretations, as well as Rawlsian philosophical arguments, to define Orthodoxy as a civilization defined by "a conception of politics radically different from the one found at the heart of Western European civilization,"[21] and to maintain that Orthodox theology informs a conception of human rights at odds with human rights norms based in Western theology.

Lossky mines the texts of early Church thinkers in order to build his argument that Orthodox Christianity's emphasis on apophaticism and mysticism expresses the pristine authenticity of Christian theology. He positions the mystical theology of Orthodoxy as essentially different from and, especially, more authentic than, the deviations and dilutions of the theology and practices of Western Christianity, whose reliance on rationalist philosophical principles produces the Scholasticism that becomes the hallmark of Roman Catholicism.[22]

Reinforcing the Orthodox constructions of the West set out by Yannaras and Lossky is Philip Sherrard's widely read work in Church history, also published in the mid-twentieth century. In *The Greek East and the Latin West: A Study in Christian Tradition*,[23] Sherrard maintains that irreconcilable philosophical views and mentalities, based on the underlying metaphysical bases of Greek Christian thought, caused the rupture between antinomies of Greek East and Latin West. Church historian Andrew Louth's narrative of religious differences between Constantinople and Rome, while sharing with Sherrard the similar title of *Greek East and Latin West: The Church AD 681–1071*,[24] adopts a somewhat less absolute position regarding the intrinsic, inevitable irreconcilability between East/Orthodoxy and West/Roman Catholic; however, his recent argument that rejects development "as an available category for Orthodox theology"[25] reinforces the doctrinal and historical foundations by which Orthodox constructions of the West are premised on ontological bases of immutable alterity.

The anti-Westernist trope in the representative scholarship on Orthodox constructions of the West during the twentieth century is also evident and reproduced in a pluralist amalgam of public-intellectual publications; official pronouncements by ecclesiastical (i.e., ordained episcopal and clerical) elites; and political leaders. Such Orthodox constructions of the West cut across conventional political-ideological lines of Right and Left. Emblematic of this was the discourse of the late Archbishop Christodoulos of Greece,[26] who critiqued the deliberately transnational objectives of European integration, declaring that the defense and survival of national identity in Greece depended on a return (as in earlier historical moments of threat) to "life-giving Greek Orthodoxy."[27] Similarly, Romanian Orthodox lay intellectuals and ecclesiastical elites regularly reminded post-Ceausescu citizens of the Orthodox Church's centrality to the triumphant survival of the "the people" over communism, and likewise, warned defensively that the Orthodox Church must defend "the nation's conscience."; accordingly, "Deputy Archbishop Gerasim Pruteanu [of Romania] . . . said that the church must enter politics for the country to preserve its Orthodox tradition and . . . that some of [the Romanian parties' legislative proposals—especially those associated with European Union notions of multiculturalism and gender/sexuality equality] . . . 'ran counter to . . . Christian Orthodox traditions.' "[28] The current patriarch of the Orthodox Church of Russia, Kirill, has long maintained that proselytizing work by non-Orthodox missionaries in post-Soviet Russia required a defensive response to Western Christian proselytizers who aimed "to destroy the unity of the people and the Orthodox faith—spiritual colonizers who by fair means or foul try to tear the people way from their church."[29]

Although only a sampling of some of the most well-known Orthodox views of the West in the twentieth century, the offerings above cohere around a unifying, internal logic expressed in the rhetoric of defensive triumphalism. Although well beyond the space limitations of this chapter, a historicized treatment of the evolution and internal interconnectedness of various Orthodox constructions of the West (a project deserving systematic investigation) points to the overweening impact of the Westphalian state system and associated secularist conception of modernity as critical factors in explaining the triumphalism and defensiveness of Orthodox constructions of the West in the late-second and early-third millennia. In this regard, the admixture of triumphalism and defensiveness, which forms the distinctive leitmotif in twentieth-century Orthodox constructions of the West, develops through the interpretation of Orthodoxy as subject-object, actor-reactor, in international relations and, more specifically, Great Power politics. The specificities of twentieth-century international relations, especially in the geographic regions identified by Dimitri Obolensky as the territories of the Byzantine Commonwealth,[30] account for the associated particularities of the defensive triumphalist rhetoric of Orthodox constructions of the West.

The international system as the centerpiece of the defensive triumphalist rhetoric is clear in the repeated observations by twentieth-century architects of Orthodox constructions of the West, who point out that the globalized wars and human rights atrocities associated with the ideological excesses of fascism and communism were the invention of Western/Occidental thought and Western states. Similarly, Orthodox constructions of the West present both Transatlantic Alliance states and international institutions in which those states hold sway as hypocritical in their failure to come to the aid of Orthodox populations[31] captive to either atheistic or religious extremism; analogous critiques characterize the European Union as a cultural homogenization project antithetical to liberal pluralism.[32] Political elites speaking in the name of Orthodoxy instrumentalized their critique of "the West" as an actor both ethically pretentious and legally reckless, in order to justify domestic and foreign policy choices whose rhetoric and discourse smacked of defensive triumphalism. The actions of Serbian Prime Minister Slobodan Milosevic and Russian Prime Minister (and now President) Vladimir Putin are emblematic in this regard.

In short, the leitmotif of defensive triumphalism in Orthodox conceptions of the West is the result of the internalization of a symbolic geography and set of material (especially economic and military) power relationships determined according to the logic of the sovereign state system. Although theoretically conceived as a system of global order in which territorially bounded units are equally sovereign due to the principle of non-intervention, the organized hypocrisy[33] of sovereignty has made for an international order marked by arbitrary violations of the principle of non-intervention (oftentimes for purposes of military and/or economic security) and wooden adherence to that same principle even in the face of massive violations of human rights and human security by states against their own citizens. The contours of the defensive triumphalism characterizing Orthodox constructions of the West has derived from and relied upon the material power inequities in the sovereign state system, which stands as the signifier of modernity. The temporal and spatial origins of the Westphalian system of sovereignty lie in the West, where, historically, religious identity was overwhelmingly Roman Catholic and Protestant Christian.

Western Constructions of Orthodoxy: Self-Image and Alterity

In his detailed treatment of the geographic and cultural evolution of the idea of Europe, J. G. A. Pocock suggests that, just as the "geographical concept of 'Europe' has moved West, to the point where it defines an Atlantic peninsula by calling it a continent . . . , the historical concept of 'Europe' has migrated, to the point where everything we mean when we say 'the history of Europe' refers to the history of the political and religious culture . . . that arose in the far-western, Latin-speaking provinces of the former Roman empire [sic]."[34] This gradual elision of West with Europe (and, eventually, with twentieth-century Transatlantic security and economic structures) and with modernity has been built on a symbolic and material set of power relations by which the narrative of history was "stolen"[35] from Orthodoxy and by which the "modern West" constructed Orthodoxy as an ontological, essentialized, Other. In this regard, critical inquiry into twentieth-century Orthodox views of the West is remarkable for revealing how the West's self-image has been built upon the successful construction of Orthodoxy as an ontologically alien, immutable Other.

Political science, including seminal works in international relations and comparative politics, has been central to the project of Western constructions of Orthodoxy in the twentieth century. It bears emphasis, however, that the epistemological project, along with the associated political and military activity, relies heavily on the bedrock of historical scholarship associated with the luminaries of the Enlightenment and quintessentially identified with the work of Edward Gibbon.[36] The nexus between political science and history is significant for two reasons. First, political scientists have transposed the historical narrative into the language and practices of state power, a reminder of the ways in which a " 'dominant symbolic framework' established by political activity [has come to] . . . embody and make manifest hegemony."[37] Second, the dominance of political science research in Western constructions of Orthodoxy, in contrast to the dominance of theologians in shaping Orthodox constructions of the West, has made for parallel monologues, rather than engaged dialogue, when it comes to problematizing and, especially, remedying the mutual (mis)perceptions embedded in the Orthodoxy-West and West-Orthodoxy antinomies.

The work of two political scientists, Francis Fukuyama and Samuel Huntington, has been seminal in shaping contemporary Western constructions of Orthodoxy.[38] Fukuyama's "The End of History?" never mentioned Orthodoxy, and Huntington's "The Clash of Civilizations" paid relatively short shrift to the "Slavic-Orthodox civilization."[39] However, both articles (and the subsequent books spawned by each) were published in journals of global repute (*The National Interest* and *Foreign Affairs*, respectively) that enjoy wide readership across scholarly and policy lines, and both authors were absolute in explaining the end of the Cold War according to a category of "West" deployed as a synonym for modernity, progress, and world order.

Fukuyama interpreted the end of the Cold War as the "triumph of the West" in the form of "the unabashed victory of economic and political liberalism"; more grand was his conclusion that the end of the Cold War meant "the end of history as such: that is, the end point of mankind's ideological evolution and the universalization of Western liberal democracy." He granted that the expansion of the West around the globe was incomplete because "the victory of liberalism has occurred primarily in the realism of ideas or consciousness and is yet incomplete in the real or material world." His confidence in the gradual globalization of Western liberal ideas—"large, unifying world views [*sic*] that . . . can include religion, culture, and the complex of moral values underlying any society"—derived from what he saw as the compelling power of the measurable superiority of market capitalism; after all, it was the consciousness that Western ideas of liberal democracy undergirded "the 'Protestant' life of wealth and risk over the 'Catholic' path of poverty and security," that had caused the collapse of state socialist regimes in Eastern Europe.[40]

Fukuyama only hinted at the Otherness of Orthodoxy vis-à-vis the Western idea in his comments on the obduracy of Russian nationalism and his pessimism about the final outcome of Soviet leader Mikhail Gorbachev's "proposed reforms, either in the sphere of economics or politics."[41] Huntington filled out and rigidified Fukuyama's intimations with an expansive argument about civilization as the determinant of historical change. Notwithstanding the inconsistencies in his use of the construct "civilization," Huntington was unambiguous and emphatic in his reduction of civilization to religion and in his proposition that the post–Cold War international order would be organized along civilizational faultlines. Therefore, the clash of civilizations would occur at "the micro-level . . . [among] . . . adjacent groups [violently struggling] . . . over the control of territory and each other" and at the macro-level, as states struggled over "military and economic power, . . . [and] control of international institutions and third parties," as they competed "to promote their particular political and religious values."[42]

There is a critical series of elisions and expansions from Fukuyama's to Huntington's arguments, which help to explain the defining features and logic of post–Cold War, Western constructions of Orthodoxy as permanently, unalterably Other. Specifically, where Fukuyama admitted contingency in the battle of ideas driving historical change, Huntington assumed certainty and permanence across lines of religious-cultural-civilizational difference. Furthermore, Huntington transformed Fukuyama's Western idea into an idea of the West, so that where Fukuyama suggested that material (economic) evidence could hold sway in the normative struggle between liberalism and nondemocratic alternatives, Huntington dismissively moved to argue for dominance in the projection of power as requisite to defend Western civilization against the inevitable threats of other civilizations whose identity he posited as inured and hostile to the West. Significantly, Fukuyama's intimations of the alterity of Russia assumed full-blown proportions in Huntington's construct of a Slavic-Orthodox civilization, a sweeping category of Otherness identified in cultural and geographic terms. Huntington presented the Slavic-Orthodox civilization as the space where Europe splits between Western Christianity and Orthodox Christianity; between the states that emerged from the Western Christian Empire and the Ottoman and Tsarist Empires; and between the states whose political and economic institutions either were informed by or rejected the political, theological, and intellectual experiences of the Renaissance, Reformation, and Enlightenment.

These twin propositions—that ideas and civilization (distilled to religion) were the motors of historical change—resonated compellingly as the new paradigm for scholars and policymakers trying to come to terms with global geopolitics in the aftermath of the Cold War. The profound significance of the Fukuyama and Huntington arguments for Western constructions of Orthodoxy lay in the fact that these global luminaries of political science theory and praxis drew on well-known historical narratives and tropes[43] to establish the parameters of the contemporary template by which Orthodoxy—*qua* set of beliefs, and territorialized churches within Westphalian states, and "peoples"[44]—came to be narrated in the historical conjuncture of contemporary geopolitics.

The elaboration and consolidation of Western constructions of Orthodoxy according to the above template occurred in response to a series of events that raised questions about the West's self-definition and anticipated hegemony. These events were the implosion of the state of Yugoslavia into conditions of substate and, then, interstate violence, concomitant with the eastward enlargement of the European Union; and, then, the geostrategic decision for the War on Terror as the U.S. (and, eventually, Transatlantic Alliance) response to the al Qaeda terrorist attacks on America.

In the first instance, political science treatments of the collapse of the Yugoslav state overwhelmingly posited religious and cultural variables, to the near exclusion of material factors, to explain the series of wars and instability in the western Balkans for nearly the entire 1990s. Indeed, there was a convergence of scholarship, statements by political leaders, and public commentaries, generating a scholar-practitioner discourse and associated policy decisions that melded identity-building and region-building; simply, religion became the cornerstone for a symbolic and operational re-mapping of Europe.[45]

Drawing on the wellspring of diachronic, historical treatments to synthesize what Maria Todorova has explicated as Balkanism,[46] and Edward Said has termed Orientalism,[47] the late twentieth-century version of the West-Orthodoxy antinomy coalesced in political science scholar-practitioner discourse. The contemporary conjuncture was merely the renewal of "West against East, the ultimate historical conflict" stretching across the

Eurasian continent, thereby positioning Eastern Orthodoxy and Islam as "strange and threatening" and fueling Zbigniew Brzezinski's call for a reconfigured Euro-Atlantic security architecture whose borders were aligned with "the Petrine Europe of the Holy Roman Empire."[48]

The fact that almost a full decade of Yugoslav-related conflict developed in tandem with the project of EU enlargement made for a synergy between the geostrategic formulation of the West-Orthodoxy antinomy on the one hand, and more generally, social science studies positing the logic of accelerated incorporation into the EU of former communist states of (Western Christian) central Europe and either the prolonged integration or permanent exclusion of the former communist states of (Orthodox Christian) southeastern Europe, on the other hand.[49] Particularly notable among the spate of political science scholarship that looked at the *longue duree* of history to explain the contemporary iteration of the West-Orthodoxy dyad were studies by regional experts whose comparative research dealt with countries with an Orthodox presence in either historical or contemporary terms. Their research frequently considered religion as either epiphenomenal or derivative and, in that regard, conformed to the standards of secularization and modernization theory, even as, paradoxically, secularization and modernization theories were undergoing a comprehensive theoretical and empirical critique in the social science literatures.

Instructive and emblematic was the scholarship of political scientists who, working on modern (signifying the nation-state period) Greece, relied on the West-Orthodoxy dichotomy to explain Greece's incomplete modernization and problematic secularization in comparison to the country's western European cohort. Nikiforos Diamandouros's work on cultural dualism and political modernization in postauthoritarian Greece[50] became the standard-bearer for scholarship that used historical-institutional analysis to argue that the cultural drag of Orthodox Christianity was an impediment to the quality of liberal democracy in Greece after the country's regime transition in 1974. Thanos Lipovats argued that the Byzantine historical experience *writ large*, which he reduced to mean the religion and culture of Orthodox Christianity, was the key causal variable in the historical "pathologies" of nationalism in Greece and, therefore, generated exclusivist forms of citizenship based on ascriptive criteria.[51] Adamantia Pollis generalized her work on Greece to posit a negative correlation between "the religious heritage of Eastern Orthodoxy, practiced in the Balkans, Russia, and other East European states," and "the Western conception of individual rights" that undergird international human rights architectures;[52] late twentieth-century problems "of institutionalizing democratic structures and processes [were] . . . complicated by the theology of Eastern Orthodoxy and the Church's relationship to the state."[53] In short, the internalization of the hegemonic Western construction of Orthodoxy is evident in, borrowing from Anastassios Anastassiadis, a *Weltanschauung* of Orthodox-relevant social theory, even as "most recent works regarding contemporary issues relevant to the Orthodox Church . . . are flawed by an absence of factual knowledge regarding the historical context."[54]

Overall, the abbreviated synopsis above of the genealogy of contemporary version(s) of the West-Orthodoxy binary underscores the reflexivity of the antinomial Western constructions of Orthodoxy. In this regard, *how* we investigate Orthodox constructions of the West necessarily involves an interrogation of Western constructions of Orthodoxy. Furthermore, the reflexive logic of these two categories has generated a mutual conceit of Otherness on the part of both Orthodoxy and the West, as the familiarity of alterity becomes a reliable source of security for the identity of Self.

Conclusion

This chapter took up the task of a critical interrogation of Orthodox constructions of the West using political science to explore this volume's central proposition: namely, that "Orthodox self-identification often engages in a distorted apophaticism . . . [by which] . . . Orthodoxy is what the 'West' is not . . . [and through which] . . . Orthodox communities not only misunderstand what Western Christians believe but, even more egregiously, . . . believe certain things about their own tradition and teachings that are historically untrue."[55]

As indicated by the aforementioned observations of this volume's editors, the conceptual categories of Orthodoxy and West comprise a knowledge regime—a way of knowing or ignoring, understanding or misunderstanding—by which Orthodox thinkers and practitioners have constructed the West as an essentialized Other. As a political scientist, I aimed to make a convincing argument that the conceptual apparatus of the Orthodoxy-West binary cannot be extricated from patterns of domination and material power relationships that are the expression of the state-centered, Westphalian system of international affairs.

The methodological choice to foreground the origins and history of the state as central to the categories of Orthodoxy and West illuminated the logical necessity of critiquing the Orthodoxy-West antinomy in tandem with analysis of the West-Orthodoxy antinomy. Because of its historical origins within the geographic locus of Western Europe and the cultural space of Western Christianity, the state, as the organizing unit of international relations and as the equivalent for modernity, became the principle metric and enforcer of Western constructions of Orthodoxy and, likewise, the principle object and agent of criticism that shaped the defensive triumphalism that unifies the diversity of Orthodox constructions of the West.

The twentieth-century focus of this volume provides a rich empirical storehouse for considering the relevance of the state to the conceptual symplegma of Orthodox-West/West-Orthodoxy. After all, the system of international relations in the twentieth century produced almost a century of regular episodes of warfare and violence—two World Wars and the Cold War. Orthodox constructions of the West in the twentieth century, drawing on deeper historical experiences, were forged, first, by the practical and normative failings of a definition of progress and modernity that the West had appropriated as its own, and second, by the existential threats and self-loathing generated by the oppressive experiences of totalitarian (communist bloc) and secular- and religious-authoritarian (Greater Middle East) regimes as self-proclaimed alternatives to the West as hostile Other. Unfortunately, the Transatlantic response to the end of the Cold War, which created the possibilities for a dramatic redress in the institutional and ethical weaknesses of the Westphalian order, aggravated and fed the defensive triumphalism of Orthodox constructions of the West; Orthodox constructions of an immutable, essentialized, hostile West were reinvigorated by the economic and military policies of the United States and the European Union, which were articulated according to the trope of normative superiority of West versus Rest (Orthodoxy in the latter category) and as justification for the West's violations of the sovereign principle of nonintervention.

Situating an investigation of the categories of Orthodoxy and West within the context of international relations is a move that coincides with recent research in political science that has begun to excavate the Orthodoxy-West/West-Orthodoxy formulations as part of the problematic of the two phenomena—globalization and religious salience—that are exercising a profound, transformative impact on the state-centered, Westphalian order. A brief comment on each of these phenomena elucidates their relevance for new ways of understanding the categories of Orthodoxy and West in twenty-first-century international relations.

Regardless of its specific form, globalization is a phenomenon driven by technologies of communication, transportation, and war, which are combining to render meaningless the territorialized borders and boundaries on which the constructions of Orthodox and West relied. Globalization has contributed to the porousness and indeterminacy of physical borders long associated with the territorial state, just as democratization projects have spread across the historical heartland of Orthodox Christianity. For the first time on a global scale, Orthodox Christians in the third millennium enjoy unprecedented opportunities for organization and action as a global, transnational, religious community. Globalizing technologies are raising questions about the obsolescence of the categories of Orthodoxy and West. Insofar as Orthodox populations live in the spaces historically understood as the West, and conversely, insofar as populations from the West cross borders into spaces once labeled as Orthodox, binaries of Orthodoxy-West are becoming pluralized and conflated. Consequently, Orthodox perceptions of the West have begun to be interrogated for their pluralized meanings, involving the combination of scrupulous empirical research with hermeneutic analysis.

In this regard, the phenomenon of globalization has created the momentum among Orthodox scholars to follow John McGuckin's exhortation to excavate, "clarify and repristinate its [Orthodoxy's] ancient and deep traditions"[56]—a project that demands unflinching critique of both Orthodox conceptions of Self and constructions of the West. In fact, there is a spate of literature that draws on new methodologies in "the ontology of borders, the study of what borders are, and the epistemology of borders, the study of what and how we know what borders are . . . ,"[57] suggestive of an emerging consensus over the need to reappraise Orthodox constructions of the West. The possibilities for a current Orthodox theology of global engagement and activism as a transnational religious community are encapsulated neatly in Archbishop Anastasios Yannoulatos's application of Orthodox thought to consider practical responses to the "abyss of hypocrisy [that] separates the general pronouncements and theoretical principles of world organizations from their actual practice in the various regions of the earth."[58] Furthermore, the involvement of political science in this new scholarship, both enabled and provoked by globalization, marks a turn towards cross-disciplinary research in Orthodox constructions of the West, so that social scientists, theologians, and humanists express the multivocality[59] of Orthodoxy and, therefore, the pluralism in Orthodox constructions of the West.

The unanticipated salience of religion in all aspects of twenty-first-century life is a phenomenon that has provoked a sea change in the study of religion and modernity,[60] with profound implications for reassessing Orthodox constructions of the West. Political science has witnessed an intellectual revolution in the theoretical assumptions and conceptual apparatuses used to problematize the meaning of modernity/ies and ideas about secularity, as well as associated issues of church-state relations in democratic polities, universal human rights norms and practices, and the ethics of war and peace.

The essentializing oppositions of Orthodox and West were built on the edifice of modernization-secularization theory, with its attendant normative assumptions and consequent prescriptive policies. The collapse of that edifice, in the face of overwhelming empirical evidence pointing to multiple modernities[61] and a plurality of secularisms,[62] has begun to foster a cross-disciplinary scholarship whose historical and comparative method has facilitated critical self-reflection in Orthodox constructions of the West, and, equally intriguing, has provoked self-criticism of Western constructions of Orthodoxy. Political science has been central to the project of rethinking modernity and secularity, creating space for engagement with other disciplines.

Research on the European Union has been especially productive in looking to institutional and systemic factors to explain the comparative absence of Orthodox Churches in democratic transitions in Europe's former communist states.[63] Political scientist Alfred Stepan has directly challenged the binary categories of West and Orthodoxy in his claim that "the major explanation for this variance [in the religion-democratization nexus] cannot lie in Orthodoxy's core religious doctrine [since for] . . . their first millennium, Eastern and Western Christianity shared the same theological doctrines."[64] Similarly, the turn to previously unavailable archival sources has contributed to revisions to what historian Deno Geanakoplos long argued was the mistaken characterization of Caesaropapism for church-state relations in the Byzantine Empire,[65] and political science research on "the Orthodox commonwealth"[66] has demonstrated a marked turn to explore "the subtle ways in which [communist-era] churches adapted to new political regimes and the role of international ecclesiastical relations."[67] More generally, the investigation of the origins of ideas and institutions of global security, concomitant with studies in the cultural geography of security,[68] have begun to contribute to a breakdown in the rigid antinomies that this volume seeks to address.

Taken as a whole, the phenomena of globalization and religious salience have produced a plethora of scholarly studies that are contributing to a lively move beyond the comfortable conceits of Otherness that had enabled the defensive triumphalism of Orthodox constructions of the West as well as the ossified contempt of Western classifications of Orthodoxy. My goal in this chapter has been to demonstrate that political science can contribute significantly to the valuable enterprise of questioning the concepts and methods by which we study Orthodox constructions of the West. The comfortable conceits of Otherness should not be overlooked and disregarded. Such self-serving postures generate the kind of cynicism, apathy, and hubris that impede dialogue and hinder understanding of similarities and differences between the two protagonists, Orthodox and West. Moreover, perpetuation of the comfortable conceits of Otherness optimizes the likelihood that self-styled representatives of both Orthodoxy and West will fail to respond efficaciously to the range of threats in which such binaries and antinomies are meaningless.

Eastern Orthodox Constructions of "the West" in the Post-Communist Political Discourse: The Cases of the Romanian and Russian Orthodox Churches

Lucian Turcescu

Romania and Russia began the process of transformation from communism to capitalism within two years of each other. The glasnost and perestroika (openness and restructuring)—the political, social, and economic reforms—implemented by the Soviet secretary of the Communist Party, Mikhail Gorbachev, revealed the major cracks in the communist system and led to its unintended demise throughout Eastern Europe and the former Soviet Union between 1989 and 1991. Romania was the last of the Soviet satellite countries to shed its communist regime in the final days of December of that momentous year of 1989. The process combined a bloody coup d'état with a popular uprising and culminated in the execution of the dictatorial couple, Nicolae and Elena Ceausescu, on Christmas Day, 1989, and their replacement with second-echelon former communists who had turned democrats overnight.

Official communism in the Soviet Union persisted a little longer. It was not until 1991 that the Union officially renounced its communist regime and disintegrated, allowing for its member states to choose whether they wanted to become independent or continue to be part of a new federation known as the Commonwealth of Independent States.

Romania and the Russian Federation also differ today; the former has been an official member of the European Union (EU) since January 2007, while the latter has not even sought membership. In order to be accepted in the EU, a country must meet a number of preaccession criteria that point to its commitment to become a liberal democracy, to demonstrate profound respect for human rights, and to join the capitalist economic union the EU represents. In 2007, Romania (along with Bulgaria) was one of the last former Soviet bloc countries to join the EU because it struggled to meet these criteria. Romania was obliged both to harmonize its legislation with that of the EU and to revisit much of its political, economic, and civic culture to bring the nation more in line with the liberal democracy it sought to become. Russia did not undergo such a process, and is, therefore, regarded as a rather unique democracy by Western standards, with many authoritarian elements still in place, as well as fewer rights and freedoms for its citizens.

In both countries, the Orthodox Church is a significant religious and political player that, like many churches in Eastern Europe, desired to be a part of the postcommunist transformation. Indeed, the Orthodox Church in Romania and Russia became an important agent in this painful transition. This essay discusses constructions of the West in the official, postcommunist political discourse of the Romanian Orthodox Church (Romanian patriarchate, or RP) and the Russian Orthodox Church (Moscow patriarchate, or MP), the two largest Orthodox churches in the world.

The Romanian Orthodox Church

According to the country's latest census (conducted in 2011), eighty-six percent of Romanians (in a population of twenty-one million) belonged to the Romanian Orthodox Church. With the latest wave of accession into the European Union (Bulgaria and Romania in 2007—two predominantly Orthodox countries), the interaction between religion and EU politics has acquired an increased significance. In a country like Romania, meeting the conditions for a successful accession to the EU was a major challenge. For example, nearly all Romanian religious groups opposed at least some of the EU requirements designed to protect minority groups against discrimination. But, as my analysis will demonstrate, with some minor pockets of Euroskeptics, the country's dominant and powerful Romanian Orthodox Church has changed its perceptions of the West in a positive direction.

To begin with, two main types of church-state relations have dominated the leadership of the Romanian patriarchate (RP) since 1989. First, under Patriarch Teoctist Arapasu (1986–2007), the RP sought a return to the model of church-state relations that it entertained in the precommunist period, in which the RP would be recognized as the national, or established, church. In doing so, Patriarch Teoctist sought a return to pre-World War II arrangements but also wanted to reconnect with the Byzantine model of *symphonia*, or harmony, between church and state. However, such a model was hardly relevant for the new postcommunist realities, as the interviews I conducted with a number of important Romanian Orthodox church leaders revealed.[1] Patriarch Teoctist and other church leaders have also sympathized with the established church model that they observed in countries such as England, where the Anglican Church is the established religion; the Scandinavian countries of Sweden, Norway, and Denmark, where the Lutheran Church plays such as role; and even Greece, where the Orthodox Church is the established church. This theoretical admiration for the "established church" model was translated into numerous calls for hierarchs of the Orthodox Church to be granted the status of unelected lifetime senators who would be present in the parliament's upper chamber. Moreover, Teoctist called on the country's legislators, successive governments, and presidents to declare his church as the national church, with privileges exceeding those offered to other religious denominations. These calls fell on deaf ears, though, and to this day the country's constitution and law on religion of 2006 do not recognize any faith as the country's national religion, but instead recognizes a rather soft separation between church and state.

Churches are, instead, recognized as "public utilities"—a concept used in predominantly Lutheran countries and derived from the history of European church-state relationships, "out of which grows the notion of a state church (or its successor) as a public utility rather than a private organization."[2] Because public utilities benefit the population as a whole, they qualify for funding through the tax system.[3] Since the European model only declares the established church a public utility, it is unclear how the Romanian model, which designates multiple religious denominations as "public utility entities," will translate in practice. Clearly, the model does not point in the direction of separation of church and state. True, the country's Law on Religious Freedom (Law 489 of 2006) does acknowledge the "important role the Romanian Orthodox Church and other churches and recognized denominations" played in the country's history and social life (Article 7.2). While this would be similar to the recognition given in Russia to the

Orthodox Church and several other religious groups, in practice it would not have the same impact on Romania's social and political life.

Teoctist and several other hierarchs proved, to a certain degree, to be admirers of the established church model present in Western countries. The same admiration for the West was not present, though, when Romania was asked to implement democratic EU requirements to eliminate discrimination in Romania's own legislation. One case in point is the explicit request for Romania, before even being considered for admission into the EU, to change Article 200 of its communist criminal code, which punished homosexuality with jail terms of up to five years. The opposition to the change was staunch, and it came from many politicians and all the religious groups, with the Orthodox Church leading the way. Numerous calls were heard for the maintenance of discrimination against what was perceived as a wrong way of life. Eventually, under pressure from the EU, the parliament voted to decriminalize homosexuality.[4]

Under the tenure of the present patriarch, Daniel Ciobotea (2007–present), things appear to have changed. The new patriarch and those around him seem to favor a model of church-state relations that could be described as "partnership and autonomy," inspired by the German system. In a personal interview I conducted in 2004, while he was still metropolitan of Iasi, Ciobotea approached the topic of partnership between church and state by indicating his admiration for the German model. When asked to comment on the Byzantine model of church-state *symphonia*, he indicated that this outdated model should be replaced by collaboration between church and state and active participation by the RP in the social life of the country. He added that:

> Democracy as we experience it today is a Western invention, which relies a lot on respect for freedom, respect for human rights, institutions, but also on a contractual understanding of human relations. One has to abide by contracts, respecting their deadlines and obligations. Unfortunately, that is not how Romanian society and Orthodox societies in general have functioned so far. Therefore, democratization presents a challenge for the Romanian society and the Orthodox Church in the sense that they have to adapt to the new contractual nature of democracy.[5]

To support his view about partnership and cooperation, during the first year after his appointment, Patriarch Daniel signed two important documents with the government on behalf of the Orthodox Church. The Protocol of Cooperation in the Area of Social Inclusion (*Protocolul de Cooperare in Domeniul Incluziunii Sociale*) was signed in October 2007, and the Protocol of Collaboration on the Medical and Spiritual Assistance Partnership (*Protocolul de Colaborare privind Parteneriatul Asistenta Medicala si Spiritualitate*) was signed in the summer of 2008. Patriarch Teoctist had signed only one such protocol, in 1995, in an effort to promote cooperation with the government in the field of medical and spiritual assistance. In contrast, Patriarch Daniel seems to place significantly greater emphasis on the capacity of this bilateral instrument to make church-state relations more transparent, predictable, and comprehensive.

The Protocol of Cooperation in the Area of Social Inclusion is meant to simplify the church-state collaboration procedures dealing with social projects, especially those benefiting disadvantaged persons and minorities. According to the document, church and state collaborate with a view towards strengthening social inclusion in Romania; promoting public debates for improving the relevant legislative and institutional framework; identifying the key priorities in the field and addressing the social needs of disadvantaged people; and exchanging information and providing assistance. Collaboration was envisioned for ten years. If unchallenged by either side, the protocol would extend beyond that time frame on a yearly basis. The government, through the Ministry of Work, Family, and Equality, pledged to include the Orthodox Church in the formulation of legislation in the field, in workshops and meetings on the topic of social inclusion, and in the activity of the National Commission for Social Inclusion. It also declared its willingness to collaborate with the church on joint projects, to inform the church about possibilities for financial support from the government, and to collaborate with the nongovernmental organizations that operate as part of, or with, the blessing of the Orthodox Church. One of the government's most important pledges was to offer spiritual assistance on the premises of governmental social service providers and to support the hiring of graduates of social work programs from the Faculties of Orthodox Theology.[6] In return, the church pledged to work with the government in providing social assistance to disadvantaged groups, to provide spiritual counseling through trained workers, to support the implementation of relevant government programs, and to offer the government information about its nongovernmental organizations. Given its unparalleled reach into rural and urban areas, the Church also vowed to identify (through its priests and social workers) and communicate to the government information about persons in need.[7]

In signing a new Protocol of Collaboration on the Medical and Spiritual Assistance Partnership, the Orthodox Church and the government, through the Ministry of Health Care, agreed to coordinate and integrate their medical, social, and spiritual assistance programs. The goal of this collaboration was to achieve "a community that is healthy from a physical, mental, social, and spiritual point of view by increasing one's awareness and involvement in actions of prevention and treatment of the practices that are damaging to one's health."[8] The protocol sought to promote health through joint programs that would raise the quality of life and promote a healthy lifestyle; to facilitate medical, social, and spiritual assistance in the country; to identify key priorities; and to address the medical and spiritual needs of those in distress. It envisaged regular meetings between church and state representatives and compelled the Church and government to assume obligations similar to those specified in the 2007 collaboration protocol.

Upon the signing of the first protocol, Patriarch Daniel emphasized its significance. According to him, the document was called for by the new 2006 Law on Religion, which recognized denominations as the government's social partners and demonstrated the commitment of the Orthodox Church and the Romanian government to help the poor, orphans, children whose parents work abroad, the elderly, and other disadvantaged groups. The social work of the church is "both a spiritual vocation and a practical necessity,"[9] and thus is to be promoted vigorously in the future.

While the two protocols were the most important of such documents, they were not the only ones. Similar documents were signed by Orthodox bishoprics and local governments. In 2008, for example, Patriarch Daniel, as the metropolitan of Bucharest, signed a protocol with the Bucharest District 1 mayor's office for the organization of common programs and activities and the restoration of local churches.[10] In 2008, 2009, and 2010, the bishopric of Giurgiu signed protocols with the Center for Antidrug Prevention, Evaluation, and Counseling for discouraging the use of alcohol, drugs, and cigarettes by children; the Giurgiu Department for Social Assistance and Child Protection for alleviating social problems like violence in the family, drug use, and child abandonment; and the gendarmerie for the organization of social, cultural, and religious activities.[11]

These partnerships represent a significant departure from the Byzantine concept of *symphonia* historically observed by the church, and the established church model upheld in the interwar and 1990–2007 periods. *Symphonia* recognized the Orthodox Church as first among denominations and a privileged partner for the state, but the church-state marriage it implemented was not a marriage of equals. Rather, it was a highly asymmetrical cohabitation where the state, in practice, took precedence over the Church in all aspects of life.[12] By contrast, the new partnerships recognized the Church and state as equals that share similar responsibilities and derive comparable benefits from mutual cooperation.

One topic that provides plenty of opportunities to reflect on relations with and attitudes towards the West is Romania's integration with the European Union. Some Orthodox monks, nuns, and faithful were apprehensive about the EU accession process and the costs it imposed on their country, but Church leaders recognized early on that they could not stop Romania's EU accession and that mounting active and open opposition to a process desired by the overwhelming majority of the population would show them to be out of step with history and, consequently, make them unnecessarily unpopular. Although some RP leaders were not excited about Europe and European values, none of them openly rejected EU eastern enlargement in general, or Romania's accession in particular.

Teoctist's conciliatory position failed to reflect the deep frustration other RP leaders felt towards the conditions the Union asked Romania to fulfill before judging it worthy of inclusion—conditions viewed as unfairly more numerous and unreasonably more stringent than those imposed on other, former communist candidate countries in central Europe. Romanians readily admit that the communist regime they endured was far worse than regimes in neighboring countries, but few recognize that Ceausescu's erratic economic policies, personality cult and megalomania, pervasive use of secret informers, and persecution of dissidents inside and outside of the Communist Party placed the country at a disadvantage that needed years of sustained effort to overcome. Similarly, Romanian politicians apparently wanted EU membership without working hard to reform their country's political culture and institutions.[13] Few Romanians recognized that the accession conditions were more stringent because their country had a wider handicap to overcome and deeper systemic problems to address.

In an influential article widely cited among theologians and the faithful, Metropolitan Bartolomeu Anania of Cluj—one of RP's most conservative but also, in some circles, most authoritative voices—noted that
Romanians "have always been Europeans, and thus one can speak not of
our 'entry' into Europe, but of our reinsertion into Europe or, more precisely, Europe's reinsertion into us." He lamented the fact that Romanians
were treated as "impoverished primitives" by the colonizing Western European countries when they themselves were the very nations responsible
for handing Romania over to the Soviet Union without much protest and
without trying to defend it from communism (an allusion to the Yalta
agreement of 1945). Consequently, Romania was assigned to the Soviet
sphere of influence. Instead of repeatedly insisting on Romania's undemo-
cratic political culture and underperforming economy, Anania reasoned,
the West should set aside its "feelings of superiority" and realize that it,
and it alone, was to blame for the country's misfortunes.

Equally disappointing was, for Anania, the West's frequent readiness
to belittle Romania's cultural riches and record of genuine accomplishments. In his words, the West "calls us 'Balkan,' although geographically
we are not part of that region" and Romanians "always had the vision of
and lived in Europe, the real Europe." That "real Europe," Anania reminded, gave the world great philosophers like Plato, Aristotle, and Sopho-
cles, a contribution invalidating the oft-cited division of the continent into
the civilized, superior West and the primitive, inferior East. The Balkans
did not deserve derogatory labels as they were Europe's roots, drawing
inspiration from "Hellenic thought, Christian spirituality, and Roman
civilization." It was this old, "real Europe" that the new Western Europe
rejected and belittled in order to propose instead "one Europe built on
economics and politics, without any trace of culture and religion." "We
don't expect spirituality on the part of the West, because it has none," Anania wrote in order to explain why Romanians "don't need this Europe . . .
[but] Europe must rediscover Romania."[14]

The metropolitan adopted a moralizing tone when discussing what exactly Europe had to offer postcommunist candidate states like Romania.
His answer amounted to a pessimistic evaluation of Western mores and a
bitter indictment of cherished, democratic values. Tolerance, trust, and
inclusiveness were to be adamantly opposed as a concerted assault on traditional Romanian values. "We are asked to tolerate those that lead us
astray in our faith. . . . All proposed forms of syncretism, from New Age

to neo-Protestant sects forming 'Evangelical' and 'Evangelizing' federa-
tions . . . are manifestations of spiritual corruption." Given the EU's un-
reasonable position, Anania considered it advisable to be intolerant towards
new religious movements entering the country and luring believers away
from the dominant Orthodox Church, the only denomination that, following him, was tied to the very core of Romanian identity.[15]

For the time being, the RP includes both pro-Western and anti-Western
hierarchs. For now, at least, the pro-Western position seems to have prevailed, especially since the powerful anti-Westerner Anania just passed
away in 2011. Yet the current economic and political crisis that the country is going through could bring dissatisfaction with the West and democratic fatigue in the predominantly Orthodox population. That, in turn,
could put pressure on the RP leadership to revise its discourse towards the
West.

The Russian Orthodox Church

The Soviet regime that lasted for almost three-quarters of a century (1917–
91) was characterized by radical antireligious policies that did away with
many of the pre-Soviet features of religious life in Russia. Many Orthodox Church leaders were imprisoned, killed, and eventually replaced with
leaders who were subservient to the regime; monasteries and churches were
closed, monks and nuns imprisoned, and religious manifestations significantly curtailed, while other churches (e.g., the Baptist Union and the
Evangelical Christian Union) were completely obliterated. According to
church records, in 1922 alone, 2,691 priests, 1,962 monks, and 3,447
nuns were killed at the time when Patriarch Tikhon and other members
of the synod, the church's collective leadership body, were imprisoned.
Recently opened secret archives prove that the crimes against the Orthodox leaders and faithful were committed on direct orders from Lenin,
whose hate for religion, especially Orthodoxy, was notorious, but accomplished by Stalin after Lenin's death in 1924.[16] By 1939, no more than one
hundred to two hundred Orthodox churches remained open in the Soviet
Union out of a prerevolutionary total of some forty-six thousand. As premier of the Soviet Union and first secretary of the Communist Party, Nikita
Khrushchev launched an aggressive state campaign to eradicate religious
sentiment. Antireligious and atheistic propaganda increased in intensity,
unauthorized church services were banned, previously authorized religious

meetings were disrupted, and numerous religious leaders were placed under arrest on trivial charges.

Following Khrushchev's ouster from power in 1964, a period of détente ensued, with antireligious propaganda focused on education more than imprisoning church leaders. By 1975, a new era of church-state relations began, whereby the state had to admit—to itself, if not to the general public—that religion would remain a permanent feature of Russian culture for the foreseeable future, and a new modus vivendi between church and state had to be initiated. Churches received small concessions ranging from registration of additional congregations and permission to renovate places of worship to the publication of several thousand Bibles and other religious books. The 1988 millennium celebration of the conversion of the Rus' to Orthodox Christianity marked the end of some seventy-years of religious persecution in the Soviet Union.[17]

According to local scholars of religion, such as Olga Kazmina, the post-Soviet religious landscape in Russia is new and in discontinuity with both the pre-Soviet and the Soviet situations.[18] Roughly three periods can be identified in the post-Soviet relations between the Russian Orthodox Church, state, and society (and they are important for understanding official Orthodox attitudes and discourse towards the West): from the early to mid-1990s, from the late 1990s to the mid-2000s, and from 2006 until today. Kazmina describes the first period as one characterized by state neutrality towards all religions, by intense foreign missionary activity and the subsequent rise of problems relating to proselytism, and by major competition between the Moscow patriarchate (MP) and Protestant missionaries. The population perceived religion as a social and cultural phenomenon during that period. While no tradition existed in Russia that considered religion a private phenomenon, the 1990 Law on Freedom of Beliefs was based on ideas of free religious choice and the privatization of religion.

The second period (late 1990s to mid-2000s) brought a strengthening of the position of the MP in Russian society, the increased correlation between religion and ethnicity, the politicization of religion, major clashes between the MP and the Roman Catholic Church over the issue of proselytism, and the rejection of the West by the MP. In fact, the MP was on better terms with non-Christian religions such as Islam, Buddhism, and Judaism, as these religions were connected traditionally with ethnic groups present in Russia. A new Law on Freedom of Religion and on Religious Associations was adopted in 1997. Unlike its 1990 predecessor, the new law connected religious life with its historical and cultural context. It was also during this time that the MP adopted important documents such as "Concept of the Rebirth of the Missionary Activity of the Russian Orthodox Church," "Bases of the Social Concept of the Orthodox Church," and "Basic Principles of the Russian Orthodox Church's Attitude to the non-Orthodox." While the state showed solidarity with and favoritism towards the MP in the late 1990s, its position changed to one of general neutrality and support for the MP during critical times in the 2000s.

The third period (since 2006) has been characterized by further strengthening of the positions of the MP and its increased influence on the Russian state and society, as well as more intense missionary activity (evidenced by a new document entitled "Concept of the Missionary Activity of the Russian Orthodox Church," issued in 2007). This period is also one of greater openness of the MP dialogue with Western Christians. As both Kazmina and others have noted, the new perceived common enemy of religion in Europe, secularism, has united the MP with the Roman Catholic Church, and even some Protestant churches, in their fight against it.[19]

The latter two periods of church-state relations can be identified as periods of opposition by the MP to Western values and religious denominations. The 1990 Law on Freedom of Beliefs—which the MP's hierarchs participated in writing—provided for unrestricted activity by all religions. The law looked at the MP as equal with all other religions and denominations based on Enlightenment ideas of state neutrality towards religion (as long as religion is regarded as a private matter). The 1990 law also opened wide the door to foreign missionaries. Following the "spiritual and moral vacuum" brought about by communist rule, many political leaders throughout Eastern Europe and the former Soviet Union argued that citizens of former communist countries would greatly benefit from exposure to religious and moral teachings previously denied to them. Religious groups were happy to oblige. Some Russian governments even recruited foreigners to teach religion. In a telling example, on November 5, 1992, before a crowd of over eight thousand Christian teachers in Anaheim, California, three officials from the Russian Ministry of Education asked educators to join The CoMission—a group formed by sixty Evangelical Christian organizations to instruct Russian public school teachers on how to teach Christian ethics. Commenting on the unusual invitation launched by the United States' former archenemy, Russian Deputy Minister of Education Alexander Asmolov said:

> While discussing the possible contacts between Russia and the United States, we usually mention the economic crisis, but this is only part of the problem. The spiritual crisis is more important. It took forty years [for Moses] to take the people of Judea from the desert. For seventy-five years we were in the desert of Communism. . . . This philosophy resulted in tragic things for the souls of people. Today we are discussing the new ways to the souls of people. . . . I want to emphasize today that Russian education is open for Christian values.[20]

The MP, to make up for its lack of proselytizing manpower, invoked the principles of ecumenism in the face of the massive and unfair proselytizing competition that confronted it. Its calls, however, went unheard by Protestant and Catholic missionaries. So, soon thereafter, the MP changed its tactic and focused on lobbying efforts in order to convince Russian legislators and politicians to protect Orthodoxy in the name of its paramount role as a "traditional denomination" that has contributed to the country's history and supported the state on many occasions in the past. According to Kazmina, the phrase "traditional denomination" became widely used in the religious, social, and political discourse during the second period, and it was applied also to denominations that were closely connected with ethnic groups settled in Russia.[21] Nationalism was also invoked, a successful lobbying tactic used by many churches to intimidate politicians.

Religious nationalism is known as phyletism—the principle of privileging race, tribe, or nation in matters of salvation—and was condemned at a council convened by Patriarch Anthimus VI in Constantinople in 1872. The patriarch reacted against the Bulgarian Orthodox Church's declaration of independence from Constantinople by declaring phyletism a heresy and excommunicating the Bulgarians.[22] The condemnation enjoyed little support in the Orthodox world at a time when many Eastern European nations were just being born and their Orthodox churches were on the way to becoming autocephalous; Orthodox churches have time and again fallen prey to that "heresy" by invoking nationalist principles in order to win political support. As the case of Russia shows, the use of nationalism succeeded in giving the MP the upper hand over other denominations in the country. As Kazmina writes, "By mid 1990s . . . the euphoria about Western values gave way to more nationalistic tendencies" among the Russian public. One should add that, as in many other cases, the transition from a communist command economy and totalitarianism to a capitalist economy and democracy has proven painful for many people. In the case of the ten Eastern European states, the carrot that kept them going was the promise of joining the European Union (eight of them joined the EU in 2004, while Romania and Bulgaria joined in 2007).

But in the case of Russia, there was no such carrot, and the population became tired of transition and became more receptive to the nationalism proclaimed by the MP. The new 1997 law, On Freedom of Conscience and Religious Association, replacing the 1990 law on religion, catered more to this new perception among Russia's population. While upholding each person's right to freedom of conscience and belief, the law recognized the historical place of the PM in the country. In its preamble, the new law singled out the "special contribution of Orthodoxy to the history of Russia and to the establishment and development of Russia's spirituality and culture."[23] Islam, Buddhism and Judaism are also recognized among Russia's traditional religions in the new law. Limits were also set on missionary activity in Russia by Western newcomers. In December 1998, at the initiative of the Russian Orthodox Church, the Inter-Religious Council of Russia was set up to include representatives of the MP, Islam, Buddhism, and Judaism.

In his 2004 monograph, *The Russian Orthodox Church: Current State and Pressing Problems* (published in Russian as *Russkaia Pravoslavnaia Tserkov': Soveremennoe Sostoianie i Aktual'nye Problemy*), Russian historian Nikolai Mitrokhin treats the MP as a political party and offers the following concise formulation of the MP's "party platform": "[The post-Soviet Church is] consistently anti-liberal, anti-Western, xenophobic in its relationship to ethnic minorities, sympathetic to the monarchical (or at a minimum, authoritarian) form of government, statist, and anti-market."[24] In her recent book, Irina Papkova agrees that Mitrokhin's statement reflects the consensus among observers of Russia's religious and political scene, although she presents a more nuanced picture of the MP.[25] In particular, a document adopted in 2000 at a major Church council, entitled "The Bases of the Social Concept of the Russian Orthodox Church" (hereafter

"Social Concept"), which has been hailed by some as an Orthodox equivalent of the Catholic *Rerum Novarum*, sets out the Church's position vis-à-vis the ideal form of government, its attitudes towards other religious groups and their proper place in Russian society, its beliefs regarding the role of the West in Russia's continuing economic and social difficulties, and the desirability of a foreign policy that would limit the West's attempts to unilaterally impose its liberal, democratic principles and capitalist values on the entire world through globalization.

In terms specifically of other Christians, the "The Basic Principles of the MP in Its Relationship with the Heterodox" (another document adopted at the 2000 church council where the "Social Concept" was adopted) affirms that, "The ties of the MP with non-Orthodox Christians . . . should be conducted in the spirit of brotherly cooperation . . . [with] the goal of coordinating actions in social life, the cooperative defense of Christian moral values, the strengthening of social harmony, [and] putting an end to proselytism on the canonical territory of the MP" (Section 6.1). While "insulting non-Orthodox believers is not acceptable," the MP does "not accept the equality of denominations" (Section 7.2).[26] As Papkova concludes by analyzing these documents, "the position of the Moscow Patriarchate is that denominations recognized by [it] as legitimately Christian are free to profess their faith on the territory of the Russian Federation but are asked not to impose it on people born into Orthodoxy."[27] This boils down to the MP's self-understanding as professing the "correct glorification" of God (literal translation of "orthodox"), unlike the sects (such as Jehovah's Witnesses) that, according to the MP, have an "erroneous glorification" of God and are destructive for society.[28] Moreover, this understanding pertains to the incorporation of American-type anticult ideology in Russian religious legislation and the MP's views on "non-traditional religions."[29]

In her carefully researched book, based in part on interviews and surveys conducted in Moscow and St. Petersburg in the spring of 2006, Irina Papkova identifies three factions inside the Orthodox Church: traditionalists, liberals, and fundamentalists. According to her, it is the traditionalists who tended to control the hierarchy after the mid-1990s, but the liberals and the fundamentalists have managed to influence some of the patriarchate's policies. The interplay among these three groups, especially their disagreements, is what renders the MP weak and incapable of speaking with one voice. These three groups have different views of the West and it is to these views that we now turn.

The traditionalists are a pragmatic, conservative group that espouses a political ideology known as *pravoslavnaia derzhavnost'* (Orthodox statism), which overlapped in important ways with the official positions of the MP until 2008. Orthodox statism is an ideology that foresees a powerful Russian state infused by renewed Orthodox values. The intellectual leadership of the *pravoslavnaia derzhavnost'* approach is associated most frequently with the circle of clergy and active laity, including politicians, connected to the Sretenskii Monastery in Moscow, headed by the monastery's abbot, Father Tikhon Shevkunov. The movement is monarchist, anti-Western, and antiglobalist, but stops short of calling "for a radical overthrow of the existing political system."[30]

While dominating the scene in the early 1990s, the liberal Orthodox seem to have been driven underground from about the mid-1990s until the mid-2000s, due to the attack on them by the other two groups.[31] The roots of liberal Orthodoxy in Russia go back to Fr. Alexander Men, who was killed in 1990, and other dissident priests such as Gleb Yakunin. The liberal wing of the MP has been associated in large part with two communities in Moscow: the parish of SS. Cosmas and Damien, under the pastorship of Father Alexander Borisov, and the community surrounding Father Georgii Kochetkov, but they also include other priests and parishes throughout the Russian Federation. Due to pushing for reform through the usage of modern-day Russian (instead of church Slavonic) in the liturgy, Fr. Kochetkov was quite compromised, because in the minds of the Russians, church reform of this type is associated with the communists who tried to introduce it in the early Soviet period in an attempt to undermine the Orthodox Church. The traditionalists associated with St. Tikhon's Theological Institute denounced the liberal reformers as heretics to Patriarch Aleksy II, and in 1998 the patriarch forbade Fr. Kochetkov from celebrating the liturgy. In the early 2000s, however, Metropolitan Iuvenalii of Krutitsa and Kolomna, a senior synod member, started protecting Fr. Kochetkov and the liberals who, in turn, pledged their allegiance to the MP hierarchy. The liberal Orthodox have also created institutions of higher learning such as the St. Andrew Biblical Theological Institute and the St. Filaret Orthodox Institute. They are prodemocratic and open towards the West, which they do not blame for Russia's ongoing ills. They think that the Russian fear of globalization is caused by a fear of foreigners and nostalgia for the Soviet empire.[32]

The Orthodox fundamentalists differ from the traditionalists in deeply distrusting the patriarchate, which they see as having betrayed the Orthodox cause through its openness to dialogue with other religions and the non-Orthodox, especially in its presence at the World Council of Churches, and by their distrust of the hierarchy in favor of relying on the charismatic elders (*startsy*).[33] Generally, the fundamentalists and their clergy do not have formal theological education, and embrace an apocalyptic worldview. They revere Tsar Nicholas II and see him as the "one who can hold back" (*Uderzhyvaiushchii*) the advance of the antichrist. Nowadays, the antichrist is globalization and the West. The patriarchate canonized Nicholas II in 2000, thus responding to the pressure that the fundamentalists had put on it. However, in numerous official statements, the patriarchate was careful to emphasize "the idea that Nicholas II is the 'Uderzhyvaiushchii' does not correspond to Orthodox doctrine."[34] The movement's ideas can be summarized as anti-Western and antimarket; staunchly monarchist and highly critical of the post-Soviet system; they would like the Russian Orthodox Church to be recognized as the state church; they are hostile to religious pluralism; they are xenophobic, openly anti-Semitic, and anti-Masonic; and they emphasize the redemptive role of Nicholas II, who is seen an apocalyptic figure.[35]

It is in this context that the current patriarch, Kirill Gundyaev, assumed the MP's leadership in 2009. Despite his rather controversial past—having been accused of being a KGB agent in the Soviet era and dubbed the "Tobacco Metropolitan" for allegedly profiting from the tax-free importation of cigarettes into the country, to the point of becoming a billionaire in the 1990s—Kirill was also actively involved in the ecumenical dialogue as the MP's official representative at the World Council of Churches starting in 1971. Clearly, his rise to power, especially towards the end of Patriarch Aleksy's reign, has led Kazmina to perceive a change in the MP's attitudes towards the West as of 2006. A more positive orientation and friendship towards the West, especially towards the Roman Catholic Church, became evident in his church's policy. After becoming patriarch in January 2009, Kirill appointed the young, talented and Western-trained—he holds a PhD in theology from Oxford University—Metropolitan Hilarion Alfeyev as the chairman of the MP's Department of External Church Relations (a position previously held by Patriarch Kirill himself). Alfeyev has been an active participant in ecumenism for many years as an official representative of the MP. As recently as September 2009, while on an official visit with Pope Benedict XVI at the Vatican, he did not even raise the issue of proselytism. Instead, a common Christian witness was proposed, defending traditional Christian values in an increasingly secular Europe.[36]

Conclusion

One can conclude that there have been several stages in the perception of the West in the official political discourse of the Romanian and Russian Orthodox Churches. First, after the communist spiritual vacuum, Orthodox faithful and leaders in both countries tended to regard the West in a positive light. Then, once Western missionaries became more visible in the two countries, there was a change in the tone towards the West. Here, the two churches part ways: while in Romania there was a generally positive perception of the West due to the country's desire to join the European Union and the accession requirements imposed on the country by the EU, the Russian Federation did not experience such a positive reception due to the fact that there has been no desire to join EU among MP leaders and the Russian faithful and politicians. What has made it possible in Russia to change perceptions of the West in some official Orthodox leadership circles is the presence of leaders such as Patriarch Kirill and Archbishop Alfeyev, who have experienced the West firsthand in their own training and ecumenical activity. This could be said about Romania, too, with a relatively young patriarch, Daniel Ciobotea, who was educated in France, Germany, and Switzerland. Ciobotea is opposed to the Euroskepticism of the older, conservative, and once-powerful metropolitan and patriarchal countercandidate, the late Bartolomeu Anania.

In this concluding section, the question must be asked whether perceptions of the West have really changed because the West is seen as more desirable by the majority of the two Orthodox churches discussed here, or simply because new leaders have come to the helm of their institutions. More research needs to be done to answer that question. But our dilemma is similar to the one that surfaced during the debate that took place some decades ago in the scientific community. As Thomas Kuhn argued in his famous *The Structure of Scientific Revolutions*, paradigm shifts occur because new, more convincing paradigms replace the old ones. Yet Kuhn quotes the opinion of the famous physicist Max Planck, who reportedly said that "a new scientific truth does not triumph by convincing its opponents and making them see the light, but rather because its opponents die and a new generation grows up that is familiar with it."[37]

PRIMACY AND ECCLESIOLOGY: THE STATE OF THE QUESTION

John Panteleimon Manoussakis

Antipapism

The phenomenon of antipapism, understood as the denial of a *primus* for the Universal Church and the elevation of such denial to a trait that allegedly identifies the whole Orthodox Church, is, properly speaking, heretical. In saying this, I am returning the favor, so to speak, to all those who have taken upon themselves the onerous task of defending Orthodoxy against all kinds of heresy. And heresy is all they see. Any difference, not only in matters of dogma, but also in liturgy, in language, in vestments, in appearance, is immediately and solemnly denounced as heresy, as every form of otherness is customarily condemned as sin.

Anticipating the reaction of some who may find such a statement dangerous and inflammatory, I wonder if it is possible that antipapism can be confused with Orthodoxy. And if there is such a possibility, is it not all the more necessary and urgent that we speak against such a false identification, distinguishing the Church to which we belong and which we serve from that party that has constructed for itself a new identity exclusively based on hatred for the office of Peter?

Nevertheless, the phenomenon of antipapism has become increasingly more observable within the Orthodox Church. Those who want to elevate their dislike for the Pope into a definition for the Orthodox Church as a whole do not realize that, if they are right, their version of the Church is reduced to little more than a religious club that can trace its origins back no earlier than the Schism of 1054—a club that would owe the raison d'être for its establishment entirely to the very opponent that it opposes. Indeed, we cannot continue to accept as genuinely Orthodox those things that are simply the opposite of what the Catholic Church believes. Orthodoxy cannot be merely reactionary, possessed, as it were, by the demonic spirit of naysaying, bereft of any creative powers of theology, where what constitutes "me" is always a negation of the "Other."[1] *Truth*, I suggest, *is antinomian and, thus, never antithetical.*[2]

For philosophy as well as for psychology, the mechanism of affirming oneself, individually or collectively, in contradistinction over and against the "Other" is well known. In fact, the more fragile one's ideological constitution, the more necessary such a strategy is. The more similar I am to my other, the more likely that this constitutive hostility becomes fiercer, because there is a greater risk that I might be confused with this "Other."[3] Western cultures have perpetuated this phenomenon through various foundational myths. The ancient city of Rome, for example, was founded by means of a fratricide between Remus and Romulus. The political function of the myth, as a foundational allegory, has been recorded and one can find analogies all the way from the "sinners" and "saints" aboard the Mayflower, to the fight for sovereignty between two English-speaking nations in Northern Ireland.[4] We could, of course, recall the archetypical case of Abel's murder of Cain, paying attention to the gloss that Scripture provides—namely, that Cain, after he had killed his brother and perhaps as a result of that, went on to become the founder of the first city.

Others contributors to this volume have written with great competence about the history of Orthodox anti-Catholicism. Allow me briefly to touch upon two cases of anti-Catholicism that occurred within the last three months in the Church of Greece[5]—cases that demonstrate, I believe, the problems that this issue creates for the Orthodox Church.

1. The first concerns an "academic" conference organized by the Metropolitan of Piraeus that took place on April 28, 2010. The topic of the conference was "Primacy, Conciliarity and the Unity of the Church." A communiqué of the conference's findings was subsequently published by the Metropolis. "Primacy," we read in the first line of this document, "has neither theological basis nor . . . ecclesiological justification."[6] The conference was attended by the organizer, the Metropolitan of Piraeus, who was also a speaker, the Metropolitan of Cythera, the Metropolitan of Glyfada, as well as the archbishop of Athens—in other words, by three members of the Holy Synod and its president, the same synod—please note—that officially autho-

rized the participation of a representing delegation to the Joint International Commission on the Theological Dialogue between the Catholic and Orthodox Churches. More recently, the same Metropolitan decided to add Pope Benedict XVI to the list of anathematized heretics that was solemnly proclaimed during the divine liturgy of the first Sunday of Lent of 2012.

2. On June 1, 2010, the Metropolitan of Cythera, one of the attendees of the aforementioned conference, decided to put the conference's conclusions into action. He sent a letter to the archbishop of Athens demanding that the Holy Synod summon the Metropolitan of Messenia, one of the members of the delegation of the Church of Greece to the dialogue with the Catholic Church, in order to publicly, orally, and in writing, retract his statement that the Church of Christ is today divided (the Metropolitan of Messenia had made a statement arguing that the division between Orthodox and Catholic constitutes a division in the Church of Christ). The Metropolitan of Cythera went so far as to suggest that, should the Metropolitan of Messenia refuse to apologize, "he cannot anymore be counted among the bishops."[7] The implication was that he should be dethroned and defrocked. In February 2012, Metropolitan of Messenia Chrysostomos submitted his resignation from his duties as representative of the Church of Greece in the International Joint Theological Dialogue with the Catholic Church. The Holy Synod of the Church of Greece accepted his resignation in the following month.[8]

These incidents are only a further confirmation of a trajectory encapsulated in the notorious *Confession of Faith* (Ὁμολογία Πίστεως)—a document that has circulated among Orthodox clergy and laity, collecting signatures and denouncing the "pan-heresy" of papism. The Ecumenical Patriarch and the Orthodox copresident of the Commission on the Theological dialogue between the Catholic and Orthodox Churches, Metropolitan of Pergamon John (Zizioulas), were so troubled by this document that they took the unprecedented step to send letters (dated September 29, 2009) to all the hierarchs of the Church of Greece, expressing their alarm at the proportions of this phenomenon and the serious dangers that it harbors for the unity of Orthodoxy itself.

These examples should suffice in providing us with some sense of both the context and the ethos with which the discussion on the Pope's primacy occurs in the Orthodox Church today. At the very least, this discussion requires that we reconsider the question of whether or not we need a *primus* in the Orthodox Church and, if so, who or what might play such a role?

The Need for Primacy

Concerning the question of whether the Orthodox Church needs a *primus*, and especially at the universal level, I will appeal to two personal experiences. In 2006, I was given permission to attend the deliberations of the International Joint Commission on the Theological Dialogue between the Orthodox and Catholic Churches, which convened, after a hiatus, in Belgrade. Although I cannot disclose details of what transpired during those sessions, since the proceedings of the commission are not public, I can, however, express my disappointment on the state of that dialogue, particularly concerning the Orthodox participation. The source of my disappointment was the paradoxical realization that we cannot unite with Rome as long as we are not united with Rome. What I mean by this is that the very absence of the authority that a *primus* would have exercised on a pan-Orthodox level hinders the efforts of remedying this institutional lacuna. The fact, in other words, that the Orthodox Churches today refuse to recognize a Rome-like primacy among themselves is the major problem in their dialogue with Rome.

The next year, in 2007, I spent the summer as a guest of the Ostkirchliches Institut in Regensburg. I shared the Institute's facilities with a number of other Orthodox scholars, mostly from Serbia and Romania. I was, if I remember correctly, the only Greek. When the first Sunday of my stay came, I realized, to my utter horror, that there were two Orthodox liturgies being celebrated at the same time in adjacent rooms: one for the Romanians and one for the Serbians. Going to either would have meant taking sides against the other—therefore, I decided to do the right thing and attend Mass at the Catholic Cathedral.

In his own contribution to this volume, Fr. Robert Taft makes an appeal for consistency on the part of the Orthodox. The demand for consistency—a reasonable and necessary condition for any dialogue—is related, in my opinion, to the question of authority. Who can speak on behalf of the Orthodox Church? Who is entitled to do so? In Dr. Kolbaba's essay, we learn of the so-called "guardians of Orthodoxy"—a phenomenon of the twelfth century that, I would argue, continues today, as vibrantly as ever. In their ferocity against the Western "Other," the contemporary guardians of Orthodoxy reject any notion of primacy, espousing and promoting an ecclesiology that they misunderstand to be democratic in its structure of equality. Among their mistakes is the conflation of the ideas of conciliarity, *sobornost*, and episcopal equality. Let me examine briefly some of the options purportedly given as the Orthodox answer to this question of authority.

The Ecumenical Council

When I was a seminarian in Athens, I was taught that, unlike the Roman Church, the highest authority in the Orthodox Church—the one authority with absolute power to decide dogmatic and canonical matters is an interpersonal (and thus impersonal) body—the Ecumenical Council.[9] By asserting such a claim, the Orthodox present a not-so-implicit critique against papal primacy, which is often caricatured as a centralized, imperialistic, and therefore totalitarian and oppressive ecclesiology. In opposition to such a structure, the Orthodox take pride in what they consider a more democratic structure. They give, however, little or no thought to the fact that the synod as a manifold body (as a gathering of bishops) presupposes the office of the One—that is, the one *primus* who, although *inter pares* as far as his sacramental faculty is concerned, remains nevertheless unequal in his primacy. Similarly, the Patriarch or the Metropolitan is also *inter pares* with the bishops who are administratively subordinate to him; yet, as the thirty-fourth Apostolic Canon makes clear, the synod cannot do anything without his consent. As the bishops are also *inter pares* with all baptized Christians, they are one with them every time that they officiate—an ecclesiological truth signified by the white *sticharion* that they, like all clerics, wear as the first piece of his liturgical vestments. And yet, despite the fact that they are *inter pares* with the faithful, the local Church cannot do anything without them, nor would the Church even exist as a community.[10]

The balanced dialectic that I have described on the universal, regional, and local levels respectively finds its articulation in the thirty-fourth Apostolic Canon mentioned earlier, which reads as follows: "The bishops of every region must acknowledge him who is first among them [*protos, primus*] and account him as their head, and do nothing of consequence without his consent; but each may do those things only which concern his own eparchy. . . . But neither let him [who is the first] do anything without the consent of the many; for so there will be unanimity, and God will be glorified through the Lord in the Holy Spirit." There is no either/or distinction between conciliarity and primacy. No council is conceivable without a *primus*.[11] Philosophically speaking, the emphasis on primacy conforms with the idea that the "one" is both logically, ontologically, and chronologically prior to the "many."

There is another reason why the Ecumenical Council cannot be considered as an *institution of authority* for the Church, without, of course, suggesting that Ecumenical Councils have no authority. The weight of the argument here falls not so much on authority itself but on the concept of the institution. An institution (θεσμός) implies both permanence and regularity, two basic characteristics lacking from the convocation of an Ecumenical Council that has more of the character of an *event* (extraordinary in nature) than that of an institution.[12]

Christ Himself

Another position that one hears often from the Orthodox is that the Church needs no *primus* because Christ is the "head" of the Church. But is this true exclusively on the universal level? Indeed, on both the regional and local levels, ecclesial structures presuppose that the bishop is Christ's living icon. No Orthodox would accept the claim that the bishop is not needed as head of either the diocese or the metropolitanate, simply because that role is filled by Christ himself. Furthermore, the naiveté of such an assertion ignores the profound theological significance of Christ's ascension.[13] Apart from the Eucharist, Christ is not with us physically; otherwise the Church's expectation of his future coming would be absurd. Moreover, saying that Christ is present in the Eucharist points to him who is physically present and who alone has the authority to celebrate the Eucharist—i.e., the bishop.

The Common Rule of Faith and Ritual

Even less needs to be said about the common rule of faith and ritual as sources of authority in the Church or as agents that could effect and represent the unity of the Church. Both faith and ritual have been proven historically and practically ineffective, as the examples that I cited in the beginning of this paper should make clear, in preserving the unity of Orthodox Churches or Orthodox communities with one another. However, a more serious consideration that begins to emerge at this point is whether the office of primacy can be exercised at any level of the Church's manifestation by something *impersonal*.

Primacy Is Personal

In Christian theology, *the principle of unity is always a person*. This simple truth can be attested on the Trinitarian, the Christological, and the ecclesiological level, demonstrating, incidentally, the interrelated nature of these three branches of theology. The mystery of the Holy Trinity places in front of us, in an eminent way, the dialectic between the One and the many, identity and difference. It is well known that what safeguards the oneness of God and prevents the doctrine of the Holy Trinity from lapsing into tritheism is the *person* of the Father. The "monarchy of the Father" indicates clearly that the coincidence and coaffirmation of unity and plurality in the Holy Trinity is exercised by a person—the Father. As the symbol of our faith, the Creed that we recite in every Eucharistic gathering attests, in its first article, the *one* God we believe in is a *person*, the *Father* ("I believe in one God, the Father the almighty.") The oneness of God is safeguarded *not* by some impersonal divine essence, but by the person of the Father.[14] Of course, any reference to the Father cannot be understood without evoking at the same time the Son, without whom the Father is not a Father. Precisely because the Father is a person, He cannot be mentioned or understood outside the relation with the other two Persons of the Holy Trinity. Therefore, the monarchy of the Father should not make us fear that the person of the Father is overemphasized at the expense of the Trinitarian communion. Rather, it is that Person, or more accurately, the personal character, that safeguards the *homoousian* community of the Holy Trinity. In a similar vein, the Christological debates, which began in the fifth century, sought, again to come to terms with the distinction between the One and the many. Here, of course, "the many" are the two natures of Christ, which became the cause of puzzlement, for the difficulty was the simultaneous affirmation of, on the one hand, the perfect divinity and perfect humanity of Christ and, on the other, of the fact that Christ was *one* . . . Again, the principle of unity, a unity "without division" and "without confusion"—as the definition of the Ecumenical Council in Chalcedon put it—is safeguarded and upheld by a person, namely, the person of the incarnate Logos.[15]

My argument is that there must be a consistency between these dogmatic claims and our ecclesiological model if we do not wish to divorce ecclesiology from theology. Ecclesiologically, then, too, the principle of unity for all and each of the three levels of ecclesial structure *must* be a person, a *primus*. Here, I invoke the unambiguous witness of the metropolitan of Bursa, Elpidophoros Lambriniadis, who, as the chief secretary of the ecumenical patriarchate, delivered a much-discussed speech at the Chapel of the Holy Cross Theological School in Brookline, stating the following:

> Let me add that the refusal to recognize primacy within the Orthodox Church, a primacy that necessarily cannot but be embodied by a *primus* (that is by a bishop who has the prerogative of being the first among his fellow bishops) constitutes nothing less than *heresy*.[16] It cannot be accepted, as often it is said, that the unity among the Orthodox Churches is safeguarded by either a common norm of faith and worship or by the Ecumenical Council as an institution. Both of these factors are impersonal while in our Orthodox theology the principle of unity is always a person. Indeed, in the level of the Holy Trinity the principle of unity is not the divine essence but the Person of the Father ("monarchy" of the Father), at the ecclesiological level of the local Church the principle of unity is not the presbyterium or the common worship of the Christians but the person of the Bishop, so too in the Pan-Orthodox level the principle of unity cannot be an idea nor an institution but it needs to be, if we are to be consistent with our theology, a person.[17]

The metropolitan of Pergamon, John Zizioulas, has devoted a number of articles to this topic (two of them recently published by Θεολογία, the official theological journal of the Holy Synod of the Church of Greece), in which he explicitly identifies primacy with a person. He writes: "Primacy is attached to a particular office or ministry and to a particular person."[18] For Zizioulas, furthermore, Church councils are an evolution of the Eucharistic assembly and therefore inexorably linked with the person who offers the Eucharist.[19]

The denial of the need for investing a particular person with the ministry of universal primacy is tantamount to the way that some Orthodox scholars (Antonios Alevizopoulos, Stergios Sakkos et al.) have attempted to interpret the primacy of Peter in Matthew 16:18–19 as referring not to Peter's person but to his confession. We witness here the same error of depersonalization as with the attempts to assign primacy either on the rule of faith, the common rite, the Ecumenical Synod, and so on. However, this is not how the Eastern Fathers understood the passage from St. Matthew's Gospel. Among the many examples, we choose a letter addressed to Pope Leo by St. Theodore the Studite:

> Because Christ the God gave to great Peter together with the keys of the kingdom the office of pastoral primacy (τῆς ποιμνιαρχίας ἀξίωμα) it is to Peter, that is, to his successor, that it is necessary to refer whatever innovation is attempted by those who err from the truth. It is this that we, the humble and least, have been always taught by our Fathers.[20]

It is interesting to note in this letter that St. Theodore affirms three points pertinent to our discussion: first, that Peter (and subsequently his successor) was given by Christ a certain primacy (ποιμνιαρχία) in accordance with the Scriptural passage of Matthew 16:18; second, that this primacy is personal, i.e., exercised by a person (Peter, Peter's successor); and third, that this was a view that was "taught always by our Fathers," that is, not a personal sentiment of St. Theodore but a perennial belief shared by the Fathers of old.

Conclusion

The history of Orthodoxy's Balkanization and the present state of its diaspora make it difficult to deny that the consequences of the heresy of antipapism—that is, the denial of a personal primacy in the Universal Church—have historically been linked to racism, which was itself condemned as a heresy in 1872 under the name of ethnophyletism. Here, racism is treated as a heresy because it ascribes the role of primacy to the nation, the *ethnos*. Thus, it commits a grave abuse of the theological principle we have described above by substituting the *person* of the *primus* with the impersonal collectivity of the nation, sacrificing the particular for the universal. Racism invests a penultimate category—that of race or language—with the authority of the ultimate, ignoring that such categories will be eschatologically overcome, as the experience of Pentecost both promises and anticipates. By doing so, national churches preclude the eschatological vision of the Gospel by realizing it in the present through a form of confessional or ethnic triumphalism. But, at the same time, we also have the phenomenon of the self-proclaimed guardians of Orthodoxy who, implicitly and illicitly, assert themselves and their criteria for Orthodoxy over the entire Church, as a type of primatial vision that supplants the legitimate structures of the Church (i.e., the bishop).

By trusting the ministry of primacy to a person, the Church defends itself against the insidious danger of idolatry, which is endemic to ideology. It elevates theories, concepts, or structures (no matter how benign or well-intended) to a normative status in the Church, which, in effect, establishes ideologies. I say this with respect to those who might prefer to see in the structure of the Church a democracy that emphasizes equality among the faithful, understanding the Church primarily as a community of equal members that cocelebrate the Eucharist—such views are open and susceptible to idolization. On the other hand, the person of the bishop, in his concreteness and not in spite of his shortcomings and failures but precisely *on account of them*, offers himself as an antidote to idolatry insofar as his humanity cannot but subject him to a process of demystification that would be difficult, if not impossible, to exercise with respect to a fleshless, impersonal construction. Finally, there are those who would perhaps feel scandalized by the fact that such a role is given to a mere human. Understandable as this concern might be, we should be mindful that the origin of this scandal is to be found nowhere else but in God's incarnation. Would those who protest today that a person (namely, the bishop) has come to occupy such a central position in our theologies and worship express the same protestations that a Nazarene man claimed to be "he who is"? Indeed, "blessed is he who shall not be scandalized" by the person of God (Mt. 11: 6, Lk. 7:23). In short, what I am trying to argue is this: It is the evident weakness of the person—and especially of the person who, as the head, cannot hide—that becomes, at the same time, his secret strength. In the words of G. K. Chesterton,

> When Christ at a symbolic moment was establishing His great society, he chose for its cornerstone neither the brilliant Paul nor the mystic John, but a shuffler, a snob, a coward—in a word, a man. And upon this rock He has built His Church, and the gates of Hell have not prevailed against it. All the empires and the kingdoms have failed, because of this inherent and continual weakness, that they were founded by strong men and upon strong men. But this one thing, the historic Christian Church, was founded on a weak man, and for

that reason it is indestructible. For no chain is stronger than its weakest link.[21]

The denial of the Pope's primacy has created a lacuna of authority in the Orthodox Church that has resulted, on the one hand, in the endless divisions of autocephalies and autonomies with multiple canonical jurisdictions over one region and, on the other, has given rise to the rogue fanaticism of para-ecclesial groups. It remains to be seen if this situation will awaken the Orthodox world from its dogmatic slumber. I hope that our Catholic brothers and sisters will learn something from our predicament. And—who knows?—one day it might take the Orthodox to convince Catholics of the necessity of the Pope's primacy.

In this paper I have concerned myself only with the task of showing that the ministry of primacy at the universal level is, from an Orthodox point of view, as necessary for the Church as it is in the diocesan and eparchial levels. Such a ministry cannot be performed save by the person of the bishop. Reality—that is, the current state of affairs on a pan-Orthodox level, as well as the Orthodox Church's theology—make it clear that neither an abstract principle nor an impersonal body can satisfactorily exercise the ministry of primacy. We have left the thorny question about the specific privileges and prerogatives in which this ministry translates untouched. This would be indeed another day's work. At least this much has been implied here: The *primus* offers witness to the Church's unity, he is a visible sign of such unity, and the means by which that unity is universally effected and proclaimed.

(In)Voluntary Ecumenism: Dumitru Staniloae's Interaction with the West as Open Sobornicity

Radu Bordeianu

Orthodox theology suffered an unhealthy influence during its "Western captivity."[1] Specifically, the overly intellectual bent of neo-Scholasticism divorced Orthodox theology from its tradition of spirituality. In line with several notable predecessors, Eastern and Western alike, Georges Florovsky called for theological education to break from the manual tradition of neo-Scholasticism. He proposed a "neopatristic synthesis"; more than a mere repetition of earlier thought, Florovsky's *ad mentem Patrum* is preachable, has spiritual benefits, and represents the key to Christian unity.[2] In a creative interaction with the West, Florovsky called for writing in the patristic spirit ("the mind of the Fathers"[3]) and for the rediscovery of the "catholic mind," which is the language of the Scriptures, the worshipping Church, and the Fathers.[4] As a historian, however, Florovsky did not write such a theology systematically.

In this brief paper, I contend that Dumitru Staniloae did produce a neopatristic synthesis. His work represents a creative development of the Orthodox patristic, spiritual, and liturgical tradition that is in dialogue with modern thought, and thus relevant for contemporary Church and social issues. To support this thesis, I present theological and biographical elements that attest to Staniloae's departure from manual theology. I then analyze his adoption of certain Western categories (namely, the three offices of Christ and the designation of seven sacraments) as instances of open sobornicity; in this section I engage with Andrew Louth, who offered a friendly criticism of Staniloae's approach. Through this essay, I

240

hope to provide a methodology of constructive engagement with the West and to correct those who falsely accuse Staniloae of being anti-ecumenical. That opinion is based on marginal aspects of his works and does not reflect a balanced reading of his corpus.

Staniloae's Engagement with the West

There are three reasons why Staniloae's engagement with the West was markedly polemical at times. First, he was not current with the developments in the theologies that he criticized because of his isolation behind the Iron Curtain. His Western encounters were mostly with Catholic and Protestant theologies of the late nineteenth and early twentieth centuries and with the classical Latin tradition, which he studied early in life as a student in the West. These theologies, of course, are frequently criticized by modern Catholic theologians as well.[5] Second, if Staniloae's criticism of Catholicism is oftentimes very sharp, it is because of his personal experience with Byzantine Catholic proselytism in his native region of Transylvania, which resorted to violence, including the bombing of monasteries and villages that opposed the union with Rome.[6] And third, Staniloae reacted against the Western influence upon Orthodox manual theology. Most of the time, this Western, neo-Scholastic influence refers to nineteenth- and twentieth-century Catholic theology, along with the surprising addition of Protestant theology. But what constitutes neo-Scholastic or manual theology? Briefly, Staniloae would have understood manual theology to be:

> An intellectualist approach to faith and the world, as opposed to an intellectual description of faith (and its logical consequences) for catechesis.[7]
>
> A method whereby philosophy is the criterion for theological truth as opposed to development, within the limits set by the Fathers.
>
> A form of theology as speculative science.[8]
>
> A concentration upon unnecessary rational speculations.[9]
>
> An overemphasis on cataphatism, to the detriment of apophatism.
>
> A lack of concern with a personal encounter with God (theology is divorced from spirituality and the life of the Church).
>
> A separation from the liturgical life of the Church (theology is not inspired by Liturgy, theology is not incorporated into Liturgy).

An ecclesiology understood through canons, organization, and order (a juridical approach), as opposed one understood through the Eucharist and sacraments (a communal approach).

A diminishment of a theocentric anthropology.

Given this view, Staniloae was prone to caricatures and unfair generalizations, especially early in his career.[10] What is more, his sources are sometimes difficult to trace.[11] Gradually, however, he became more receptive to changes in Catholic theology, especially concerning its more sacramental, spiritual ecclesiology. He was certain that schism could not endure.[12] Roberson considers that this change was determined by Staniloae's direct involvement with ecumenism:

> Staniloae's experience as a participant at the second plenary session of the international Catholic-Orthodox dialogue at Munich in 1982 seems to have caused him to greatly moderate his views on the Catholic Church. In an interview published in 1988, he stated that Orthodoxy and Catholicism "are not divided by essential differences." . . . He emerged hopeful that a solution may even be found to the problem of the papacy which would integrate the bishop of Rome into the communion of the Church in a way acceptable to the Orthodox.[13]

Staniloae dedicated much energy to the study of ecclesiology and ecumenism. As a thematic bibliography shows,[14] he contributed sixty-five articles and many references in his other writings to the cause of Christian unity. He praised the ecumenical movement and its purpose to reestablish the unity of the Church.[15] He also encouraged Orthodox theologians to study the teachings of other churches in an irenic spirit.[16] Indeed, any consideration of Staniloae's attitude towards the West must take into consideration Staniloae's attitude towards ecumenism, based upon the then current developments of Western theologies (rather than his condemnation of an outdated neo-Scholasticism).

Staniloae's Departure from Neo-Scholasticism

Staniloae's attitude towards the West changed over time, probably because his theology moved from a rejection of neo-Scholasticism to a positive affirmation of neopatristic synthesis. According to several commentators, he was the first Orthodox theologian to successfully break away from the manual tradition.[17] This affirmation does not diminish the importance of previous theologians who embarked on the same quest, but they were more concerned with historical and nonsystematic theology than Staniloae (e.g., Florovsky). He regarded theology as a personal experience rather than an abstract philosophical system and emphasized the complementarity between cataphatism and apophatism (as opposed to a contemporary like Lossky, who insisted upon the primacy of apophatism).[18] He achieved this kind of theology by drawing from three sources: revelation (Scripture and Tradition), Liturgy, and contemporary thought.

The first source of his theology is revelation, and it may appear that Staniloae's understanding of revelation is not biblical enough. To be sure, he occasionally prefers what we might call "logical speculation" and he does not reference Scripture consistently. But his theology is profoundly biblical—his systematic theology does not simply use the Bible for decorative purposes. Many of Staniloae's arguments are rooted in implicitly biblical concepts or derived directly from exegetical analysis. He even dedicated entire books to biblical theology, such as *The Evangelical Image of Jesus Christ.*[19]

The other aspect of revelation that informed his theology is the patristic tradition of the Church. Staniloae studied the Church Fathers thoroughly, reading the Greek authors in their original language and translating many of their works, such as the Romanian *Philokalia* in twelve volumes.[20] He filled the translations with commentary, often informed by Western scholarship. But Staniloae believed that reading the Fathers was not sufficient— their work needed to be advanced and their insights, which were limited by historical context, needed to be made current.[21] This is why he wrote in the foreword to his *Dogmatics*: "We tried to understand the teaching of the Church in the spirit of the Fathers, but, at the same time, to understand it as we think that they would have understood it today. I believe that they wouldn't ignore our times, as they didn't ignore theirs."[22]

The second source of Staniloae's theology is the Liturgy.[23] In his book *Spirituality and Communion in the Orthodox Liturgy*, for example, he builds a communion ecclesiology on the foundation of the Liturgy and, vice versa, explains the theological, communal aspects of the Liturgy. The worshipping Church is both the source and the interpretative lens of Staniloae's theology.

A third source is contemporary thought, engaging, among others, with Buber, Heidegger, and various Russian émigrés. Due to communist isolation, however, Staniloae was not heavily influenced by his contemporaries.

In fact, he was the victim of an unjust communist trial, which resulted in a five-year imprisonment. Staniloae preferred not to talk about these terrible five years in which he was mentally and physically abused through violent interrogations, isolation, hunger, and beatings.[24] Moreover, Staniloae confessed later that he learned the Jesus Prayer in prison.[25] He also admitted that those years of incarceration taught him that theology was not sufficiently in touch with the people. For Staniloae, the need to distance the Romanian Church from the manual styles of neo-Scholasticism was directly related to his attempt to reunite dogma and spirituality.[26]

Born and raised in communist Romania, I have bitter memories of this oppressive regime. When I began to study Staniloae, my inclination was to emphasize the negative consequences of living and writing under communist isolation. But recently, I have interviewed Roman Braga, a Romanian intellectual and hieromonk who knew Staniloae closely—they were convicted at the same trial. Braga was the first to point me to the positive consequences of writing under communist persecution. By being isolated from the West and even from the rest of the Orthodox world—says Braga—Staniloae developed a positive affirmation of the Orthodox faith, as opposed to a theology in opposition to other theologians. His theology could thus grow naturally, without being framed by polemics originating outside his tradition. I agree. But this does not mean that isolation is good in and of itself. One can only wonder how Staniloae's theology would have been enriched by more meaningful dialogues with other theologians. His limited (though intense) encounter with the West, however, is most helpful for contemporary ecumenism, especially concerning open sobornicity.

Open Sobornicity

In 1971, Staniloae wrote an article entitled "Open Sobornicity," a term aptly summarized by Lucian Turcescu as the acceptance of every valid theological insight in other theological traditions without running the risk of doctrinal relativism.[27]

Staniloae wrote this article as a positive reaction to the "Scripture and Tradition" document of the Faith and Order meeting in Aarhus (1964). The document notes the unity of the Gospel as reflected in diverse, complementary, or even contradictory biblical testimonies.[28] These testimonies reflect the diversity of God's actions in different historical circumstances and the diversity of human answers to God's actions. The

document recommends, in what Staniloae calls a justified and wise declaration, that biblical interpreters should not attach themselves to just one
biblical passage, as central as it may seem, because this would lead to a
misunderstanding of the richness and variety of the Bible. Staniloae, ap-
plying this recommendation to ecclesiology, argues that most schisms
derive from the unilateral attachment to a single scriptural passage without regard to the diversity of the Bible. Church unity became understood
not as a balanced unity of apparently contradictory points, but as a uniformity that suppressed the complexity of ecclesial life. Staniloae notes:

> The restoration of unity is for Western Christianity a matter of aban-
> doning the plane of exclusivist alternatives. It must rediscover the
> spirit of Orthodoxy which does not oppose one alternative or the
> other, but embraces in its teaching and equilibrium the points af-
> firmed by both forms of Western Christianity. . . . Of course, we
> must not pride ourselves with a satisfactory actualization of Ortho-
> doxy on the plane of spirituality and with efficacy in the lives of the
> faithful.[29] Besides this, Orthodox sobornicity nowadays must be en-
> riched with the spiritual values actualized by Western Christians.[30]

Staniloae's concern here is to call both sides to action and counteract
triumphal attitudes temp Orthodoxy from being open to Western values.
All churches need to learn from each other not only in order to maintain
diversity, but also to come to a symphonic unity without uniformity,[31] just
as the Scripture is unitary and diverse at the same time. Being confined
within one's own limits means to regard a certain experience of God's actions as ultimate and exclusive; this results in a limited experience of God.
However, God's actions in different historical contexts, although valuable, have a relative value in the sense that only if we search for the other
manifestations of God's revelation and bring them together in unity do
we find God fully. Concretely, Staniloae believed that Orthodoxy could
benefit from Catholicism by strengthening its unity, while it could learn
from Protestantism to give greater value to all instances of God's revelation. Staniloae concludes:

> Sobornicity is more than embracing in common all the modes of
> revelation and expression of God into the world or in life. . . .
> Sobornicity is also an increasingly comprehensive and embracing
> openness towards God who is above these [revelations]; it is a

continuous advancement in God's infinitely spiritual richness. This sobornicity that is *open*, transparent, and continuously surpassed, also implies a certain *theological pluralism* [emphases added].[32]

These considerations are not intended in a relativistic sense, as if there is no unique truth of revelation. Nor do they negate the understanding of the Orthodox Church as the one that possesses the fullness of truth. Instead, this view of sobornicity advances the idea that Orthodoxy can be enriched (even corrected) by other historical instances of God's revelation. At the same time, Staniloae added, Orthodoxy can bring an important contribution to the ecumenical movement by looking for the living spiritual core in doctrinal formulations. Rather than regarding its doctrinal formulae as rigid expressions opposed to equally rigid expressions used by the other churches, Orthodoxy should seek to uncover the living meanings of the doctrines of the other churches. The spiritual effects of these doctrines might be identical, despite differences in semantics and terminology, as is often (though not always) the case.[33] Not surprisingly, Staniloae adds: "Western theology often leads towards the same spiritual and mystical core of Revelation, and so by this path comes to merge with Orthodox theology."[34] Thus, Staniloae proposes a "spiritual interpretation" of dogmas as a means towards unity.

How is open sobornicity implemented concretely, here and now, when the East does not have Eucharistic communion with the West? Staniloae answers that it is through "spiritual intercommunion," a form of intercommunion that consists in study, common prayer, and action among Christians.[35] This intercommunion leads to open sobornicity because, through its exercise, "the Holy Spirit multiplies the 'connections' among Churches, [connections] through which their life in Christ may be transmitted from one Church to another, thus becoming more and more alike."[36]

In his own special way, despite his occasional polemical tone, Staniloae was considerably open to the West. He applied open sobornicity both knowingly and unknowingly. He relied on Western philosophers and theologians, and biblical and patristic scholarship. He also adopted the positive influences that Western theology had upon Orthodoxy, such as the three offices of Christ and the designation of seven sacraments, sometimes unaware of their Western origin.

The Three Offices of Christ

According to Andrew Louth, Staniloae makes the mistake of adopting a form of Orthodox manual theology that was influenced by Western theology. Louth notes:

> Christ's work of redemption is presented in terms of Christ's three-fold office as Prophet, Priest, and King. Fr. Dumitru declares that it is patristic (without any references), but it was only with Calvin's *Institutes* that the notion of Christ's threefold office assumed the structural significance with which he invests it. There is nothing wrong with an Orthodox borrowing from Calvin, though it would be gracious to admit it: Fr. Dumitru, however, was probably borrowing from Orthodox Dogmatics. But it is this dependence on the structure of earlier Orthodox Dogmatics (which borrowed their structure from Catholic and Protestant models) that may conceal dangers.[37]

First, there is no doubt that Christ's threefold office as Prophet, Priest,[38] and King is a theological construct consecrated by Calvin.[39] But it is certainly present in the biblical and patristic traditions[40] and, more importantly, it has become a part of the Orthodox ecclesiastical tradition. To suggest otherwise is to argue that the Holy Tradition of the Orthodox Church does not adapt to present challenges—that it exists only as a museum piece trapped in a mythical past. For Staniloae, it was perfectly acceptable that the adaptability of Orthodox theology to express itself in contemporary parlance could include the borrowing of valid concepts from other, non-Orthodox theological sources, so long as there was sufficient biblical and patristic grounds to do so. While Staniloae was likely unaware that the model of the three offices of Christ originated with Calvin, I take this use of that Western construction to be an example of his open sobornicity.

Louth's second criticism is that Staniloae's use of the traditional dogmatic structure may conceal dangers. Louth did not provide a more specific description of these dangers. Nor did he offer an alternative manner of presenting Christ's offices. Staniloae does both: He exposes some dangers of Scholastic descriptions of the three offices and departs from them. He reacts against Bulgakov's sharp separation of the three offices, as if before his Passion, Christ was only Prophet, during his Passion only Priest, and then at the end of his ministry only King.[41] Moreover, Staniloae criticizes the separation of the prophetic aspect of pastoral life from the priestly and kingly offices (to which Staniloae sometimes refers as the works of illumination, sanctification, and perfection, respectively). This separation is symptomatic of the Scholastic strict delimitation between theology, spirituality, and pastoral life, rooted in the separation between reason, feeling, and will, thus not looking at the human being as a whole. On the contrary, Staniloae argues, biblical and patristic writings point to the interdependence between these human capacities; hence, the three offices are sometimes designated as one ministry, that of sanctification.[42] Staniloae's discussion of the three offices of Christ goes well beyond a cold over-systematization of Christology, and is ultimately a theology with spiritual consequences: namely, our participation in Christ's three offices.

In summary, the notion of the threefold office of Christ originated with Calvin, and, if taken to its extreme, conceals the dangers of rationalization of theology, of separation between theology and spirituality, and—I might add in light of Staniloae's critique of Bulgakov—of the clear separation of the three offices, contrary to the Scriptures. Departing from such theology, Staniloae presents a neopatristic synthesis that leads to an encounter with God through participation in Christ's three offices in the Church through the Spirit without claiming to exhaust the mystery of God's saving presence in our lives.

The Designation of Seven Sacraments

Louth also criticizes Staniloae for adopting the Latin designation of seven sacraments:[43]

> The idea of seven sacraments, distinct and set apart from other sacramental acts, is a Western idea that only emerges in the twelfth century. It was only accepted by the Orthodox under pressure from the West, explicitly, by the Emperor Michael VIII Paleologos after the Council of Lyon (1274), and in reaction against Protestant influence by such as Dositheos and Peter Mogila. In the West it was bound up with the notion of Dominical institution and the mystique of the number seven. It is made easier in the West by the clear separation of baptism and confirmation. Fr. Dumitru has to keep to this separa-

tion, although it corresponds to no reality in Orthodox practice, and finds himself defending the Dominical institution in a very forced way. It also leads him to misunderstand some of the ingenuity devoted to this topic by Catholic theologians such as Karl Rahner. It also means that he draws a veil over the variety of ways in which sacraments are treated by the Fathers, very nearly sealing himself off from some of the sources of his theology (e.g., Nicholas Kabasilas, whom he quotes a good deal, both of whose major works, his *Commentary on the Divine Liturgy* and his *Life in Christ*, presuppose a rather different, more Dionysian approach to the sacraments). Here, it seems to me, the structure has become a strait-jacket, though what is pressed into the strait-jacket is often arresting and profoundly moving (it also means that some of his sacramental teaching appears elsewhere in his teaching on creation as a gift bearing the mark of the cross, for instance).[44]

Did Staniloae indeed defend the Dominical institution of all the sacraments "in a forced way"? A careful reading of *Dogmatics* (the basis of Louth's critique) shows that the "Dominical institution" is at best marginal. For example, Staniloae's treatment of marriage shows absolutely no dependence upon the "Dominican institution,"[45] and elsewhere Staniloae acknowledges that Christ did not explicitly institute all the sacraments. Instead, the Apostles have applied different events in Jesus's life or his sayings to their pastoral necessities, resulting in the sacraments.[46]

Furthermore, Louth considers that the demarcation of the seven sacraments from other sacramental acts is a Western idea that emerged only in the twelfth century.[47] He implies that Staniloae is unaware of the lateness of this development. But Staniloae is not only aware of this, but his discussion of the Western development is far more precise than Louth's.[48] Thus, unlike Staniloae's "involuntary acceptance" of a Western doctrine discussed above, he is aware that the number seven, designating the sacraments, originated in the West, and yet he adopts it. Was this an instance of open sobornicity?!

Ware, too, would probably disagree with Louth's criticism. While he believes that the idea of the formalization of seven sacraments is of Western origin, he also states that the setting apart of the seven sacraments from other sacramental acts is actually found in early Eastern Fathers well before the twelfth century. As is well known, there was no consensus on the number of the sacraments in the patristic period (it often ranged from two to ten) and those who identified seven actually included some liturgical acts other than "the seven," such as monastic tonsure.[49] It is not surprising that the Eastern Church, too, would want to settle the issue—that Staniloae advocates a solution first articulated in the West, I regard as another instance of open sobornicity.

In the passage cited above, Louth further criticizes Staniloae for failing to adopt a "Dionysian approach" to sacraments. Since Louth does not provide any further clarifications, one is left to presume that his criticism refers to Dionysius's combination of baptism and chrismation.[50] Louth contends that the separation between baptism and chrismation corresponds to no reality in Orthodox practice. But a more careful reading of Dionysius shows that the anointing of Myron does not refer exclusively to the completion of baptism, but also to the consecration of new church buildings—implying that it is a sacrament that can stand on its own. Moreover, Louth overlooks the fact that a person who has been baptized validly elsewhere is received in the Orthodox Church through chrismation, unaccompanied by baptism.[51] Hence, chrismation can actually be administered separate from baptism, and Staniloae was correct to count them as distinct sacraments.[52]

Finally, Staniloae repeatedly stresses that Eastern theology emphasizes the spiritual experience, the encounter with God, that the sacraments produce. The Church in its totality becomes a sacrament because Christ (the sacrament of God who is the origin of all sacramentality) unites himself with the Church and sustains the Church's continuous growth as a sacrament.[53] Such descriptions of the sacraments in no way conceal the dangers mentioned by Louth. Instead, they clearly reveal Staniloae's careful borrowing of Western concepts in the process of open sobornicity.

Louth, of course, is not an unsympathetic critic of Staniloae. He is actually very appreciative of Staniloae's contribution and notes that he wrote the *Dogmatics* under considerable restraints. In 1976, the Romanian Orthodox Church was begrudgingly granted permission by the Communist Party to publish a handbook of dogmatics for theological institutes. Knowing that the book would have to gain the approval of censors, Staniloae was forced to write his *Dogmatics* in the Scholastic form of Russian manuals.[54] As I have argued, Staniloae was able to produce a volume that was Scholastic in form but decisively non-Scholastic in content. It is worth noting, however, that Staniloae's adoption of Christ's threefold office and his appropriation of the seven sacraments both predate Communism.

I submit that it was Staniloae's choice to affirm Christ's threefold office and the seven sacraments because they were consistent with his understanding of open sobornicity. Through his creativity, Staniloae presented an intrinsically Orthodox theology that was enriched, not corrupted, by Western categories.

Can the West Influence the East?

Can Orthodox theologians introduce new categories that are not found in the Fathers? Can they adopt categories that originate in other Christian theologies and adapt them to Orthodox purposes? Despite criticizing Staniloae for doing precisely that, Louth responds elsewhere in the affirmative.[55] Before him, Florovsky did not call for the simple repetition of old patristic formulae, but for theologizing according to "the mind of the Fathers" in dialogue with others. For his part, Staniloae rejects the claim that manual theologies supply comprehensive formulae repeated mechanically because they inhibit the progress of theological thought. In contrast, he argues: "Today we think that the terms of every dogmatic formulation indicate—as though they were signposts—the entrance where we are admitted to the depths of the abyss, but we do not think that they assign limits to these depths."[56]

Staniloae constructively used Western insights to reach new depths of Orthodox theology. As previously stated, even concepts that are not of Orthodox origin can be incorporated into Orthodox ecclesial tradition, as long as they are consonant with Scripture and tradition, concerned with a personal encounter with God, and balance cataphatism with apophatism. Rather than being perceived as the foe, the West becomes the friend that helps the East develop its own legacy. East and West acknowledge the revealing work of God in each other, a revelation that extends beyond the patristic era.

One could propose two brief examples where Eastern theology, in its encounter with the West, might progress. First, we should reopen the discussion about the number of sacraments. In the context of a divided Christendom, the distinction between sacraments and sacramentals[57] is necessary; the Orthodox allow different forms of prayer with other denominations, but, as a general rule, prohibit sharing in the sacraments. There are, however, some notable exceptions, which include: (1) Any validly baptized Christian can be received in the Orthodox Church through chrismation without needing a second baptism; (2) the Orthodox Church currently performs the sacrament of marriage, even if only one of the recipients is Orthodox, and the US Joint Committee of Orthodox and Catholic Bishops decided to allow concelebrated weddings, a decision that, to my knowledge, has not been implemented yet;[58] and (3) the Orthodox Church recognizes some of the ordinations of other denominations. Concerning the latter, Staniloae was at the forefront of the ecumenical effort. As early as 1956, he argued that Anglican priests should be received in the Orthodox Church without reordination.[59] One should not draw too many conclusions from exceptions, but, at the same time, these exceptions point to the need to reevaluate the extent to which the Orthodox Church does not share in sacramental communion with other churches. Perhaps we should be more specific, and note that it is really only one sacrament for which the Orthodox Church does not share some level of sacramental communion with other Christian denominations—the Eucharist.

Second, in its encounter with the West, the East might rediscover apophatism. I refer here neither to Christos Yannaras's "apophatism of the person" (understood as the infinite possibilities of encountering the human or divine person),[60] nor to Staniloae's experiential apophatism. I believe that Orthodox theology excels in these regards. Instead, I refer to negative theology, where terms do not fully express the divine mystery. This is the aspect of apophatism that Lossky has consecrated, precisely in his most vehement criticism of the West for its lack of apophatism. And yet, it seems that contemporary Western, not Eastern, theologians are most determined to find new ways to express the Trinitarian theology and alternatives to the person-nature terminology.[61] Perhaps discouraged by these Western attempts, Eastern theologians did not follow the same path. And yet, the Cappadocians were adamant that God is above our linguistic categories, and Orthodox theologians need to produce a neopatristic synthesis that would bring to light the divine mystery, revealing more and more the superabundant, luminous darkness of the Trinity. In recent times, the West seems to lead the path in the direction traced by the Cappadocians or the Areopagite.

Conclusion

Staniloae played a critical role in moving Orthodox theology beyond the manual tradition, and he did so through a constructive engagement with the West. In the process, Staniloae helped to establish a valuable methodology, that of open sobornicity, which offers a platform for future ecumenical initiatives. What is perhaps most remarkable about Staniloae's achievement is that his receptivity to the Western categories of the three offices of Christ and the seven sacraments enabled him to achieve a level of neopatristic theology that so many other modern Orthodox theologians have advocated but not delivered themselves. In Staniloae's hands, however, a Western-inspired neopatristic synthesis balances cataphatism and apophatism, embraces a personal encounter with God, is rooted in the biblical, patristic, and liturgical traditions of the Church, and engages contemporary thought. In short, it is Orthodox theology.

NOTES

Orthodox Naming of the Other: A Postcolonial Approach / George E. Demacopoulos and Aristotle Papanikolaou

We thank Ben Dunning and Paul Gavrilyuk for their many helpful suggestions to an earlier version of this essay.

1. As is well known, Constantinopolitan missionaries to the Balkans helped to develop and encouraged the use of Slavonic in the Balkans, whereas Frankish missionaries insisted on Latin. The debate came to a head when the Byzantine missionaries Cyril and Methodius were arrested by the Franks and sent to Rome for trial where they were ultimately vindicated.

2. So many Greek have emigrated to Australia that it is commonly believed that Melbourne has the highest Greek population of any city outside of Athens.

3. By "imagined" we do not mean that they are fictional or deliberately untrue, but that they are comprised of presumptions and assumptions that are not based upon empirical encounters with the other.

4. There is no textual evidence to indicate that Christians in the first millennium identified themselves as Eastern or Western in order to differentiate themselves from one another. It is true, of course, that in the documents surrounding the Council of Ephesus (431), the language of "Easterners" is applied to the "heretical" supporters of John of Antioch in order to differentiate their theology from that of the See of Alexandria and Rome, even though neither of the latter are ever referred to in the same documents as "Westerners."

5. As numerous scholars have shown, the Roman Empire was not converted to Christianity overnight simply because Constantine legalized the religion. Some of the most important studies of the past generation include Ramsey McMullen's *The Christianizing of the Roman Empire* (New Haven, Conn.: Yale University Press, 1984), Robin Lane Fox, *Pagans and Christians* (New York: Knopf, 1987), and Averil Cameron's *Christianity and the Rhetoric of Empire* (Berkeley: University of California Press, 1994).

6. Of course, the experience of Eastern Christians living under Muslim rule in these regions was decidedly different.

7. John Chrysostom's appeal to Innocent of Rome at the time of his exile provides a famous example.

8. While it is true that Gregory's Eastern correspondence was larger than anyone else of his day, it is also true that he has the largest surviving correspondence of anyone from the ancient world.

9. For the many problems of the Augustine-versus-the-East narrative that all too frequently haunts theological and historical scholarship, see Demacopoulos and Papanikolaou, *Orthodox Readings of Augustine*.

10. In particular, this was true for Basil of Caesarea and Cyril of Alexandria.

11. For this history, see the excellent work of A. Edward Sieciensky, *The Filioque: History of a Doctrinal Controversy* (Oxford: Oxford University Press, 2010), especially 51–71.

12. Ibid., 69.

13. Ibid.

14. Ibid., 98.

15. Tia Kolbaba, *Inventing Latin Heretics: Byzantines and the Filioque in the Ninth Century* (Kalamazoo: Medieval Institute Publications, 2008).

16. In 1339, Barlaam of Calabira informed the papal court: "That which separates the Greeks from you is not so much a difference in dogma as the hatred of the Greeks for the Latins provoked by the wrongs they have suffered" (Barlaam of Calabira, *MPG* 151.1332. Translated by D. Geanakoplos in his *Byzantine East and Latin West* [New York: Barnes and Noble, 1966], 91). Concerning Barlaam's career, see Tia Kolbaba, "Barlaam the Calabrian: Three Treatises on Papal Primacy, Introduction, Edition and Translation," *Revue des études byzantines* 53 (1995): 41–115, especially 50–63.

17. Constantine Stilbes was the first to publish a series of grievances against the crusaders. Writing from exile in 1213, Stilbes produced a catalogue of criticisms, ranging from theological errors of the clergy to criminal actions by crusaders. His criticisms were comprehensible by a wide audience. Stilbes's text is important because it serves as a point of demarcation—prior to 1213 there had been several Byzantine critiques of Latin doctrine (*filioque*, Papal primacy, etc.), but Stilbes's criticisms, and many that followed, took a much more aggressive ap-

proach to Roman theology and Latin abuses in the East. See Jean Darrouzès, "Le mémoire de Constantin Stilbès contre les Latins," *Revue des Études byzantines* 21 (1965): 50–100. See, also, Michael Angold, "Greeks and Latins after 1204: The Perspective of Exile," in *Latins and Greeks in the Eastern Mediterranean after 1204*, ed. B. Arbel et al. (London: Frank Cass, 1989), 63–86.

18. Demetrios Chomatenos, the bishop of Ochrid, Serbia (ca. 1216–36) became the leading proponent of clerical opposition to the Latins on the Greek mainland. Of course, the fact that he was so insistent suggests two important things. First, we can assume that the interaction he so frequently critiqued must have been quite common. Second, that he came to have a personal investment (theological, political, or otherwise) in perpetuating a radical distinction between Orthodox and Latin teaching. For a critical edition of his letters and canonical judgments, see Gunter Prinzing, ed., *Demetrii Chomateni: Ponomata Diaphora* (Berlin: Walter de Gruyter, 2002).

19. An analysis of the Frankish experience in both the Peloponnesus of Greece, as well as the regions around Thessaloniki, in fact, demonstrates that the Franks enjoyed a good relationship with their Greek laborers, possibly even better than that of the Byzantine lords who had preceded them. See Angold, *The Fourth Crusade: Event and Context* (London: Longman, 2003), 139f.

20. In this regard, Homi Bhabha's interest in the work of Franz Fanon could prove to be especially rewarding as Bhabha explores the extent to which the colonized can actually disrupt (through mimicry and mockery) the sensibilities of the colonizer. See, especially, Bhabha, "Interrogating identity: Frantz Fanon and the Postcolonial Prerogative" and "Of Mimicry and Man: The Ambivalence of Colonial Discourse," in his *The Location of Culture* (London: Routledge, 1994), 57–93 and 121–31.

21. Gennadios Scholarios probably serves as the best example here. In contrast to the apologetic narrative that posits Scholarios as having abandoned his fascination with Thomas Aquinas at roughly the same time that he came under the influence of Mark of Ephesus (i.e., in the 1440s), we note that Scholarios actually published an epitome for Thomas's *Summa contra gentiles* and *Summa theologica* in 1464, more than fifteen years after he began his vociferous condemnation of the Council of Florence.

22. Gregory Palamas's critique, however brief, of syllogistic reasoning surely had more to do with his condemnation of Barlaam's reliance on pre-Christian authors than it was a critique of Western-styled Scholasticism. See, for example, his *Triads* in the section on apophaticism.

23. Angold, *The Fourth Crusade*, 202–3. It is noteworthy that many of the Greek landowners in the Peloponnesus were able to come to a peaceful solution with their Frankish overlords, in large part Frankish settlers in the Peloponnesus were the most tolerant of Eastern Christian religious traditions.

24. On the links between Orthodox and Hellenistic identity that emerged, for the first time, in the wake of the Fourth Crusade, see James Skedros, "Hellenism and Byzantium," *St. Vladimir's Theological Quarterly* 54 (2010): 345–63.

25. See Angold, *The Fourth Crusade: Event and Context* (Harlow, U.K.: Pearson Longman, 2003), especially 202–3.

26. The widely divergent interpretations of the quintessential "Western" theologian, Augustine of Hippo, provides an excellent case in point. See Demacopoulos and Papanikolaou, "Augustine and the Orthodox: The 'West' in the East," in Demacopoulos and Papanikolaou, *Orthodox Readings of Augustine*, 11–40.

27. The Ottoman millet system allowed different religious sects to self-govern according to their confessional inclinations (Muslims, Orthodox Christians, Armenian Christians, Jews, etc.). During the sixteenth and seventh centuries, a patriarchate of Serbia emerged and was granted independent status. In the nineteenth century, the Bulgarian Church was also granted independence from the Orthodox millet, which was governed by the patriarch of Constantinople.

28. For a revisionist view that suggests that the Third-Rome title was not actively pushed until the nineteenth century, see, especially, Marshall Poe, "Moscow, the Third Rome: The Origins and Transformations of a 'Pivotal Moment,'" *Jahrbücher für Geschichte Osteuropas* 49 (2001): 412–29.

29. According to Donald Ostrowski, the claim actually emerged from an inter-Russian contest for primacy between the See of Moscow and the See of Novgorod. See Ostrowski, *Muscovy and the Mongols: Cross-Cultural Influences on the Steppe Frontier* (Cambridge: Cambridge University Press, 2002), especially 219–33. See also Daniel Roland, "Moscow—The Third Rome or New Israel?," *The Russian Review* 55 (1996): 591–614.

30. Poe's examination on this point is compelling. He notes that Filofei's interest in promoting the title was directly linked to an attempt to convince the secular leaders of Russia of the need to adhere to the traditional tenets of the Orthodox confession (Poe, "Moscow, the Third Rome," especially 416–18).

31. See Demacopoulos, "The Popular Reception of the Council of Florence in Constantinople, 1439–53," *St. Vladimir's Theological Quarterly* 42 (1997): 347–71.

32. J. L. Black, *Citizens for the Fatherland: Education, Educators, and Pedagogical Ideals in Eighteenth-Century Russia* (New York: Columbia University Press, 1979).

33. On clerical education, see Gregory Freeze, *The Russian Levites: Parish Clergy in the Eighteenth Century* (Cambridge, Mass.: Harvard University Press, 1977).

34. See Alexander Sydorenko, *The Kievan Academy in the Seventeenth Century* (Ottawa: Ottawa University Press, 1977) and Black, *Citizens for the Fatherland*, 17.

35. See Demacopoulos and Papanikolaou, "Augustine and the Orthodox," 21.

36. "The fascinating area of Russian religious philosophy therefore falls outside the proper scope of this volume, even though there will be several references

to its influence." See Mary B. Cunningham and Elizabeth Theokritoff, "Who Are Orthodox Christians? A Historical Introduction," in *The Cambridge Companion to Orthodox Christian Theology*, ed. Mary B. Cunningham and Elizabeth Theokritoff (Cambridge: Cambridge University Press, 2008), xvi.

37. The grave error, from Romanides's perspective, was that the Franks lacked a concept of deification and the philosophical capacity to distinguish between God's essence and his energies. On the many anachronisms in Romanides's critique, see Demacopoulos and Papanikolaou, "Augustine and the Orthodox," especially 28–33. See, also, Demacopoulos, "History, Postcolonial Theory, and Some New Possibilities for Recovering the Theological Past," in *Neo-Patristic Synthesis or Post-Patristic Theology: Can Orthodox Theology Be Contextual?*, ed. Pantelis Kalaitzidis (Volos, Greece: Volos Theological Academy, forthcoming).

38. For evidence that Augustine did not reject *theosis*, see Demacopoulos and Papanikolaou, *Orthodox Readings of Augustine*.

39. See Aristotle Papanikolaou, *The Mystical as Political: Democracy and (Non-Radical) Orthodoxy* (Notre Dame, Ind.: University of Notre Dame Press, 2012). See, also, Rowan Williams, ed., *Sergius Bulgakov: Towards the Orthodox Political Theology* (London: T&T Clark, 2001).

40. See Papanikolaou, *The Mystical as Political*, especially ch. 1.

41. John P. Burgess, "Christ and Culture Revisited: Contributions from the Recent Russian Orthodox Debate," *Journal of the Society of Christian Ethics* 31:2 (2011): 55–74.

42. The phrase "subaltern" originated with Antonio Gramsci, who likely employed the term to refer to the marginalized lower-class worker who cannot control his or her social status. The term was first appropriated by a group of postcolonial theorists working on the Asian Subcontinent, known as the Subaltern Studies Group. Spivak, a member of the group, critiqued what she believed to be a reckless use of the term. See Leon de Kock, "Interview with Gayatri Chakravorty Spivak: New Nation Writers Conference in South Africa," *A Review of International English Literature* 23 (1992): 29–47.

43. Gayatri Spivak, "Can the Subaltern Speak?," in *Marxism and the Interpretation of Culture*, ed. C. Nelson and L Grossberg (Urbana: University of Illinois Press, 1988), 271–313.

44. See, especially, Bhabha's essays "The Other Question" and "Of Mimicry and Man," in his *Location of Culture* (London: Routledge, 1994), 94–131. For Bhabha, the subaltern not only "speaks back" to the colonizer through an appropriation and transformation of the mechanisms of cultural domination, but also subversively mimics the colonizer in the process.

45. See Bhabha, "The Commitment to Theory," in his *Location of Culture*, especially 31–35.

46. Long before Samuel Huntington's provocative essay on the future of world conflict, Orthodox historians and theologians were explaining the Eastern Orthodox / Roman Catholic divide as a clash of cultural ideologies. See Huntington, "The Clash of Civilizations," presented at the *American Enterprise Institute* (1992).

47. Fr. Florovsky repeatedly made the claim that the Russian theological tradition of his day had abandoned (through Western influence) the purity of a late-ancient Christian Hellenism. See, for example, his "Christianity and Civilization," *St Vladimir's Seminary Quarterly* 1.1 (1952), 13–20. For more on this, see the excellent essay in this volume by Paul Gavrilyuk.

48. Indeed, one of the most fascinating ways of viewing the modern Orthodox quest for an authentic Orthodox identity, unfettered by Western influence, is to examine the extent to which the spokesmen for this narration employ the tools and terminology of the Western intellectual tradition in their search for and narration of Eastern purity. Whether it is the historicist narratives of Florovsky and Rominides or the philosophical metasystem of Yannaras, there is little denying the extent to which the twentieth-century spokesmen of Orthodox identity have been trained in and have resorted to the academic tools of the Western academic enterprise to achieve their goals.

49. For Bhabha, mimicry is intrinsic to the colonial discourse, a discourse between the colonizer and the colonized; it affords the colonizer a way of making the colonized like its master, but because the discourse is similar, rather than identical ("almost the same but not quite"), there remains enough difference to justify colonial rule. Reciprocally, for the colonized, mimicry offers a mechanism of subversion, which ultimately undermines or has the potential to undermine the colonial project insofar as it creates an alternative "normative knowledge." For Bhabha, however, any recognition of the subversive effects of mimicry remain subconscious (Bhabha, "Of Mimicry and Man," in *Location of Culture*). See also Huddart, 60.

50. While space will not permit an exhaustive analysis of his theory, it is worth noting that Bhabha seems to suggest that the process of subversive mimicry is subconscious, even though it can be recognized after the fact and thereby can be transformed into a strategy of resistance.

51. Perhaps one of the most remarkably ironic examples of this "use the West to condemn the West" is provided by Fr. Michael Azkoul in his *The Influence of Augustine of Hippo on the Orthodox Church* (Lewiston, N.Y.: Mellon Press, 1991).

52. Chakrabarty, *Provincializing Europe: Postcolonial Thought and Historical Difference* (Princeton: Princeton University Press, 2008), 237–55.

53. The primary exception to this rule would be the increasing community of scholars who view Jesus and/or Paul as "resisting empire." For an important survey of postcolonial studies in the field of New Testament studies, see Stephen

Moore, *Empire and the Apocalypse: Postcolonialism and the New Testament* (Sheffield, U.K.: Sheffield Phoenix Press, 2006).

54. Ann Joh, for example, has argued that the ancient Korean concept of *jeong* provides the modern theologian with a vocabulary and conceptual framework missing in colonial (i.e., Western European) Christianity, and that it is only through the insight of *jeong* that we can adequately understand what she calls the "double gesture" of the cross. For Joh, the double gesture relates to the way in which the cross simultaneously (and subversively) affirms that it represents both pain and suffering as well as love and compassion (Ann Joh, *The Heart of the Cross: A Postcolonial Christology* [Louisville, Ky.: Westminster John Knox Press, 2006]).

55. Young carefully differentiates the categories of "imperialism" and "colonialism," arguing that there is a fundamental difference between the empires of Rome or Byzantium and the colonial projects of Western Europe in the early modern period. While Young's thesis works for the examples he provides, it does not seem to apply to the Norman and Venetian "colonies" in the East during the era of the Crusades, nor does it account for the Eastern Christian and Western Christian interaction that occurred within the Ottoman empire (Robert Young, *Postcolonialism: An Historical Introduction* [Oxford: Blackwell's, 2001], especially 16–43).

Perceptions and Realities in Orthodox-Catholic Relations Today: Reflections on the Past, Prospects for the Future / Robert F. Taft, S.J.

Abbreviations used in the notes

AAS = *Acta Apostolicae Sedis.*
DHGE = *Dictionnaire d'histoire et de géographie ecclésiastiques.*
DSp = *Dictionnaire de spiritualité.*
ECJ = *Eastern Churches Journal.*
ECP = Eastern Christian Publications, Fairfax, VA.
GCS = Die griechischen christlichen Schriftsteller.
OCA = *Orientalia Christiana Analecta.*
OCA 251 = Robert F. Taft, ed., *The Christian East: Its Institutions & Its Thought. A Critical Reflection.* Papers of the International Scholarly Congress for the 75th Anniversary of the Pontifical Oriental Institute, Rome, May 30–June 5, 1993 (OCA 251, Rome 1996).
OCP = *Orientalia Christiana Periodica.*
ODB = *The Oxford Dictionary of Byzantium,* ed. A. Kazhdan et al., 3 vols. (New York: Oxford University Press, 1991).

OKS = *Ostkirchliche Studien.*
OSBM = *Ordo Sancti Basilii Magni.*
PIO = Pontificio Istituto Orientale, Rome.
SL = *Studia liturgica.*

1. Translated from the French as reported in *Irénikon* 73 (2000): 112.

2. Translated from the French as reported in *Irénikon* 66 (1993): 135. In the same vein, the *Irénikon* obituary of Protopresbyter John Meyendorff, noted Orthodox historian and theologian and a personal friend of mine, says he had "a friendship for many Catholics and Catholic institutions that was exigent and sometimes severe" (*Irénikon* 65 [1992]: 544).

3. For an Orthodox affirmation of the "sister Churches" theology, see Metropolitan Maximos (Aghiorgoussis) of Pittsburgh, "Toward Healing of Wounds: The Balamand Statement," ECJ 4, no. 1 (1997): 6–23, especially 15. For the Catholic point of view, see Michael A. Fahey, S.J., *Orthodox and Catholic Sister Churches: East Is West and West Is East* (The Père Marquette Lecture in Theology, Marquette University, Milwaukee, Wis. 1996). Note especially 7–14 on the history of the expression "sister Churches" in Catholic usage.

4. Concrete instances in Robert F. Taft, "The Problem of 'Uniatism' and the 'Healing of Memories': Anamnesis, not Amnesia," Annual Kelly Lecture, The University of St. Michael's College of the University of Toronto, Toronto, ON, Canada, December 1, 2000 *Logos* 41–42 (2000–2001): 155–96, here 176–80; reprinted in Mark M. Morozowich, ed., *Saints—Sanctity—Liturgy. For Robert Francis Taft, S.J. at Seventy, January 9, 2002. Symposium Papers and Memorabilia* (Fairfax, VA: ECP, 2006) 201–42, here 221–26; German translation: "Das Problem des 'Uniatismus' und der 'Heilung der Errinerungen': Anamesis, nicht Amnesia," *ContaCOr*, Collegium Orientale Eichstätt und Oriens Occidens e. V., Eichstätt, Germany 4, no. 2 (2002): 102–25.

5. Published in the journal *Edinaja Cerkov'—One Church*, the official organ of the Russian Orthodox exarchate of the patriarchate of Moscow in the United States. I have been unable to recover the exact reference to this statement, which I cite here from my student notes of many years ago. For a very different vision of what Jesuit work for Russia should comprise, see Vincenzo Poggi, "*Le travail futur*, d'après Philippe de Régis S.J. (1897–1955)," OCP 58 (1992): 5–21.

6. Chapter 8 of the new *Cambridge History of Christianity*, vol. 5: *Eastern Christianity*, ed. Michael Angold (Cambridge: Cambridge University Press, 2006) furnishes a recent example.

7. This has been detailed in a recent study every Jesuit should read: Ernst Chr. Suttner, "Jesuiten—Helfer und Ärgernis für die Kirchen des Ostens," *Der christliche Osten* 49, no. 2 (1994): 80–95. Fr. Suttner, Professor Emeritus of the University of Vienna, is a Catholic priest, visiting professor at my Jesuit-run Pontifical Oriental Institute in Rome, and no enemy of the Jesuits.

8. In none of this am I judging anyone's motives or good will, but good will, the cheapest of all virtues, cannot be used to excuse mistakes before the bar of history, but only at the Last Judgment. Three recent books illustrate all too painfully what a comedy of errors modern Catholic policy toward the Christian East, and especially toward Russia, has been: Giuseppe M. Croce, *La Badia Greca di Grottaferrata e la Rivista "Roma e l'Oriente." Cattolicesimo e ortodossia fra unionismo ed ecumenismo (1799–1923), con appendici e documenti inediti,* 2 vols. (Vatican: Libreria Editrice Vaticana, 1990); Angelo Tamborra, *Chiesa cattolica e Ortodossia russa. Due secoli di confronto e dialogo. Dalla Santa Allianza ai nostri giorni* (Cinisello Balsamo: Edizioni Paoline, 1992); Léon Tretjakewitsch, *Bishop Michel d'Herbigny SJ and Russia. A Pre-Ecumenical Approach to Christian Unity* (Das östliche Christentum, Neue Folge, Bd. 39. Würzburg: Augustinus-Verlag, 1990). In this context it is not irrelevant to emphasize that the first two of these books are by Catholic authors. It is not often (if indeed ever) that one sees such devastatingly honest self-criticism of Orthodox activities from the pen of an Orthodox writer.

9. For all historical Jesuit figures mentioned, see *Diccionario histórico de la Compañía de Jesús. Biográfico-temático,* ed. Charles E. O'Neill, S.J. and Joaquín M. Domínguez, S.J., 4 vols. (Rome: Institutum Historicum S.I./Madrid: Universidad Pontificia Comillas, 2001).

10. Translated James Brodrick, *The Progress of the Jesuits (1556–79)* (Chicago: Loyola University Press, 1986), 245, from *Monumenta Historics Societatis Iesu: Monumenta Ignatiana,* series prima, 6:74.

11. Namely, the period before 1773–1814, when the Jesuit order was suppressed as a result of pressure from the Bourbon monarchies.

12. I put the word "Uniatism" in quotation marks because it is now continuously used by some authors as a pejorative term of contempt, like "papist." I believe that to use it as a name for Eastern Catholics can be gratuitously offensive. To permit without demur its use in official Catholic-Orthodox ecumenical documents is impermissible and ultimately counter-productive. Here, I use the term "Uniatism" in precisely that pejorative sense, just as a Catholic might use the term "papalism" for some exaggerated interpretations of the Petrine office without meaning thereby "Catholicism." Because it is *that* phenomenon of "Uniatism" too—i.e., not just the reality of Eastern Christians in union with Rome but the prejudicial way that phenomenon, those groups, and their history are viewed, rightly or wrongly—which like everything else in history must be studied with objectivity and fairness.

13. I have expressed my views on the whole question in the study cited above in note 4.

14. For a fair and objective analysis of the problem by a Catholic priest-scholar, see Ernst Chr. Suttner, *Church Unity: Union or Uniatism? Catholic-Orthodox*

Ecumenical Perspectives (Rome: Centre for Indian and Inter-religious Studies, and Bangalore: Dhamaram Publications, 1991). For a scholarly sociological analysis of the phenomenon, see Josef Macha, *Ecclesiastical Unification: A Theoretical Framework Together with Case Studies from the History of Latin-Byzantine Relations* (Rome: PIO, 1974).

15. Kallistos T. Ware, "Orthodox and Catholics in the Seventeenth Century: Schism or Intercommunion," in *Schism, Heresy and Religious Protest*, ed. D. Baker, Studies in Church History 9 (Cambridge: Cambridge University Press, 1972), 259–76, here 259–60. Published in serial without wide diffusion, this article has not received the attention it deserves. In addition, See most recently Giuseppe Croce, "Les Églises orientales," in *L'Âge de raison (1620/30–1750)*, ed. Marc Venard et al., vol. 9: (Paris: Desclée, 1997), 539–612. Among the sources Croce cites, see especially Georg Hofmann, "Athos e Roma," *Orientalia Christiana* 5, no. 2 (Rome: PIO 1925); id., *Vescovadi cattolici della Grecia,* I: *Chios*, Orientalia Christiana 34 (Rome: PIO 1934); II: *Tinos*, OCA 107 (Rome: PIO 1936); III: *Syros*, OCA 112 (Rome: PIO 1937); IV: *Naxos*, OCA 115 (Rome: PIO 1938); V: *Thera-Santorino*, OCA 130 (Rome: PIO 1941). On Hofmann, a veritable devourer of archives, see Vincenzo Poggi, "Patriarchi ecumenici e peregrinazioni archivistiche di Georg Hofmann S.J. (1885–1956)," in *Le Patriarcat de Constantinople aux XIVe au XVIe siècles: Rupture et continuité*, Actes du colloque international, Rome, 5–6–7 décembre 2005. Dossiers byzantins—7 (Paris: Centre d'études byzantines néo-helléniques et sud-est européennes, Écoles des Hautes Études en Sciences Sociales, 2007): 73–90. I am indebted to my confrère and colleague Fr. Poggi for providing me with an offprint of his precious study. On the Jesuits among the Greeks, see also Vitalien J. Laurent, "La mission des Jésuites à Naxos de 1627 à 1643," *Echos d'Orient* 33 (1934): 218–26, 354–75; 34 (1935): 97–105, 179–204, 350–67, 473–81. I am grateful to my friend and colleague Msgr. Croce for assisting me in locating again these references to sources I had read long ago.

16. "Toutes les formes de la *commmunicatio in sacris*" (Croce, "Les Églises orientales," 605).

17. Ibid. 605–7; Croce, *La Badia Greca di Grottaferrata*, especially vol. 1, 131ff, 258–65, 295–305; vol. 2, chap 4, especially 265–82; Carlo Gatti & Cirillo Korolevskij, *I riti e le chiese orientali*, vol. 1 (the only volume to appear): *Il rito bizantino e le Chiese Bizantine* (Genova-Sampierdarena: Libreria Salesiana Editrice, 1942): 423–35.

18. See the detailed account of this insanity in Croce, *La Badia Greca di Grottaferrata* 2:267–82 plus the invaluable footnotes.

19. Recently among the large number of books on the topic: Margaret MacMillan, *The Uses and Abuses of History* (New York: Modern Library, 2008).

20. A ghastly crime recently preserved for posterity, lest we dare to forget, in an anthology of photos recording the horrors man can inflict upon man: James

Allen et al., *Without Sanctuary: Lynching Photography in America* (Santa Fe, N. Mex.: Twin Palms Publishing, 2000).

21. Yves Congar, *After Nine Hundred Years: The Background of the Schism between the Eastern and Western Churches* (New York: Fordham University Press, 1959); Robert B. Eno, *The Rise of the Papacy*, Theology and Life Series 32 (Wilmington, Del.: Michael Glazier, 1990); Jean-Marie R. Tillard, *The Bishop of Rome* (Wilmington, Del.: Michael Glazier, 1983); Tillard, *Church of Churches: The Ecclesiology of Communion* (Collegeville: The Liturgical Press, 1992); Francis Dvornik, *Byzantium and the Roman Primacy* (New York: Fordham University Press, 1966).

22. Dvornik, *Byzantium and the Roman Primacy.*

23. For an objective account of these events and their aftermath, the latest study is Johannn Marte & Oleh Turij, *Die Union von Brest (1596) in Geschichte und Geschichtsschreibung: Versuch einer Zwischenbilanz*, PRO Oriente (Lviv, Ukraine: Institut für Kirchengeschichte der Ukrainischen Katholischen Universität, 2008). See also Borys A. Gudziak, *Crisis and Reform: The Kyivan Metropolitanate, the Patriarchate of Constantinople, and the Genesis of the Union of Brest*, Harvard Series in Ukrainian Studies (Cambridge, Mass.: Ukrainian Research Institute—Harvard University Press, 1998); Ambroise Jobert, *De Luther à Mohila: La Pologne dans la crise de la Chrétienté, 1517–1648*, Collection historique de l'Institut d'études slaves (Paris: Institut d'études slaves, 1974). For briefer accounts, see Sophia Senyk, "Vicissitudes de l'Union de Brest au XVIIe siècle," *Irénikon* 65 (1992): 462–87; Senyk, "The Background of the Union of Brest," *Analecta OSBM* 21 (1996): 103–44; Silverio Saulle, "L'Unione di Brest. Genesi e sviluppi storici," *Studi sull'Oriente cristiano* 2, no. 1 (1998): 137–64; and 2, no. 2 (1998): 137–67.

24. Before the era of "Uniatism" at the end of the sixteenth century, Rome had worked for a general reunion with the Orthodox while at the same time striving for conversions to the Latin rite. See for example, the July 18, 1231 bull of Gregory IX in Atanasius G. Welykyj, ed., *Documenta Pontificum Romanorum Historiam Ucrainae Illustrantia (1075–1953)*, 2 vols., Analecta OSBM, series II, section III (Rome: PP. Basiliani, 1953–54), vol. 1 (1075–1700) 19–20, and numerous other pertinent documents; also James J. Zatko, "The Union of Suzdal, 1222–52," *The Journal of Ecclesiastical History* 8 (1957): 33–52, here 36; Albert M. Ammann, *Kirchenpolitische Wandlungen im Ostbaltikum bis zum Tode Alexander Newski's: Studien zum Werden der russischen Orthodoxie*, OCA 105 (Rome: PIO 1936), ch. 3.3.

25. Cited in Cyrille Karalevskij [*sic*], "Le clergé occidental et l'apostolot dans l'Orient asiatique et gréco-slave," extrait de la *Revue apologétique* (1923); 25n3 = *Revue apologétique*, 18e année—tome 35 (oct.-mars 1922–23) 276 note 3. The French stormy petrel and scourge of "Uniatism," Jean-François-Joseph Charon, a.k.a.

Cyril Korolevskij, born in Caen on December 16, 1878, and died in Rome on April 19, 1959, took a while to decide what his name was to be, from Charon, to Karalevskij, or Korolevskij/Korolevsky. On K. see Eugène Tisserant, "Father Cyril Korolevsky. A Biographical Note," in *Metropolitan Andrew (1865–1944)*, by Cyril Korolevsky, translated and revised by Serge Keleher (L'viv: Stauropegion, 1993) 17–36; also Croce, *La Badia Greca di Grottaferrata* 2:32–54, 283–96, and the further references there, 33–35 note 71; and now especially the massive Cyrille Korolevskij, *Kniga bytija moego (Le livre de ma vie : Mémoires autobiographiques*, Texte établi, édité et annoté par Giuseppe M. Croce, Collectanea Archivi Vaticani 45 [Vatican: Archives Secrètes Vaticanes 2007]).

26. See the work cited in note 22 above. In the well-informed, balanced, and objective view of historian Ambroise Jobert, "The Union of Brest is not the work of Polish or Roman policies. The Ruthenian bishops, irritated by the reforms of [Constantinopolitan patriarch] Jeremias II, requested it, the Polish court decided, not without hesitation, to risk it, and Rome received the Ruthenians into union without making any precise commitments in their regard" (*De Luther à Mohila* 343).

27. For the theological significance of this unique and historic act, see Pierre Gervais, "La demande de pardon de Jean-Paul II et ses implications théologiques," *Nouvelle revue théologique* 123 (2001): 4–18; also "Chronique des Églises," *Irénikon* 3–4 (2000): 455–61.

28. SOP=*Service orthodoxe de presse* 247 (April 2000): 14.

29. "Bischof Pawel: 'Mea culpa ist der Orthodoxie unnötig.'" KNS press interview in Vienna as reported by G. Illmeier in *Pressespiegel pro Oriente* Nr. 115 (2000): 19–20: see also *Glaube in der 2. Welt* 28, no. 6 (2000): 6–7.

30. In the Italian original: "Di tutte le discordanze tra le Chiese d'Oriente e d'Occidente quella che può essere compresa più è il perché e il come la Chiesa d'Occidente ha fondata la sua speranza nella sua forza mondana." And again "Le Chiese ortodosse dell'Oriente non hanno mai cercato il potere mondano e non hanno mai appoggiato la loro esistenza e vita su di esso": Gianni Valente, Intervista con Bartolomeo I, patriarca ecumenico di Costantinopoli: "Le radice dello scisma: un pensiero mondano nella Chiesa," in *30 GIORNI NELLA CHIESA E NEL MONDO. Mensile internazionale diretto da Giulio Andreotti* (January 2004); text also available online at http://www.30giorni.it/it/articlo.asp?id=2524.

31. See Abram M. Hubbell, "The *Codex Justinianus* and the Forced Conversion of the Jews in Early Byzantine Society," (*Shifting Frontiers in Late Antiquity II*: "*The Transformation of Law and Society During Late Antiquity*," University of South Carolina, Columbia, SC, March 12–16, 1997) published in the Congress Acta. See http://www.sc.edu/Itantsoc/shifprg2.htm. I have a printout of this paper but have not yet seen the published Congress Acta.

32. Nina G. Garsoïan, "Secular Jurisdiction over the Armenian Church (Fourth-Seventh Centuries)," in *Okeanos: Essays Presented to Ihor Ševčenko*, ed.

Cyril Mango and Omeljan Pritsak, Harvard Ukrainian Studies 7 (Cambridge, Mass.: Harvard University Press 1983): 228; Garsoïan, "The Armenian Church between Byzantium and the East," in *Treasures in Heaven: Armenian Art, Religion, and Society* (symposium organized by Thomas F. Mathews and Roger S. Wieck, The Pierpont Morgan Library, New York, N.Y., May 21–22, 1994): 3–12, here 7 and the references in 11n25. See also Suttner, *Church Unity* 39ff.

33. See James F. Coakley, *The Church of the East and the Church of England: A History of the Archbishop of Canterbury's Assyrian Mission* (Oxford: Clarendon Press, 1992), 216–34.

34. Jean-Claude Roberti, *Les Uniates*, Fides 44 (Paris: Cerf 1992): 102–7; William S. Schneirla, "The Western Rite in the Orthodox Church," *St. Vladimir's Seminary Quarterly* 2, no. 2 (1958): 20–46, and the discussion in *St. Vladimir's Seminary Quarterly* 2, no. 4 (1958): 37–38, 3; and no. 1 (1959): 36–37; Johannes Madey, "Orthodox Churches and Western Liturgies," *Christian Orient* 19 (1998): 193–96; *Missel orthodoxe: Rit occidental Gallican de s. Germain de Paris (6e siècle)*. Italique pré-Célestinien (début 5e siècle). Missel ou livre de la synaxe liturgique approuvé et authorisé pour les églises orthodoxes de rit occidental relevant du Patriarcat de Moscou. Version française officielle établie sur le texte latin original. Édition revue et typique (Collection "Documents liturgiques," supplément de la revue "Contacts," n° 38/39, 2e/3e trim. 1962, Paris 1962) with further bibliography on 96. According to a recent report, the Western-rite Orthodox Vicariate under the jurisdiction of the Antiochian Orthodox Christian Archdiocese of North America has twenty-seven parishes: ECJ 6, no. 3 (1999): 150. See also the blog *Unique photos posted on the blog of reader Michael, from ROCOR's British diocese*, and the website http://ad-orientem.blogspot.com/search/label/western%20rite for photos of Western-rite Orthodox liturgies concelebrated by Archbishop Alexis van der Mensbrugghe and Metropolitan Anthony Bloom of the Russian Orthodox Church (Moscow patriarchate), and by Russian Orthodox Church Outside Russia (ROCOR) Archbishop St. John of Shanghai and San Francisco.

35. See, for example, the disclaimer of Greek-Orthodox theologian Soterios Varnalides, "L'ecclésiologie de l'uniatisme dans la création des exarchats de Constantinople et d'Athènes," *Irénikon* 65 (1992): 400–22, here 400: "l'uniatisme . . . a crée dans l'histoire de l'Église et dans la théologie chrétienne une ecclésiologie artificielle, inconnue jusqu'alors et étrangère à l'Église unie des premiers siècles. Même après le schisme et jusqu'à maintenant elle est inconnue à l'Église orthodoxe." See also ibid. 420.

36. See Milton V. Anastos, "The Transfer of Illyricum, Calabria and Sicily to the Jurisdiction of the Patriarchate of Constantinople in 732–33," in *Silloge bizantina in onore di Silvio Giuseppe Mercati*=Studi bizantini e neoellenici 9 (1957): 14–31; Francis Dvornik, "La lutte entre Byzance et Rome à propos de

l'Illyricum au IXe siècle," *Mélanges Charles Diehl*, vol. 1 (Paris: Librairie Ernest Leroux 1930): 61–80; Venance Grumel, "L'annexion de l'Illyricum oriental, de la Sicile et de la Calabre au Patriarcat de Constantinople," in *Mélanges Jules Lebreton* II = *Recherches de science religieuse* 40 (1951–52): 191–200.

37. Examples in Suttner, *Church Unity*, 38–43.

38. On the history of the Byzantines in S. Italy see Vera von Falkenhausen, "I bizantini in Italia," in *I bizantini in Italia*, ed. Guglielmo Cavallo et al., Antica Madre, collana di studi sull'Italia antica (Milan: Libri Scheiwiller 1982), 1–136.

39. As modern studies continue to show, Medieval Latin ecclesiastical rule in areas of the Orthodox East was like the shepherding of Little-Bo-Peep compared to what the Latins suffered under the Russian Orthodox in the Tsarist empire. Greek dioceses in lands under the control of the Italian maritime city-states, as in the islands of the Aegean, automatically came under Latin ecclesiastical rule as well. The same was true in the Latin Kingdoms the Crusaders carved out for themselves in the Middle East, where Latin hierarchies were imposed on the conquered lands. But this was long before the East-West schism had hardened after the seventeenth century (see Ware, "Orthodox and Catholics in the Seventeenth Century," 259–76), and on the parish level the Orthodox clergy and people were pretty much left alone (see Brand, Cutler, "Latin Empire," ODB 2:1184). For example, in thirteenth-century Cyprus under Latin domination, the Orthodox were free to elect their own bishops. See Gregorios A. Ioannides, "Il manoscritto Barberini greco 390: edizione e commento liturgico" (PhD diss., Rome: PIO, 2000), 337; and most recently, Christopher H. MacEvitt, *The Crusades and the Christian World of the East: Rough Tolerance*, The Middle Ages Series (Philadelphia: University of Pennsylvania Press, 2008).

40. *A History of the Crusades*, Kenneth M. Setton, general editor, vol. 2. *The Later Crusades, 1189–1311*, ed. Robert Lee Wolff and Harry W. Hazard, 2nd ed. (Madison: The University of Wisconsin Press, 1969), 145, 162. Before the rise of national states, great commercial centers around the Mediterranean basin like Venice and Genoa had large communities of merchants resident in Constantinople.

41. *Chronicle* 22, 13 (12): churches and holy places were destroyed and laity as well as clergy massacred, including the envoy subdeacon John: "Inter quos virum venerabilem, Iohannem nomine, sancte Romane ecclesie subdiaconum, quem pro negociis ecclesie dominus papa illuc direxerat, comprehendentes, in contumeliam ecclesie decollaverunt, caput eius ad caudam canis immunde religantes." *Willhelmi Tyrensis Archiepiscopi Chronicon*, ed. Robert B.C. Huygens, 2 vols., Corpus Christianorum series Latina, continuatio mediaevalis 63–63A (Turnhout: Brepols 1986); 63A:1023. William's *Chronicle* is the major source for relations between Byzantium and the Crusader states: see Michael McCormick,

"William of Tyre," ODB 3:2197–8; Charles M. Brand, Anthony Cutler, "Andronikos I Komnenos," ODB. 1:94, and "Latin Empire," ODB 2:1183–5.

42. *The Later Crusades* 181ff, tells the story in detail.

43. Of course none of that justifies what the Crusaders did, but a dose of truth might help to re-dimension traditional Orthodox slanted views on the issue and apportion responsibilities where they belong—certainly not to the Catholic Church, in whose name Pope Innocent III bitterly condemned the Crusaders' horrific actions in no uncertain terms: see ibid. 180, 185. Interestingly, the immediate aftermath to the Fourth Crusade does not seem to have provoked, even among the Greeks, the universal revulsion that it does today. Some Byzantine nobles joined the Latins and some Orthodox Greeks even fought for Latin Emperor Henry against the Byzantine armies: See *The Later Crusades*, 180, 185; Brand, Cutler, "Latin Empire," ODB 2:1184.

44. See Raymond Janin, "Evsévedès, Benjamin," DHGE 16:221; Sébastien Ronzevalle, "Un épisode de l'histoire contemporaine des Églises d'Orient: captivité et délivrance d'un évéque grec," *Études* 80 (August 1858); 528–36. Curiously, I can find no reference to Evsevidis in the official sources for the Catholic hierarchy available to me, not even in Remegius Ritzer & Perminus Sefrin, *Hierarchia Catholica medii et recenrioris aevi . . .* vol. 8: 1846–1903 (Padua: 1979); ibid., vol. 9: 1903–22 (Padua: Ex Typographia "Il Messagero di S. Antonio" 2002). *Damnatio memoriae?*

45. Further evidence of this well-documented Russian Orthodox persecution of Catholics, both Roman and Eastern, can be found most recently in Simon, *Pro Russia* ch. 2 passim. The evidence is especially damning, coming as it does from this markedly pro-Russian author.

46. P. Bernard, "André Bobola," DHGE 2: 1641–44.

47. Vasyl' Lencyk, *The Eastern Catholic Church and Czar Nicholas I*, Praci Filosoficno-Filolohicnoho Fakul'tetu 2 (Rome, N.Y.: Ukrainian Catholic University, 1966), 83ff and the literature cited 124–25n70.

48. On the well-documented persecution of Catholicism under Nicholas I, see Adrien Boudou, *Le Saint-Siège et la Russie: Leurs rélations diplomatiques au XIXe siècle*, 2 vols. (Paris: Plon-Nourrit et C.ie, 1922–26), 1:209–48, and, most recently, Alan J. Reinerman, "Metternich, Pope Gregory XIV, and Revolutionary Poland, 1831–1842," *The Catholic Historical Review* 86 (2000): 603–19, here 612–19, who speaks of Nicholas I's "systematic decatholicisation" of Poland, fully and historically Roman Catholic from time immemorial. Regarding the persecution of the Greek Catholics, see Lencyk, *The Eastern Catholic Church and Czar Nicholas I*, especially ch. 8 and 128ff. Concerning the 1829 suppression of the Cholm Eparchy and the violence and deaths accompanying it, see Luigi Glinka, *Diocesi ucraino-cattolica di Cholm: liquidazione ed incorporazione alla Chiesa russo-ortodossa, sec. XIX*, Analecta OSBM Series 3, Sectio 1, Opera vol. 34

(Rome: PP. Basiliani 1975), especially 54–55, 85, 91ff. Similar material is detailed in Andrej Piattchits, "A Latin Altar and an Orthodox Throne: Roman Catholicism in Nineteenth-Century Belarus," *Diakonia* 34 (2001): 109–28, especially 117ff.

49. Killing thirteen and eleven faithful, respectively, on the two occasions (Glinka, *Diocesi ucraino-cattolica di Cholm*, 85–86).

50. It has been reactivated as a men's monastery since the fall of the Soviet Union. In 2006 it had thirty monks. See Brakhaus-Ephron, *Enciklopedicheskij Slovar'* 82+4 supplementary vols. (St. Peterburg: 1890–1907), 17:109; and especially N. B. Alatarceva, "Goloseevskij v chest' Pokrova presvjatoj Bogorodicy muzheskoj monastyr,'" in the excellent new post-Soviet *Pravoslavnaja Enciklopedija* (Moscow 2000–): 11:712, with photo and further bibliography. Needless to say, the Russian encyclopedias consulted have no entry for Sokolski, on whom see the best, serenely objective available history of the origins of this Church by Bulgarian Orthodox author Ivan Elenkov, *La Chiesa cattolica di rito bizantino-slavo in Bulgaria dalla sua cosituzione nel 1860 fino alla metà del XX sec*, trans. from the Bulgarian by Neli Radanova (Sofia: Montecchi Editore 2000), 73–75; see Ritzer-Sefrin, *Hierarchia Catholica* 8:162. On Popov's episcopate, see Elenkov chaps. 3–5 passim.

51. Among the examples that could be given is one cited by Tamborra, *Chiesa cattolica e ortodossia russa* 182: when Princess Zinaida Volkonskaja became a Catholic in 1833, Tsar Nicholas I ordered that her property be confiscated, that her minor children be taken away from her, and that she be confined to an Orthodox monastery. On Volkonskaja, see also Simòn, *Pro Russia*, 53–57. Of course, the West at an earlier period knew this sort of thing too. In England, for example, Catholics suffered the same thing at Anglican hands: in 1593 an Act of Parliament decreed that the children of recusants (i.e., those who refused to accept the established Anglican Church) over seven years old "are to be committed to others to be educated." Only at the end of the eighteenth century could English Catholics legally own, inherit, and transfer property, and only in 1828 were their civil rights restored. The difference is that, in the meantime, Catholics and Anglicans have learned something from their turbulent earlier history: see below at note 82.

52. Details in Taft, "The Problem of 'Uniatism' and the 'Healing of Memories': Anamnesis, not Amnesia," 167–76.

53. Velo Salo, "The Catholic Church in Estonia, 1918–2001," *The Catholic Historical Review* 88 (2002): 281–92, here 281.

54. See Robert F. Taft, "Ecumenical Scholarship and the Catholic-Orthodox Epiclesis Dispute," OKS 45 (1996): 201–26; Taft, "The Epiclesis Question in the Light of the Orthodox and Catholic Lex orandi Traditions," in *New Perspectives on Historical Theology: Essays in Memory of John Meyendorff*, ed. Bradley Nassif

(Grand Rapids, Mich.: William B. Eerdmans, 1996), 210–37; Taft, "Jesuits at the End of the Twentieth Century. Questionnaire Imago Mundi: Interview with Robert F. Taft, S.J.," in Morozowich, ed., *Saints—Sanctity—Liturgy*, 137–71, here 145–47.

55. On this issue, see the important recent publications of Basilio Petrà, *Preti sposati per volontà di Dio? Saggi su una Chiesa a due polmoni*, Nuovi saggi teologici 59 (Bologna: Edizioni Dehoniane 2004); Petrà, "Preti sposati per volontà di Dio? Alcune risposte e ulteriori riflessioni," *Rivista di teologia morale* 159 (2008): 407–18; Petrà, "Married Priesthood: Some Theological 'Resonences,'" *Logos* 50, no. 3–4 (2009): 459–79; Petrà, & Lawrence Cross, "Married Priests: At the Heart of Tradition," *Nicolaus* 36 (2009): 117–35. Fr. Petrà, an Italian Catholic priest of Greek ancestry, is easily one of the best authors writing on Orthodox theology today. By way of contrast, see the historical argumentation in a recent piece in the Vatican daily *L'Osservatore romano* (Saturday, March 13, 2010) 5: Stefan Heid, "Quella luce che cambia la vita." See also the same author's book, *Zölibat in der frühen Kirche: Die Anfänge einer Enthaltsamkeitspflicht für Kleriker in Ost und West* (Paderborn, Germany: Ferdinand Schöningh, 1998); English trans. *Celibacy in the Early Church: The Beginnings of a Discipline of Obligatory Continence for Clerics in East and West* (San Francisco: Ignatius Press, 2000). See also the recent theological congress: *XV Convengo della Facoltà di Teologia "Il Celibato sacerdotale: teologia e vita,"* (Pontificia Università, Santa Croce, Rome, Italy [billed as held under the patronage of the Vatican Congregation for the Clergy], March 4–5, 2010). For its tone, see the websites http://www.pusc.it/teo/conv/conv10/ and http://www.zenit.org/article-28589?/=english. The references to these sites I owe to my graduate assistant Daniel Galadza.

56. See Mary M. Schaefer, *Twelfth-Century Latin Commentaries on the Mass: Christological and Ecclesiological Dimensions* (PhD diss., Notre Dame University, 1983; accessed through Ann Arbor: University Microfilms International, 1983); Schaefer, "Twelfth-Century Latin Commentaries on the Mass: The Relationship of the Priest to Christ and to the People," SL 15 (1982): 76–86, especially 80–82. A master of medieval Latin Eucharistic theology, to be read and meditated by the many Roman-Catholic theologians in need of being brought down to earth and put in touch with historical reality, is Gary Macy of Santa Clara University. See his *Theologies of the Eucharist in the Early Scholastic Period* (Oxford: Clarendon Press, 1984); Macy, *Treasures from the Storeroom: Medieval Religion and the Eucharist* (Collegeville: Liturgical Press, 1999). See also his excellent essay "Impasse passé: Conjugating a Past Tense," in *Proceedings of The Catholic Theological Society of America* 64 [= Proceedings of the Sixty-fourth Annual Convention, Halifax, Nova Scotia, June 4–7, 2009], ed. J. Y. Tan (2009): 1–20, here especially 8. I am indebted to Prof. Macy for providing me a copy of his seminal paper.

57. See note 56.

58. Basile de Césarée, *Sur le Saint-Esprit*, introduction, text, translation, and notes by Benoit Pruche, 2nd ed., Sources chrétiennes 17bis (Paris: Cerf 1968). See Myrolsavl Ivan Lubatchiwskyj, "Des heiligen Basilius liturgischer Kampf gegen den Arianismus. Ein Beitrag zur Textgeschichte der Basiliusliturgie," *Zeitschrift für katholische Theologie* 66 (1942): 20–38.

59. *Decr. S. Officii* March 8 (May 23) 1957, AAS 49 (1957): 370 = Heinrich Denzinger, *Enchiridion symbolorum, definitionum et declarationum de rebus fidei et morum*, ed. Peter Hünermann with Helmut Hoping, 42 ed. (Freiburg: Herder, 2009) §3928; see also AAS 48 (1956) 716–25.

60. See for example Placide de Meester, "De concelebratione in ecclesia orientali, praesertim secundum ritum byzantinum," *Ephemerides liturgicae* 37 (1923): 101–10, 145–54, 196–201, here 101: "Definitur concelebratio sensu latissimo, sensu strictiori, sensu strictissima sumpta," and "concelebratio mere caerimonialis." See Jean-Michel Hanssens, "De concelebratione missae in ritibus orientalibus. De eius notione et modis, usu praesenti et historia," *Divinitas* 10 (1966): 482–559 (repr. Rome 1966): 483–84 and passim. On the whole question see the excellent summary of Bernhard Schultze, "Das theologische Problem der Konzelebration," *Gregorianum* 36 (1955): 212–71, 215–16 and note 6, 218–32.

61. Bernard Botte, "Note historique sur la concélébration dans l'église ancienne," *La Maison-Dieu* 35 (1953): 9–23, holds this view strongly, whereas Jean-Michel Hanssens, "De concelebratione eucharistica in ritibus orientalibus," *Periodica de re morali, canonica, liturgica* 16 (1927): 142–54, 181–210; 17 (1928): 93–127; 21 (1932): 193–219, here 144, 219, asserted that his distinction between "ceremonial" and "sacramental" concelebration was a merely ritual distinction that did not prejudge whether what he deemed "ceremonial" concelebration could have been a "real" participation of the concelebrants in the consecration of the gifts.

62. French original: *Essai sur la théologie mystique de l'Église d'Orient* (Paris: Aubier, 1944): "La mystique de l'imitation [du Christ] que l'on peut trouver en occident est étrangère à la spiritualité orientale, qui se definit plutôt comme *une vie dans le Christ*." (p. 212). "La voie de l'imitation du Christ n'est jamais pratiquée dans la spiritualité de l'Église d'Orient" (p. 242). The same nonsense is repeated in the English trans. *The Mystical Theology of the Eastern Church* (Cambridge: James Clarke, 1957), 215, 243.

63. On Hausherr and his writings, see his *Hésychasme et prière* (Pont. Institutum Studiorum, 1966), ix–xi, which gives his bibliography up to that date; also Thomáš Špidlík, "In Memoriam Irenée Hausherr S.J. (7-6-1891—5-12-1978)," OCP 45 (1979): 159–65, with Hausherr's later writings indicated.

64. Irenée Hausherr, "L'imitation de Jésus Christ dans la spiritualité byzantine," *in Mélanges offerts au R. P. Ferdinand Cavallera* . . . (Toulouse: Institut

catholique 1948): 231–59; reprinted in Hausherr's *Études de spiritualité orientale*, OCA 183 (Rome: PIO 1969): 217–45.

65. On the imitation of Christ theme in the history of Christian spirituality from the New Testament though the fathers and beyond, see the lengthy studies by several authors in DSp 7.2, 1536–1601, and on Kempis's classic, DSp 7.2, 2338–68. On its place in Russian spirituality, see Stanislav Janežič, *Imitazione di Cristo secondo Tihon Zadonskij*, PIO Tesi di Laurea (Trieste: Tipografia Coana 1962). On topic of East-West differences and pseudo-antitheses, see the thorough discussion and references in Gerhard Podskalsky, "Entwicklungslinien des griechisch-byzantinischen theologischen Denkens (bis zum Ende der Turkokratie)," OKS 47 (1998): 34–43, especially 35–36. On the Orthodox tendency to overdo the East-West distinction/antithesis, see Podskalsky, "Ostkirchliche Theologie in der Weltkirche: Alternative (Antithese), Annex oder Allheilmittel?" OCA 251:531–541; Dorothea Wendebourg, "'Pseudomorphosis'—ein theologisches Urteil des Axiom der kirchen- und theologiegeschichtlichen Forschung," ibid., 565–89, reprinted in English translations as "'Pseudomorphosis': A Theological Judgment as an Axiom for Research in the History of Church and Theology," *The Greek Orthodox Theological Review* 42 (1997): 321–42; and most recently, Johannes Oeldemann, "Pseudomorphose oder Komplementarität? Historische Entwicklung und heutige Bewertung gegenseitige Einflüsse der Theologie in Ost und West," in *Ost- und Westerweiterung in Theologie: 20 Jahre Orthodoxe Theologie in München*. ed. Theodor Nikolaou with Konstantin Nikolakopoulos and Anargyros Anapliotis, Münchener Universitäts Schriften, Reihe: Veröffentlichungen des Instituts für Orthodoxe Theologie, Bd. 9, Erzabtei St. Ottilien (Eresing, Germany: EOS Verlag 2006): 51–60.

66. Another, contemporary translation I have found in the Russian sources available to me is the second edition of a translation by a certain Speranskov published in Moscow: Tipografija V. Ja. Barbej Mjasnic. Georgiev. Per. Boejkovoj. 1877, with the approval of the censors at the Moscow Spiritual Academy. I am indebted to my colleague, PIO professor of Russian Church History, Constantin Simon S.J., for assisting me in my search for Russian editions of Kempis.

67. The basic work on Pobedonostsev is Robert F. Byrnes, *Pobedonostsev: His Life and Thought* (Bloomington: Indiana University Press, 1968): on P's work as Procurator of the Synod, see ch. 8; on his translation of *The Imitation*, see 286.

68. Cited in the *SEIA Newsletter on the Eastern Churches and Ecumenism*, no. 150 (March 31, 2008) 4.

69. See for instance Miguel Arranz, ed., *I penitenziali bizantini*, Kanonika 3 (Rome: PIO 1993): 49–58, with its "Number and Species of Sins," its "Seven Carnal Sins"; similarly in Frans van de Paverd, *The Kanonarion by John, Monk and Deacon, and Didascalia Patrum*, Kanonika 12 (Rome: PIO 2006), passim.

70. George Dennis, "Popular Religious Attitudes and Practices in Byzantium" OCA 251:253 and note 43.

71. Epiphanios of Salamis, *Panarion*, ed. Karl Holl, 3 vols. (GCS 25, 31, 37, Leipzig: J.C. Heinrich'sche Buchhandlung 1915–33; repr. GCS Neue Folge 13, Berlin: Walter de Gruyter 2006); Euthymios Zigabenos (or Zigadenos), *Panoplia dogmatica*, PG 130:10–1362.

72. *The Rudder*, trans. D. Cummings (Chicago: The Orthodox Christian Educational Society, 1957).

73. See Vassa Larin "What is 'Ritual Impurity' and Why?," *St. Vladimir's Theological Quarterly* 52 (2008): 275–92.

74. In his review in *Sobornost'* series 3, no. 12 (Winter 1952): 584–86 of: Nicodemus the Hagiorite, *Unseen Warfare* . . . (London: Faber & Faber 1952, repr. Crestwood, N.Y.: St. Vladimir's Seminary Press 1978). On this wonderful hieromonk who entered into communion with the Orthodox Church in 1928, see the excellent biography of Élizabeth Behr-Sigel, *Lev Gillet: A Monk of the Eastern Church*, trans. Helen Wright (Oxford: Fellowship of St. Alban and St. Sergius 1999).

75. See Yannis Spiteris, "Attuali tendenze nella teologia greca," OCP 71 (2005): 299–314, here 309–10.

76. As for example the author of a recent article seems to do: Jean-Claude Larchet, "La théologie des énergies divines: l'enjeu, les difficultés et les perspectives du dialogue entre catholiques et orthodoxes," *Logos* 50 (2009): 369–85,

77. See de Halleux's "Palamisme et scolastique," *Revue théologique de Louvain* 4 (1973): 409–42; de Halleux, "Palamisme et tradition," *Irénikon* 48 (1975): 479–93; both reprinted in de Halleux, *Patrologie et œcuménisme: Recueil d'études* (Bibliotheca Ephemeridum Theologicarum Lovaniensium 93, Leuven: University Press—Peeters 1990): 782–830. For de Halleux's own evaluation of his work as an ecumenical patristic scholar, see his "Une vie consacré à l'étude et au service de l'Orient chrétien," in *Il 75° anniversario del Pontificio Istituto Orientale: Atti delle celebrazioni giubilari, 15–17 ottobre 1992*, ed. Robert F. Taft and James Lee Dugan, a cura di OCA 244 (Rome: PIO 1994): 40–54.

78. *Anthologion tou holou eniautou* (Rome: Vatican, 1967–80) here vol. 2 (1974): 676–83. Of course some Catholic theologians have attacked Palamism as, indeed, have some Orthodox theologians: on Palamas in Orthodox theological debate see Yannis Spiteris, *Palamas: la grazia e l'esperinze: Gregorio Palamas nella discussione teologica*, Pubblicazioni del Centro Aletti 17 (Rome: Lipa 1996): 114–23.

79. Luca Bianchi, *Monasteri icona del mondo celeste: La teologia spirituale di Gregorio Palamas* (Bologna: EDB—Edizioni Dehoniane 2010).

80. Just a few off the top of my head, in alphabetical order: *Bessarione, Bollettino della Badia Greca di Grottaferrata, Christian Orient, ContaCOr, Der christli-*

che Osten, Diakonia, Eastern Churches Journal, Eastern Churches Quarterly, Eastern Churches Review, Echos d'Orient, Ephrem's Theological Journal, Irénikon, Istina, Journal of St. Thomas Christians, Le Muséon, Logos: A Journal of Eastern Christian Studies (Ottawa), *Logos* (Slovakia), *One, One in Christ, Oriens Christianus; Orientalia Christiana, Orientalia Christiana Periodica, Oriente cristiano, Ostkirchliche Studien, Nicolaus, Pokrov, Proche-orient chrétien, Revue des études byzantines, Roma e l'Oriente, Russia cristiana* (formerly *L'altra europa*), *Simvol, Stoudion, Studi sull'Oriente Cristiano, The Harp: A Review of Syriac Oriental Ecumenical Studies, The Journal of Eastern Christian Studies, Thomas Christian Heritage, Urha—The Way. A Journal of Theology,* etc., Some of these rank among the major international scholarly journals on the Christian East today, along with *Oriens Christianus* founded under Catholic auspices by Anton Baumstark but now under secular academic direction. Of course, some of the older journals suffering, inevitably, from the limited mentality of the times, were "unionistic" in approach. My point is not to support their orientation but to insist that one cannot say Catholicism ever ignored the Christian East. In that light, one can, perhaps, understand the perplexity of "Westerners," accustomed to dealing with facts, at the following opening sentence of a recent article by two Serbian Orthodox: "In the Western literature and periodicals there is an inadmissible [*sic.*] small number of articles, studies and books dealing with either Orthodoxy in general or the Serbian Orthodoxy and the Serbian Orthodox Church in particular": D.B. Djordjevic and B. Djurovic, "Secularization and Orthodoxy: The Case of the Serbians," *Orthodoxes Forum* 7 (1993): 215. Incidentally, the journal containing the complaint cited above is published by the Institut für Orthodoxe Theologie within the Faculty of Catholic Theology of the University of Munich. So much for objectivity.

81. I list a number of them in Robert F. Taft, "Eastern Catholic Theology—Is There Any Such Thing? Reflections of a Practitioner," *Logos* 38 (1998): 13–58, here 38–47.

82. See Archbishop of Canterbury Dr. Rowan Williams, "Pardon Is the Word. Shakespeare, Edmund Campion, and the Grace of Forgiveness," *America* (March 1, 2010): 18–20.

Byzantines, Armenians, and Latins: Unleavened Bread and Heresy in the Tenth Century / Tia Kolbaba

1. General discussions of Byzantine identity are ubiquitous in the historical literature. Some notable examples: Paul Magdalino, "Hellenism and Nationalism in Byzantium," in *Tradition and Transformation in Medieval Byzantium*, Article 14 (London: Variorum, 1991); Magdalino, *The Empire of*

Manuel I Komnenos, 1143–1180 (Cambridge: Cambridge University Press, 1993), ch. 5; Évelyne Patlagean, "Byzance, le barbare, l'hérétique et la loi universelle," in *Ni Juif ni Grec: Entretiens sur le racisme, sous la direction de Léon Poliakov* (Paris: École des hautes études en sciences sociales, 1978); Charlotte Roueché, "Defining the Foreign in Kekaumenos," in *Strangers to Themselves: The Byzantine Outsider*, ed. Dion Smythe (Aldershot, U.K.: Ashgate/Variorum, 1998; Society for the Promotion of Byzantine Studies Publications 8), 203–14.

2. Judith Herrin, *The Formation of Christendom* (Princeton: Princeton University Press, 1987), 140.

3. A notable exception is Karl Leyser, "The Tenth Century in Byzantine-Western Relations," in *Relations between East and West in the Middle Ages*, ed. Derek Baker (Edinburgh: Edinburgh University Press, 1973), 29–63. Leyser's account is concerned primarily with political and diplomatic interaction.

4. Jonathan Shepard, "Aspects of Byzantine Attitudes and Policy towards the West in the Tenth and Eleventh Centuries," *Byzantinische Forschungen* 13 (1988): 67–118, especially 68.

5. For an account of which Greek complaints about Latin theology and religious practice were emphasized in which periods, see Tia Kolbaba, "Byzantine Perceptions of Latin Religious 'Errors'—Themes and Changes from 850 to 1350," in *The Crusades from the Perspective of Byzantium and the Muslim World*, ed. Angeliki E. Laiou and Roy Parvis Mottahedeh (Washington, D.C.: Dumbarton Oaks Press, 2001), 117–43.; repr. in *Doctrine and Debate in the Eastern Christian World*, 300–1500, ed. Averil Cameron and Robert Hoyland (Aldershot, U.K.: Ashgate, forthcoming).

6. Later, of course, the Germanic Arians would force the West to deal with a new phase of this controversy, but that is a separate history from the one I am concerned with here. On East-West differences in the fourth-century controversy, see Gilbert Dagron, "Les temps des changements (fin Xe—milieu XIe siècle)," in *Histoire du christianisme des origines à nos jours*, ed. Jean-Marie Mayeur et al., vol. 4, *Éveques, moines et empereurs (610–1054)* (Paris: Desclée, 1993), 343.

7. For some of the best recent discussions of theological differences—real and imagined—between Greeks and Latins, see George Demacopoulos and Aristotle Papanikolaou, *Orthodox Readings of Augustine* (Crestwood, New York: St. Vladimir's Theological Seminary Press, 2008).

8. For a survey of East-West relations in the fourth to eighth centuries, see Herrin, *Formation*, 100–25.

9. Note, for example, Herrin's statement (*Formation*, 345) that "There is no evidence that Christian communities outside Italy were even aware of the eastern initiative in regard to artistic representation [i.e., of iconoclasm], which is not surprising in view of Byzantine isolation from Transalpine Europe. The use of icons was not widespread in other western churches."

10. Aidan Nichols, *Rome and the Eastern Churches: A Study in Schism* (Edinburgh: T&T Clark, 1992), 182–83, 210; Aristeides Papadakis and John Meyendorff, *The Christian East and the Rise of the Papacy: The Church 1071–1453 A.D.* (Crestwood, N.Y.: St. Vladimir's Seminary Press, 1994), 14, 55.

11. For my argument it does not matter whether the Frankish objections represent *more* than a misreading of the *Acta* of 787. It has been argued—I think rightly—that Frankish theologians had fundamental objections to icon-veneration that would have surfaced even if their translation had been accurate. See, for example, Gilbert Dagron, "L'iconoclasme et l'établissment de l'Orthodoxie (726–847)," in Mayeur, *Histoire*, vol. 4, 128, 148–50; Herrin, *Formation*, 426–43.

12. The Nicene-Constantinopolitan Creed contains the following statement about the Holy Spirit: "[We believe in] the Holy Spirit, the Lord, the Giver of Life, who proceeds from the Father." In the sixth century, Spanish churches added the phrase "and from the Son [Latin: *filioque*]" to this statement as part of a response to groups who subordinated the Son to the Father ("Adoptionists" and "Arians"). This addition spread from Spain to the Frankish lands and eventually (though only in the eleventh century) to Rome. The claim of Latins that the Greeks had removed the *filioque* from the Creed stemmed from their belief that the so-called Athanasian Creed, which contains the *filioque*, was written by St. Athanasius the Great, who was also believed to be the author of the Nicene Creed. Westerners in Spain and the Kingdom of the Franks assumed that the Greeks had tried to "suppress" that part of the Creed. On the doctrinal controversy, the authoritative work is now A. Edward Siecienski, *The Filioque: History of a Doctrinal Controversy* (Oxford: Oxford University Press, 2010). See also Nichols, *Rome and the Eastern Churches*, 195–98.

13. Richard Haugh, *Photius and the Carolingians: The Trinitarian Controversy* (Belmont, Mass: Nordland, 1975).

14. Photios, Patriarch of Constantinople. "Encyclica ad sedes orientales," in *Photius: Epistulae et Amphilochia*, ed. B. Laourdas and L.B. Westerink (Leipzig: Teubner, 1988), vol. 1, ep. 2. On the composition—or rather compilation—of the various parts of this letter, see Tia Kolbaba, *Inventing Latin Heretics: Byzantines and the* Filioque *in the Ninth Century* (Kalamazoo: Medieval Institute Publications, 2008), ch. 4; Paul Speck, "Die griechischen Quellen zur Bekehrung der Bulgaren und die zwei ersten Briefe des Photios," in *Polupleuros Nous: Miscellanea für Peter Schreiner zu Seinem 60. Geburtstag*, ed. C. Scholz and G. Makris (Munich: K.G. Saur, 2000), 353–57.

15. Jules Gay, *L'Italie méridionale et l'empire byzantin depuis l'avènement de Basil Ier jusqu'a la prise de Bari par les Normands* (Paris: A. Fontemoing, 1904; Bibliothèque des Écoles Françaises d'Athénes et de Rome 90); Vera von Falkenhausen, "Between Two Empires: Southern Italy in the Reign of Basil II," in

Byzantium in the Year 1000, ed. Paul Magdalino, *The Medieval Mediterranean*, vol. 45 (Leiden: Brill, 2003), 135–60.

16. For example, Photios's letter to the Archbishop of Aquileia: Photios, Patriarch of Constantinople, "Archiepiscopo Aquileiae," in *Photius: Epistulae et Amphilochia*, (Leipzig: Teubner, 1985), vol. 3, ep. 291. See also Kolbaba, *Inventing Latin Heretics*, ch. 6.

17. *The Oxford Dictionary of Byzantium*, ed. Alexander Kazhdan (Oxford: Oxford University Press, 1991), s.v. "Neilos of Rossano"; André Guillou, "Grecs d'Italie du Sud et de Sicile au Moyen Age: Les moines," *Mélanges d'Archéologie et d'Histoire* 75 (1963), 79–110, repr. in Guillou, *Studies on Byzantine Italy* (London: Variorum Reprints, 1970), Article 12, 101–2; Oliver Rousseau, "La visite de Nil de Rossano au Mont-Cassin," in *La chiesa greca in Italia dall'VIII al XVI secolo*, vol. 2 (= *Italia Sacra* 22; Padova: Editrice Antenore, 1973), 1111–37; G. da Costa-Louillet, "Saints de Sicile et d'Italie méridionale aux VIIIe, IXe et Xe siècles," *Byzantion* 29–30 (1959–60), 148–64; P. G. Giovanelli, ed., *Bios kai politeia tou hosiou patros hēmōn Neilou tou Neou* (Grottaferrata: Badia di Grottaferrata, 1972); Italian translation of and extensive notes on the Vita: P. G. Giovanelli, *San Nilo di Rossano, fondatore di Grottaferrata* (Grottaferrata, 1966).

18. Michel Balard, "Amalfi et Byzance (xe–xiie siècles)," *Travaux et mémoires du Centre de Recherche d'Histoire et Civilisation de Byzance* 6 (1976): 85–95.

19. G.A. Loud, "Montecassino and Byzantium in the Tenth and Eleventh centuries," in *The Theotokos Evergetis and Eleventh-Century Monasticism*, ed. Margaret Mullett and Anthony Kirby (Belfast: Belfast Byzantine Texts and Translations, 1994); repr. in Loud, *Montecassino and Benevento in the Middle Ages* (Aldershot, U.K.: Ashgate, 2000), 37.

20. Thomas F.X. Noble, *The Republic of St. Peter: The Birth of the Papal State, 680–825* (Philadelphia: University of Pennsylvania Press, 1984), 204–11.

21. Jane Carol Bishop, *Pope Nicholas I and the First Age of Papal Independence* (PhD Diss., Columbia University, 1980).

22. See, for example, Papadakis and Meyendorff, *Christian East*.

23. Mahlon H. Smith, *And Taking Bread. . . . Cerularius and the Azyme Controversy of 1054* (Paris: Éditions Beauchesne, 1978). Before Smith, Jean Darrouzès had published a short note on the Greek-Latin-Armenian connection: "Notes: Une faux *Peri ton azumon* de Michel Cérulaire," *Révue des études byzantines* 25 (1967), 288–91. Later Darrouzès published three critical documents for this topic: "Trois documents de la controverse gréco-arménienne," *Révue des études byzantines* 48 (1990), 89–153.

24. Gérard Dédéyan, "L'immigration arménienne en Cappadoce au xie siècle," *Byzantion* 45 (1975): 41–117; here 49.

25. Dédéyan, "L'immigration armenienne," 52.

26. Gilbert Dagron, "Minorités ethniques et religieuses dans l'orient byzantin à la fin du xe et au xie siècle: l'immigration syrienne," *Travaux et Mémoires* 6 (1976; Recherches sur le xie siècle), 177–216.

27. Dagron, "Minorités ethniques," 207: "There was not one policy of the empire with regard to Jacobite Syrians or Monophysite Armenians, but at least two: the first, tolerance, at Melitene or at Sebaste, the other, intolerance, at Antioch."

28. On the importance of Armenian soldiers in the Byzantine armies of the tenth century, see Eric McGeer, *Sowing the Dragon's Teeth: Byzantine Warfare in the Tenth Century*, Dumbarton Oaks Studies 33 (Washington, D.C.: Dumbarton Oaks, 1995).

29. Dagron, "Minorités ethniques," 199.

30. Magdalino, *Empire of Manuel I*, ch. 5. Compare John Haldon's description of Byzantium after Justinian: *Byzantium in the Seventh Century: The Transformation of a Culture* (Cambridge: Cambridge University Press, 1990), 297: "From Justinian's reign, neo-Chalcedonian universalism and a single orthodoxy start to become the keynote values of early Byzantine society and the state. The marginalisation and exclusion of non-conforming groups becomes increasingly apparent under Justinian's successors. The unity of state and church, the future salvation of the *oikoumene*, depends upon their partnership in orthodoxy. To be different was dangerous."

31. Magdalino, *Empire of Manuel I*, 386.

32. Mark Whittow, *The Making of Byzantium, 600–1025* (Berkeley: University of California Press, 1996), 336–37.

33. On Phokas's request and the synod's denial, see Joannes Skylitzes, *Synopsis Historiarum*, ed. J. Thurn (Vienna: CFHB, 1973), 273–75; Venance Grumel, *Les regestes des actes du patriarcat de Constantinople*, 2nd rev. ed., Jean Darrouzès, vol. 1, fasc. 2 and 3, "Les regestes de 715 à 1206" (Paris: Institut français d'études byzantines, 1989), no. 790.

34. Some of their responses to the threat are reflected in actions of the standing synod in Constantinople: Grumel, *Regestes*, no. 838, 839, 846.

35. We only rarely hear the voices of the opponents in these debates—that is, those who were marrying Chalcedonians to non-Chalcedonians and who presumably considered the similarities between the two groups more important than the differences. Living on the border between Islamic and Christian lands probably influenced their perception that the common quality of being Christians outweighed the differences about the one or two natures of Jesus Christ. As Fredrick Barth wrote, "It is important to recognize that although ethnic categories take cultural differences into account, we can assume no simple one-to-one relationship between ethnic units and cultural similarities and differences. The features that are taken into account are not the sum of 'objective' differences, but

only those that the actors themselves regard as significant"; Barth, introduction to *Ethnic Groups and Boundaries: The Social Organization of Culture Difference*, ed. Barth (Bergen-Oslo: Universitets Forlaget and George Allen & Unwin, 1969), 14. Compare Dimitri Obolensky, "The Balkans in the Ninth Century: Barrier or Bridge," BF 13 (1988), 63: "I will merely point out that the Slav rulers of the Balkans continued to behave, through much of the Middle Ages, as though [a schism between Eastern and Western Christendom] did not exist." I would suggest that the existence or nonexistence of a schism depends upon it being in someone's interest either to emphasize or to downplay difference.

36. Grumel, *Regestes*, no. 846.

37. Herrin, *Formation*, 285–86.

38. G.A. Rhalles and M. Potles, *Syntagma tōn theiōn kai hierōn kanonōn tōn te hagiōn kai paneuphēmōn apostolōn, kai tōn hierōn oikoumenikōn kai topikōn synodōn, kai tōn kata meros hagiōn paterōn: ekdothen syn pleistais allais ten ekklēsiastikēn katastasin diepousais diataxesi, meta tōn archaiōn exegetōn kai diaphorōn anagnōsmatōn*, vol. 2, 373–74 (Canon 32), 379 (Canon 33), 436 (Canon 56), 543 (Canon 99). English translation at http://www.newadvent.org/fathers/3814.htm, accessed March 18, 2011.

39. Dagron, "L'iconoclasme et l'établissment de l'Orthodoxie," 96–97.

40. Andrew Sharf, *Byzantine Jewry from Justinian to the Fourth Crusade* (London: Routledge & Kegan Paul, 1971), 107–8.

41. Sharf, *Byzantine Jewry*, 112–13.

42. Sharf, *Byzantine Jewry*, 116; Smith, *And Taking Bread*, 113.

43. Sharf, *Byzantine Jewry*, 123; Smith, *And Taking Bread*, 117.

44. Smith, *And Taking Bread*, 117.

45. The fundamental study of this process is Alain LeBoulluec, *La notion d'hérésie dans la littérature grecque IIe–IIIe siècles: Tome 1. De Justin à Irénée* (Paris: Études augustiniennes, 1985). See also Averil Cameron, "How to Read Heresiology," *Journal of Medieval and Early Modern Studies* 33, no. 3 (Fall 2003): 476–77; Hervé Inglebert, "L'histoire des hérésies chez les hérésiologues," in *L'Historiographie de l'Église des premiers siècles*, ed. Bernard Pouderon and Yves-Marie Duval (Paris: Beauchesne, 2001; Théologie historique 114), 105–25. For the influence of this system on Byzantine responses to Islam, see Adel-Théodore Khoury, *Polémique byzantine contre l'Islam (VIIIe–XIIIe s.)* (Leiden: Brill, 1972), 354–56. For a fascinating discussion of how this kind of classification of heresies both influenced and then was influenced by Roman and Byzantine legal practice, see Caroline Humfress, "Roman Law, Forensic Argument and the Formation of Christian Orthodoxy (III–VI Centuries)," in *Orthodoxie, Christianisme, Histoire / Orthodoxy, Christianity, History*, ed. Susanna Elm, Éric Rebillard, and Antonella Romano (Rome: École française de Rome, 2000), 125–47.

46. Greek arguments in defense of leavened bread rely on the Gospel of John's account of the Last Supper, in which the supper occurs before the days of unleavened bread and Jesus is crucified before the Passover. Latins tend to focus on the synoptic gospels, in which the supper is a Passover meal.

47. On the earlier practice of naming heretics after their real or legendary founder, see LeBoulluec, *Notion d'hérésie*, 60–62.

48. Dagron, "Les temps des changements," 336–37; Dagron, "Minorités ethniques," 214.

49. Cameron, "How to Read Heresiology," 484.

"Light from the West": Byzantine Readings of Aquinas / Marcus Plested

1. William of St-Thierry, *Epistola ad fratres de Monte Dei* 1 (*Sources Chrétiennes* 223), 144. All translations are my own unless otherwise specified.

2. Raffaele Cantarella, ed., "Canone greco inedito di Giuseppe vescovo di Methone in onore di San Tomaso d'Aquino," *Archivum Fratum Prædicatorum* 4 (1934), 153.

3. Demetrios gives us this information in his own hand and in Latin at the end of MS *Vaticanus graecus* 616. The translation was completed at the monastery of St George of the Mangana, the same monastery to which his patron John VI Kantakuzene had recently retired, taking the monastic name Joasaph. Kydones was the μεσάζων (chief minister) of John VI, a post he was also to hold under John V and Manuel II.

4. Martin Jugie, "Palamas, Grégoire" and "Palamite, Controverse," *DTC* 11 (Paris, 1932), 1735–1818; Gerhard Podskalsky, *Theologie und Philosophie in Byzanz: Der Streit um die theologische Methodik in der spätbyzantinischen Geistesgeschichte (14./15. Jahrhundert)* (Munich: C.H. Beck, 1977).

5. Rowan Williams, "The Philosophical Structures of Palamism," *Eastern Churches Review* 9 (1977): 27–44.

6. This tired and artificial dichotomy has long outlived any usefulness it might once have had. The contrast between the neopatristic school, hidebound by the dead weight of received tradition, and the more philosophically oriented and self-consciously modern Russian religious school is a commonplace within contemporary Orthodox studies. See, for example, Paul Vallière, *Modern Russian Theology: Bukharev, Soloviev, Bulgakov: Orthodox Theology in a New Key* (Edinburgh: T&T Clark, 2000), where the sympathies are very much with the Russian religious school. In fact, neopatristic theologians such as Georges Florovsky were deeply rooted in the religious philosophy of the Russian Silver Age (and motivated by the concerns of modernity), while theologians of the Russian religious

school such as Sergius Bulgakov were profoundly immersed in and engaged with the patristic tradition.

7. Sergius Bulgakov, "The Eucharistic Dogma" in *The Holy Grail and the Eucharist*, trans. Boris Jakim (Hudson, N.Y.: Lindisfarne Books, 1997), 76–83. The article was originally published in 1930 in the Russian émigré journal *Put'* (*The Way*).

8. "By the dogma of the *Filioque*, the God of the philosophers and savants is introduced into the heart of the Living God, taking the place of the *Deus absconditus, qui posuit tenebras latibulum suum*. The unknowable essence of the Father, Son, and Holy Spirit receives positive qualifications. It becomes the object of natural theology: we get 'God in general,' who could be the god of Descartes, or the god of Leibnitz, or even perhaps, to some extent, the god of Voltaire and of the de-christianized Deists of the eighteenth century." Vladimir Lossky, "The Procession of the Holy Spirit in Orthodox Trinitarian Doctrine" in his *In the Image and Likeness of God* (Crestwood, N.Y.: St. Vladimir's Seminary Press, 1976), 88.

9. Ibid., 80. In contrasting the Trinitarian theologies of East and West, Lossky is perfectly aware of his debt to Theodore de Régnon's *Études de théologie positive sur la Sainte Trinité*, citing him in support of his contrast between the Latin emphasis on essence and the Greek accent on person (ibid., 78n10).

10. The recapture of Gallipoli in 1366 by Amadeus of Savoy and its brief return to the Byzantine fold could not reverse the process of Turkish expansion into Europe.

11. Christos Yannaras, Ὀρθοδοξία καὶ Δύση στὴ Νεώτερη Ἑλλάδα (Athens, 1992), 489; English translation: Peter Chamberas and Norman Russell, *Orthodoxy and the West* (Brookline, Mass.: Holy Cross Orthodox Press, 2006), 61. I refer in the first instance to the original Modern Greek, but also draw on this fine and elegant translation. This is in deference to Yannaras, who has expressed reservations concerning the English translation. Thanks to Norman Russell for information on Yannaras's position.

12. Yannaras, Ὀρθοδοξία καὶ Δύση στὴ Νεώτερη Ἑλλάδα, 62 [English translation: 27].

13. Christos Yannaras, "Orthodoxy and the West," *Eastern Churches Review* 3 (1971), 287. Note especially the denial of *participation* in Thomas—precisely the theme that forms the lynchpin of the "Radical Orthodox" reading of Thomas: see John Milbank and Catherine Pickstock, *Truth in Aquinas* (London: Routledge, 2000). While Thomas is, for Radical Orthodoxy, the "answer" to secularism, for Yannaras (as for Lossky, Meyendorff, and Sherrard), Thomas is unmistakably its progenitor. It is piquant to note that Yannaras cites not an Eastern but a Western source for his intuition: "Heidegger has assured us that Descartes represents the natural end result of Western scholasticism" (Ibid., 286).

14. Philip Sherrard, *Greek East and Latin West: A Study in the Christian Tradition* (Oxford: Oxford University Press, 1959). Yannaras says little of his connection with or indebtedness to the work of Philip Sherrard, with whom he was at one time on very close terms. He is more forthcoming on the decisive contribution of Demetrios Koutroubis, a seminal and almost Socratic figure for many of the Greek theologians of the "golden decade" of the 1960s. Koutroubis was instrumental in introducing a whole generation to the riches of the theology of the Russian Orthodox disaspora.

15. Yannaras, "Orthodoxy and the West," 296–98.

16. Yannaras acknowledges that the historical account in the book is "necessarily brief and schematic" and goes on to observe: "The critique of Western theology and tradition which I offer in this book does not contrast 'Western' with something 'right' which as an Orthodox I use to oppose something 'wrong' outside myself. I am not attacking an external Western adversary. As a modern Greek, I myself embody both the thirst for what is 'right' and the reality of what is 'wrong': a contradictory and alienated survival of ecclesiastical Orthodoxy in a society radically and unhappily Westernized. My critical stance towards the West is self-criticism; it refers to my own wholly Western mode of life." Yannaras, *Orthodoxy and the West: Hellenic Self-Identity in the Modern Age,* trans. by Norman Russell (Brookline, Mass.: Holy Cross Greek Orthodox Press, 2007), viii–ix.

17. Giovanni Mercati, ed., *Notizie di Procoro e Demetrio Cidone, Manuela Caleca e Theodore Meliteniota ed altri appunti per la storia della teologia e della letteratura bizantina del secolo XIV,* 359–403. See also *Letter* 33 for Demetrios's esteem of Thomas's philosophical culture in *Démétrius Cydonès: Correspondance,* ed. Raymond-Joseph Loenertz, Studi e Testi 186 (Vatican City, 1956), 64–66.

18. Demetrios Kydones, *Apology,* 365.77–84.

19. Demetrios Kydones, *Apology,* 383.53–57.

20. Demetrios Kydones, *Apology,* 399.83.

21. See Evangelos Moutsopoulos, 'L'Hellénisation du Thomisme au XIVe siècle,' *Annuaire Scientifique de la Faculté de Philosophie de l'Université d'Athènes* 24 (1975), 131–36; Photios Demetracopoulos, "Demetrius Kydones' Translation of the *Summa Theologica,*" *JÖB* 32 (1982), 311–19; and Athanasia Glycofrydi-Leontsini, "Demetrius Cydones as a Translator of Latin Texts," in *Porphyrogenita: Festschrift Julian Chrysostomides,* ed. Charalambos Dendrinos et al. (Aldershot, U.K.: Ashgate, 2003), 175–85.

22. On the life and times of Demetrios Kydones, see Raymond-Joseph Loenertz, "Démétrius Cydonès I: De la naissance à l'année 1373," *OCP* 36 (1970), 47–72 and "Démétrius Cydonès II: De 1373 à 1375," *OCP* 37 (1971), 5–39; Frances Kianka, "The Apology of Demetrius Cydones: A Fourteenth-Century Autobiographical Source," *Byzantine Studies* 7 (1980), 51–71 and "Demetrius Cydones: Intellectual and Diplomatic Relations between Byzantium and the

West" (Diss. Fordham University 1981); Norman Russell, "Palamism and the Circle of Demetrius Cydones," in *Porphyrogenita*, 153–74; and Judith Ryder, *The Career and Writings of Demetrius Kydones: A Study of Fourteenth-Century Byzantine Politics, Religion and Society* (Leiden: Brill, 2010).

23. Demetrios Kydones, *Oratio pro subsidio latinorum* (PG 154 977D).

24. Prochoros Kydones, *De essentia et operatione* I–II (PG 151 1191–1242), which is attributed here, wrongly, to Gregory Akindynos; Manuel Candal, "El libro VI de Prócoro Cidonio [sobre la luz tabórica]," *OCP* 20 (1954), 247–96. Books I–V are largely composed of extract from Thomas whereas Book VI (on the light of Thabor) is his own work. On Prochoros, see Thomas Tyn, "Prochoros und Demetrios Kydones: der byzantinische Thomismus des XIV Jahrhunderts," in *Thomas von Aquino: Interpretation und Rezeption*, ed. W.P. Eckert (Mainz: Matthias-Grünewald, 1964), 837–912 and Norman Russell, "Prochoros Cydones and the fourteenth-century understanding of Orthodoxy," in *Byzantine Orthodoxies: Papers from the Thirty-Sixth Spring Symposium of Byzantine Studies*, ed. Andrew Louth and Augustine Casiday (Aldershot, U.K.: Ashgate, 2006), 75–91.

25. There were many of these, notably Manuel Kalekas, Maximos, Theodore, and Andrew Chrysoberges, and Manuel Chrysoloras.

26. See Reinhard Flogaus, *Theosis bei Palamas und Luther* (Göttingen: Vandenhoeck & Ruprecht, 1997); "Der heimliche Blick nach Westen: zur Rezeption von Augustins *De Trinitate* durch Gregorios Palamas," *JÖB* 46 (1996), 275–97; "*Palamas and Barlaam Revisited:* A Reassessment of East and West in the Hesychast Controversy of 14th Century Byzantium," *St. Vladimir's Theological Quarterly* 42 (1998), 1–32; and "Inspiration–Exploitation–Distortion: The Use of St Augustine in the Hesychast Controversy," in *Orthodox Readings of Augustine*, ed. George Demacopoulos and Aristotle Papanikolaou (Crestwood, N.Y.: St. Vladimir's Seminary Press, 2008), 63–80.

27. See especially his *Apodictic Treatises* and *Letters to Barlaam*, ed. Panayiotis Chrestou, *Syngrammata*, vol. 1 (Thessaloniki, 1988), 23–153, 225–95. In the closely related *First Letter to Akindynos* 8 (Ibid., 211.3–5), Palamas writes that "we have in truth been taught by the Fathers to syllogize about [theological matters], and no one would write even against the Latins because of this."

28. Printed in *PG* 154 372–692.

29. E. Voordeckers and F. Tinnefeld, eds., *Iohannis Cantacuzeni: Refutationes duae prochori cydonii et disputatio cum Paulo Patriarcha Latino epistulis septem tradita* (CCSG 16: Turnhout, 1987).

30. John Kantakuzene, *Refutatio* I 16 (CCSG 16: Turnhout), 22–24.

31. Demetrios Kydones, *Apology*, 391.28.

32. Emmanuel Candal, ed., *Neilos Kabasilas et theologia S. Thomae de processione Spiritus Sancti* (Vatican, 1945) and Théophile Kislas, ed., *Nil Kabasilas: Sur le Saint Esprit* (Paris: Les Éditions du Cerf, 2001).

33. Meyendorff, *Byzantine Theology* (New York: Fordham University Press, 1983), 107. This line of thought is pursued in Joost van Rossum's "Palamism and Church Tradition: Palamism, its Use of Patristic Tradition, and its Relationship with Thomistic Thought" (PhD. diss., Fordham University, 1985).

34. See Ioannis Polemis, *Theophanes of Nicea: His Life and Works* (Vienna: Wiener Byzantinistische Studien 20, 1996), 87–112, 122–25.

35. See John Demetracopoulos, "Nicholas Kabasilas's *Quaestio de rationis valore*: an anti-Palamite defense of secular wisdom," *Βυζαντινά* 19 (1998): 77–83. This anti-Palamite reading seems to me a little exaggerated.

36. See Hugh Barbour, *The Byzantine Thomism of Gennadios Scholarios* (Vatican City: Libreria Editrice Vaticana, 1993), 43; Asterios Argyriou, *Macaire Macrès et la polémique contre l'Islam* (Vatican City: Biblioteca Apostolica Vaticana, 1986) and Argyriou, "La *Dialexis* de Joseph Bryennios avec un Ismaelite," *Epeteris Hetaireias Byzantinon Spoudon* 35 (1967), 141–95.

37. Stylianos Papadopoulos, ed., Καλλίστου Ἀγγελικούδη κατα Θωμᾶ (Athens, 1970). See also the companion volume, Συνάντησις ὀρθοδόξου καὶ σκολαστικῆς θεολογίας (Thessaloniki, 1970). Also Ivan Christov, "Kallistos Angelikoudes's Critical Account of Thomistic and Orthodox Anthropology," *Synthesis Philosophica* 39 (2005), 73–83 and Ioannis Polemis, "Notes on Two Texts Dealing with the Palamite Controversy," in *Realia Byzantina* [*Byzantinsches Archiv* 22: Festschrift Apostolos Karpozilos] (Berlin, 2009), 207–12.

38. On Scholarios, see Marie-Hélène Blanchet, Georges-Gennadios Scholarios (Paris: Institut Français d'Etudes Byzantines, 2008) and Hugh Barbour, *The Byzantine Thomism of Gennadios Scholarios*. Scholarios's complete works have long been edited: Louis Petit, Xenophon Side¥ride's and Martin Jugie, eds., *Oeuvres complètes de Georges Scholarios*, 8 vols. (Paris, 1928–36).

39. Scholarios, *Oeuvres complètes*, vol. 6, 179. Scholarios explicitly targets the Franciscans here.

40. Scholarios, *Oeuvres complètes*, vol. 6, 1. This is a marginal note in Gennadios's abridged version of the *Prima secundae*.

41. Martin Jugie neatly turns this lament on Scholarios, lamenting that he had been born on the Bosphorus and not the Tiber. "Georges Scholarios et Saint Thomas d'Aquin," *Mélanges Madonnet* I (Paris: Vrin, 1930), 435.

42. Scholarios, *Oeuvres complètes*, vol. 6, 177. Scholarios goes on to praise the universal patristic foundations of Thomas's teaching, drawing attention to his use of Latin and Greek Fathers alike.

43. "It is not enough to refute or reject western errors or mistakes—they must be overcome through a new creative act." This "new creative act" is described as "a historiosophical exegesis of the western religious tragedy," one in which "the centuries-old experience of the Catholic west must be studied and diagnosed by Orthodox theology with greater care and sympathy than has been the case until

now." Georges Florovsky, *Ways of Russian Theology*, vol. 2 (Vaduz: Bücherver-triebsanstalt, 1987), 301–3.

44. Georges Florovsky, Review of Lossky's *Mystical Theology of the Eastern Church* (London: James Clarke, 1957), *The Journal of Religion* 38 (1958): 207–8.

45. Vladimir Lossky, Review of Eric Mascall, *Existence and Analogy* (London: Longmans, Green & Co., 1949), *Sobornost* 1950, 295–97. Gilson was to furnish a warm and moving tribute to Lossky in the preface to the posthumously published *Théologie négative et connaissance de Dieu chez Maître Eckhart* (Paris: Vrin, 1960).

46. This essay is essentially an adumbration of the content and themes of my *Orthodox Readings of Aquinas* (Oxford: Oxford University Press 2012). There is much here that is simply sketched or briefly mentioned but that receives due attention and amplification in that work.

From the "Shield of Orthodoxy" to the "Tome of Joy": The Anti-Western Stance of Dositheos II of Jerusalem (1641–1707) / Norman Russell

1. For a closely argued presentation of this view, see Stelios Ramfos, *Yearning for the One: Chapters in the Inner Life of the Greeks*, trans. Norman Russell (Brookline, Mass.: Holy Cross Orthodox Press, 2011). Ramfos believes that the Western philosophical and spiritual tradition can stimulate Orthodoxy to remedy a defective sense of interiority inherited from Byzantium.

2. Christos Yannaras is a leading exponent of this view. See his *Orthodoxy and the West*, trans. Peter Chamberas and Norman Russell (Brookline, Mass.: Holy Cross Orthodox Press, 2006). It should be noted, however, that Yannaras does not simply treat the West as the "Other." "My critical stance towards the West," he says, "is self-criticism; it refers to my own wholly Western mode of life" (*Orthodoxy and the West*, ix). What Yannaras objects to is not the West as such but an Orthodoxy that has so absorbed Western values and cultural attitudes that it has become "religionized" and consequently no longer expresses a living relationship with God.

3. Chrysostomos Papadopoulos, "Dositheos, patriarchēs Hierosolymōn (1641–1707)," *Nea Siōn* 5–6 (1907), 97–168; I. Pomerantsev, "Ierusalimiskii patriarkh Dosifei II (1669–1707g.)," *Istoricheskii ocherk, Soobshcheniia Imperatorskago Pravoslavnago Palestinskago Obshchestva* 19 (1908): 1–32; Aurelio Palmieri, *Dositeo, patriarca greco di Gerusalemme (1641–1707): Contributo alla storia della teologia greco-ortodossa nel secolo XVII* (Florence: Liberia Editrice Fiorentina, 1909). For a full bibliography on Dositheos, see Klaus-Peter Todt, "Dositheos II.

von Jerusalem," in *La théologie byzantine et sa tradition II (XIIIᵉ–XIXᵉs.)*, ed. Carmelo Giuseppe Conticello and Vassa Conticello (Turnhout: Brepols Publishers, 2002), 659–720.

4. Papadopoulos, "Dositheos," cited by Palmieri, *Dositeo*, 5.

5. Palmieri, *Dositeo*, 93.

6. Ioannis N. Karmiris, *Dogma—Dogmatikē—Dogmatōn Historia: Dositheos Hierosolymōn kai hē Homologia tou*. Offprint from vol. 2 of the *Thrēskeutikē Enkyklopaideia*. (Athens, 1937).

7. Ioan V. Durǎ, *Ho Dositheos Hierosolymōn kai hē prosphora autou eis tas Roumanikas chōras kai tēn ekklēsian autōn* (Athens: n.p., 1977), 38.

8. Gerhard Podskalsky, *Griechische Theologie in der Zeit der Türkenherrschaft (1453–1821)* (Munich: C. H. Beck, 1988), 282.

9. By "ecumenicity" I mean Orthodoxy's sense of being the one catholic and apostolic Church, not necessarily in an exclusive sense, but neither simply as the Church's Eastern branch or expression. For a concise overview of the period, see Paschalis M. Kitromilides, "Orthodoxy and the West: Reformation to Enlightenment," in *The Cambridge History of Christianity: Eastern Christianity*, ed. Michael Angold (Cambridge: Cambridge University Press, 2006), 187–209.

10. The main source for the life of Dositheos is the biographical sketch with which his nephew and successor, Chrysanthos (1707–31), prefaced the posthumous publication of Dositheos's *Historia peri tōn en Hierosolymois patriarcheusantōn* (History of the patriarchs of Jerusalem) (Bucharest, 1715). The fundamental modern discussion is still Palmieri, *Dositeo*. See also Palmieri's article "Dosithée," *Dictionnaire de Théologie Catholique*, vol. 4 (1911), 1788–1800, and most recently Todt, "Dositheos," 659–70.

11. It was long believed that Dositheos's family name was Notaras, like that of his nephew. Towards the end of the nineteenth century, however, Kyrillos Athanasiades drew attention to an autograph document in the archive of the Metochion of the Holy Sepulchre at Constantinople in which Dositheos refers to his father as *to genos Skarpetē*. Athanasiades, *Sotēr* 14 (1891), 289; cited by Palmieri, *Dositeo*, 6.

12. The canonical age for the diaconate (as laid down by Canon 14 of the Quinisext Ecumenical Council) was twenty-five. Monasteries often received child oblates on whom minor orders were conferred at an early age, but to be raised to the diaconate at the age of eleven was highly unusual. Dositheos himself attests to the fact that he became a deacon at the monastery under Kyr Gregory (Athanasiades, *Sotēr* 14 [1891], 290; cited by Palmieri, *Dositeo*, 7).

13. The Acts of the Council of Jerusalem (1672), which Dositheos probably drew up himself, are written (as one would expect) in a strongly classicized form of the language. His historical writings, however, are in the normal paratactic style of the period. Many of his letters, even to heads of state and senior ecclesiastics, are written in a lively vernacular.

14. Cited by Palmieri, *Dositeo*, 8.

15. On Nektarios, see Podskalsky, *Griechische Theologie*, 244–48.

16. The synod met at the Metochion of the Holy Sepulchre at Constantinople, which remained throughout the Ottoman period the *konak*, or official residence, of the patriarchs of Jerusalem in Constantinople.

17. Again, he was dispensed from the canonical age requirement, which, following earlier precedent, had been set at thirty for the presbyterate by Canon 14 of the Quinisext Council of 692. As Lewis Patsavos has remarked, however, in Eastern canon law the maturity of candidates was always a more important consideration than fulfilment of the age requirements (Lewis Patsavos, *A Noble Task: Entry into the Clergy in the First Five Centuries* [Brookline, Mass.: Holy Cross Orthodox Press, 2007], 273–77).

18. Palmieri, *Dositeo*, 13. The piastre was a silver coin approximately equal to the Venetian ducat (the international currency of the time). In today's terms, the sum raised by Dositheos was equivalent to about US$750,000.

19. During the seventeenth century, a good deal of the trade of the Ottoman Empire began to be concentrated in the hands of Greeks. As *kürçübaşi*, head of the Constantinopolitan guild of furriers, Manolakis controlled the important fur trade. On his career and benefactions, chiefly concerning the founding of schools, see Apostolos E. Vakalopoulos, *Historia tēs Makedonias 1354–1833* (Thessaloniki: n.p., 1969), 414–15; English translation: *History of Macedonia 1354–1833*, trans. Peter Megann (Thessaloniki: Institute of Balkan Studies, 1973), 446.

20. Nikousios, who had studied medicine in Italy, began his career as a doctor. He came to the attention of the government through helping the Kapudan Pasha (grand admiral of the Ottoman fleet) negotiate the treaty with Venice in 1669 that ceded Crete to the Ottoman Empire. This led to the creation of the office of grand dragoman, or official interpreter to the Sublime Porte (the Ottoman imperial government), with Nikousios as its first holder. On the importance of this office, which gave the Greeks direct access to the grand vizier and the sultan, see Philip Mansel, "Viziers and Dragomans," in *Constantinople: City of the World's Desire 1453–1924* (London: John Murray, 1995).

21. "More than most of his predecessors," says Mansel, "Louis XIV liked to pose as the champion of the Catholic Church" (*Constantinople*, 196). Cooperation between France and the Ottoman Empire went back to the previous century, when the rivalry between Francis I and the Holy Roman Emperor, Charles V, made an alliance with Austria's powerful enemy to the east highly attractive to the French. The first Franco-Ottoman capitulations (treaty terms) were signed on October 18, 1569. They were of immense value to the French. According to Halil Inalcik, "At the beginning of the seventeenth century there were about a thousand French vessels active in the Levant, and the volume of trade rose to

thirty million livres, half of France's total trade" (*The Ottoman Empire: The Classical Age 1300–1600* [London: Phoenix, 1994], 137). By the time of Dositheos this trade had been much reduced, largely as a result of the rise of the English Levant Company. But in 1673 de Nointel was able to negotiate the renewal of the capitulations on terms favourable to France. It was probably in this connection that de Nointel was instructed to put pressure on Jerusalem in the Catholic interest.

22. Palmieri, *Dositeo*, 26–28. The grand vizier was the sultan's chief minister. An *iradé* was an imperial decree issued by the Sublime Porte. De Nointel turned out to be a source of irritation to the Porte and was recalled in 1678 (Mansel, *Constantinople*, 196–97).

23. On Cyril's *Confession*, see Klaus-Peter Todt's notice in his "Kyrillos Lukaris," in Conticello and Conticello, *La théologie byzantine et sa tradition II (XIIe—XIXes.)*, 634–35. There is an English translation in George A. Hadjiantoniou, *Protestant Patriarch: The Life of Cyril Lucaris (1572–1638), Patriarch of Constantinople* (Richmond, Va.: John Knox Press, 1961), 141–45. Hadjiantoniou, a Greek Evangelical, had no hesitation in claiming Cyril for Protestantism: "One of the greatest men who ever sat on the Ecumenical Throne of Constantinople was a Calvinist" (*Protestant Patriarch*, 103). For a balanced, recent assessment of Cyril, see Kitromilides, "Orthodoxy and the West," 193–202. In Kitromilides's view, "The Protestant alliance was conceived as a major weapon in the defence of Orthodoxy, not as an end in itself" (195).

24. Dositheos's arguments in favor of forgery were accepted by many Greek scholars (including Papadopoulos) right up to the Second World War (Hadjiantoniou, *Protestant Patriarch*, 102–3). Today it is generally acknowledged that Cyril was the author of the *Confession of Faith* attributed to him.

25. Nikousios is described by Dositheos as "an extreme zealot for the [Orthodox] faith" (preface to his *Homologia orthodoxou pisteōs*, Bucharest, 1690; reproduced in Emile Legrand, *Bibliographie hellénique du dix-septième siècle* [Paris: Picard, 1894], 2:202). He was happy to satisfy the Western appetite for information on where the Orthodox stood with regard to points of controversy between Catholics and Protestants, supplying the embassy of the States General (the Dutch embassy), for example, with a copy of Syrigos's *Confession*, which was printed in a Latin translation in Antwerp in 1668 at the expense of the Dutch in spite of Nikousios's willingness to pay for the edition himself (Legrand, *Bibliographie hellénique*, 2:204–5, citing a letter of de Nointel). Foucqueret's edition of the *Shield of Orthodoxy* was twice reprinted in Paris (in 1678 and 1715). There is an English translation by J. N. W. B. Robertson, *The Acts and Decrees of the Synod of Jerusalem, Sometimes Called the Council of Jerusalem, Holden under Dositheus, Patriarch of Jerusalem in 1672* (London: Thomas Baker, 1899).

26. Palmieri, *Dositeo*, 18, citing the edition of the *Homologia orthodoxou pisteōs* published by Mesoloras in *Symbolikē tēs orthodoxou Anatolikēs Ekklēsias* (Athens: n.p., 1893), 57.

27. Palmieri, *Dositeo*, 22. Palmieri points out that Ecumenical Patriarch Dionysios IV confirmed the orthodoxy of Dositheos's *Confession* but refrained from using the term *metousiōsis* (transubstantiation). Dositheos was to modify his view of purgatory, though not of transubstantiation, as we shall see below, as a result of his study of late Byzantine authors. For discussions of his theological approach to these issues, see Timothy Ware, *Eustratios Argenti: A Study of the Greek Church under Turkish Rule* (Oxford: Oxford University Press, 1964), 11–15; Todt, "Dositheos," 696–706.

28. Aymon, *Monumens authentiques de la religion des grecs* (The Hague: n.p., 1708). Aymon regards the Acts of the synod as fraudulent. Palmieri concurs (*Dositeo*, 16–17), in that the document purporting to be the Acts seems to have been drawn up beforehand and simply subscribed by the participants. If so, this would not have been the first time the Acts of a council had been produced in this way.

29. The reception of the *Targa* by the Orthodox in the Ottoman Empire is described by Dositheos in his *Historia peri tōn en Hierosolymois patriarcheusantōn*, 1177: "In the year one thousand six hundred and fifty eight there came to Constantinople and to the Eastern Church in general from France the so-called *Targa*; and having received authorization from the government, the Patriarch Parthenios the fourth wrote to the City and to Galata, and indeed also to Smyrna and every city and Orthodox land against it. And having bought up the *Targa*, the Orthodox burned a great many copies of it in the market places, and it became a great source of shame for the papists."

30. From the (Latin) Dedicatory Epistle of the *Targa tēs pisteōs tēs Rōmaikēs Ekklēsias* addressed to the Marquis de Ventelay, at the time Louis XIV's ambassador to the Ottoman Emperor, reproduced in Legrand, *Bibliographie hellénique*, 2:104–5.

31. On the activities of the Jesuits in the Ottoman Empire, see Charles A. Frazee, *Catholics and Sultans: The Church and the Ottoman Empire 1453–1923* (Cambridge: Cambridge University Press, 1983), 72–74, 81–83, 114–18, 123–25. For much of the seventeenth century many Orthodox metropolitans welcomed Jesuits into their churches to preach and hear confessions. For some well-documented cases, see Ware, *Eustratios Argenti*, 16–29; also Ware, "Orthodox and Catholics in the Seventeenth Century: Schism or Intercommunion?" in *Schism, Heresy and Religious Protest*, ed. D. Baker (Cambridge: Cambridge University Press, 1972), 259–76. Ware notes a hardening of attitudes around 1700, which he attributes principally to Orthodox alarm at "the success of Latin penetration and propaganda . . . made worse by the policy of concealment which the western clergy adopted" (*Eustratios Argenti*, 24).

32. The *ulema* was the organized body of Muslim religious scholars who administered the *şeriat*, or system of Islamic law, in the Ottoman Empire. Halil Inalcik comments that as in Muslim theory "the state is subordinate to religion," it was the duty of the secular authority to put the judgments of the *ulema* into practice (*The Ottoman Empire*, 171).

33. Steven Runciman, *The Great Church in Captivity* (Cambridge: Cambridge University Press, 1968), 272–73.

34. Peter Mackridge has described this aptly as "a kind of privatization of Ottoman rule in the region" (*Language and National Identity in Greece, 1766–1976* [Oxford: Oxford University Press, 2009], 41). On Dositheos's relations with the Danubian provinces, Nicolae Iorga, *Byzance après Byzance* (Bucharest, 1935; repr. 1971), especially chs. 7 and 8, is still valuable.

35. Dositheos, *Historia*, 1236, reproduced in Legrand, *Bibliographie hellénique*, 2:401, together with Dositheos's dedicatory letter to John Doukas, voivode of all Moldo-Wallachia, from his first publication, in which he praises Doukas for his stout defense of Orthodoxy and his support for the press. Besides paying for the fount (equivalent to nearly US$25,000 at today's values), Dositheos also supplied Metrophanes with paper from Adrianople.

36. For a full register of Dositheos's publications, see Todt, "Dositheos," 670–83.

37. Legrand, *Bibliographie hellénique*, 2:407–8. Allix's translation is prefaced by a dedicatory epistle addressed to Thomas, Archbishop of Canterbury. Le Quien's refutation was published under the pseudonym Stephanus de Altimura with the title *Panoplia contra Schisma Graecorum qua Romana et Occidentalis ecclesia defenditur Adversus Criminationes Nectarii . . . .*

38. Legrand, *Bibliographie hellénique*, 2:578; Todt, "Dositheos," 670–71.

39. Legrand, *Bibliographie hellénique*, 2:635; Todt, "Dositheos," 671. On Maximos Peloponnesios, see Podskalsky, *Griechische Theologie*, 154–56.

40. Legrand, *Bibliographie hellénique*, 2:632; Todt, "Dositheos," 671, 673. On Meletios Syrigos, see Podskalsky, *Griechische Theologie*, 207–13.

41. Legrand, *Bibliographie hellénique*, 2:632; Todt, "Dositheos," 678, 680–81.

42. *Encheiridion kata tēs Kalvinikēs Phrenovlaveias* (Bucharest, 1690), IIIb.

43. *Encheiridion*, IIIa.

44. Ware, *Eustratios Argenti*, 13–15; Todt, "Dositheos," 696–99.

45. Ware, *Eustratios Argenti*, 150–53. See Todt, "Dositheos," 713–20, for a German translation of the two versions of Article 18 on purgatory.

46. Ware, *Eustratios Argenti*, 153–54.

47. Todt, "Dositheos," 680.

48. *Tomos katallagēs* (Jassy, 1692), viii; quoted by Palmieri, *Dositeo*, 49. The "single shepherd" is presumably Jesus Christ, in accordance with the usual

Orthodox position on the papacy. But the phraseology does suggest the influence of the papal monarchical ideology.

49. Palmieri draws attention to the many codices in the patriarchal libraries of Jerusalem and the Metochion of the Holy Sepulchre containing documents collected by Dositheos with notes written in his own hand (*Dositeo*, 92).

50. On Allatius, see Podskalsky, *Griechische Theologie*, 213–19.

51. *Tomos katallagēs*, viii; Palmieri, *Dositeo*, 48–49. The first edition of Allatius's *Enchiridion* was issued in 1658.

52. *Tomos agapēs* (Jassy, 1698), 1–7 (dedicatory letter addressed to the reader); Palmieri, *Dositeo*, 56–57.

53. Legrand, *Bibliographie hellénique*, 3:42–43.

54. Ligarides and Karyophylles were both alumni of the Greek College in Rome. Ligarides (c. 1609–78) was sent to the East by Propaganda in 1641, and from 1643 was employed by the Patriarch Parthenios I and his successors Parthenios II and Joannikios II to preach and hear confessions. In 1652 he transferred his allegiance to Orthodoxy, whereupon Paisios of Jerusalem made him archbishop of Gaza. Never trusted by Dositheos, who deposed him in 1671, he spent most of his remaining years in Russia. His criticism of hesychasm (he referred to Palamas as a polytheist) belongs to his Catholic phrase (V. Grumel, "Ligaridès, Paisios," *Dictionnaire de Théologie Catholique* 9 [1926], 749–57; Podskalsky, *Griechische Theologie*, 39 no. 114: 251–58). Karyophylles (c. 1566–1633), after a brief period in his native Crete, spent most of his life engaged in scholarly work in Rome. He wrote a refutation of Cyril Loukaris's *Confession* and was the Greek translator of Bellarmine's *Dottrina Christiana Breve* (Podskalsky, *Griechische Theologie*, 181–83). Defenders of hesychasm included Nektarios of Jerusalem, in his book against the papal primacy; the Likhoudes brothers, who in 1690 made a note of a debate between a Jesuit and a Greek on hesychasm (Podskalsky, *Griechische Theologie*, 39); and a group of theologians at Ioannina, led by Bessarion Makres, who engaged in a three-year disputation (from 1696 to 1699) on hesychasm with another Orthodox group led by George Sougdoures (Dura, *Dositheos Hierosolymōn*, 35, citing P. Christou, "Hēsychastikai anazētēseis eis ta Iōannina peri to 1700," *Klēronomia* 1, no. 2 [1969]: 337–52). Makres was supported by his metropolitan, Clement of Ioannina, with both of whom Dositheos was in close touch.

55. The introductory essay occupies pages 12–114. The Palamite texts that follow are the very substantial *Antirrhetics* of Philotheos Kokkinos against Gregoras and the much shorter *Hagioritic Tome* of 1340, the *Synodal Tomes* of 1341, 1351, and 1368, and Palamas's *Confession of Faith* of 1343–44. Dositheos was well read in the hesychast literature of the fourteenth century. In the *Shield of Orthodoxy* (1690) he also mentions John Cantacuzenos, who "demonstrated through the holy Fathers [in his *Refutation of Prochoros Cydones*] that the divine

grace and divine energy are uncreated" (Legrand, *Bibliographie hellénique*, 2:465).

56. *Tomos charas* (Rimnic, 1705), β, cited by Palmieri, *Dositeo*, 68. Dositheos distinguishes between the *filioque* as a heresy, and the papal monarchy as a blasphemy.

57. Dositheos had first "blown the sacred trumpet" on the Jesuits in a Letter to the Reader published in 1699 in his edition of the *Confession of Peter Mogila* (Legrand, *Bibliographie hellénique*, 3:68–75), where he identifies the "order of the Jesuits" as one of the four beasts (along with the Lutherans, the Calvinists, and the Gregorian calendar) that had appeared in the sixteenth century. The blasphemies he objects to are the Jesuits' soteriological exclusivism ("they say that he who does not believe in the pope of Rome is godless and cannot attain salvation"), and the way their propaganda had unsettled the Russians. For example, they converted Mary, the daughter of the Grand Duke Basil, to papism, and caused her to lament that her father was in hell: "To make her feel better, the Jesuits went and dug and exhumed her father's bones from the grave, and baptized them according to the Latin rite" (Legrand, *Bibliographie hellénique*, 3:69). They also spread the slander that Cyril of Constantinople was a Calvinist, with the result that the Russians sent representatives to Theophanes of Jerusalem (Paisios's predecessor from 1606 to 1644), who had ordained the tsar's father, Philaret of Moscow, and was then at Jassy, to ask if this was true (Legrand, *Bibliographie hellénique*, 3:71).

58. During the negotiations at Karlowitz the French demanded the deposition of Dositheos, but this was successfully resisted by Mavrokordatos.

59. Mansel, *Constantinople*, 145.

60. The exarchate lasted from 1577 to 1790. The exarch was always the titular metropolitan of Philadelphia (the last city in western Asia Minor to fall to the Turks).

61. For an entertaining account of contacts between the Orthodox and the Church of England, see Runciman, "The Church and the Churches: The Anglican Experiment," in Runciman, *Great Church*.

62. This was the option followed by many of the bishops of the patriarchate of Antioch, which led to a schism in 1724 between those in favor of union with Rome and those who rejected it. See Ware, *Eustratios Argenti*, 28–30; Frazee, *Catholics and Sultans*, 132–37, 199–207.

63. Cited and translated by James Cracraft from Peter the Great's collected letters (*Pis'ma i bumagi imperatora Petri Velikago* [St. Petersburg: n.p., 1887–1962], 2:715–21) in *The Church Reform of Peter the Great* (London: Macmillan, 1971), 125.

64. Cracraft, *Church Reform*, 4.

65. In 1691, after the French had secured control of the Holy Places for the Franciscans, Dositheos wrote to Peter the Great in terms that the Ottoman gov-

ernment, had they known, might well have thought treasonable: "Destroy the Tatars and Jerusalem will be yours. Alexander the Great went to the war with the Persians not for God's sake but for the sake of his fellow tribesmen. All the more reason that you should be vigilant and make every effort to drive off your wicked neighbors for the sake of the holy places and our Orthodox faith" (Letter of March 18, 1691, cited by Lindsey Hughes from S. M. Soloviev, *History of Russia*, vol. 25, *Rebellion and Reform: Fedor and Sophia*, trans. Lindsey Hughes [Gulf Breeze, Fla: Academic International Press, 1989], 116–19, in Lindsey Hughes, *Russia in the Age of Peter the Great* [New Haven: Yale University Press, 1998], 352). Dositheos (and perhaps his recipient's advisers) would have been aware that in the work of the Byzantine historians, "Persians" was the code word for "Turks."

66. Moscow had always had a filial relationship with Constantinople as the source of its Orthodox faith, a relationship strengthened in 1589 when Metropolitan Job of Moscow was consecrated patriarch by Jeremias II of Constantinople. Within the ecumenical patriarchate Dositheos seems to have had a special responsibility for Russian affairs. This ensured some continuity. During Dositheos's patriarchate (1669–1707) the ecumenical throne changed hands no fewer than fifteen times (see Podskalsky, *Griechische Theologie*, 400). The fullest account of Dositheos's relations with Russia is N. F. Kapterev, "Snosheniia patriarkha Dosifeia s russkim pravitel'stvom pri Petre Velikom," reprinted in Kapterev, *Sobranie Sochinenii* (Moscow: Dukhovnaia Akademiia, 2008), 2:181–252.

67. On the Likhoudes brothers, see Martin Jugie, "Likhoudès (Les Frères)," *Dictionnaire de Théologie Catholique*, vol. 9 (1926), 757–60.

68. Letter of June 2, 1702, cited by Cracraft, *Church Reform*, 125n63. Dositheos repeated the same sentiments in almost the same words in a letter to Stefan Iavorskii (Kallinikos Delikanes, *Patriarchika Engrapha*, vol. 3 [Constantinople: Patriarchal Press, 1905], no. 33 bis, Letter of Dositheos to Stephen of Ryazan, 218–25, especially 222). Delikanes assigns this letter to 1704. Cracraft, working from the Russian sources, dates it to November 15, 1703 (*Church Reform*, 126).

69. Iavorskii was appointed metropolitan of Ryazan and remained *locum tenens* of the patriarchal throne of Moscow from Adrian's death in 1700 to the abolition of the patriarchal office in 1721.

70. Delikanes, *Patriarchika Engrapha*, 3:223.

71. Delikanes, *Patriarchika Engrapha*, 3:221.

72. Palmieri, "Dosithée," 1791.

73. Todt, "Dositheos," 706.

74. Dositheos, *Historia*, 1217.

75. Letter to Stephen of Ryazan, Delikanes, *Patriarchika Engrapha*, 3:224.

76. From Dositheos's epilogue to the *Shield of Orthodoxy*, trans. Robertson, in *Acts and Decrees*, 177.

The Burdens of Tradition: Orthodox
Constructions of the West in Russia
(late 19th–early 20th cc.)/
Vera Shevzov

1. As examples of the numerous studies of this topic, see Nicholas V. Riasanovsky, *Russia and the West in the Teaching of the Slavophiles: A Study in Romantic Ideology* (Cambridge, Mass.: Harvard University Press, 1952); Peter K. Christoff, *An Introduction to Nineteenth-Century Slavophilism: A Study in Ideas*, vol. 1–4 ('s-Gravenhage: Mouton, 1961–91); Andrzej Walicki, *The Slavophile Controversy: History of a Conservative Utopia in Nineteenth-Century Russian Thought* (Oxford: Clarendon, 1975); Stefan Reichelt, "Die Kirche des Ostens und des Westens in der russichen religiösen Philosophie," in *Russische Religionsphilosophie und Theologie um 1900*, ed. Karl Pinggéra (Marburg: N. G. Elwert, 2005), 95–107; Susanna Rabow-Edling, *Slavophile Thought and the Politics of Cultural Nationalism* (Albany: State University of New York Press, 2006); Laura Engelstein, *Slavophile Empire: Imperial Russia's Illiberal Path* (Ithaca, N.Y.: Cornell University Press, 2009).

2. Peggy Heller, "The Russian Dawn: How Russia Contributed to the Emergence of 'the West' as a Concept," in *The Struggle for the West: A Divided and Contested Legacy*, ed. Christopher S. Browning and Marko Lehti (New York: Routledge, 2010), 34.

3. Vasilii Pevnitskii (1832–1911), a graduate of the Kiev Theological Academy and professor of homiletics, maintained that Slavophiles were not interested in Orthodox thought per se, but only as it concerned "foreign faiths." See V. N. Pevnitskii, "Rech' o sud'bakh bogoslovskoi nauki v nashem otechestve," *Trudy Kievskoi Dukhovnoi Akademii* (November–December 1869): 201. Also see comment by M. Krasniuk, "Religiozno-filosofskoe uchenie prezhnikh slavianofilov," *Vera i razum* 2 (August 1900): 180. For Orthodox academic accounts of the history of the Slavophiles, see V. Zavitnevich, *Znachenie pervykh Slavianofilov v dele uiasneniia idei narodnosti i samobytnosti* (Kiev: n.p., 1891). Vladimir Zavitnevich (1853–1927) was a graduate of St. Petersburg Theological Academy, a professor of Russian history at Kiev Theological Academy, and an active publicist.

4. As an example, see Robin Aizlewood, "Revisiting Russian Identity in Russian Thought: From Chaadaev to the Early Twentieth Century," *The Slavonic and East European Review* 78, no. 1 (January 2000): 20–43.

5. Most of Russia's theological and devotional journals began publication in the second half of the nineteenth century, beginning in the period of reform during the reign of Alexander II. Journals that began publication at this time included *Dushepoleznoe chtenie* (1860–1917), *Pravoslavnoe obozrenie* (1860–91),

Pravoslavnyi sobesednik (1855–1917), *Strannik* (1860–1917), *Trudy Kievskoi Dukhovnoi Akademii* (1860–1917) among numerous others.

6. The earliest Orthodox polemics with the Christian "West" or "Latins" carried out in Rus' were authored by Greek hierarchs and churchmen who were serving in this outpost of the Byzantine commonwealth. See Ieromonakh Avgustin, "Polemicheskaiia sochineniia protiv latinian, pissanyia v russkoi tserkovi v XI–XII v. v sviazi s obshchim istoricheskim izyskaniem otnositel'no raznostei mezhdu vostochnoiu i zapadnoiu tserkoviu," *Trudy Kievskoi Dukhovnoi Akademii* (June 1867): 352–420; (September 1867): 461–521. In his insightful work on Russia and the Christian West, Wil van den Bercken has noted that the thirteenth century marks a turning point when Russian's Orthodox self-image is affected by the schism between the Roman Catholics and the Byzantine East. See Wil van den Bercken, *Holy Russia and Christian Europe: East and West in the Religious Ideology of Russia* (London: SCM Press, 1999), 122–26.

7. *The Russian Primary Chronicle: Laurentian Text*, trans. and ed. Samuel Hazzard Cross and Olgerd P. Sherbowitz-Wetzor (Cambridge, Mass.: Medieval Academy of America, 1953), 115–16.

8. V. V. Rozanov, "Russkaia tserkov'," in *Pravoslavie—Pro et Contra: Osmyslenie roli Pravoslaviia v sud'be Rossii so storony deiatelei russkoi kul'tury i tserkvi*, comp. V. F. Fedorov (St. Petersburg: Izd-vo Russkogo khristianskogo gumanitarnogo in-ta, 2001), 113.

9. Shebatinskii was a graduate of Kiev Theological Academy. Konstantin Shebatinskii, "Istoricheskii genesis idei Moskvy—Tret'iago Rima v XV v.," *Vera i razum* 1, no. 13 (1908): 289–90.

10. V. V. Zenkovskii, "Ideia Pravoslavnoi kul'tury," Fedorov, *Pravoslavie—Pro et Contra*, 259.

11. A. P. Lopukhin, "Sovremennyi Zapad v religiozno-nravstvennom otnoshenii," *Khristianskoe chtenie*, no. 9–10 (1885): 488. Lopukhin (1852–1904) was a graduate of St. Petersburg Theological Academy, where he also taught courses in comparative theology and ancient history. He spent three years serving as a reader in the St. Nicholas Church in New York City, the result of which was a book on religion in America.

12. For a description of Orthodox seminary education in the eighteenth century, see Gregory L. Freeze, *Russia Levites: Parish Clergy in the Eighteenth Century* (Cambridge, Mass.: Harvard University Press, 1977).

13. Iosif Vladimirov, "Poslanie nekoego izugrafa Iosifa k tsarevu izugrafu i mudreishemu zhivopistsu Simonu Fedorovichu," in *Drevne-russkoe iskusstvo, XVII vek* (Moscow: Nauka, 1964), 28; V. Illarionov, "Ikonopistsy-Suzdal'tsy," *Russkoe obozrenie*, 32 (March–April 1895): 735; N. Trokhimovskii, "Ofeni," *Russkii vestnik* 63 (June 1866): 577–78.

14. Examples where authors mention a need to search for the essence of Christianity, Sviashchennik P. Linitskii, "Po povodu zashchity slavianofil'stva v Pravoslavnom obozrenii," *Trudy Kievskoi Dukhovnoi Akademii* (January 1884): 88–89; N. Glubokovskii, "Pravoslavie po ego sushchestvu," *Khristianskoe chtenie* (January 1914): 3–22. Also printed in English translation as Nicholas Glubokovsky, "Orthodoxy in Its Essence," *The Constructive Quarterly* 1, no. 2 (June 1913): 282–303. Petr Linitskii (1839–1906) was professor of philosophy at Kiev Theological Academy. N. Glubokovskii (1863–1937) was professor of New Testament at St. Petersburg Theological Academy. He died in emigration in Sophia, Bulgaria.

15. Lopukhin, "Sovremennyi Zapad," 451.

16. Arkhimandrit Feodor (A.M. Bukharev), "O sovremennosti v otnoshenii k pravoslaviiu" in *O Pravoslavii v otnoshenii k sovremennosti* (St. Petersburg: n.p., 1906) 55–56; Lenitskii, "Po povodu zashchity slavianofil'stva," 88–89; Arkhimandrit Vladimir Troitskii, "A. S. Khomiakov i drevne-tserkovnye polemisty," *Vera i razum*, no. 18 (1911): 731–48.

17. V. V. Zenkovskii, *Russian Thinkers and Europe*, trans. Galia S. Bodde (Ann Arbor, Mich.: J. W. Edwards, 1953), 48.

18. Glubokovskii, "Pravoslavie po ego sushchestvu," 13.

19. E. Smirnov, "Slavianofily i ikh uchenie v otnoshenii k bogoslovskoi nauke," *Strannik* (February 1877): 203. Protopresbyter Evgenii Smirnov (b. 1845) was a graduate of St. Petersburg Theological Academy and served in the embassy church in London.

20. Also see observation by Pevnitskii, "Rech' o sud'bakh bogoslovskoi nauki," 190–91; I. Osinin, "Rech' chitannaia v torzhestvennom sobranii S. Peterburgskoi Dukhovnoi Akademii ekstraordinarnym professorom I. T. Osininym, 17-go fevralia 1872," *Khristianskoe chtenie* (March 1872): 1; Nikolai Sergievskii, "Vzgliad na proshedshee i nadezhdy v budushchem," *Pravoslavnoe obozrenie* (January 1870): 19. A graduate of St. Petersburg Theological Academy, Ivan Osinin was born in 1835 in Copenhagen, where his father served as a reader in the embassy church. He taught German at St. Petersburg Theological Academy before eventually becoming involved in women's education in Russia. Also a graduate of St. Petersburg Theological Academy, Protopresbyter Nikolai Sergievskii (1827–92) was professor of theology at Moscow University.

21. Nikolai Barsov, "Novyi metod v bogoslovii," in *Istoricheskie, kriticheskie i polemicheskie opyty* (St. Petersburg, n.p., 1870), 7. Barsov (1839–1903) was a graduate of St. Petersburg Theological Academy, where he eventually became professor of homiletics.

22. For an overview of the features of this new theological approach, see Sergievskii, "Vzgliad na proshedshee," *Pravoslavnoe obozrenie* (January 1870): 1–31; (February 1870): 195–243; Barsov, "Novyi metod v bogoslovii," 6. For

an example of the type of engagement that these authors advocated, see the essay on Christianity and the notion of progress by the graduate of St. Petersburg Theological Academy and professor of patristics, P. I. Shalfeev (d. 1862). P. Shalfeev, "Khristianstvo i progress," *Khristianskoe chtenie* (January 1861): 1–51.

23. Sergievskii, "Vzgliad na proshedshee," 225. For examples of similar Orthodox apologetics for modernity and progress, see "Sovremennost'," *Trudy Kievskoi Dukhovnoi Akademii* 2 (1860): 48; V. V. V., "Khristainstvo i progress," *Khristianskoe chtenie* (January 1878): 117–35.

24. *U Troitsy v Akademii: Iubileinyi sbornik istoricheskikh materialov* (Moscow: n.p., 1914), 229.

25. Paul Valliere, *Modern Russian Theology: Bukharev, Soloviev, Bulgakov. Orthodox Theology in a New Key* (Edinburgh: T&T Clark, 2000), 19–106.

26. Bukharev, "O sovremennosti v otnoshenii k pravoslaviiu," 60.

27. P. Znamenskii, "Bogoslovskaia polemika 1860-kh godov ob otnoshenii pravoslaviia k sovremennoi zhizni," *Pravoslavnyi sobesednik* (May 1902): 651; Sergievskii, "Vzgliad na proshedshee," (January 1870): 25–27; "K nabliudaiushchim za sovremennostiu," *Pravoslavnyi sobesednik* (June 1864): 109–28.

28. "O prepodavanii bogoslovskikh nauk v russkikh universitetakh," *Pravoslavnoe obozrenie* (January 1864): 39. Nikolai Barsov maintained that until Orthodox theologians became more adept in the art of apologetics, they should freely draw on the works of their Western Christian counterparts. Barsov, "Novyi metod v bogoslovii," 11.

29. M. Moroshkin, "Obozrenie inostrannoi sovremennoi bogoslovskoi zhurnalistiki," *Pravoslavnoe obozrenie* (February 1864): 39; Pevnitskii, "Rech' o sud'bakh bogoslovskoi nauki," 208.

30. For observations regarding support for unification among the Christian churches, see Barsov, "Novyi metod v bogoslovii," 1–3; I. Osinin, "Rech', chitannaia v torzhestvennom sobranii"; M. G. Koval'nitskii, "O znachenii natsional'nago elementa v istoricheskom razvitii khristianstva," *Trudy Kievskoi Dukhovnoi Akademii* (November 1880): 289; "Prizyv k soedineniiu tserkvei," *Tserkovnyi vestnik*, no. 29 (1894): 449–51; no. 30 (1894): 465–67; no. 31 (1894): 481–83. For the notion that the Roman Catholic and Orthodox Churches could find a common language by means of the ecclesiology of the Catholic modernists and early Slavophiles, see S. Troitskii, "Soedinenie tserkvei i modernizm," *Strannik* (April 1908): 519–40. For examples of Orthodox reactions to the representation of Orthodox Christians among modern Protestants and Catholics, see S. M. B-yi, "Po povodu napadok na vizantizm i obriadnost' v russkoi pravoslavnoi tserkvi," *Vera i tserkov'* 2, no. 7 (1900): 227–45; A. Mal'tsev, "Russkaia tserkov' po izobrazheniiu rimsko-katolicheskago pisatelia," *Khristianskoe chtenie* (September–October 1894): 262–85.

31. Sergievskii, "Vzgliad na proshedshee," 236. As examples of this type of dry presentation, see the pastoral discussions for common believers, Protoierei Ioann Pospelov, "Nepravda Rimsko-Katolikov," *Dushepoleznoe chtenie* (September 1907): 112–22; Protoierei Ioann Pospelov, "Nepravda Liuteran," *Dushepoleznoe chtenie* (October 1907): 220–39.

32. Smirnov, "Slavianofily i ikh uchenie," 200–202.

33. Barsov, "Novyi metod v bogoslovii," 6.

34. An excellent essay on how Khomiakov's theological work was understood to satisfy contemporary theological needs, see Barsov, "Novyi metod v bogoslovii." The search for essential experiential differences between Russian Orthodoxy and Western forms of Christianity can be seen in the travelogues published by priests and academic theologians who traveled to the West. See, for example, "Pis'ma pravoslavnago puteshestvennika o *tserkovnom sostoianii zapada*," *Khristianskoe chtenie* 1 (1862): 367–99; Aleksei Vvedenskii, "Svetlyi prazdnik u nas i zagranitsei," *Dushepoleznoe chtenie* (April 1902): 686–92; Protoierei Kl. Fomenko, "Vostok, zapad i Rossiia v religiozno-nravstvennom otnoshenii: istoricheskii ekskurs i sovremennyia nabliudeniia," *Trudy Kievskoi Dukhovnoi Akademii* (March 1903): 382ff.

35. *U Troitsy v Akademii*, 221–22; 227–32; A. D. Kaplin, "Slavianofily i ikh vozzreniia v russkoi dorevoliutsionnoi tserkovnoi istoriografii," *Visnik Kharkivskogo natsionalnogo universitetu im. V. N. Karazina*, no. 594 (Istoriia), vyp. 35 (Kharkiv: "SD," 2003): 262. Also see comments by Pevnitskii, "Rech' o sud'bakh bogoslovskoi nauki," 200.

36. N. I. Barsov, "O znachenii Khomiakova v istorii otechestvennago bogosloviia: polemicheskaia zametka," *Khristianskoe chtenie* 1 (1878): 306–9; Vasilii Pevnitskii, on the other hand, felt that Khomiakov led the way in clarifying the essence of Orthodoxy for "the Russian mind" (Pevnitskii, "Rech' o sud'bakh bogoslovskoi nauki," 190).

37. Krasniuk, "Religiozno-filosofskoe uchenie prezhnikh slavianofilov," 110.

38. Aleksei Khomiakov, "Po povodu broshiury g-na Loransi," in Khomiakov, *Sochineniia Bogoslovskie* (Moscow: n.p., 1907. Reprint, St. Petersburg: Nauka, 1995), 88.

39. Khomiakov, "Po povodu broshiury g-na Loransi," 74.

40. Khomiakov, "Po povodu broshiury g-na Loransi," 104.

41. Khomiakov, "Tserkov' odna," in Khomiakov, *Sochineniia Bogoslovskie*, 41.

42. Khomiakov, "Po povodu broshiury g-na Loransi," 67.

43. Khomiakov, "Po povodu broshiury g-na Loransi," 75.

44. Barsov, "Novyi metod v bogoslovii," 19.

45. Khomiakov, "Po povodu broshiury g-na Loransi," 104; "Po povodu odnogo okruzhnogo poslaniia Parizhskogo arkhiepiskopa," in Khomiakov, *Sochineniia Bogoslovskie*, 146, 157.

46. Khomiakov, 157–58; for a good short summary of this point, see Troitskii, "A. S. Khomiakov i drevne-tserkovnye polemisty," 734.

47. Khomiakov, "Po povodu odnogo okruzhnogo poslaniia," 159.

48. Khomiakov, "Po povodu odnogo okruzhnogo poslaniia," 124–25.

49. Khomiakov, "Po povodu broshiury g-na Loransi," 91.

50. Glubokovskii, "Pravoslavie po ego sushchestvu," 13.

51. Edward C. Thaden, "The Beginnings of Romantic Nationalism in Russia," *American Slavic and East European Review* 13, no. 4 (December 1954): 500–521; Boris Groys, "Russia and the West: The Quest for Russian National Identity," *Studies in Soviet Thought* 43 (1992): 185–98; Susanna Rabow-Edling, *Slavophile Thought*, 65–71.

52. Rabow-Edling, *Slavophile Thought*, 1–5.

53. Khomiakov, however, stood apart from his Slavophile colleagues with respect to the amount of emphasis he placed on nationality in his understanding of Orthodoxy. For instance, he had once stated, with respect to Konstantin Aksakov's views of Orthodoxy, "though sincere, [they are] too local and too subordinate to nationality and consequently not completely adequate" (Konstantin Shebatinskii, "Znachenie religii, kak kul'turnago faktora, v mirosozertsanii starykh slavianofilov," *Vera i razum* 2 [January 1909]: 206).

54. Rabow-Edling, *Slavophile Thought*, 63, 70–71, 136.

55. This summary is based on Barsov, "Novyi metod v bogoslovii," 14–44; Krasniuk, "Religiozno-filosofskoe uchenie prezhnikh slavianofilov," *Vera i razum* 1 (August 1900): 93–121; *Vera i razum* 2 (August 1900): 174–86; Shebatinskii, "Znachenie religii," 205–14. Also see Joseph L. Wieczynski, "Khomyakov's Critique of Western Christianity," *Church History* 38, no. 3 (Summer 1969): 291–99.

56. A. S. Khomiakov, "Pis'mo k izdateliu," *Sochineniia Bogoslovskiia*, 165.

57. Khomiakov, "Po povodu broshiury g-na Loransi," 87.

58. A. V. Gorskii, "Zamechaniia A. V. Gorskago na bogoslovskie sochineniia A. S. Khomiakova," *Bogoslovskii Vestnik* (November 1900): 518, 520. *U Troitsy v Akademii*, 545–48. Sergievskii, "Vzgliad na proshedshee," (February 1870): 240. Petr Simonovich Kazanskii (1819–78) was a graduate of Moscow Theological Academy and professor of history at the same academy.

59. *U Troitsy v Akademii*, 548.

60. Pevnitskii, "Rech' o sud'bakh bogoslovskoi nauki," 203. Also see criticism of Linitskii, quoted in F. Smirnov, "Bogoslovskoe uchenie Slavianofilov," *Pravoslavnoe obozrenie* (October 1883): 287.

61. F. Ternovskii, "Dva puti dukhovnago razvitiia," *Trudy Kievskoi Dukhovnoi Akademii* (April 1864): 378–402. Ternovskii (1838–84) was a graduate of Moscow Theological Academy and a professor of Church history at Kiev University.

62. Ternovskii, "Dva puti," 386.

63. Ivantsov-Platonov, *U Troitsy v Akademii*, 227–32.

64. Sergievksii, "Vzgliad na proshedshee," (February 1870): 240.

65. Bukharev, "O sovremennosti v otnoshenii k pravoslaviiu," 259–73.

66. E. A. L., "Nash prakticheskii papism i prakticheskoe protestantstvo: k sovremennym tserkovnym voprosam," *Strannik* (November 1905): 757–95.

67. Bukharev, "O sovremennosti v otnoshenii k pravoslaviiu," 260–61, 263.

68. Bukharev, "O sovremennosti v otnoshenii k pravoslaviiu," 263.

69. Bukharev, "O sovremennosti v otnoshenii k pravoslaviiu," 260–61.

70. Bukharev, "O sovremennosti v otnoshenii k pravoslaviiu," 278–85.

71. Lopukhin, "Sovremennyi Zapad," 478.

72. The following is based on A. Katanskii, "Kharakteristika pravoslaviia, Rimskago katolichestva i protestantstva: obshchii ocherk," *Khristianskoe chtenie* (January 1875): 1–32. Katanskii (1836–1919) was a graduate of St. Petersburg Theological Academy.

73. Katanskii, "Kharakteristika pravoslaviia," 31.

74. Glubokovskii, "Pravoslavie po ego sushchestvu," 31–32.

75. Lopukhin, "Sovremennyi Zapad," *Khristianskoe chtenie* (November–December 1885): 677.

76. Wieczynski, "Khomiakov's Critique," 298.

77. Arkhimandrit Ilarion (Troitskii), "Edinstvo tserkvi i vsemirnaia konferentsiia khristianstva," *Bogoslovskii vestnik* (January 1917): 6. Troitskii referred specifically to the views held by his more liberal colleague, Protopresbyter P. Ia Svetlov (1861–41), a graduate of Moscow Theological Academy.

78. Arkhimandrit Ilarion (Troitskii), "Edinstvo tserkvi," 15. Other Orthodox academics made the distinction between unity in form and a more mystical unity in spirit. See Koval'nitskii, "O znachenii natsional'nago elementa," 428.

79. For a discussion of Soloviev's views on nationalism, see Greg Gaut, "Can a Christian Be a Nationalist? Vladimir Solov'ev's Critique of Nationalism," *Slavic Review* 57, no. 1 (Spring 1998): 77–94. For a discussion of his views on church unity, see Valliere, *Modern Russian Theology*, 173–92. Tolstoy's views on patriotism elicited responses from Orthodox academics and clergy that often included their views on nationality and nations and the distinction between patriotism and nationalism. For instance, see I. I. Dobroserdov, "Khristianstvo i patriotizm," *Vera i tserkov'* 5 (1902): 709–41.

80. D. Vvedenskii, "Obshchekhristianskoe edinenie i natsional'naia samobytnost' narodov," *Vera i tserkov'* 3 (1901): 375. Dmitrii Vvedenskii (1873–1954) taught Church and biblical history in the Vifansk Seminary and later biblical history at Moscow Theological Academy.

81. S. Levitskii, "Printsip narodnosti i vopros o soedinenii tserkvi s tochki zreniia pravoslaviia," in S. Levitskii, *Pravoslavie i narodnost'* 196–229.

82. S. V. Troitskii, "Soedinenie tserkvei i modernizm," *Strannik* (April 1908): 533. Sergei Troitskii (1878–1972), a graduate of St. Petersburg Theological Academy, was a canon lawyer who taught at the University of Novorossisk and, following his emigration, at the University of Belgrade.

83. F. Andreev, "Moskovskaia dukhovnaia akademiia," *Bogoslovskii vestnik* (October–December 1915): 563–644.

84. Troitskii, "A. S. Khomiakov i drevne-tserkovnye polemisty."

85. Barsov, "Novyi metod v bogoslovii," 6.

86. Fr. Alexander Men, "Otets Pavel Florensky," http://www.vehi.net/men/florensky.html. Accessed January 2, 2012.

87. Pavel Florensky, "Okolo Khomiakova (Kriticheskie zametki)" in Florensky, *Sochineniia v chetyrekh tomov* (Moscow: Mysl', 1996), vol. 2, 313–16.

Florovsky's Neopatristic Synthesis and the Future Ways of Orthodox Theology / Paul L. Gavrilyuk

Earlier versions of this paper were presented at the Methodology Seminar, St. Tikhon's Orthodox University, Moscow, Russia in September 2009; "Neopatristic Synthesis or Post-Patristic Theology" Conference, Volos Theological Academy, Volos Greece in June 2010; and "Orthodox Constructions of the West" Conference, Fordham University, New York in June 2010.

1. See Alexander Schmemann, "*In Memoriam* Fr. Georges Florovsky," *St. Vladimir's Seminary Quarterly* 23 (1979): 133: "And even if he himself failed to clarify and to explain what he meant by the 'neopatristic synthesis' as the goal of the Orthodox theological task; if, in the last analysis, the historian in him seems to have been more articulate than the theologian, his work will remain an essential milestone, indeed an inescapable and decisive term of reference for all future developments of Orthodox theology." George H. Williams ("Georges Vasilievich Florovsky: His American Career [1948–65]," *Greek Orthodox Theological Review* 11 [1965]: 106) remarks that Florovsky "has not completed his patristic synthesis."

2. Andrew Blane, ed., *Georges Florovsky: Russian Intellectual, Orthodox Churchman* (Crestwood, N.Y.: St. Vladimir's Seminary Press, 1993) contains three important biographies of Florovsky by A. Blane, Mark Raeff, and George H. Williams.

3. As Florovsky reminisced later: "I read Soloviev, who is the father of this trend [i.e., sophiology], when I was sixteen, was awakened, troubled, fascinated and impressed" ("The Renewal of Orthodox Theology, Florensky, Bulgakov and the Others," unpublished typescript, 3). The author is grateful to Brandon Gal-

laher for bringing this invaluable paper to his attention. This paper, which apparently was delivered as a public lecture to an English-speaking audience, should be dated to the early years of Florovsky's American period.

4. Synthesis as a central direction of Soloviev's philosophy of all-unity is emphasized in Florovsky, "Reason and Faith in the Philosophy of Solov'ëv," *Continuity and Change in Russian and Soviet Thought*, ed. E. J. Simmons (Cambridge, Mass.: Harvard University Press, 1955), 283–97.

5. Florovsky dedicated to Soloviev one of his earliest published review articles, "Novye knigi o Vladimire Solovieve," *Izvestiia Odesskago Bibliographicheskago Obshchestva pri Imperatorskom Novorossiiskom Universitete* 1.7 (1912), 237–55. In this piece Florovsky was concerned to defend Soloviev against the charge of philo-Catholicism, arguing that "in the depth of his soul Soloviev was Orthodox, not Catholic, that the spirit of his philosophy is the authentic spirit of Greek-Eastern orthodoxy, and the idea of his philosophy—the idea of Godmanhood, the idea[s] of the church, the idea of total knowledge, free all-unity—are suggested by patristic thought; these ideas were developed during the era of the ecumenical councils," 238. In the emigration, Florovsky came to doubt Soloviev's orthodoxy.

6. *Put'* 1, no. 1 (1925): 3.

7. 'Iz proshlogo russkoi mysli', *Izvestiia Odesskago Bibliographicheskago Obshchestva pri Imperatorskom Novorossiiskom Universitete* 1.10 (1912), 382.

8. Nikolai O. Lossky, Anton V. Kartashev, and Georges Fedotov were also working on related themes during this period, although their monographs would appear in print years later.

9. Florovsky notes in his "Review of Matthew Spinka's *Christian Thought from Erasmus to Berdiaev*," *Church History* 31 (1962): 470: "We are in the stage of crisis, of critical transition, of desperate search."

10. *Iskhod k Vostoku* (1921).

11. *Na Putiakh*, 1922 and *Rossiia i Latinstvo*, 1923, respectively.

12. In 1927, the Eurasians announced their ideological platform, which began with the following two theses: "1. Russia represents a unique world. The historical destinies of this world by and large are fulfilled *separately* from the destiny of the countries that lie to the West (Europe), as well as to the south and east (Asia). 2. This unique world should be called Eurasia. Peoples who live within the limits of this world are capable of such forms of mutual understanding and brotherly living, which are difficult to achieve in relations to the peoples of Europe and Asia. In regards to its territory, the present-day [1927] USSR comprises the main core of this world" (P. N. Savitskii, ed., *Evraziiskaia khronika* 9 [1927]: 3; emphasis in the Russian original).

13. N. A. Danilevsky, *Rossiia i Evropa* (Moscow: Kniga, 1991), 162–72.

14. *Der Untergang des Abendlandes* (1918).

15. "We must understand that in some sense, Bolshevism and Latinity, International and Vatican, in a historical and empirical sense are coworkers and partners. For both of the forces have risen against the fortress of the Orthodox Spirit, a fortress in which lies Russia's might. The Orthodox children who are converted into Latinity, when they enter Catholic schools (sometimes parents who have been tempted [by Latinity] become accomplices in such a conversion) as well as the Orthodox folk, who become involved in Latinity succumbing to external and internal temptations—may be compared and contrasted with the victims of Bolshevik purges. The latter cause flesh to perish, yet we believe that by the mercy of God they will find spiritual salvation. Those who convert to Latinity may satisfy their material wellbeing; yet they perish spiritually, they depart from the full Truth to the perversion of the Truth, from Christ's Church to a society which sacrificed the ecclesial foundations to man's hubris" (Petr Savitsky, *Rossiia i Latinstvo* [Berlin, n.p., 1923], 11).

16. "Pis'mo v redaktsiiu 'Puti' P. P. Suvchinskogo, L. P. Karsavina, G. Florovskogo, P. Savitskogo, Pr. N. S. Trubetskogo, Vl. N. Il'ina," *Put'* 2 (1926): 247; Florovsky, "Okameneloe beschuvstvie (Po povodu polemiki protiv evraziistva)," *Put'* 2 (1926): 242–47. On Eurasianism, see Marlène Laruelle, *Russian Eurasianism: An Ideology of Empire* (Washington, D.C.: Woodrow Wilson Center Press, 2008).

17. Andrew Blane, ed., *Georges Florovsky: Russian Intellectual, Orthodox Churchman,* 39.

18. Florovsky, *Puti russkago bogosloviia* (Paris: YMCA, 1937/1983), xv.

19. "The Problem of Old Russian Culture," *Slavic Review* 21 (1962): 13.

20. *Puti russkago bogosloviia*, 49.

21. For Florovsky's cautious and critical appreciation of the Slavophile movement, see his lecture "*Vechnoe i prekhodiashchee v uchenii russkikh slavianofilov*" ("The Eternal and the Temporal in the Teaching of the Russian Slavophiles"), in *Slavianski Glas* (Sofia, n.p., 1921), 1:59–77.

22. *Puti russkago bogosloviia*, 89.

23. "The Legacy and the Task of Orthodox Theology," *Anglican Theological Review* 31 (1949): 68.

24. In a later review article, Florovsky observes that "Vladimir Solovyov is an episode in the history of German Idealism and can be fully understood only in the context of what is usually denoted as *Spätidealismus*, a rather neglected phase of the idealistic religious philosophy which was quite vigorous in the sixties and seventies of the last [nineteenth] century" (Review of *Christian Thought from Erasmus to Berdiaev* by Matthew Spinka, *Church History* 31, no. 4 [1962]: 470). For a more balanced treatment of Soloviev, see Florovsky, "Reason and Faith in the Philosophy of Solov'ëv," 283–97.

25. See P. Gavrilyuk, "Georges Florovsky's Monograph *Herzen's Philosophy of History*: The New Archival Material and the Reconstruction of the Full Text," *Harvard Theological Review* 106 (2013), forthcoming.

26. For the discussion of this period in Florovsky's life, see N. K. Gavriushin, "Chtoby istoshchilos' uporstvo razdora: Shtrikhi k portretu G. V. Florovskogo," *Simvol* 27 (2004): 201–40.

27. *Vostochnye Ottsy IV veka* (Paris: YMCA, 1931), 5. Florovsky mentions "the need for a new synthesis" as early as 1928 in his review article "Protivorechiia origenizma" (The Contradictions of Origenism), *Put'* 18 (1929): 107.

28. Berdiaev opened his devastating critique of *The Ways of Russian Theology* with the following line: "Fr. Georges Florovsky's book has the wrong title, it should have been called 'The Waywardness of Russian Theology,' or given the breadth of material that he covers, 'The Waywardness of Russian Thought,' or 'The Waywardness of Russian Spiritual Culture'" ("Ortodoksiia i chelovechnost," *Put'* 53 [1927]: 668).

29. "Westliche Einflüsse in der russischen Theologie" and "Patristics and Modern Theology," *Procès-Verbaux du Premier Congrès de Théologie Orthodoxe à Athènes (29 Novembre—6 Décembre 1936)* (Athens: Pyrsos, 1939), 212–31 and 238–42.

30. As Harnack's *Das Wesen des Christentums* (1900) is commonly summarized.

31. The current title of this journal is *St. Vladimir's Theological Quarterly*.

32. "Christianity and Civilization," *St. Vladimir's Seminary Quarterly* 1, no. 1 (1952): 13–20, here 14, emphasis in the original; reprinted in *CW* 2: 121–30. This point is also emphasized in Florovsky's "Review of Karl Friz's *Die Stimme der Ostkirche*," *Theology Today* 7, no. 4 (1951), 559–60 and in "Review of Paul J. Alexander's *The Patriarch Nicephorus of Constantinople*," *Church History* 28, no. 2 (1959): 205. See also *In Ligno Crucis: The Patristic Doctrine of the Atonement* (1936–39), Princeton Archive, first draft of the introduction: 4, second draft: 2. I am grateful to B. Gallaher for supplying this document to me.

33. "Christian Hellenism," 10.

34. Florovsky, "The Ethos of the Orthodox Church," *The Ecumenical Review* 12, no. 2 (1960): 187. It should be noted that this seminal paper, presented on this occasion to the Orthodox Consultation on Faith and Order in Kifissia, Greece, August 16–18, 1959, was based in part on the review of Nicholas N. Glubokovskii's work, the Russian version of which was rejected for publication by P. Florensky. See Sergei Polovinkin, "Invektiva skoree, chem kritika: Florovskii i Florenskii," in *Issledovaniia po istorii russkoi mysli*, vol. 6, ed. M. A. Kolerov (Moskva: Modest Kolerov, 2004), 66–68.

35. Alexis Klimoff, "Georges Florovsky and the Sophiological Controversy," *St. Vladimir's Theological Quarterly* 49, no. 1–2 (2005): 67–100.

36. Russian adjective *oblichitel'noe* could also be translated as "accusatory" or "condemning."

37. *Puti russkago bogosloviia*, 514–15.

38. "The Legacy," 70. See A. Schmemann, *For the Life of the World* (Crestwood, N.Y.: St. Vladimir's Seminary Press, 1998; first published in 1963): "The Western captivity of Orthodox theology has been vigorously denounced by the best theologians of the last hundred years and there exists today a significant movement aimed at the recovery by our theology of its own genuine perspective and method. The return to the Fathers, to the liturgical and spiritual traditions which were virtually ignored by the 'theology of manuals,' is beginning to bear fruit."

39. "Patristic and Modern Theology," 242, emphasis in the original.

40. "The Christian Hellenism," *Orthodox Observer* 442 (1957): 10.

41. "Quest for Christian Unity: The Challenge of Disunity" (1955), Princeton archive, Box 3, f.11. The author is grateful to B. Gallaher for providing this reference.

42. "The Legacy," 66–67.

43. See Florovsky's critique of A. Toynbee in "The Ethos of the Orthodox Church," 198.

44. See Florovsky's review of Emilios Inglessis's *Maximos IV: L'Orient Conteste L'Occident*, *Journal of Ecumenical Studies* 9 (1972): 622–23.

45. Florovsky, *In Ligno Crucis*, first draft of the introduction, Princeton Archive, 4 (pagination absent in the original): "St. Augustine and even St. Jerome were no less Hellenistic than St. Gregory of Nyssa and St. Chrysostom. And St. Augustine introduced Neoplatonism into Western theology. Pseudo-Dionysios was influential in the West no less than in the East, from Hilduin up to Nicolas of Cusa. And St. John of Damascus was an authority both for the Byzantine Middle Ages and for Peter Lombard and Thomas Aquinas. Thomism itself is Hellenistic. In England, the Caroline divines were obviously Hellenistic in tendency. And one of the greatest contributions of the Tractarian Movement was just this move back to the Greek Fathers." Later in the same document, he adds that "Medieval Scholasticism was perhaps overburdened with unreformed philosophy" (6).

46. See Florovsky, *Vostochnye Ottsy IV veka*, 224–33.

47. Andrew Blaine, *Georges Florovsky*, 155.

48. Florovsky, "The Christian Hellenism," 9.

49. Florovsky, "Bogoslovskie otryvki," *Izbrannye bogoslovskie stat'i* (Moscow: Izdatel'stvo 'Probel', 2000), 130; "Patristics and Modern Theology," 241.

50. Florovsky, "Tvar' i tvarnost," in *Izbrannye bogoslovskie stat'i*, 37–70; "Protivorechiia origenizma," *Put'* 18 (1928): 107–14; "Bogoslovskie otryvki," 131; "St. Gregory Palamas and the Tradition of the Fathers," *CW* 1: 105–20. In "The Renewal of Orthodox Theology: Florensky, Bulgakov and the Others" (unpub-

lished typescript, 10–11), Florovsky states that the philosophical categories for expressing these "patristic" insights were provided by Charles Renouvier's *Essai d'une classification du doctrine philologique* (1886).

51. "Bogoslovskie otryvki," 130.

52. In "Predicament of Christian Historian," 163, Florovsky states that German Idealism was "a relapse into Hellenism," meaning pagan, pre-Christian Hellenism. For discussion, see Williams, "Georges Vasilievich Florovsky," 93.

53. Despite some considerable differences of emphasis, a similar line of criticism emerges from the pages of Vladimir Lossky's *Mystical Theology of the Eastern Church*.

54. Florovsky, "Dom Otchii," *Izbrannye bogoslovskie stat'i* (Moscow: Izdatel'stvo "Probel," 2000), 9.

55. Florovsky, "The Function of Tradition in the Ancient Church," *CW* 1: 73–92.

56. "One can best be initiated into the spirit of the Fathers by attending the offices of the Eastern Church, [e]specially in Lent and up to Trinity Sunday," writes Florovsky in the first draft of the introduction to *In Ligno Crucis*, 8.

57. For Florovsky's use of the expression "the mind of the Fathers," see "The Ethos of the Orthodox Church," 189–91; "The Lamb of God," *Scottish Journal of Theology* 4 (1951): 16; "The Lost Scriptural Mind," *CW* I: 9–16. Florovsky's account of historical knowledge bears a striking similarity to the ideas developed in R. G. Collingwood's *Essays in the Philosophy of History* (1965).

58. For a valuable discussion of Möhler as a source of the concept of intellectual intuition, see Brandon Gallaher, "Waiting for the Barbarians," *International Journal of Systematic Theology* (forthcoming). An equally plausible source is Berdiaev, *Filosofiia svobody* (Philosophy of freedom), ch. 1.

59. "Bogoslovskie otryvki," 128: "It is sheer misunderstanding to speak of the 'development of dogmas.' The dogmas do not develop or change, they are utterly unchangeable and untouchable, even in their external verbal form," (my translation). See Williams, "Georges Vasilievich Florovsky," 88n221 and 99n255.

60. See especially Vladimir Lossky's posthumously published Sorbonne lectures, *The Vision of God* (Bedfordshire: Faith Press, 1973).

61. Florovsky, "Le corps du Christ vivant: Une interprétation orthodoxe de l'Église," in *La sainte Église Universelle: Confrontation oecuménique* (Paris: Delachaux et Niestlé, 1948), 12; "Christ and His Church, Suggestions and Comments," in *L'Église et les Églises* II (1954): 164. On this point, see J. Zizioulas, *Being as Communion* (Crestwood, N.Y.: St. Vladimir's Seminary Press, 2002), 124, 158n67.

62. Williams, "Georges Vasilievich Florovsky," 86.

63. A. Klimoff, "Georges Florovsky and the Sophiological Controversy," 97–98. The indirect target was always Bulgakov, who presumably wrote *The Lamb of*

God in part to counter Florovsky's criticism of the insufficiently Christocentric character of sophiology. I believe that the inspiration for this charge comes from Berdiaev's earlier dictum regarding the Russian Silver Age, that the intelligentsia came to believe in Sophia without believing in Christ. Florovsky later took up a critique of Florensky in a lecture, "The Renewal of Orthodox Theology," 6 (unpublished typescript): "I was shocked to find that the 800 page book [Florensky's *The Pillar and Ground of the Truth*] on the Christian Theodicy has no chapter on Jesus Christ at all."

64. *Vostochnye Ottsy piatogo-vos'mogo veka*, 26.

65. "Predicament of the Christian Historian," *CW* II: 31–66. Such extrapolations of ancient heresies were common in Russian religious thought, beginning with Vladimir Soloviev, as well as Florensky, Berdiaev, Bulgakov, and Karsavin.

66. Florovsky, "Kniga Melera o Tserkvi," *Put'* 7 (1927): 128–30.

67. Fergus Kerr, *Twentieth Century Catholic Theologians* (Oxford: Blackwell, 2007), 31.

68. Marcellino D'Ambrosio, "*Ressourcement* Theology, *Aggiornamento*, and the Hermeneutics of Tradition," *Communio* 18 (1991): 538.

69. Cited in Marcellino D'Ambrosio, "*Ressourcement* Theology, *Aggiornamento*, and the Hermeneutics of Tradition," 541.

70. Florovsky, "The Oxford Conference on Patristic Studies, September, 1955," *St. Vladimir's Seminary Quarterly* 4 (1955–56): 60.

71. Florovsky, *Puti russkago bogosloviia*, xv. See the section of this chapter titled "The Waywardness of Russian Theology and the True Way of the Church Fathers."

72. The staunch anti-Westernism of Florovsky's student Fr. John Romanides, as well as the works and public statements of the Old Calendarist Archbishop Chrysostomos of Etna, come to mind.

73. For groundbreaking work in this arena, see George E. Demacopoulos and Aristotle Papanikolaou, eds., *Orthodox Readings of Augustine* (Crestwood, N.Y.: St. Vladimir's Seminary Press, 2008).

Eastern "Mystical Theology" or Western "Nouvelle Théologie"?: On the Comparative Reception of Dionysius the Areopagite in Lossky and de Lubac / Sarah Coakley

1. The classic text in question is, of course, *The Mystical Theology of the Eastern Church* (Crestwood, N.Y.: St. Vladimir's Seminary Press, 1976), originally published in French as *Essai sur la théologie mystique de l'Église d'Orient* (Paris: Aubier, 1944). Readers should note that some of the footnote material in the original French is cut or changed in the English edition.

2. I already hinted at the ecumenical significance of this time-span's engagement with the Dionysian theme in my introduction to *Re-Thinking Dionysius the Areopagite*, ed. Charles Stang and Sarah Coakley (Oxford: Wiley-Blackwell, 2009), 1–10, at 4, 6. This is a volume that traces some of the major historic receptions of the Dionysian corpus and their modern and contemporary significance: see especially Paul L. Gavrilyuk, "The Reception of Dionysius in Twentieth-Century Eastern Orthodoxy," 177–93, at 182–86, for relevant remarks on Lossky.

3. The most substantial theological treatments in English to date are Rowan Williams, "The Theology of Vladimir Nikolaievich Lossky: An Exposition and Critique" (D.Phil. diss., Oxford University, 1976, Bodleian Library), now published in Russian as Уильямс Роуэн. Богословие Владимира Лосского. Изложение и критика, trans. Dar'ia Morozova and Iurii Vestel' (Kiev, Dukh i litera, 2009); and Aristotle Papanikolaou, *Being With God: Trinity, Apophaticism, and Divine-Human Communion* (Notre Dame, Ind., Notre Dame University Press, 2006). See also Papanikolaou's analysis of Lossky's Dionysian rendering of analogy in "Created for Communion: Vladimir Lossky on Creation and the Divine Ideas," in *Metropolitan Methodios of Boston: A Festal Volume*, ed. George Dion Dragas (Boston: Greek Orthodox Metropolis of Boston, 2009), 650–69. Surprisingly little attention is given in these works, however, to Lossky's interrelations with his Catholic scholarly hosts and friends in Paris. The first chapter of Williams's unpublished thesis (especially 21–28) does give a very useful, but brief, account of the relations between Lossky and his Parisian interlocutors, in which Williams is mainly reliant on the testimony of Lossky's friend, Olivier Clément, for biographical details: See Clément's substantial memorial essay, "Vladimir Lossky, un théologien de la personne et du Saint-Esprit," *Messager* 30–31 (1959): 137–206, which is reprinted (lightly edited, and with an additional new section on the *filioque*) in Olivier Clément, *Deux Passeurs: Vladimir Lossky et Paul Evdokimov* (Genève: Labor et Fides, 1985).

4. This was a term that was originally applied critically: See Hans Boersma, *Nouvelle Théologie and Sacramental Ontology: A Return to Mystery* (Oxford: Oxford University Press, 2009), and Jürgen Mettepenningen, *Nouvelle Théologie—New Theology: Inheritor of Modernism, Precursor of Vatican II* (New York: T&T Clark, 2010), for recent accounts of the origins and background of the New Theology movement. The central interest of the circle of French Catholic theologians who attracted this characterization was a resistance to a modernizing, neo-Scholastic rendition of Thomas's theology which was primarily interested in rational apologetics, and forgetful of Thomas's own debts to the patristic heritage, especially to Augustine and to the Greek patristic corpus.

5. Leo XIII's encyclical *Aeterni Patris* (August 1879) riposted modern trends in secular philosophy by proposing a normative return to the Christian philosophy

of Thomas Aquinas, and by reading "reason" in Thomas as an autonomous "stepping-stone" to faith. The later requirement by Pius X of an "anti-Modernist oath" (September 1910), further required assent by all clergy and seminary teachers to the "certainty" of the arguments for God's existence "by the natural light of reason from the created world." It was the rigidity of this rendition of Thomas's understanding of the relation between reason and faith that revulsed the de Lubac circle as much as it did Lossky.

6. As we shall see below, Lossky was to drive a wedge between Western negative theology and what he regarded as a superior Greek apophatic theology; but for the meantime we shall gloss over this somewhat problematic semantic distinction.

7. The "experimentalism" of a then-fashionable interest in "mystic" states should, of course, be distinguished here from the burgeoning *philosophical* existentialism of Heidegger in Germany or Sartre in France (and of a certain shadow of Kierkegaard behind them). Nonetheless, one can detect a confluence of these diverse strands of thinking in Lossky's *Mystical Theology*, as we shall discuss below.

8. Nicholas Lossky, "Theology and Spirituality in the Work of Vladimir Lossky," *Ecumenical Review* 51 (1999): 288–93, here 288.

9. See again Lossky, "Theology and Spirituality," 288.

10. See Rowan Williams, "Lossky, the *Via Negativa* and the Foundations of Theology" (originally published as "The *Via Negativa* and the Foundations of Theology: An Introduction to the Thought of V. N. Lossky," in *New Studies in Theology*, ed. Stephen Sykes and Derek Holmes, 1 [London: Duckworth, 1979], 95–117), now in *Wrestling with Angels*, ed. Mike Higton (London: S.C.M., 2007), 1–24. Williams's doctoral thesis (see above, note 3) is mainly taken up with demonstrating the ironic continuity of Lossky's thought with that of his father and his circle (despite his rhetorical announcements to the contrary). In parallel, my short study here uncovers the indebtedness of Lossky to his Catholic intellectual surroundings in France, again despite rhetorical insistences to the opposite.

11. See especially M. Henri-Charles Puech, "La ténèbre mystique chez le pseudo-Denys l'Aréopagite et dans la tradition patristique," *Études Carmélitaines* (1938): 33–53; and the influential study of Nyssen, Jean Daniélou, *Platonisme et Théologie Mystique* (Paris: Aubier, 1944). There is good evidence that Daniélou and Lossky knew each other quite well through the *Dieu Vivant* circle (see below, notes 37 and 56), although I know of no surviving correspondence between them.

12. See *Oeuvres Complètes de Pseudo-Denys d'Aréopagite,* ed. Maurice de Gandillac (Paris: Aubier, 1943). Papanikolaou (*Being with God*, 165n14) suggests that Lossky may have first come to an interest in Dionysius via his doctoral study of Eckhart. The issue of Dionysius's status in relation to Neoplatonic thought would have also come up immediately in Lossky's early study of the Greek fa-

thers in Paris, especially in the light of recent European scholarly debate on Dionysius's relation to Neoplatonism: See, for example, Hugo Koch, *Pseudo-Dionysius Areopagita in seiner Beziehungen zum Neuplatonismus und Mysterienwesen* (Mainz: Franz Kirchheim, 1900), and H. F. Müller, *Dionysios, Proklos, Plotinos: Ein historischer Beitrag zur neuplatonischen Philosophie* (Münster: Aschendorff, 1918), both of whom Lossky already engages with critically in his first published article.

13. Vladimir Lossky, "La Théologie Négative dans la Doctrine de Denys L'Aréopagite," *Revue des Sciences Philosophiques et Théologiques* 28 (1939): 204–21. Note that Williams, "Lossky, the *Via Negativa* and the Foundations of Theology," 19n1, mistakenly assigns this article to the year 1936; and Papanikolaou (*Being with God*, 208) mistakenly assigns it to 1930. The earlier, Russian, version of the essay had appeared in *Seminarium Kondakovianum* 3 (1929): 135–44.

14. See "La Théologie Négative," 210n1, where Lossky accuses both Koch and Müller of "overestimating" the influence of Neoplatonism on Dionysius.

15. Lossky, *Mystical Theology*, 29–32.

16. Lossky, *Mystical Theology*, 29–30. Only a brief reference is made to Koch here in the English translation (24n1), though we know from "La Théologie Négative" that polemics against both Koch and Müller hover in the background. Later, however, in *The Vision of God*, trans. Asheleigh Moorhouse (London: Faith Press, 1963), 99, Lossky was to adopt a significantly more eirenic approach to Koch's position, acknowledging that Koch had indeed demonstrated the close connection between Proclus and Dionysius, but still insisting that Dionsyius is a "Christian thinker *disguised as a neo-Platonist*" (my italics), rather than *vice versa*.

17. Lossky, *Mystical Theology*, 30.

18. Lossky, *Mystical Theology*, 29.

19. Lossky, *Mystical Theology*, 31 (my italics), 32.

20. On which Wayne Hankey has perhaps most scathingly waxed of late: See his "Misrepresenting Neoplatonism in Contemporary Christian Dionysian Polemic: Eriguena and Nicholas of Cusa versus Vladimir Lossky and Jean-Luc Marion" (unpublished paper prepared for the *American Catholic Philosophical Quarterly*, http://classics.dal.ca./Files/Misrepresenting_Neoplatonism_for_ACPQ.pdf).

21. For a sympathetic recent intellectual biography of Gilson that sets this issue in context, see Francesca Aran Murphy, *Art and Intellect in the Philosophy of Étienne Gilson* (Columbia: University of Missouri Press, 2004), especially ch. 6, "Christian Philosophy," 102–29.

22. Rowan Williams (in conversation) has drawn my attention to a possible influence from Georges Florovsky's celebrated paper "Offenbarung, Philosophie und Theologie," *Zwischen den Zeiten* Heft 6 (München, 1931), trans. Richard Haugh as "Revelation, Philosophy and Theology," in *Collected Works of Georges*

Florovsky, vol. 3: *Creation and Redemption* (Belmont, Mass.: Nordland Press, 1976), 21–40. It is unclear that Lossky had any direct knowledge of Barth's theology himself, however, though he does occasionally cite him fleetingly.

23. Lossky, *Mystical Theology*, 42. ·

24. Lossky even mentions the Thomist shibboleth of "pure nature" at one point, fervently distancing Eastern thought from its presumptions.

25. *Mystical Theology*, 57–58, citing the French Jesuit Théodore de Régnon's *Études de théologie positive de la Sainte Trinité*, vol. 1 (Paris: Victor Retaux, 1892), 433. Michel René Barnes has famously drawn attention to the fact that Lossky is here drawing, again ironically, on a *Western* author to level this particular charge of the West's moving from the one to the three: See Barnes's "De Régnon Reconsidered," *Augustinian Studies* 26 (1995): 51–79. However, it should be added that this is not a straightforward use by Lossky of de Régnon, who himself never intended his comparison of two starting points in Trinitarian thinking to be utilized disjunctively, nor to form a gulf between Latin and Greek *patristic* Trinitarian thinking. Indeed de Régnon, like Lossky later, is himself countering the already-rigidified Scholasticism of his day, and seeking to overcome it through a return to patristic sources: on this point. see Kristin Hennessy, "An Answer to de Régnon's Accusers: Why We Should Not Speak of 'His' Paradigm," *Harvard Theological Review* 100 (2007): 179–97.

26. Lossky, *Mystical Theology*, 52.

27. Lossky, *Vision of God*, 104, my italics.

28. Lossky, *Vision of God*, 105, my italics.

29. Vladimir Lossky, *Théologie Négative et Connaissance de Dieu chez Maître Eckhart* (Paris: Vrin, 1960). The most important sections comparing Dionysius and Eckhart are to be found on pages 18–25 and 61–64.

30. Lossky, *Théologie Négative*, 21.

31. Lossky, *Théologie Négative*, 61.

32. See "The Mystical Theology," in *The Complete Works of Dionysius the Areopagite*, trans. Colm Luibheid (London: S.P.C.K., 1987), 136 (PG 1000B); 138 (PG 1025B).

33. Lossky, *Mystical Theology*, 37.

34. Lossky, *Mystical Theology*, 38.

35. Lossky, *Mystical Theology*, 38.

36. It suggests, of course, that only Dionysius has a fully "experiential" and "revelatory" account of divine darkness: See Rowan Williams's excellent analysis of Lossky's position on this issue in "Lossky, the *Via Negativa* and the Foundations of Theology," especially 2–5. Another influential attempt to tidy up the difference between Dionysius's account of divine darkness and Thomas's (which of course itself draws directly on Dionysius's corpus) is to be found in Josef Pieper, *Silence of St. Thomas: Three Essays*, trans. John Murray and Daniel O'Connor

(London: Faber and Faber, 1957). The argument here is that for Thomas the darkness is an epistemological one (the effect on us of an over-abundance of divine light), whereas for Dionysius the darkness is intrinsic to God's being "beyond Being." I am, myself, unclear whether either Dionysius or Thomas is so consistent on this point as to make the contrast a sure one. Certainly Lossky's account over-polemicizes the difference, as well as covertly inflecting it with distinctly modern understandings of "experience" and "revelation."

37. Williams briefly discusses the importance of this circle, and its attendant friendships, for Lossky's intellectual development in Chapter 1 of his doctoral thesis (see note 3, above). He is here partly reliant on oral testimony from Olivier Clément, and more scholarly work deserves to be done on the interactions forged here. The group, an ecumenical one that also involved Jewish philosophers such as Wahl, was founded at the very end of the war (1945) in Paris, and for a while produced a journal of the same name to which Lossky, Wahl, de Lubac, Daniélou, von Balthasar, Chenu, and other like-minded reforming theological luminaries contributed. Lossky's involvement was, however, relatively short-lived: See note 56, below.

38. Rowan Williams makes this point in "Lossky, the *Via Negativa* and the Foundations of Theology," 17–18, as well as more extensively in his doctoral thesis. Tomasz Weclawski's *Zwischen Sprache und Schweigen: Eine Erörterung der theologishen Apophase im Gespräch mit Vladimir N. Lossky und Martin Heidegger* (München: Minerva-Fachserie, 1985) makes some interesting and prescient comparisons between Heidegger's attack on "onto-theology" and Lossky's "apophaticism," though without claiming any direct influence.

39. Donald Allchin suggested a Kierkegaardian influence of this sort in A. M. Allchin, "Vladimir Lossky: The Witness of an Orthodox Theologian," *Theology* 72 (1969): 203–9, at 204.

40. Papanikolaou helpfully draws attention to this repetitive theme in Lossky in Chapter 3 of *Being with God*.

41. See *Mystical Theology*, 43. So Christology and Trinitarianism are completely compatible with this antinomy: Here Lossky is implicitly responding to Western critiques of the coherence of the essence/energies distinction in its Palamite form. By contrast, Illtyd Trethowan, O.S.B., finds this "antinomic" account of the Godhead by far the least convincing side of Lossky's theology. It confuses, according to Trethowan, epistemology with ontology: "All we need to do is to distinguish our knowledge of [God], which is always limited, from God himself." See Illtyd Trethowan, "Lossky on Mystical Theology," *The Downside Review* 92 (1974): 239–47, here 244.

42. See *A Study of Gregory Palamas* (orig. French 1959), trans. George Lawrence (London: Faith Press, 1964), and *Christ in Eastern Christian Thought* (orig. French 1969) (Crestwood, N.Y.: St. Vladimir's Seminary Press, 1975) for his critiques of the Neoplatonic/Dionysian dangers for Orthodox thought, and

especially for Christology. Meyendorff, in contrast to Lossky, reads Palamas as finally taming and correcting those strands in Eastern Christian thought which were primarily associated with Platonism and Neoplatonism (for him Origen, Evagrius, Dionysius), rather than manifesting the climax of a "Dionysian" hegemony.

43. Surprisingly, I have not been able to find any comments on Lossky's changes of mind, or interlocutions with his critics, in the existing secondary literature. Again, this line of research is worthy of extension.

44. Lossky, *In the Image and Likeness of God* (orig. French, 1967), ed. John H. Erickson and Thomas E. Bird, with an introduction by John Meyendorff (Crestwood, N.Y.: St. Vladimir's Seminary Press, 1974).

45. See Maurice de Gandillac, *La Sagesse de Plotin* (Paris: Vrin, 1952), which was especially critical of Lossky's assault on the Neoplatonic tradition; and, among other assessments, the insightful review of Lossky's work by the Jesuit Sebastian Tyszkiewicz, "La spiritualité de l'Église d'Orient selon M. Vladimir Lossky," *Gregorianum* 31 (1950): 605–12, which takes Lossky forcibly to task for his radical manipulation of the Eastern tradition into an eccentric reading of Dionysius.

46. See *In the Image and Likeness of God*, ch. 1, especially 24–25, for an acknowledgement of the force of Gandillac's criticism of Lossky's earlier position, but a maintaining of the insistence that the Trinity in Dionysius surpasses any possibility of a "transpersonal Unity" (27).

47. Lossky, *Image and Likeness*, ch. 2, especially 37–40.

48. Étienne Gilson, *Théologie Négative et Connaissance de Dieu chez Maître Eckhart*, 9–11, in which Gilson comments that it must have been a "secret affinity" (11) that drew Lossky to the thought of Eckhart in the first place, despite all his criticisms of his "Western" failings. Gandillac, interestingly, did the editorial work for the volume (see 7–8), which appeared in a series under the overall editorship of Gilson.

49. *Le Thomisme: Introduction au système de S. Thomas d'Aquin*, 5th. ed. (Paris: Vrin, 1944); English translation: *The Christian Philosophy of St. Thomas Aquinas*, trans. L. K. Shook (London: Gollancz, 1957): see 136–41.

50. *Christian Philosophy of St. Thomas Aquinas*, 136–41.

51. *Théologie Negative et Connaissance de Dieu chez Maître Eckhart*, 24n38.

52. Étienne Gilson, *The Mystical Theology of St. Bernard*, trans. A. H. C. Downes (London: Sheed and Ward, 1940): "The influence exerted on the Cistercian mysticism by Dionysius is very difficult to estimate" (25). Note especially the careful discussion of the fourth, ecstatic, moment of love in Bernard's *de diligendo deo* and of whether its language may perhaps indicate an influence from Dionysius's *Mystical Theology*, which Gilson doubts, surmising that, if anything, it must be an indirect influence via Maximus the Confessor (and Erigena) (26–28).

It is surely not a coincidence that Lossky subsequently published an article on Bernard's theological semantics which takes issue at various points with Gilson's analysis; see V. Lossky, "Études sur la Terminologie de Saint Bernard," *Archivum Latinitatis Medii Aevi* 17 (1943): 79–96. Behind these two publications must lie an ongoing exchange between Gilson and Lossky on the Western assimilation of Dionysius.

53. See Étienne Gilson, *Les Tribulations de Sophie* (Paris: Vrin, 1976), 48–49. Francesca Murphy kindly drew my attention to this passage, in which Gilson objects to the project of a new polemical Thomist *defense* of the "West," given that "No western theology is better qualified to dialogue with the East than Thomas [himself]" since "Thomas . . . is full of the Greek Fathers."

54. Étienne Gilson and Henri de Lubac, *Letters of Étienne Gilson to Henri de Lubac*, trans. Mary Emily Hamilton (San Francisco: Ignatius Press, 1988)

55. My thanks to Philip McCosker for asking Père Chantraine this question on my behalf not long before Chantraine died. For his unfinished biography of de Lubac, see Georges Chantraine, *Henri de Lubac* (Paris: Éditions du Cerf, 2007–9).

56. See again note 37, above. The first issue of the journal *Dieu Vivant* from 1945 contains, inter alia, an article by Lossky on Gregory Palamas, an article by von Balthasar on Kierkegaard and Nietszche, a review of de Lubac's *Corpus Mysticum* by Chenu, and a review of a book by Barth (*Deux Textes*) in French. Within three years, however (as Rowan Williams briefly discusses in Chapter 1 of his doctoral thesis), Lossky had left the *Dieu Vivant* group after a falling-out over the anti-Western polemics of the patriarchate of Moscow, to which Lossky remained doggedly committed.

57. See Nicholas Lossky, "Theology and Spirituality," 293.

58. See Hans Urs von Balthasar, *Prufet alles: das Gute behaltet* (Ostfildern: Schwabenverlag, 1986), 9; in English, trans. Maria Shrady, *Test Everything: Hold Fast to What Is Good* (San Francisco: Ignatius Press, 1989), 11–12.

59. See Hans Urs von Balthasar, *Parole et mystère chez origène* (Paris: Cerf, 1957) Balthasar, *Presence and Thought: Essay on the Religious Philosophy of Gregory of Nyssa*, trans. Marc Sebanc (San Francisco: Ignatius Press, 1995), and Balthasar, *Cosmic Liturgy: The Universe According to Maximus Confessor*, trans. Brian E. Daley (San Francisco: Ignatius Press, 2003). It is worth noting that Balthasar's later utilization of Dionysius in his *Glory of the Lord* shows an interesting indication of interaction with, and appreciation of, Lossky's *Mystical Theology*: see Hans Urs von Balthasar, *The Glory of the Lord*, vol. 2: *Classical Styles*, orig. 1962 (Edinburgh: T&T Clark, 1984), especially 145, 171. Von Balthasar concurs with Lossky that Dionysius cannot be dismissed as a Platonist interloper into the Christian fold.

60. The original French is Henri de Lubac, Préface to *La Mystique et les Mystiques*, ed. A. Ravier (Paris: Desclée de Brouwer, 1965), 7–39; translated as

"Mysticism and Mystery," in *Theological Fragments*, trans. Rebecca Howell Balinski (San Franciso: Ignatius Press, 1989), 35–69.

61. de Lubac, *Theological Fragments*, 52.

62. de Lubac, *Theological Fragments*, especially 53–59.

63. de Lubac, *Theological Fragments*, 49 (for brief mention of Dionysius), 67 (for suspicions about Eckhart and Tauler), and 60–61, 65 (for laudatory remarks on Origen). For a useful secondary assessment of de Lubac on the subject of mysticism, see Jean-Pierre Wagner, "Henri de Lubac et la Mystique," *Revue des sciences religieuses* 71 (1997): 90–103.

64. For these themes critical of Dionysius in *Medieval Exegesis*, see vol. 1, trans. Mark Sebanc (Edinburgh: T&T Clark, 1998), 172–73; vol. 2, trans. E. M. Macierowski (Edinburgh: T&T Clark, 2000), 180, 194–96; vol. 3, trans. E. M. Macierowski (Edinburgh: T&T Clark, 2009), 321–23, 413–14. The article by Chenu that de Lubac regularly draws upon for this criticism is Marie-Dominique Chenu, "Lecture de la Bible et Philosophie," in *Mélanges offerts à Étienne Gilson de l'Académie Française* (Paris: Vrin, 1959), 161–71, see especially 169–71.

65. See Chenu, "Lecture de la Bible et Philosophie," 171. Anders Nygren, *Agape and Eros: A Study of the Christian Idea of Love*, orig. 1932–39, trans. Philip S. Watson (London: S.P.C.K., 1953) had been published in French in 1944. It had been somewhat critically reviewed in the first issue of *Dieu Vivant* 1 (1945): 139–41, by Pierre Burgelin, but overall it exercised enormous influence ecumenically, and greatly intensified the presumption that Platonism and Christianity were incompatible opposites. The most celebrated English-language riposte to the thesis was to come from Martin D'Arcy, *The Mind and the Heart of Love, Lion and Unicorn: A Study in Eros and Agape* (London: Faber and Faber, 1945).

66. Henri de Lubac, *Surnaturel: Études Historiques* (Paris: Vrin, 1946). De Lubac's later *Augustinianism and Modern Theology*, trans. Lancelot Sheppard (New York: Herder and Herder, 1969) closely follows the first part of the earlier *Surnaturel*.

67. John Milbank, *The Suspended Middle: Henri de Lubac and the Debate Concerning the Supernatural* (London: S.C.M., 2005), 5.

68. Milbank, *Suspended Middle*, 5.

69. Henri de Lubac, *La Mystère du Surnaturel* (Paris: Aubier, 1965), frontispiece (but the quotation from Dionysius is omitted in the English translation). *The Mystery of the Supernatural*, trans. Rosemary Sheed (New York: Crossroad, 1998), 24, 68–69. 286.

70. David Grumett, *De Lubac: A Guide for the Perplexed* (London: T&T Clark, 2007). I am particularly grateful to Dr. Grumett for illuminating correspondence on this point; in de Lubac's case the more positive embrace of the apophatic at this later stage in his career may also be connected with his new

interest in Buddhism and Buddhist-Christian thought: see de Lubac, *La Mystère du Surnaturel*, chs. 6 and 7.

71. Henri de Lubac, *The Discovery of God*, trans. Alexander Dru with Mark Sebanc and Cassian Fulsom (Edinburgh: T&T Clark, 1996), 141.

72. Henri de Lubac, *The Christian Faith: An Essay on the Structure of the Apostles' Creed*, trans. Richard Arnandes (San Francisco: Ignatius Press, 1986), 255.

73. In his preface to Lossky, *The Vision of God*, 5, Meyendorff writes: "As a controversialist and apologist, Vlaidmir Lossky was sometimes intransigent and harsh. However in the last years of his life one sees him developing more and more that serene wisdom which made his personality so engaging."

74. Nicholas Lossky, "Theology and Spirituality," 293. Antoine Arjakovsky, in conversation, has suggested that these eirenic comments from Nicholas Lossky may be somewhat overstated for ex post facto diplomatic purposes. Olivier Clément, in contrast, writes affectionately of Lossky as having "un tempérament de guerrier" right up to the end (Clément, "Vladimir Lossky," 205).

75. I would like to record my gratitude to Johannes Börjesson, David Grumett, Paul Gavrilyuk, Philip McCosker, Francesca Murphy, Rowan Williams, and Antoine Arjakovsky for invaluable assistance in developing the themes in this paper.

The Image of the West in Contemporary Greek Theology / Pantelis Kalaitzidis

This paper is based on my as-yet-unpublished thesis, "Greekness and Antiwesternism in the Greek Theological Generation of the '60s" (PhD diss., School of Theology, University of Thessaloniki, 2008) [in Greek], as well as on two of my previous papers: "The Discovery of Greekness and Theological Antiwesternism in the Theological Generation of the '60s," in *Turmoil in Postwar Theology: The "Theology of the '60s,"* ed. P. Kalaitzidis, Ath. N. Papathanasiou, and Th. Abatzidis (Athens: Indiktos Publications, 2009), 429–514 [in Greek] (a French version of this volume, *Le renouveau de la théologie grecque contemporaine: des années soixante à nos jours*, which results from a conference in Paris on April 15–16, 2010, organized by the Volos Academy for Theological Studies in collaboration with the Ecumenical Center *Istina*, the St. Sergius Orthodox Theological Institute, the journal *Contacts*, and the portal of Orthodox news www.orthodoxie.com, will be published by Éditions du Cerf); and "Orthodoxy and Hellenism in Contemporary Greece," *St. Vladimir's Theological Quarterly* 54 (2010): 365–420.

1. "Greek" theology refers to Orthodox Christian theology that originates in Greece, and does not designate all contemporary Orthodox theology.

2. G. Florovsky, "The Legacy and the Task of Orthodox Theology," *Anglican Theological Review*, 31 (1949): 65–71. See Florovsky, "Some Contributors to 20th Century Ecumenical Thought," in *Ecumenism II: A Historical Approach*, vol. 14, *Collected Works of G. Florovsky* (Belmont, Mass.: Nordland, 1989), 209–10; and Florovsky, "The Ways of Russian Theology," *Aspects of Church History*, vol. 4, *Collected Works of G. Florovsky* (Buchervertriebsanstalt/Vaduz-Europa, 1987), 201–4.

3. See P. Kalaitzidis, "From the 'Return to the Fathers' to the Need for a Modern Orthodox Theology," *St. Vladimir's Theological Quarterly* 54 (2010): 5–36, especially 19–23. For an overview on the Greek theologians of the 1960s, see Kalaitzidis, *Turmoil in Postwar Theology*.

4. J. S. Romanides, *The Ancestral Sin*, trans. George S. Gabriel (Ridgewood, N.J.: Zephyr Publishing, 2002).

5. M. Begzos, *The Future of the Past: A Critical Introduction to Orthodox Theology* (Athens: Armos, 1993), 92 [in Greek].

6. See, representatively, Fr. G. Metallinos, *Protopresbyter John S. Romanides: The "Prophet of Romanity": A Profile through Unknown or Little-Known Texts* (Athens: Armos, 2003) [in Greek]. See also the laudatory comments made by Metropolitan Hierotheos (Vlachos) of Nafpaktos and Agios Vlasios at Romanides's funeral (67f). See also G. D. Dragas, introduction to J. Romanides, *An Outline of Orthodox Patristic Dogmatics*, ed. and trans. G. D. Dragas (Rollinsford, N.H.: Orthodox Research Institute, 2004), iv–xv. See also C. Yannaras, *Orthodoxy and the West*, trans. Peter Chamberas and Norman Russell (Brookline, Mass.: Holy Cross Orthodox Press, 2006), 275–78.

7. P. Ranson, "Avant Propos," in *Saint Augustin*, ed. P. Ranson (Lausanne: L'Age d'Homme, 1988), 7. For a different assessment of Romanides's interpretation of Augustine, see the introduction to *Orthodox Readings of Augustine*, ed. George Demacopoulos and Aristotle Papanikolaou (Crestwood, N.Y.: St. Vladimir's Seminary Press, 1987). I have not yet seen specific studies on Romanides with regard to the issues raised in this paper, apart from brief references by M. Begzos, *The Future of the Past*, 92–95 [in Greek] (which contains a critique of Romanides's "neo-romanticism of ethnophyletism"). Apart from the book by Fr. Metallinos, to which I already referred, there is also the comprehensive approach to Romanides's work and teaching that was attempted by Andrew J. Sopko in his study with the characteristic title: *Prophet of Roman Orthodoxy: The Theology of John S. Romanides* (Dewdney, B.C.: Synaxis Press, 1998). Yiannis Spiteris dedicates a special chapter to Romanides's theology in his work *La teologia ortodossa neo-greca*, 279–95, including Romanides's theology, in fact, somewhat paradoxically, in the so-called neo-Orthodox movement, and criticizing it for anti-Westernism and rather arbitrary historical interpretations and conclusions. Fr. Metallinos takes a negative stance toward Spiteris's views in his book on Ro-

manides (21–47), while Archimandrite Chrysostomos Savvatos (now metropolitan of Messinia, in Kalamata, Greece) takes a positive approach to it (with only some reservations about specific parts) in his review in *Theologia* 65 (1994): 200–205 [in Greek].

8. See, for example, his early English papers: J. S. Romanides, "An Orthodox Look at the Ecumenical Movement," *The Greek Orthodox Theological Review* 10 (1964): 7–14; "A Greek Orthodox View of Ecumenism," *Orthodox Observer* 535 (November 1964): 335, 339; and *Orthodox Observer* 537 (December 1964): 370–71.

9. J. S. Romanides, "Remarks of an Orthodox Christian on Religious Freedom," *The Greek Orthodox Theological Review* 8 (1962–63): 127–32.

10. J. S. Romanides, "Islamic Universalism and the Constitution of Medina," in *A Work of Appreciation: Festschrift to Professor V. M. Vellas*, ed. A. P. Hastoupis (Athens: n.p., 1969), 614–18.

11. J. S. Romanides, *Romanity, Romania, Rumeli* (Thessaloniki: Pournaras, 1975) [in Greek]; a third edition, updated with an additional chapter, was published in 2002 [in Greek].

12. It should be noted here that Romanides's idea of Romanity does not include the Orthodox Slavs, who in his writings are almost always conspiring, with the Franks, against the "Romans."

13. *Orthodoxos Typos*, no. 255 (March 25, 1976).

14. *Orthodoxos Typos*, no. 309 (March 25, 1978).

15. J. S. Romanides, *Franks, Romans, Feudalism, and Doctrine: An Interplay between Theology and Society* (Brookline, Mass.: Holy Cross Orthodox Press, 1981).

16. Fr. Metallinos, *Protopresbyter John S. Romanides*, 50.

17. Published by Domos, Athens, 1989.

18. J. S. Romanides, *The Ancestral Sin*, xv [in the 1989 Greek edition]. Influenced, in all likelihood, by Fr. Romanides's ideas and overall thrust, Theodoros Zisis (now protopresbyter) spoke about "the Great Powers' cultural agenda, which aided in the liberation and creation of modern Greece in order to distance it from the East and unite it with the West"; see Zizis, "Theology in Greece Today," *Epopteia* 91 (1984) (dedicated to the topic of Modern Hellenism): 581 [in Greek].

19. See J. S. Romanides, "Introduction to the Theology and Spirituality of Romiosyne over and against Francosyne," in J. S. Romanides-D. Kontostergiou, *Romans or Romoi Fathers of the Church: The Works of Gregory Palamas I: In Defense of the Holy Hesychasts. Triads I* (Thessaloniki: Pournaras, 1984), 11–33, 49–194 [in Greek].

20. J. S. Romanides, *Patristic Theology*, foreword by Fr. George Metallinos, edited with notes by Monk Damascene of the Holy Mountain (Thessaloniki:

Parakatathiki Publications, 2004), 30 [in Greek]: "But Orthodoxy is not a *religion*. Orthodoxy is not a religion like all the other religions. Orthodoxy is distinguished by one unique characteristic, which is not found in the other religions. This is its anthropological and therapeutic aspect. In this it differs. Orthodoxy is a therapeutic course that treats the human person."

21. See the website www.romanity.org for more details concerning the reproduction, propagation, and reception of these ideas.

22. Christodoulos K. Paraskevaides (metropolitan of Demetrias), *The Europe of Spiritual Values and the Role of the Greek Orthodox and Our Paideia: A Talk to Teachers (Volos, 01/30/1995)* (Athens, 1995), 8 [in Greek]: "The Greek saints Cyril and Methodius worked 'as Greek representatives of the Latins to the Slavs against the Franks' to prevent Frankish invasion and estrangement." Another section of the same talk by then-Metropolitan Christodoulos, clearly inspired by Romanides, reads: "But the Frankification [of Europe] later with the Franco-Germanic storm and the Thomistic theology of Scholasticism led to the post-Charlemagne estrangement that abandoned the ascetic spirit of the East, replacing it with a simple sociology bereft of any transcendent element" (8–9).

23. See, in contrast to this severe presentation, for à French-speaking audience, the pertinent criticisms of the well-known Roman Catholic theologian A. de Halleux, "Une vision orthodoxe grecque de la romanité," *Revue Théologique de Louvain* 15 (1984): 54–66.

24. Fr. Metallinos, *Protopresbyter John S. Romanides*, 67.

25. See J. S. Romanides, *Romanity*, 259f, 271f.

26. See, for example, one of Fr. Romanides's later articles, "Religion is a Neuro-biological Sickness and Orthodoxy Its Cure," in *Orthodoxy, Hellenism, Journey into the Third Millenium*, vol. 2 (Mount Athos: Holy Monastery of Koutloumousiou, 1996), 67–87, which contains his views concerning the Orthodox Catholic Tradition and the Ecumenical Councils as "companies of psychiatric clinics." He explicated these same views more systematically in "Ecclesiastical Councils and Culture," *Theologia* 66 (1995): 646–80, in which he not only espouses the view that the Ecumenical Councils are "companies of psychiatric clinics" (654) that guide the local psychiatric clinics (i.e., the local Churches) in the treatment of the faithful/patients through the vision of God (*theoptia*), but also identifies the Kingdom of God with the *hic et nunc* experiences of the vision of God, which renders the mystery of baptism unnecessary (656n14) and the resurrection mere window-dressing. See also the critical observations of Fr. Nicholas Loudovikos, *Closed Spirituality and the Sense of Self: The Mysticism of Power and the Truth of Nature and Person* (Athens: Ellinika Grammata, 1999), 206–7 [in Greek]; S. Yangazoglou, "Eucharistic Ecclesiology and Monastic Spirituality: The Question of Gerontism," in Kalaitzidis, *Turmoil in Postwar Theology*, 615–18 [in Greek].

27. Fr. George Metallinos's attempt to explain away this problem lacks historical accuracy, frequently appealing to errors in chronology and fact; see *Protopresbyter John S. Romanides*, 27–28, with many contradictions on 43, 45.

28. I offer a more detailed analysis of Romanides's anti-Westernism in my previous writings: "Greekness and Antiwesternism in the Greek Theological Generation of the '60's," 75–109 [in Greek]; "The Discovery of Greekness and Theological Antiwesternism in the Theological Generation of the '60's," 439–53 [in Greek]; and "Orthodoxy and Hellenism in Contemporary Greece," 408–12. A different approach and appreciation of Romanides's politico-theological synthesis is offered by D. P. Payne, "The Revival of Political Hesychasm in Greek Orthodox Thought: A Study of the Hesychast Basis of the Thought of John S. Romanides and Christos Yannaras" (PhD diss., Graduate Faculty of Baylor University, J. M. Dawson Institute of Church-State Studies, 2006), 383–443.

29. A. Louth, Introduction to *On the Absence and Unknowability of God: Heidegger and the Areopagite*, by C. Yannaras, trans. H. Ventis (London: T&T Clark, 2005), 1, dramatically expands this, arguing that "Christos Yannaras is without doubt the most important living Greek Orthodox theologian." See Aristotle Papanikolaou's review of this book in *Modern Theology* 23 (2007): 301–4.

30. Oliver Clément, "Situation de la parole théologique selon la tradition orthodoxe," preface to the French translation of Yannaras's book: *De l'absence et de l'inconnaissance de Dieu, d'après les écrits aréopagitiques et Martin Heidegger*, trans. J. Touraille (Paris: Éditions du Cerf, 1971), 9. See R. Williams, "Eastern Orthodox Theology," in *The Modern Theologians: An Introduction to Christian Theology since 1918*, ed. D. F. Ford and R. Muers (Malden, Mass: Blackwell, 2005), 583; and B. Petrà, "Christos Yannaras," *Credere Oggi* 24, 2 (2004): 121n140.

31. This Greek conception of philosophical thought largely summarizes one of his first philosophical works, *Philosophie sans rupture*, trans. A. Borrély (Genève: Labor et Fides, 1986). This was originally published in two volumes in Greek in 1980 and 1981.

32. See on this point my analysis in "Orthodoxy and Hellenism in Contemporary Greece," 393–405, in the section titled: "The Cultural Hermeneutics of Fr. Georges Florovsky's 'Christian Hellenism': i) The 'Greek Orthodoxy' of the 'Unbroken Continuity of Greek Thought' Theory of the Neo-Orthodox—Primarly Christos Yannaras and Fr. Vasileios Gontikakis."

33. See C. Yannaras, "The Decision *De Oecumenismo* of the Second Vatican Council and Orthodoxy's Nationalism," in Yannaras, *Being Honest with Orthodoxy: Modern Greek Theological Essays* (Athens: Astir Publications, 1968), 98–109 [in Greek].

34. See on this Y. Spiteris, *La teologia ortodossa neo-greca*, 304.

35. S. Gounelas, "A Return to Greek Roots or a March toward the Eschaton? A Critical View of Some of Christos Yannaras's Positions on Hellenocentrism

and Greek Orthodoxy," in Gounelas, *Crisis of Culture, Crisis of Man: A Loss of Meaning* (Athens: Armos, 1997), 358 [in Greek].

36. English translation: *Orthodoxy and the West: Hellenic Self-Identity in the Modern Age*, trans P. Chamberas and N. Russell (Brookline, Mass: Holy Cross Orthodox Press, 2006).

37. English original: Erwin Panofsky, *Gothic Architecture and Scholasticism* (Latrobe, Pa.: Archabbey Press, 1951).

38. English translation: M.-D. Chenu, *Is Theology a Science?*, trans. A. H. N. Green-Armytage (New York: Hawthorn Books, 1959).

39. English translation: Étienne Gilson, *History of Christian Philosophy in the Middle Ages* (New York: Random House, 1955).

40. C. Yannaras, *On Himself* (Athens: Icarus, 1995), 72–74 [in Greek].

41. C. Yannaras, *Contra Religion* (Athens: Icarus, 2006) [in Greek].

42. See, for example, the interview with Yannaras by the Orthodox theologian Michel Stavrou: C. Yannaras, "Orient-Occident. La signification profonde du schisme. Un entretien avec Christos Yannaras," *Service Orthodoxe de Presse (SOP)* no. 150 (August–September 1990), 32–34.

43. C. Yannaras, *Red Square and Uncle Arthur* (Athens: Domos, 1986), 90 [in Greek].

44. See C. Yannaras, *Contra Religion*, 119–37, 186–202, 210–11, 213–23, 293–308 [in Greek]. For a critique of "religionization" in the Orthodox East, see also the last theological work by Yannaras, *The Enigma of Evil* (Athens: Ikaros, 2008) [in Greek]. For an analysis of the development of this term in Yannaras's thought, see Basilio Petrá's contribution to this volume.

45. See for example, Yannaras, *Orthodoxy and the West in Modern Greece*, 26–28 [in Greek]; "Nature and History in the Book of Revelation," *Synaxis* 56 (1995): 44 [in Greek]; "Orthodoxy and International Affairs," in *Resistance to Estrangement* 3 [in Greek]; "Capitalism and Fundamentalism," in *Resistance to Estrangement* 210 [in Greek]; *The Inhumanity of the Right* (Athens: Domos, 1998), 46n1 [in Greek]; "A Timely Proposal for Celebration," in *Greek Preparedness for European Integration: Critical Timely Detections: Chronography 1999* (Athens: Libanis, 2000), 375 [in Greek]; "Greek Catholicity and Western Universalism," 218–19 (the exact same text under the title: "The Schism as a Cultural Rift in Europe" in *Party Politics: When Citizens Vote for the Plundering of Their Lives* [Athens: Patakis, 2004], 119–39), and especially on this particular issue, 127–28 [in Greek]; "Church and Culture," *Synaxis* 88 (2003): 13–14 [in Greek]; *Contra Religion*, 144–46, 225–27 [in Greek]; "What is the Future for Europe?," in *Battling Hopelessness* (Athens: Hestia Publications, 2007): 13–15 [in Greek]; "On an Incongruous Ecology (and Christmas)," in *The Collapse of the Political System in Greece Today*, Columns 2007 (Thessaloniki: Ianos, 2008), 276 [in Greek].

46. *Orthodoxy and West in Modern Greece*, 39–42. This analysis is omitted in the English translation of this work.

47. For more, see M. Begzos, *The Future of the* Past, 54–56, 85 [in Greek]; P. Dimitras, "L'antioccidentalisme grec," *Contacts* 128 (1984): 350–58; V. Makrides, "Neoorthodoxie-eine religiöse Intellektuellenströmung im heutigen Griechenland," in *Die Religion von Oberschichten: Religion, Profession, Intellektualismus*, ed. P. Antes and D. Paahnke (Marburg, Diagonal-Verlag, 1989), 279–89; "Le rôle de l'Orthodoxie dans la formation de l'antieuropéanisme et l'antioccidentalisme grecs," in *Religions et transformations de l'Europe*, ed. G. Vincent and J.-P. Willaime (Strasbourg: Presses Universitaires de Strasbourg, 1993), 103–16; "Byzantium in Contemporary Greece: The Neo-Orthodox Current of Ideas," in *Byzantium and the Modern Greek Identity*, ed. D. Ricks and P. Magdalino (Aldershot, U.K.: Ashgate, 1998), 141–53; V. Makrides and D. Uffelmann, "Studying Eastern Orthodox Anti-Westernism: The Need for a Comparative Research Agenda," in *Orthodox Christianity and Contemporary Europe: Selected Papers of the International Conference held at the University of Leeds, England, in June 2001*, ed. J. Sutton and W. van den Bercken (Leuven: Peeters, 2003), 87–120. See also A. Heraclides, *Greece and the "Danger from the East"* (Athens: Polis Publications, 2001), 81–126 [in Greek]; and F. Terzakis, *Irrationalism, Fundamentalism and Religious Revival: The Colors of the Chessboard* (Athens: Ellinika Grammata, 1998), 59–68 [in Greek]. For Yannaras's own view on fundamentalism, see "The Dilemma: Modernization-Fundamentalism," in *"Generous in Small Measure": Instructions for Use* (Athens: Patakis, 2003), 264–76 [in Greek]; "The American Matrix of Fundamentalism," in *Logic Begins with Love* (Athens: Ikarus, 2004), 53–56 [in Greek]; and *Contra Religion*, 174–78 [in Greek].

48. For the "West" in Russia, see Vera Shevzov's contribution to this volume.

49. See C. Yannaras, *De l'absence et de l'inconnaissance de Dieu*.

50. Yannaras's recent (May 2011) discourse on the occasion of the conferment of his *honoris causa* doctorate from Holy Cross Greek Orthodox School of Theology in Boston, Massachusetts, gives the impression of a shift in his thinking—Yannaras strongly criticizes Orthodox fundamentalists and neoconservatives for their fanatical anti-Westernism and their obstinate reaction against meetings with Christians of other traditions and against the ecumenical dialogue, which they consider a fallacy and a betrayal of Orthodoxy. For a more detailed analysis of Yannaras's thought, see P. Kalaitzidis, "Greekness and Antiwesternism in the Greek Theological Generation of the '60's" (PhD diss., School of Theology, University of Thessaloniki, 2008), 209–543 [in Greek]; "The Discovery of Greekness and Theological Antiwesternism in the Theological Generation of the '60's," in Kalaitzidis, *Turmoil in Postwar Theology*, 479–514 [in Greek]; "Orthodoxy and Hellenism in Contemporary Greece," 393–405. On the same topic, see also Y. Spiteris, *La theologia orthodossa neo-greca*, 296–322; and Kristina Stöckl,

Community after Totalitarianism: The Russian Orthodox Intellectual Tradition and the Philosophical Discourse of Political Modernity (Franfurt a. Main: Peter Lang, 2008), 128–31, 151–62.

Christos Yannaras and the Idea of
"Dysis" / Basilio Petrà

This English translation of my Italian text is the work of Norman Russell, a well-known scholar and a dear friend of mine, to whom I am greatly and deeply grateful.

1. For a very careful study of Yannaras's idea of the West and for a large bibliography, see Pantelis Kalaitzidis, "Greekness and Antiwesternism in the Greek Theological Generation of the '60s" (PhD diss., School of Theology, University of Thessaloniki, 2008), 209–584 [in Greek], and "The Discovery of Greekness and Theological Antiwesternism in the Theological Generation of the '60s," in *Turmoil in Postwar Theology: The "Theology of the '60s,"* ed. P. Kalaitzidis, Ath. N. Papathanasiou, and Th. Abatzidis (Athens: Indiktos Publications, 2009), 429–514, esp. 479–514 [in Greek]. See also C. Stamoulis, *Lot's Wife and Contemporary Theology* (Athens, Indiktos, 2008), 131–57 [in Greek].

2. On the importance of Dostoevsky in Yannaras's life, see Yannaras, *The Red Square and Uncle Arthur* (Athens: Domos, 1986), 35 [in Greek]. This book is a kind of diary of Yannaras's journey to Russia in May 1982.

3. "Peri ēthikōn protupōn: Me anafora ston Alyosha Karamazov," in Yannaras, *Honest*, 92–97.

4. Yannaras, *Honest*, 155–56.

5. On May 2, Yannaras has the chance to stand in front of the monument to Pushkin in the homonymous square of Moscow, and recalls this discourse of Dostoevsky's: "I stood there, for a while, deeply moved." Yannaras, *The Red Square and Uncle Arthur*, 80–81.

6. Yannaras, *Honest*, 33.

7. Georges Florovsky, *Ways of Russian Theology. Part two*, vol. 6 of the *Collected Works*, trans. Robert L. Nichols (Büchervertriebsanstalt: Vaduz 1987), 302.

8. Yannaras, *Honest*, 33–34.

9. Yannaras, *Honest*, 35–36.

10. Yannaras, *Honest*, 36.

11. Yannaras, *Honest*, 157.

12. Yannaras, *Honest*, 156.

13. Yannaras, *Honest*, 172.

14. Yannaras, *Honest*, 172.

15. Yannaras, *The Freedom of Morality: Essays for an Orthodox Vision of Ethics* (Athens, 1970), 10 [in Greek].

16. Yannaras, *Honest*, 38.

17. Yannaras, *Honest*, 38.

18. Yannaras, *Honest*, 38–39.

19. Yannaras, *Honest*, 40.

20. Yannaras, *Honest*, 51.

21. Yannaras, *Honest*, 54.

22. See "Heretical Orthodoxy?" reprinted in Yannaras, *Honest*, 59–73.

23. See Yannaras, "Heretical Orthodoxy?"

24. See the article "Eros and Celibacy. The Drama of a Christianity without Eros" reprinted in, *Honest to Orthodoxy*, 74–83.

25. See "Iconoclasts: The Conservatives of Orthodoxy," reprinted in Yannaras, *Honest*, 84–91.

26. See "Hellenic and Ecumenical Orthodoxy," reprinted in Yannaras, *Honest*, 42–49.

27. See "The Decree of Oecumenismo of the Second Vatican Council and the Nationalism of Orthodoxy," reprinted in Yannaras, *Honest*, 98–109.

28. Yannaras, *Honest*, 11.

29. See Yannaras, *Honest*, 98–109; "The People of God," reprinted in Yannaras, *Honest*, 178–190.

30. See "A Comment on 'The Death of God,'" reprinted in Yannaras, *Honest*, 113–25. Yannaras quotes Martin Heidegger, *Holzwege* (Frankfurt: Klostermann, 1963); he underlines the interpretation of nihilism given by Heidegger in the footsteps of Nietzsche, and somehow anticipates his own future ideas. Not by chance, with respect to the original text published in *Synoro*, he adds a reference to his work of 1967.

31. The category of perdition, as it is presented in Sartre's thought, is given particular attention by Yannaras in *Honest*, 120–123, and in the answer to A. Terzakis in *Epocej* (Epochs), which is also reprinted in *Honest*, 133–146.

32. See Yannaras, "Person and Eros: Theological Essay of Ontology," *Deukalión* 3, no. 10 (1974): 145: Yannaras refers to his doctoral dissertation in Thessaloniki, *The Ontological Content of the Theological Concept of Person* (Athens, 1970) as the first version of his work, adding: "It was one of the phases of the endeavour to study themes connected with the present writing—one among other phases that preceded and others that followed since about the end of 1966, when this endeavour started, up to the present time."

33. Yannaras, *Memories* (Athens: Ikaros, 1995), 48 [in Greek].

34. Yannaras, *Memories*, 45.

35. Yannaras, *Memories*, 47.

36. Yannaras, *Memories*, 50.

37. The book has been translated by J. Touraille: *De l'absence et de l'inconnaissance de Dieu d'après les écrits aréopagiques et Martin Heidegger*, with a preface by Olivier Clément (Paris: Du Cerf, 1971). It was the first of Yannaras's books to be translated into a Western language. Clément's preface, entitled "Situation de la parole théologique selon la tradition orthodoxe," is a long essay (almost a fourth of the entire book).

38. Yannaras, *De l'absence*, 64.

39. Yannaras, *De l'absence*, 65. Yannaras quotes from Heidegger, *Holzwege* (1963 ed.), 239–240.

40. Yannaras, *De l'absence*, 65–66.

41. Yannaras, *De l'absence*, 73.

42. Yannaras, *De l'absence*, 73.

43. Yannaras, *De l'absence*, 99. Yannaras mentions the following names: Gregory of Nyssa, Basil the Great, Gregory the Theologian, Maximus the Confessor, John Damascene, and Gregory Palamas.

44. Yannaras, *De l'absence*, 87–88.

45. Yannaras, *De l'absence*, 105.

46. Yannaras, *De l'absence*, 120.

47. Yannaras, *On the Absence and Unknowability of God: Heidegger and the Areopagite* (London: T&T Clark, 2007), 72.

48. Yannaras, *Memories*, 74–75.

49. Yannaras, *Party Power: When Citizens Vote for the Pillage of Their Life* (Athens: Pataki, 2002), 238 [in Greek]. Yannaras, *The Enigma of Evil* (Athens: Ikaros, 2008), 244 [in Greek].

50. It is well known that, for Heidegger, the Latin translation of the Greek terms is really a translation into a different way of thinking the experimentation of being, and it is precisely through such a translation that we have the beginning of the flattening of the ground of Western thought. This topic is fully present in "Der Ursprung des Kunstwerkes," the first essay of the *Holzwege (Heideggers Gesamtausgabe*, 5:7–8). Yannaras underlines the novelty of the Heideggerian reading of Plato and Aristotle in the Prologos to the first edition of his work *Person and Eros*.

51. See Yannaras, *A Sketch of Introduction to Philosophy*, vol. 2 (Athens: Domos, 1981), 29–31 [in Greek].

52. Yannaras, *The Neo-Greek Identity* (Athens: Grigori, 1978), 99–100 [in Greek].

53. The insistence of Yannaras upon such a continuity of the Greek way of thought marks a relevant difference from Zizioulas's idea of the Christian "Ontological Revolution": cf. A. Papanikolaou, *Being with God: Trinity, Apophaticism, and Divine-Human Communion* (South Bend, Ind.: University of Notre Dame Press, 2006), 73–89.

54. See the enthusiastic article of Yannaras in *Tribune*, July 9, 1977, "A Discourse before the Common Market," where he presents the essay by John Zizioulas: "From Mask to Person." Reprinted in Yannaras, *Neo-Greek Identity*, 93–101 [in Greek].

55. In Yannaras, *Orthodoxy and the West: Theology in Greece Today* (Athens: Editions Athina, 1972), 136 [in Greek].

56. Yannaras, *Cultural Diplomacy: Pre-theory of a Greek Planning* (Athens: Ikaros, 2001), 95 [in Greek].

57. Yannaras, *Neo-Greek Identity*, 94–95.

58. Yannaras, *Cultural Diplomacy*, 93–94.

59. The first and most meaningful work in this direction is represented by *Person and Eros*. Yannaras considers the first edition of this work to be *The Ontological Content of the Theological Concept of Person*; the second is the edition of 1974, published by *Deukalion* in Athens; the third edition, still in print, is the one published by Papazisi (Athens). The fourth edition is the one published in 1987 by Domos (Athens): in this edition we lose the subtitle, *Theological Essay on Ontology*. The same publishing house, Domos, published the seventh edition in 2006. The centrality of the category of relation becomes direct and formal in the book *Ontology of Relation* (Athens: Ikaros, 2004) [in Greek].

60. Of great interest on this topic is the interview given by Yannaras to Michel Stavrou and published in Yannaras, *An Interview, Synaxē* 34 (1990): 69–78 [in Greek]. Yannaras increasingly accepts the idea that the Schism has its roots, on the one hand, in the Augustinian approach to gnoseology and to ontology, and on the other, in the assumption of a dominating role of the Germanic tribes in the West, especially of the Franks (without, however, arriving at Romanidis's radical positions): see Yannaras, "Schism as Cultural Split of Europe" in Yannaras, *Party Power*, 119–139 [in Greek]. This is the text of a paper read in 2000 at the *Fondazione Giovanni Agnelli*. For a challenge to Yannaras's interpretation of Augustine, see *Orthodox Readings of Augustine*, ed. George Demacopoulos and Aristotle Papanikolaou (Crestwood: St. Vladimir's Seminary Press, 2008), esp. 32–35.

61. See Yannaras, *Truth and Unity of the Church* (Athens: Grigori, 1977), 148 [in Greek].

62. The paper was published with the same title in *Orthodoxy, Life and Freedom: Essays in Honour of Archbishop Iakovos*, ed. A.J. Philippou (Oxford: Studion Publications, 1973), 130–147. The Greek text is published together with another text—already published in French (*La théologie en Grèce aujourd'hui*)—in *Orthodoxy and the West*.

63. Yannaras, *Orthodoxy and the West*, 134–135.

64. The work where these attacks initially emerge is *The Freedom of Morality*. As we have already mentioned, the first Greek edition of this inspiring book has

the subtitle *Essays for an Orthodox Vision of Ethics*. Because of violent reactions to it, Yannaras prepared a second edition, largely revised and published by Grigori (Athens) in 1979, leaving out the subtitle; a third edition, seemingly revised but almost the same as the second, has been published by Ikaros in 2002. As known, the most organic and systematic endeavour to criticize the influence of the West in Greece is his *Orthodoxy and the West* (Brookline, Mass.: Holy Cross Orthodox Press, 2006).

65. Yannaras, *Truth and Unity*, 128.

66. Yannaras, *Freedom* (1979 ed.), 306.

67. Yannaras, *Red Square*, 90.

68. Yannaras, *Red Square*, 90–91.

69. Yannaras, *Red Square*, 93.

70. Later published by Domos (Athens) in 1988 and translated into English as *On the Absence and Unknowability of God*.

71. Yannaras, *On the Absence*, 56.

72. Yannaras, *On the Absence*, 53.

73. The English translation is *Orthodoxy and the West: Hellenic Self-Identity in the Modern Age* (Brookline, Mass.: Holy Cross Press, 2006).

74. Yannaras, *Orthodoxy and the West*, 44.

75. Yannaras, *Orthodoxy and the West*, 56.

76. See Yannaras, *The Inhumanity of Right* (Athens: Domos, 1998), 138, 141, 148, 228 [in Greek]; and Yannaras, *The Speakable and the Unspeakable: The Linguistic Limits of Metaphysics* (Athens: Ikaros, 1999), 313 [in Greek], where Yannaras speaks about the "twin religionization" (Catholic and Protestant) of the ecclesial event; also, Yannaras, *Party Power*, 131, 138, 245–248, 250.

77. Yannaras, *Ontology of Relation*, 151–161.

78. Yannaras, *Against Religion* (Athens, Ikaros, 2006).

79. Yannaras, *Against Religion*, 265–308.

80. Yannaras, *Against Religion*, 271.

81. Because of his vision of the prelapsarian condition, Yannaras is drawn to a new reading of original sin: see *Ontology of Relation*, 175–191.

82. Yannaras, *Enigma*, 123.

83. Yannaras, *Enigma*, 157.

84. Yannaras, *Against Religion*, 313.

85. There is also a latent presence of the language and of the thought of Berdiaev; on this, see B. Petrà, "Personalist Thought in Greece in the Twentieth Century: A First Tentative Synthesis," *The Greek Orthodox Theological Review* 50 (2005) nos. 1–4, 2–48.

Religion in the Greek Public Sphere:
Debating Europe's Influence / Effie Fokas

1. Peter Berger, "The Desecularisation of the World," in *The Desecularisation of the World: Resurgent Religion and World Politics*, ed. P. Berger (Grand Rapids, Mich.: William B. Eerdmans, 1999), 9.

2. "It is not fanciful to predict that there will be similar developments [to Western European secularization] in Eastern Europe, precisely to the degree that these countries too will be integrated into the new Europe." Berger, "The Desecularization of the World," 10. This statement was repeated in Berger, "Secularism in Retreat," in *Islam and Secularism in the Middle East*, ed. J. Esposito and A. Tamini (New York: New York University Press, 2000), 44, and was expressed more boldly during a London School of Economics Forum on Religion seminar devoted to the topic of his retraction statement on November 12, 2008, at the LSE.

3. For example, see David Martin, *A General Theory of Secularization* (New York: Harper & Row, 1978) and David Martin, "Is There an Eastern European Pattern of Secularization?," in *Religion: Problem or Promise? The Role of Religion in the Integration of Europe*, ed. S. Marincak (Kosice: Orientala et Occidentalia, 2008), 129–44.

4. Of course, Martin was well ahead in this field in speaking in terms of differing degrees and kinds of secularization since his 1978 *General Theory of Secularization*, while most theorists were generalizing on the basis of a monolithic European secularization or a monolithic American secularization.

5. Martin, "Eastern European Pattern?," 130.

6. Ibid., 132. The relation of religion to democracy, and specifically of Orthodoxy to democracy, is an important subject worthy of a separate study. For more on this subject, see Elizabeth Prodromou, "The Ambivalent Orthodox," *Journal of Democracy* 15 (2004): 62–75.

7. Ibid., 133.

8. Ibid., 144.

9. Ibid., 133–34.

10. Their conclusion is not based exclusively on Orthodox contexts but is applied to certain Catholic and Protestant cases as well. Loek Halman and Veerle Draulans, "How Secular is Europe?" *British Journal of Sociology* 57 (2005): 263–88.

11. See Slavica Jakelić, "Secularization, European Identity, and 'The End of the West,'" *The Hedgehog Review* 8 (2006): 133–39, 136.

12. Peter Katzenstein, "Multiple Modernities as Limits to Secular Europeanization?," in *Religion in an Expanding Europe*, ed. T. Byrnes and P. Katzenstein (Cambridge: Cambridge University Press, 2006), 2.

13. Sabrina Ramet, "The Way We Were—and Should Be Again? European Orthodox Churches and the 'Idyllic Past,'" in *Religion in an Expanding Europe*, 148.

14. T. Byrnes, "Transnational Religion and Europeanization," in *Religion in an Expanding Europe*, 293.

15. Constantine Danopoulos, "Religion, Civil Society, and Democracy in Orthodox Greece," *Journal of Southern Europe and the Balkans* 6 (2004): 51.

16. A. Pollis, "Eastern Orthodoxy and Human Rights," *Human Rights Quarterly* 15 (1993): 355. See also Daniel Payne, "The Clash of Civilisations: The Church of Greece, the European Union and the Question of Human Rights," *Religion, State and Society* 31 (2003): 261–71.

17. Prodromou, "The Ambivalent Orthodox," 62–75.

18. Jose Casanova, *Public Religions in the Modern World* (Chicago: University of Chicago Press, 2004).

19. However, Martin does concede the important role of active maintenance of this relationship. Drawn from a personal communication, August 29, 2008.

20. From a range of perspectives and disciplines, and mainly but not exclusively on the Greek case: Sia Anagnostopoulou, "The Historicity of the 'National Role' of the Church of Greece," in *Structures and Relations of Power in Contemporary Greece: Proceedings of the 7th Scientific Conference* (Athens: Panteion University, 2000), 349–52; P. Dimitropoulos, *State and Church: A Difficult Relationship* (Athens: Kritiki, 2001); P. Kalaitzidis, *Orthodoxy and Modernity: Prologue* (Athens: Indiktos, 2007); Nikos Kokosalakis, "Religion and Modernization in 19th Century Greece," *Social Compass* 34 (1987): 223–42; Nikos Kokosalakis, "Greek Orthodoxy and Modern Socio-Economic Change," in *Religion and the Transformation of Capitalism*, ed. R. Roberts (London: Routledge, 1995), 248–65; Nikos Kokosalakis, "Orthodoxie Grecque, Modernité et Politique," in *Identités Religieuses en Europe*, ed. G Davie and D. Hervieu-Léger (Paris: La Découverte, 1996), 131–51; Nikos Kokosalakis, "Orthodoxy and Social Change in Modern Greek Society," *Synaksi* 62 (1997): 101–8; Vasilios Makridis, "Aspects of Greek Orthodox Fundamentalism," *Orthodoxes Forum* 5 (1991): 49–72; Vasilios Makridis, "Le Rôle de l'Orthodoxie dans la Formation de l'Antieuropéanisme et l'Occidentalisme Grecs," in *Religions et Transformations de l'Europe*, ed. G. Vincent and J.-P. Willaime (Strasbourg: Presses Universitaires de Strasbourg, 1993), 103–16; Vasilios Makridis, "Conflicting views on Byzantium in Contemporary Greece: Romeic/Neoorthodox vs. Hellenic/Neopagan" (paper presented at conference on "Byzantium and Modern Greek identity," King's College, London, May 1996); A. Manitakis, "The Autocephalous Church of Greece between State and Nation," in *Structures and Relations of Power in Contemporary Greece*, 327–42; A Manitakis, *The Relations of the Church with the Nation-State* (Athens: Nefeli, 2000); P. Vassiliadis, "Orthodox Christianity," in *God's Rule*, ed. J. Neusner (Washington D.C.: Georgetown University Press, 2003), 85–106.

21. Victor Roudometof, "The Evolution of Greek Orthodoxy in the Context of World Historical Globalization," in *Orthodox Christianity in 21st Century Greece: The Role of Religion in Politics, Ethnicity and Culture*, ed. V. Roudometof and V. Makrides (Aldershot, U.K.: Ashgate, 2010), 29.

22. See Effie Fokas, "Greek Orthodoxy and European Identity," in *Contemporary Greece and Europe*, ed. A. Mitsos and E. Mossialos (Aldershot, U.K.: Ashgate, 2000), and Effie Fokas, "Greece: Religion, Nation and European Identity," in *Citizenship and Ethnic Conflict: Challenging the Nation-State*, ed. H. Gulalp (New York: Routledge, 2006).

23. By "full separation" I mean less the legal and constitutional framework of church-state relations and more the informal and pervasive interaction between the two spheres, led and maintained by individual religious and political leaders usually with reference (explicit or implicit) to the relationship between Orthodoxy and Greek national identity. As Theoni Stathopoulou notes, "although the constitutional arrangements of church-state relations in Greece, even the special privileges given to the church, are not very different from those in the rest of Europe, the visibility of the church in the public sphere is high—mainly due to the way religion is diffused in everyday life" (Stathopoulou, "Faith and Trust: Tracking Patterns of Religious and Civic Commitment in Greece and Europe: An Empirical Approach," in *Orthodox Christianity in 21st Century Greece*, 196).

24. Ibid., 197.

25. Martin, "Eastern European Pattern?," 130.

26. "What needs underlining here is precisely the unproblematic and undifferentiated nature, thus far, of the relation of Orthodoxy to national identity. Culture and religion, in Greece and Orthodox Eastern Europe generally, are woven without seam throughout" (Martin, "Eastern European Pattern?," 144). The "thus far" in this passage is also indicative of Martin's concession that the religion-national identity link is not inevitable.

27. Greece was the first state to be convicted under the European Convention article protecting freedom of religion and belief (Article 9) in the watershed *Kokkinakis v. Greece* case of 1993, and was the defendant in nine of the twelve subsequent cases where religious freedom was supported (with seven of them involving Jehovah's Witnesses). See James Richards and J. Shoemaker, "The European Court of Human Rights, Minority Religions, and the Social Construction of Religious Freedom," in *The Centrality of Religion in Social Life: Essays in Honour of James A. Beckford*, ed. Eileen Barker (Aldershot, U.K.: Ashgate, 2008), 103–16.

28. In fact, Berger indicates more specifically: "The closer a society moves towards Europe, the more it will come under the influence of European *secularity*" (my emphasis). See Peter Berger, "Orthodoxy and Global Pluralism," *The Journal of Post-Soviet Democratization* 13 (2005): 437–47.

29. This is a European Court of Human Rights decision of November, 2009, in a case raised by Soile Lautsi, the mother of two children attending Italian public schools, who argued that the presence of the crucifix in the school class-rooms violated her right to educate her children in accordance with her own re-ligious (or nonreligious) beliefs (Article 2 of the ECHR) and breached the principle of the secularism of the Italian state. The European Court of Human Rights ruled in Lauti's favor, finding the display of the crucifix in violation of Article 2 of Protocol No. 1, the right of parents to educate their children in ac-cordance with their religious or philosophical beliefs, and Article 9, the right to freedom of thought, conscience, and religion. The Italian State sought and won a referral of the case to the Grand Chamber of the European Court of Human Rights. That hearing took place on June 30, 2010, with an unprecedented num-ber of states, associations, and individuals allowed to intervene in the hearing with statements either for or against the original ruling. The final decision was not yet released at the time of this writing. One of the interventions was from law professor Joseph Weiler; for his critique of the original Lautsi ruling, see Jo-seph Weiler, "Editorial: Lautsi: Crucifix in the Classroom Redux," *European Journal of International Law* 21 (2010): 1–6. See also Susanna Mancini, "The Crucifix Rage: Supranational Constitutionalism Bumps against the Counter-Majoritarian Difficulty," *European Constitutional Law Review* 6 (2010): 6–27.

30. "Critical Mr. Ieronymos," *Kathimerini*, November 24, 2009, 5 [in Greek].

31. In the identity-card issue, the controversy began May 8, 2000, when the interview with then–Justice Minister Michalis Stathopoulos—in which he indi-cated that reference to religion should be removed from the national-identity cards—appeared in the newspaper *Ethnos*; and in the religious-symbols issue, it began on November 4, 2009, one day following the European Court of Human Rights decision on the case (although reference is also made to one article dated December 25, 2009, and thus beyond the six-week period).

32. For an overview of the identity-card issue from a discourse analysis per-spective, see Y. Stavrakakis, "Religion and Populism: Reflections on the 'Politi-cised' Discourse of the Greek Church," discussion paper no. 7, presented at Hellenic Observatory (London School of Economics and Political Science, May 2002). From a press analysis perspective, see L. Molokotos-Liederman, "The Greek ID Cards Controversy: A Case Study on Religion and National Identity in a Changing European Union," *Journal of Contemporary Religion* 18 (2003): 291–315. See also the discussion of the identity-card issue in N. Alivatos, *The Uncertain Modernisation* (Athens: Polis, 2001), 311–20. Finally, see A. Anas-tassiadis, "Religion and Politics in Greece: The Greek Church's 'Conservative Modernisation' in the 1990s," *Questions de Recherche* 11 (2004): 1–32. See also A. Manitakis, "The Autocephalus Church," 327–42; and P. Dimitropoulos, *State and Church*.

33. "Christodoulos: Voluntary the Inscription of Religion," *Ethnos*, May 15, 2000, 19 [in Greek].

34. M. Antoniadou, "Christodoulos from the Pulpit: Let There Be a Referendum for the New Identity Cards," *To Vima*, May 15, 2000, A3 [in Greek].

35. "Referendum for the People to Judge," *Ethnos*, May 15, 2000, 18 [in Greek].

36. *Sofianopoulos and Others v. Greece*, December 20, 2001.

37. On this topic, see Effie Fokas, "A New Role for the Church? Reassessing the Place of Religion in the Greek Public Sphere," in *Hellenic Observatory Papers on Greece and Southern Europe* (GreeSE), Paper Series 17 (London School of Economics, 2008).

38. Antoniadou, "Christodoulos from the Pulpit" [in Greek].

39. Grigoris Kalokairinos, "Why the Hierarchy Chose Ieronymos as Archbishop," *To Vima*, Februrary 17, 2008, 20 [in Greek].

40. Nikos Sifounaki, "This Is How We Want the Church," *Eleutherotypia* February 10, 2008 [in Greek].

41. Kostas Bougatsos, "Casus Belli the . . . Removal of Religious Symbols," *Eleutheros Typos*, December 5, 2009, 14 [in Greek].

42. "Critical Mr. Ieronymos," 5 [in Greek].

43. Thanos Tstatsi, "Ieronymos against the 'Ostracism' of the Religious [Symbols]," *Eleutherotypia*, November 24, 2009, 22 [in Greek].

44. Tstatsi, "Ieronymos," 22 [in Greek].

45. George Gilson, "Fighting for an Authentic Faith," *Athens News*, December 25, 2009. Earlier in the interview, Ieronymos states: "One might conclude we have entered the realm of the irrational, but the roots of the decision are in eighteenth-century Enlightenment . . . [that have] reached Greece. . . . All these efforts boil down to one thing—pushing the Church to the margins."

46. Most interestingly, the reaction of certain Greek Orthodox leaders indicates that, through its decision, the European Court of Human Rights may be inadvertently influencing a situation wherein the Greek Orthodox Church (and surely others) will increasingly seek to interpret religious symbols as national symbols in efforts to "protect" them from "European harm." To the extent to which this trend materializes, Europe will be steering the Church towards even greater emphasis on national identity than is already the case. The cited cleric made the statement at a public seminar held at a Greek theological institute in May, 2010.

47. See "Critical Mr. Ieronymos," 5

48. The same, however, applies to Italy in the *Lautsi* case, where, for example, the minister of education declared that "No ideological European Court can negate our identity." Cited in Ersi Vatou, "Vatican Declares Its Anger," *Eleutherotypia*, November 4, 2009, 23 [in Greek]. In other words, Orthodox Greece is not exceptional in this regard.

49. This point brings to mind a point made by Aziz al-Azmeh about perceptions of Islam, which, however, applies also to Orthodoxy (in fact, in many of the papers presented at the conference from which this paper originates, one could easily substitute "Islam" for "Orthodoxy" at certain points in discussions of relations with the West): "We can surely assume that among the permanent acquisitions of the social and human sciences is the realization that ideological and other forms of collective representation are unthinkable without internal change and structural bearing. And it is a fact that this acquisition is almost invariably put to use in the study of contemporary ideologies, mass movements and other phenomena of European histories and realities. But it is not generally put to use regarding *phenomena islamica*, which are regarded as generically closed, utterly exotic, repellently mysterious, utterly exceptionalist." See Aziz Al-Azmeh, *Islams and Modernities* (London: Verso, 1993), 1.

Shaking the Comfortable Conceits of Otherness: Political Science and the Study of "Orthodox Constructions of the West" / Elizabeth H. Prodromou

The epigraph to this article comes from Valerie Hotchkiss and Patrick Henry, "An Introduction to the Essays," in *Orthodoxy & Western Culture: A Collection of Essays Honoring Jaroslav Pelikan on His Eightieth Birthday*, ed. Valerie Hotchkiss and Patrick Henry (Crestwood, N.Y.: St. Vladimir's Seminary Press, 2005), 27.

1. Maria Todorova, *Imagining the Balkans*, updated ed. (New York: Oxford University Press, 2009), 19.

2. Jose Casanova, "Cosmopolitanism, the Clash of Civilizations, and Multiple Modernities," *Current Sociology* 59, no. 2 (2011): 257.

3. I use the term "modern," as is the commonplace in political science, to mean the historical period that inaugurated the sovereign-state system originating in the Peace of Westphalia. For a standard reference, with expansive bibliography on modernity's origins with the Peace of Augsburg in 1555 and, more specifically, with the Treaties of Westphalia in 1648, see Daniel Philpott, *Revolutions in Sovereignty: How Ideas Shaped Modern International Relations* (Princeton, N.J.: Princeton University Press, 2001).

4. For an effort to mine and apply Orthodox concepts to current debates on war in international relations, see Alexandros K. Kyrou and Elizabeth H. Prodromou, "Debates on Just War, Holy War, and Peace: Orthodox Christian Thought and Byzantine Imperial Attitudes towards War," in *Orthodox Perspectives on War*, ed. Perry Hamalis and Valerie Karras (South Bend, Ind.: University of Notre Dame Press, forthcoming 2013).

5. Aristotle Papanikolaou and George Demacopoulos, "Conference Aims" (prospectus of Orthodox Constructions of the West, Second International Conference of the Orthodoxy in America Lecture Series, Bronx, N.Y., June 2010), www.fordham.edu/mvst/conference10/orthodox/index.html.

6. Papanikolaou and Demacopoulos, "Conference Aims." The causes and consequences of the demonstrated ambivalence by some Orthodox Churches towards the ideas and institutional voices perceived as the dominant arbiters of liberal democratic politics has been a general theme in my scholarship, and my intellectual (not to mention professional and personal) unease with the discursive and behavioral critiques of liberal democracy that are voiced by Orthodox scholars (whether speaking independently or as, and along with, official representatives of Orthodox Churches) has rested on my arguments that categorical condemnations of liberalism and of liberal democracy derive from an essentialized, ossified, and therefore, ultimately, erroneous interpretation of Orthodox theology. Indeed, there is a growing body of scholarship—cutting across academic disciplines, Orthodox ecclesiastical jurisdictions, and languages—that positions Orthodox theology as supportive of and compatible with the universal human rights that inform liberal democracy. For examples, see Elizabeth H. Prodromou, "Beyond the Dickensian Paradoxes of Human Rights: Reconceptualizing Proselytism, Rediscovering Evangelism," in *Violence and Christian Spirituality: An Ecumenical Conversation*, ed. Emmanuel Clapsis (Brookline, Mass.: World Council of Churches Press and Holy Cross Orthodox Press, 2007), 222–35; Elizabeth H. Prodromou, "Christianity and Democracy: The Ambivalent Orthodox" in *World Religions and Democracy*, ed. Larry Diamond, Mark F. Plattner, and Philip J. Costopoulos (Baltimore, Md.: Johns Hopkins University Press, 2005), 132–45. A fuller sampling includes the following, all of which have helpful bibliographies: James H. Billington, "Orthodoxy and Democracy," *Journal of Church and State* 49, no. 1 (January 2007); Konstantinos Delikonstanstanis, *Ta Dikaiōmata tou anthrōpou: Dytiko Ideologēma ē oikoumeniko ēthos?* (Human Rights: Western Ideology or Universal Norm?) (Thessaloniki, Greece: Kyriakidis, 1995); Pantelis Kalaitzidis, *Orthodoxia kai Neōterikotēta: Prolegomena* (Orthodoxy and Modernity: Prolegomena) (Athens, Greece: Indiktos, 2007); Daniela Kalkandjieva, "Pre-Modern Orthodoxy: Church Features and Transformations," *Etudes Balkaniques* 46, no. 4 (2010), 166–95; Stephen White and Ian McAllister, "Orthodoxy and Political Behavior Behavior in Postcommunist Russia," *Review of Religious Research* 41 (2000): 359–72; Elizabeth H. Prodromou, "Orthodox Christianity and Pluralism: Moving beyond Ambivalence?," in *The Orthodox Churches in a Pluralist World: An Ecumenical Conversation*, ed. Emmanuel Clapsis (Brookline, Mass.: World Council of Churches, 2004), 22–46; and Stavros Zoumboulakis, "Sēmeiōseis gia tē christianikē strofē tou Giorgou Theotoka" (Notes on the Christian Turn of Giorgos Theotokas), in *Christianoi*

ston Dēmosio Chōro: Pistē ē Politistikē Tautotēta? (Christians in the public sphere: Faith or cultural identity?) (Athens, Greece: I.D. Kollarou, 2010).

7. I am indebted to Jane Ellis's insightful and thorough work for my notion of defensive triumphalism. I draw from her examination of the tension between defensiveness and triumphalism that has characterized the Orthodox Church of Russia since the dissolution of the Soviet Union. See Jane Ellis, *The Russian Orthodox Church: Triumphalism and Defensiveness* (New York: Palgrave Macmillan, 1996).

8. There is a vast literature on the origins of the state at the Peace of Westphalia in 1648. Useful works that are standards in the field of political science and that are especially helpful for the arguments in this chapter include Hedley Bull, *The Anarchical Society* (New York: Columbia University Press, 2002); Robert Jackson, *Sovereignty: The Evolution of an Idea* (New York: Polity Press, 2002); and Stephen D. Krasner, *Sovereignty: Organized Hypocrisy* (Princeton, N.J.: Princeton University Press, 1999).

9. For a superb synopsis of Pelikan's body of work as an expression of the integration of Orthodoxy and West, see John H. Erikson, "Jaroslav Pelikan: The Living Legend in Our Midst," in *Orthodoxy & Western Culture: A Collection of Essays Honoring Jaroslav Pelikan on His Eightieth Birthday*, ed. Valerie Hotchkiss and Patrick Henry (Crestwood, N.Y.: St. Vladimir's Seminary Press, 2005) and Hotchkiss and Henry, "An Introduction," *Orthodoxy & Western Culture*.

10. Jaroslav Pelikan, "A Personal Memoir: Fragments of a Scholar's Autobiography," in Hotchkiss and Henry, *Orthodoxy & Western Culture*, 42.

11. The late twentieth and early twenty-first centuries have witnessed a spate of political science works that debate the sustainability of the Westphalian state, but notwithstanding empirical evidence and theoretical arguments regarding the *denouement* of the state established through the Westphalian process, the international order remains largely state-organized. For interesting treatments regarding the state and sovereignty, see Richard Falk, *The Declining World Order: America's Imperial Geopolitics* (New York: Routledge, 2004); Hent Kalmo and Quentin Skinner, eds., *Sovereignty in Fragments: The Past, Present, and Future of a Contested Concept* (Cambridge: Cambridge University Press, 2011); and Steven Krasner, *Power, the State, and Sovereignty: Essays on International Relations* (New York: Routledge, 2009).

12. Vasilios N. Makrides and Dirk Uffelmann, "Studying Eastern Orthodox Anti-Westernism: The Need for a Comparative Research Agenda," in *Orthodox Christianity and Contemporary Europe*, ed. Jonathan Sutton and Wil van den Bercken (Leuven, Netherlands: Peeters Publishers, 2003).

13. This is the title of Philip Sherrard's widely read work, which has been reproduced and reiterated in various incarnations by other scholars. See Philip Sherrard, *The Greek East and the Latin West: A Study in the Christian Tradition* (Oxford: Oxford University Press, 1959). A more recent work that utilizes nearly

the same title is Andrew Louth, *Greek East and Latin West: The Church AD 681–1071*. vol. 3, *The Church in History* (Crestwood, N.Y.: St. Vladimir's Seminary Press, 2007).

14. A recent popular, but accessible and historically sound, treatment on this point is Lars Brownsworth, *Lost to the West: The Forgotten Byzantine Empire That Rescued Western Civilization* (New York: Random House, 2009).

15. Still considered a seminal work on the Great Schism is Steven Runciman, *The Eastern Schism: A Study of the Papacy and the Eastern Churches during the XIth and XIIth Centuries*, updated re-issue (Eugene, Oreg: Wipf & Stock, 2005).

16. The quintessential expression of the Eastern Orthodox Church vis-à-vis the hostility of the Roman Catholic Church is the 1204 sacking of Constantinople by Western Christian Crusaders. Steven Runciman, *A History of the Crusades*, 3 vols. (Cambridge: Cambridge University Press, 1987).

17. By theological, I mean thinkers whose work in theology included the, by-now, standard disciplines of systematic theology (dogmatics), patristics and canon law, and church history.

18. Milica Bakic-Hayden helpfully points out, it is not "difference as such" that alone matters; rather, the criterion "by which we select one difference as more 'profound' or decisive for the relationship [between Orthodoxy and the West] than another." See Milica Bakic-Hayden, "What's So Byzantine about the Balkans?," in *Balkan as Metaphor: Between Globalization and Fragmentation*, ed. Dusan I. Bjelic and Obrad Savic (Cambridge, Mass.: MIT Press, 2002), 65.

19. By paradigmatic, I mean those scholarly works that have become so widely referenced and cited, whether in support or rejection, as to be regarded as seminal representations of Orthodox constructions of the West. For excellent introductions to the foundational texts, primarily in the disciplines of theology (whether in the sub-disciplines of dogmatics or church history) and philosophy, see Pantelis Kalaitzidis, Th. N. Papathanasiou, and Th. Abatzidis, eds., *Anataraches sti Metapolemiki Theologia: H "Theologia tou '60"* (Turmoil in postwar theology: The "theology of the '60s") (Athens, Greece: Indiktos, 2009); and Paul Valliere, *Modern Russian Theology: Bukharev, Soloviev, Bulgakov: Orthodox Theology in a New Key* (Grand Rapids, Mich.: William B. Eerdmans, 2000).

19. Christos Yannaras, *Orthodoxia kai Dysi sti Neoteri Ellada* (Orthodoxy and the West in Modern Greece) (Athens, Greece: Domos Press, 1992).

20. For example, see Christos Yannaras, *Person and Eros*, trans. Norman Russell (Brookline, Mass.: Holy Cross Orthodox Press 2007); Christos Yannaras, *The Freedom of Morality* (Crestwood, N.Y.: St. Vladimir's Press, 2004); Christos Yannaras, *I Apanthropia tou Dikaiomatos* (The Inhuman Character of Human Rights) (Domos Press, Athens 1998); Christos Yannaras, "Human Rights and the Orthodox Church," October 4, 2002, http://jbburnett.com/resources/yannaras/yannaras_rights&orth.pdf.

21. Christos Yannaras, "A Note on Political Theology," *St. Vladimir's Theological Quarterly* 27:1 (1983): 53.

22. See his seminal work, Vladimir Lossky, *The Mystical Theology of the Eastern Church*, trans. Fellowship of St. Alban and St. Sergius (Cambridge: James Clarke, 1957). For more on Lossky's thought, see Aristotle Papanikolaou, *Being with God: Trinity, Apophaticism and Divine-Human Communion* (South Bend, Ind.: University of Notre Dame Press, 2006).

23. See note XIV.

24. Also, see note XIV.

26. Christodoulos was the primate, or leading hierarch, of the Orthodox Church in Greece (i.e., the Autocephalous Church of Greece), and held the seat of Archbishop of Athens and All Greece. There has been a notable expansion in the social science literature on Orthodoxy in Greece since the end of the Cold War, especially generated by virtue of interest in the nexus between religion and geopolitics in southeastern Europe. Useful sources that include bibliographic references and citations helpful for exploring the triumphalist and defensive aspects of Orthodox constructions of the West include Paschalis Kitromilides and Thanos Veremis, eds., *The Orthodox Church in a Changing World* (Athens, Greece: Hellenic Foundation for European and Foreign Policy, and Center for Asia Minor Studies, 1998); Victor Roudometoff and Vasilios N. Makrides, eds., *Orthodox Christianity in 21st Century Greece: The Role of Religion in Culture, Ethnicity and Politics* (Aldershot, U.K.: Ashgate, 2010). For an excellent treatment of the same issues, from the discipline of theology, see Pantelis Kalaitzidis, ed., *Critical Approaches to the Theology of the '60s* (Athens: Indiktos Publications, 2008).

27. Quoted in Victor Roudometof, "The Evolution of Greek Orthodoxy in the Context of World Historical Globalization," in Roudometof and Makrides, *Orthodox Christianity in 21st Century Greece*, 32.

28. All three quotes are cited in Lavinia Stan and Lucian Turcescu, *Religion and Politics in Post-Communist Romania* (Oxford: Oxford University Press, 2007), 124–25.

29. Quoted in Daniel P. Payne, "Spiritual Security, the Russian Orthodox Church, and the Russian Foreign Ministry: Collaboration or Cooptation?," *Journal of Church and State* 52, no. 4 (2010): 3.

30. Dimitri Obolensky, *The Byzantine Commonwealth: Eastern Europe, 500–1453* (New Haven, Conn.: Phoenix Press, 2000).

31. This has been a particular critique by Russian Orthodox intellectuals and ecclesiastical officials in the face of the tendency by social scientists to simplistically present the Russian Orthodox Church during the Soviet period as a willing collaborator of the Soviet state and, therefore, to ignore differentiation within the Church vis-à-vis Soviet policies and, especially, to overlook the comprehen-

sive human rights abuses of the Soviet state against Russian Orthodox Christians. In short, the Western construction of Orthodoxy as essentially and willingly authoritarian in its political orientation and collaborationist and/or apologist in its behavior vis-à-vis communist states informs the defensive features of Orthodox constructions of the West. This same perspective flows from the conventional—if, by now, critically deconstructed and analyzed—construct of Caesaropapism long mis-applied to studies of the Orthodox Church. A standard reference, with useful bibliography that speaks to the origins of the defensive features of Orthodox constructions of the West, is Jane Ellis, *The Russian Orthodox Church: A Contemporary History* (Bloomington: Indiana University Press, 1986).

32. Representative of this perspective were the debates associated with controversy over the removal of religious designation from national identity cards in Greece. For an analysis of the theoretical and methodological approaches to religion, identity, and politics in Greece, with a very helpful bibliography on anti-Westernist reactions to the identity card controversy, see Tassos Anastassiadis, "Challenging the Modernization-Secularization Dogma: The Identity Cards Crisis in the '90s and the Church's 'Conservative Renovation,'" (Paper presented at the first LSE PhD Symposium on Modern Greece, London, U.K., June 2003), http://www2.lse.ac.uk/europeanInstitute/research/hellenicObservatory/pdf/1stSymposium/Anastassiadis.pdf. For an expansion, with associated references, on the same subject, see Anastassiadis, "An Intriguing True-False Paradox," in Roudometof and Makrides, *Orthodox Christianity in 21st Century Greece*. See also the essay in this volume by Effi Fokas, "Religion in the Greek Public Sphere: Debating Europe's Influence."

33. Krasner, *Sovereignty*.

34. J. G. A. Pocock, "Some Europes in Their History," in *The Idea of Europe: From Antiquity to the European Union*, ed. Anthony Pagden (New York: Cambridge University Press, 2002), 60.

35. This is Pocock's term. See ibid.

36. Edward Gibbon, *The History of the Decline and Fall of the Roman Empire*, 6 vols. (1776–1788; reprint, New York: Everyman's Library, 2010).

37. David Laitin, *Hegemony and Culture* (Chicago: University of Chicago Press, 1986), 19, quoted in Milica Bakic-Hayden and Robert M. Hayden, "Orientalist Variations on the Theme 'Balkans': Symbolic Geography in Recent Yugoslav Cultural Politics," *Slavic Review* 51, no. 1 (Spring 1992): 3.

38. Francis Fukuyama, "The End of History," *The National Interest* 16 (Summer: May-June 1989); and Samuel P. Huntington, "The Clash of Civilizations," *Foreign Affairs* 72, no. 3 (Summer 1993). Both authors expanded on their respective arguments in subsequent monographs with near-identical titles to their much-ballyhooed articles. See Francis Fukuyama, *The End of History and the Last*

Man (New York: Free Press, 1992; 2006), and Samuel P. Huntington, *The Clash of Civilizations and the Remaking of World Order* (New York: Simon & Schuster, 1996). It bears emphasis that, when he published his arguments about the end of history, Fukuyama held the position of deputy director of the State Department's Policy Planning Staff in the administration of President George H. W. Bush.

39. This is Huntington's formulation, first presented in "Clash," 25.

40. All quotes in this paragraph are drawn from Fukuyama, *The End of History*, 3, 4, 5, 7.

41. The peaceful dissolution of the Soviet Union was still two years away at the time of Fukuyama's prognostications about glasnost and perestroika (Ibid., 10).

42. All quotes are from Huntington, "Clash," 24.

43. Huntington, for example, utilized a map drawn from William Wallace's work, *The Transformation of Western Europe* (New York: Council on Foreign Relations, 1992), to build his arguments about the cultural-religious geography and strategic imperatives of EU enlargement. Accordingly, Huntington proposed that "the most significant dividing line in Europe, as William Wallace has suggested, may well be the eastern boundary of Western Christianity in the year 1500 . . . [where the] . . . peoples to the east and south of this line are Orthodox or Muslim . . . [and] . . . historically belonged to the Ottoman or Tsarist Empires and *were only lightly touched by the shaping events in the rest of Europe*" (italics mine). Huntington, "Clash," 30.

44. Huntington, "Clash," 30.

45. For a relevant discussion, with extensive citations and bibliography, see Elizabeth H. Prodromou, "Paradigms, Power, and Identity: Rediscovering Orthodoxy and Regionalizing Europe," *European Journal of Political Research* 39 (September 1996). The discursive trope was cast thusly in the lead-up to the collapse of Yugoslavia: There was the desire to exit on the part of the "Roman Catholic republics . . . the country's most advanced and politically enlightened region . . . [in the face of] bullying Orthodox Christian republics" and incompatibility of "the authoritarian traditions of the dominant Orthodox Church [which] have helped fashion intense nationalism but have not fostered participatory democracy." These quotations, drawn from *The New York Times* (1989) and *The Washington Post* (February 9, 1990), are cited in Prodromou, "Paradigms," 130.

46. Todorova, *Imagining the Balkans*.

47. Edward Said, *Orientalism* (New York: Vintage Books, 1978).

48. The quotations are from Robert Kaplan, *Balkan Ghosts: A Journey through History* (New York: St. Martin's Press, 1993), *The New York Times* (April 6, 1990), and Zbigniew Brzezinski, "A Plan for Europe," *Foreign Affairs* 74, no. 1 (1995); all citations are drawn from Prodromou, "Paradigms," 29–30.

49. A representative account of the deployment of the West-Orthodoxy binary in discussions about EU enlargement is found in George Schopflin, "Central Europe: Definitions Old and New," in *In Search of Central Europe,* ed. George Schopflin and Nancy Wood (New York: Polity Press, 1989) and George Schopflin, "Postcommunism: The Problems of Democratic Construction," *Daedalus* 123, no. 3 (1994). For a broader elaboration of this point, see Prodromou, "Paradigms."

50. Nikiforos Diamandouros, *Cultural Dualism and Political Modernization in Post-Authoritarian Greece* (Madrid: Instituto Juan March, 1994).

51. See Thanos Lipovats, *H Psychopathologia tou Politikou* (The Psychopathology of the Political) [in Greek]. Lipovats makes a related argument in "Orthodoxos Christianismos kai Ethnikismos: Duo Ptyches tis Synchronis Ellinikis Politikis Koultouras" (Orthodoxy and Nationalism: Two aspects of Contemporary Greek Culture), in *Elliniki Epitheorisi Politikis Epistimis* (Greek Review of Political Science) 2 (October 1993).

52. Both quotations are drawn from Adamantia Pollis, "Eastern Orthodoxy and Human Rights," *Human Rights Quarterly* 15 (1993), 339–40.

53. Ibid, 340.

54. Anastassiadis, "An Intriguing True-False Paradox," 40.

55. Papanikolaou and Demacopoulos, "Conference Aim."

56. John A. McGuckin, "The Issue of Human Rights in Byzantium and the Orthodox Christian Tradition," in *Christianity and Human Rights: An Introduction,* ed. John Witte Jr. and Frank S. Alexander (New York: Cambridge University Press, 2010), 188.

57. Henk van Houtum, "The Geopolitics of Borders and Boundaries," *Geopolitics* 10 (2005): 674.

58. Anastasios Yannoulatos, "Globalization and Religious Experience," in Yannoulatos, *Facing the World: Orthodox Christian Essays on Global Concerns* (Crestwood, N.Y.: St. Vladimir's Seminary Press, 2003), 184.

59. I use the term as deployed by Alfred Stepan in "Religion, Democracy, and the 'Twin Tolerations,'" *Journal of Democracy* 11, no. 4 (October 2000), 45.

60. The literatures that have developed over the past two decades to study the unanticipated salience of religion and modernity (where the latter is conceived largely in terms of the Westphalian marker) are remarkably interdisciplinary and have been led by inquiries in political science and sociology. For an exceptionally expansive source of citations on the constructs of multiple modernities, plural secularisms, and more generally, the evolving salience of religion in the public sphere, see the website of the Social Science Research Council (SSR), entitled "The Immanent Frame," http://blogs.ssrc.org/tif/.

61. The concept of multiple modernities had its formative elaboration by Shmuel N. Eisenstadt, "Multiple Modernities," *Daedalus* 129, no. 1 (Winter

2000): 1–29. For a lively discussion and cross-disciplinary elaboration on the concept, see Shmuel N. Esisenstadt, ed., *Multiple Modernities* (Piscataway, N.J.: Transaction Publishers, 2002).

62. For an incomparably rich source of citations on the constructs of multiple modernities, plural secularisms, and more generally, the evolving salience of religion in the public sphere, see the website of the Social Science Research Council (SSR), entitled "The Immanent Frame," http://blogs.ssrc.org/tif/.

63. See, for example, Timothy A. Byrnes and Peter J. Katzenstein, eds., *Religion in an Expanding Europe* (Cambridge, U.K.: Cambridge University Press, 2000).

64. Stepan, "Religion, Democracy, and the 'Twin Tolerations,'" 52.

65. Deno Geanakoplos, "Church and State in the Byzantine Empire: A Reconsideration of The Problem of Caesaropapism," *Church History: Studies in Christianity and Culture* 34, no. 4 (December 1965): 381–403.

66. Paschalis M. Kitromilides, *An Orthodox Commonwealth* (Aldershot, U.K.: Ashgate, 2007).

67. Lucian N. Leustean, "Eastern Christianity and the Cold War: An Overview," in *Eastern Christianity and the Cold War, 1945–1991*, ed. Lucian N. Leustean (New York: Routledge, 2010).

68. An accessible introduction to the ways in which culture and, specifically, ideas about the equivalence of the West and modernity have shaped security studies and security policy is Pinar Bilgin's "The 'Western-Centrism' of Security Studies: 'Blind Spot' or Constitutive Practice," *Security Dialogue* 41, no. 6 (December 2010): 615–22. Bilgin observes that "Western-centrism is no mere 'blind-spot' but has been constitutive of security studies. The end result is security knowledge that is not only parochial but also peripheral," 620.

Eastern Orthodox Constructions of "the West" in the Post-Communist Political Discourse: The Cases of the Romanian and Russian Orthodox Churches / Lucian Turcescu

1. In 2004, I conducted personal interviews with Metropolitan Nicolae Corneanu of Banat, Metropolitan Daniel Ciobotea of Iasi, and Archbishop Andrei Andreicut of Alba Iulia.

2. Grace Davie, "Is Europe an Exceptional Case?," *International Review of Mission* 95, nos. 378/379 (July/October 2006): 251.

3. Ibid.

4. For an extensive presentation and discussion of this issue, including examples, see Lavinia Stan and Lucian Turcescu, *Religion and Politics in Post-Communist Romania* (New York: Oxford University Press, 2007), 171–97.

5. Personal interview with Daniel Ciobotea, metropolitan of Moldova and archbishop of Iasi, conducted by Lucian Turcescu on June 11, 2004, Iasi, Romania.

6. Established after 1990 in Romania, the social work section of the Faculty of Orthodox Theology is meant to train social workers who will assist the bishops and priests in their missionary and social work, but also work in orphanages and homes for the elderly that are in the care of the RP.

7. "Protocol de Cooperare in Domeniul Incluziunii Sociale intre Guvernul Romaniei si Patriarhia Romaniei," October 2, 2007, available at: http://www .patriarhia.ro/ro/opera_social_filantropica/biroul_pentru_asistenta_social_ filantropica_2.html, accessed May 4, 2010.

8. "Protocol de Cooperare privind Parteneriatul Asistenta Medicala si Spirituala," (July 25, 2008): 1, available at http://www.basilica.ro/_upload/doc/ 1216886201076490400.pdf, retrieved May 4, 2010.

9. "Cuvant al Prea Fericitului Patriarh Daniel," October 12, 2007, author's copy.

10. "Protocol de parteneriat intre Patriarhia Romana, Arhiepiscopia Bucurestiului si Consiliul Local al Sectorului 1 Capitala," November 13, 2008, available at: http://www.basilica.ro/ro/stiri/protocol_de_parteneriat_intre_patriarhia_romana_arhiepiscopia_bucurestilor_si_consiliul_local_al_sectorului_1_capitala. html, accessed May 4, 2010.

11. "Protocol de cooperare intre Episcopia Giurgiului si Centrul de Prevenire, Evaluare si Consiliere Antidrog Giurgiu," March 31, 2008, available at: http:// www.basilica.ro/ro/stiri/protocol_de_cooperare_intre_episcopia_giurgiului_si_ centrul_de_prevenire_evaluare_si_consiliere_antidrog_giurgiu_.html, "Protocol de colaborare in domeniul asistentei sociale la Giurgiu," Radio Trinitas, August 5, 2009, available at: http://www.basilica.ro/ro/stiri/protocol_de_colaborare_in_domeniul_asistentei_sociale_la_giurgiu.html, and "Parteneriat in organizarea de activitati social-culturale si religioase la Giurgiu," available at: http://www.basilica.ro/ro/stiri/parteneriat_in_organizarea_de_activitati_social _culturale_si_religioase_la_giurgiu.html, accessed May 4, 2010.

12. Stan and Turcescu, *Religion and Politics in Post-Communist Romania*, 25.

13. Tom Gallagher, *Romania and the European Union: How the Weak Vanquished the Strong* (Manchester, U.K.: Manchester University Press, 2009), passim.

14. Bartolomeu Anania, "Ce ne ofera Europa?," *Evenimentul Zilei* (April 16, 1998). Available at: http://orthodoxmedia.com/opinie, accessed April 10, 2007.

15. Ibid.

16. Nicolas Werth, "A State against Its People: Violence, Repression, and Terror in the Soviet Union" in *The Black Book of Communism: Crime, Terror, Repression*, ed. Stephane Courtois, Nicolas Werth, Jean-Louis Panne, trans. J. Murphy

and M. Kramer (Cambridge, Mass.: Harvard University Press, 1999), 124–26. See also Timothy Snyder, *Bloodlands: Europe between Hitler and Stalin* (New York: Basic Books, 2010), 29.

17. Walter Sawatsky, "Protestantism in the USSR," in *Protestantism in Eastern Europe and Russia: The Communist and Post-Communist Eras,* ed. Sabrina P. Ramet (Durham, N.C.: Duke University Press, 1992), 237–60.

18. Olga Kazmina, "The Russian Orthodox Church, State and Society in Post-Communist Russia," unpublished paper delivered at the 2009 annual conference of the American Academy of Religion, Montreal, November 1–3, 2009. In what follows, I am drawing on Kazmina's paper, which she kindly shared with me after the conference.

19. Daniel P. Payne and Jennifer M. Kent, "An Alliance of the Sacred: Prospects for a Catholic-Orthodox Partnership against Secularism in Europe," *Journal of Ecumenical Studies* 46 (2011): 41–66.

20. CoMission Press Conference (1992), 11. Quoted in Perry Lynn Glanzer, *The Quest for the Russian Soul: Evangelicals and Moral Education in Post-Communist Russia* (Waco, Tex.: Baylor University Press, 2002), 1.

21. Besides the Slavs (Russians, Ukrainians, and Belarusians), who account for about eighty-five percent of Russia's population, three main ethnic groups and a handful of isolated smaller groups reside within the federation. The Altaic group includes mainly speakers of Turkic languages widely distributed in the middle Volga, the southern Ural Mountains, the North Caucasus, and above the Arctic Circle. The main Altaic peoples in Russia are the Balkars, Bashkirs, Buryats, Chuvash, Dolgans, Evenks, Kalmyks, Karachay, Kumyks, Nogay, and Yakuts. The Uralic group, consisting of Finnic peoples living in the upper Volga, the far northwest, and the Urals, includes the Karelians, Komi, Mari, Mordovians, and Udmurts. The Caucasus group is concentrated along the northern slopes of the Caucasus Mountains; its main subgroups are the Adyghs, Chechens, Cherkess, Ingush, and Kabardins, as well as about thirty Caucasus peoples collectively classified as Dagestani. Sources: "Russia," ch. 4: "Ethnic, Religious, and Cultural Setting" in *The Library of Congress Country Studies: Russia* available at http://memory.loc.gov/frd/cs/rutoc.html (accessed on May 22, 2011).

22. In 1945, reconciliation took place between Constantinople and Sophia with the full recognition of Bulgarian autocephaly within the limits of the Bulgarian state.

23. An English translation of the Russian Law on Freedom of Conscience and Religious Associations can be found here: http://www2.stetson.edu/~psteeves/relnews/freedomofconscienceeng.html, accessed May 22, 2011.

24. Nikolai Mitrokhin, *Russkaia Pravoslavnaia Tserkov': Sovremennoe Sostoianie i Aktual'nye Problemy* (Moscow: Novoe Literaturnoe Obozrenie, 2004),

265. Quoted in Irina Papkova, *The Orthodox Church and Russian Politics* (New York: Oxford University Press, 2011), 16.

25. Papkova, *Orthodox Church and Russian Politics*, 16–17.

26. Osnovnye Printsipy Otnosheniia k Inoslaviiu Russkoi Pravoslavnoi Tserkvi, Section 7.2, http://www.mospat.ru/ru/documents/attitude-to-the-non-orthodox. Quoted in Papkova, *Orthodox Church and Russian Politics*, 33–34.

27. Ibid.

28. Marat S. Shterin and James T. Richardson, "Effects of the Western Anti-Cult Movement on Development of Laws Concerning Religion in Post-Communist Russia," *Journal of Church and State* 42 (2000): 247–71.

29. Papkova, *Orthodox Church and Russian Politics*, 81.

30. Ibid., 47–53.

31. Ibid., 53–60.

32. Ibid., 58.

33. Ibid., 61–67.

34. Ibid., 64.

35. Ibid., 66–67.

36. Payne and Kent, "An Alliance of the Sacred."

37. Quoted in Thomas S. Kuhn, *The Structure of Scientific Revolutions*, 2nd ed. (Chicago: University of Chicago Press, 1970), 151.

Primacy and Ecclesiology: The State of the Question / John Panteleimon Manoussakis

1. A case in point would be the Photian invention of monopatrism as a reaction to the *filioque*. The question here is *not* the monarchy of the Father but Photius's addition in his *Mystagogy* of the formula *ek monou tou patros* regarding the procession of the Holy Spirit, an addition that was certainly much more of an arbitrary (and polemical) innovation than the *filioque* some centuries earlier. By this addition, Photius sought to create a new dogmatic position for Eastern pneumatology—namely, that the Holy Spirit proceeds *only* from the Father or from the Father *alone*, the not-so-silent implication being that the Second Person of the Holy Trinity is not involved in any way (either *from* Him or *through* Him) in the procession of the Holy Spirit. For an Orthodox criticism of Photius's monopatrism, see Sergius Bulgakov, *The Comforter*, translated by Boris Jakim (Grand Rapids, Mich.: William B. Eerdmans, 2004), in particular 97–100 and 137–8.

2. I have in mind Pavel Florensky's excellent analysis of the antinomian character of the Christian truth, understood as the integration of antitheses that are to be found within any dogmatic assertion. See *The Pillar and Ground of the Truth*, translated and annotated by Boris Jakim (Princeton, N.J.: Princeton University Press, 1997).

3. For a philosophical discussion of the demonization of otherness as a process of forming and affirming one's identity, see Richard Kearney's *Strangers, Gods and Monsters: Interpreting Otherness* (London: Routledge, 2002). Of course, the dialectic of other versus same goes as far back as the Eleatic Stranger in Plato's *Sophist*.

4. For a theoretical analysis of such historical paradigms, see Kearney, *Strangers, Gods and Monsters*.

5. Bear in mind that this text was delivered in June 2010.

6. "Πορίσματα" as published on the official site of the Metropolis of Piraeus, http://www.imp.gr/Nea.htm.

7. "ούδε ως Επίσκοπος δύναται του λοιπού να λογίζεται," Letter of the metropolitan of Cythera to the archbishop of Athens (June 1, 2010, Protocol Number 493, published at the ecclesiastical news agency amen.gr).

8. Press release of the Holy Synod (March 5, 2012) in http://www.ecclesia.gr/greek/holysynod/holysynod.asp?id=1488&what_sub=d_typou.

9. See Panayiotis Trempelas, "Ἀνωτάτη δ' ἀρχὴ τῆς καθόλου Ἐκκλησίας εἶναι ἡ Οἰκουμενικὴ Σύνοδος," in Δογματικὴ τῆς Ὀρθοδόξου Καθολικῆ Ἐκκλησίας, vol. 2, (Athens: O Sotir, 1979), 402. The *Dogmatics* of Christos Androutsos (1907) also agree: "ἀλλ' ἂν ὁ ἐπίσκοπος εἶνε ὁ ἀνώτατος φορεὺς τῆς ἐκκλησιαστικῆς ἐξουσίας, εἶνε φανερὸν ὅτι ἀνωτάτη ἀρχὴ τῶν μὲν ἐπὶ μέρους Ἐκκλησιῶν εἶνε ἡ σύνοδος τῶν ἐπισκόπων, πασῶν δὲ τῶν Ὀρθοδόξων Ἐκκλησιῶν τὸ σύνολο τῶν ἐπισκόπων" (Athens, Typografeion tou Kratous), 287.

10. This is the ecclesiological structure reflected in such apostolic writings as St. Ignatius of Antioch's *Letters*, in the ancient canons of the Church, like the aforementioned thirty-fourth Canon of the Holy Apostles, but also, and more importantly, in ancient liturgical practices, most of them still preserved in Orthodox praxis. A now-classic discussion of the role of the bishop for the local church is the doctoral dissertation of John D. Zizioulas *Eucharist, Bishop, Church: The Unity of the Church in the Divine Eucharist and the Bishop during the Three First Centuries*, translated in English by Elizabeth Theokritoff (Brookline, Mass.: Holy Cross Orthodox Press, 2001).

11. John Zizioulas, "Recent Discussions on Primacy in Orthodox Theology," in *The Petrine Ministry: Catholics and Orthodox in Dialogue*, ed. Walter Cardinal Kasper (New York: Newman, 2006), 231–248, here 242. See also "Η Ευχαριστιακή Εκκλησιολογία στην Ορθόδοξη Παράδοση," *Θεολογία* 80 (2009): 23.

12. See John Zizioulas "Ο Συνοδικός Θεσμός: Ιστορικά, εκκλησιολογικά και κανονικά προβλήματα," *Θεολογία* 80 (2009): 20–1.

13. For a discussion of the bearing of the Ascension on ecclesiology, see Douglas Farrow, *Ascension and Ecclesia: On the Significance of the Doctrine of the*

Ascension for Ecclesiology and Christian Cosmology (Grand Rapids, Mich.: William B. Eerdmans, 1999).

14. The identification of God's oneness with the person of the Father was, according to John Zizioulas, one of the two fundamental "leavenings" of patristic theology. For the history of this groundbreaking association and its theological implications, see his *Being as Communion* (Crestwood, N.Y.: St. Vladimir's Seminary Press, 1985), 40 and ff. See also Chapter 3, "The Father as Cause: Personhood Generating Otherness" in his *Communion and Otherness* (London: T&T Clark, 2006), 113–54. In this last text, Metropolitan Zizioulas draws some significant consequences of the Father's monarchy for ecclesiology (especially 145–49).

15. For the capital implications of Chalcedonian Christology, see Zizioulas's *Communion and Otherness*, especially ch. 7, 250–85.

16. This is, indeed, supported by a number of patristic texts. We mention here the most representative of them—namely, St. Cyril's of Jerusalem sermons where "the axiom of monarchy" is explicitly identified with "the axiom of the Father's fatherhood": St. Basil's treatise, *Contra eunomium* (especially vol. 1: 20, 24, 25; vol. 2: 12; vol. 3: 6), and Chapter 18 of his *De spiritu sanctu*; and the *Theological Orations* of St. Gregory Nazianzen. For a discussion of the patristic sources on the monarchy of the Father, see Atanasije Jevtić's *Χριστός Ἀρχὴ καὶ Τέλος* (Athens: Goulandri-Horn, 1983), 222–26, as well as Lossky's third chapter from his *Mystical Theology of the Eastern Church* (Crestwood, N.Y.: St. Vladimir's Seminary Press, 1976). For Metropolitan John Zizioulas, primacy is a matter of dogma, therefore any anomaly with regard to it constitutes heresy; see John Zizioulas, "Recent Discussions on Primacy in Orthodox Theology" in Kasper, *Petrine Ministry*, 237. Also, Zizioulas, "Ο Συνοδικός Θεσμός": "ο διαχωρισμός των διοικητικών θεσμών της Εκκλησίας απο το δόγμα δεν είναι απλώς ατυχής, είναι και επικίνδυνος," 5–6.

17. Elpidophoros Lambriniadis, "Challenges of Orthodoxy in America and the Role of the Ecumenical Patriarchate," a speech delivered at the Chapel of the Holy Cross Greek Orthodox School of Theology on March 18, 2009. Posted on the official website of the Church of Greece (http://www.ecclesia.gr/englishnews/default.asp?id=3986), accessed June 25, 2010.

18. John Zizioulas, "Recent Discussions on Primacy in Orthodox Theology" in Kasper, *Petrine Ministry*, 243.

19. See Zizioulas, "Ο Συνοδικός Θεσμός."

20. Theodore the Studite, *Letter 33* (*PG* 99, 1017). The Greek reads as follows: "᾿Επειδήπερ Πέτρῳ τῷ μεγάλῳ δέδωκε Χριστός ὁ Θεὸς μετὰ τὰς κλεῖς τῆς βασιλείας τῶν οὐρανῶν, καὶ τὸ τῆς ποιμνιαρχίας ἀξίωμα, πρὸς Πέτρον, ἤτοι τὸν αὐτοῦ διάδοχον, ὁτιοῦν καινοτομούμενον ἐν τῇ καθολικῇ ᾿Εκκλησία παρὰ

τῶν ἀποσφαλλομένων τῆς ἀληθείας, ἀναγκαῖον ἀναφέρεσθαι. Τοῦτο τοιγαροῦν δεδιδαγμένοι καὶ ἡμεῖς οἱ ταπεινοὶ καὶ ἐλάχιστοι, ἐκ τῶν ἀνέκαθεν ἁγίων Πατέρων ἡμῶν."

21. G. K. Chesterton, "Mr. Bernard Shaw" from *Heretics* in *G. K. Chesterton's Collected Works*, vol. 1 (San Francisco: Ignatius Press, 1986), 70.

(In)Voluntary Ecumenism: Dumitru Staniloae's Interaction with the West as Open Sobornicity / Radu Bordeianu

I am deeply grateful to the Wimmer Family Foundation for offering me a grant to research this theme. A modified version of this chapter has appeared in my book, *Dumitru Staniloae: An Ecumenical Ecclesiology* (New York: Continuum/T&T Clark, 2011).

1. Alexander Schmemann, *Great Lent: Journey to Pascha* (Crestwood, N.Y.: St. Vladimir's Seminary Press, 1974), 131.

2. Georges Florovsky, "Patristic Theology and the Ethos of the Orthodox Church," in *Aspects of Church History, Collected Works*, vol. 4 (Belmont, Mass.: Nordland, 1975), 17–18, 22, 29. Concerning neopatristic synthesis, Florovsky wrote: "It should be more than just a collection of Patristic sayings or statements. It must be a *synthesis*, a creative reassessment of those insights that were granted to the Holy Men of old. It must be *Patristic*, faithful to the spirit and vision of the Fathers, *ad mentem Patrum*. Yet, it must also be *Neo*-Patristic, since it is to be addressed to the new age, with its own problems and queries." Florovsky's "Address at 80 Years of Age" in "A Sketch of the Life of Georges Florovsky," in *Georges Florovsky: Russian Intellectual and Orthodox Churchman*, ed. Andrew Blane (Crestwood, N.Y.: St. Vladimir's Seminary Press, 1993), 154. For an overview of Florovsky's application of neopatristic synthesis to various theological themes, see George H. Williams, "The Neo-Patristic Synthesis of Georges Florovsky," in Blane, *Georges Florovsky: Russian Intellectual and Orthodox Churchman*, 287–329, especially 292.

3. Georges Florovsky, "St. Gregory Palamas and the Tradition of the Fathers," in *Bible, Church, Tradition: An Eastern Orthodox View*, vol. 1 in *Collected Works of Georges Florovsky*, (Belmont, Mass.: Nordland Publishing, 1972), 107–08. In the same article (105–6, 114, 120), Florovsky recommends going beyond "archaic formulas," and a simple "appeal to antiquity," providing Gregory Palamas as an example of the "creative extension of ancient tradition" "in complete conformity with the mind of the Church," as opposed to a "theology of repetition."

4. Florovsky, "The Church: Her Nature and Task," in *Bible, Church, Tradition*, 58. Florovsky, "Patristic Theology," 181–82.

5. Ronald G. Roberson, "Contemporary Romanian Orthodox Ecclesiology: The Contribution of Dumitru Staniloae and Younger Colleagues," (PhD diss., The Pontifical Oriental Institute in Rome, 1988), 163–64.

6. Despite these considerations, Ion Bria remarks that "he has a profound sense of the unity of all Christians and he never adopts an attitude of anti-ecumenism." Ion Bria, "The Creative Vision of Dumitru Staniloae: An Introduction to his Theological Thought," *Ecumenical Review* 33, no. 1 (1981): 57. See also Stefan L. Toma, *Traditie si actualitate la pr. Dumitru Staniloae* (Tradition and actuality in Fr. Dumitru Staniloae) (Sibiu: Agnos, 2008), 237–45.

7. Anna Williams's contrast between Origen and the Enlightenment is illuminating in this sense: "[Origen's] purpose is nonetheless quite different from that of the Enlightenment thinkers who made natural arguments for the existence of God, for he declares that the faith is not something that needs to be proved by human reason, and that his purpose in pursuing particular points is only to follow the inquiry where it logically leads. The line between the two is very fine, of course, and Origen does not trouble to explain where he would draw it. It seems to run between the differing sorts of intention, the desire, which he implicitly repudiates, to look intellectually strong in the eyes of the world, and the rightful wish to inform inquirers about the faith in a way that is readily graspable, this latter purpose being one also of catechesis, and hence not one a Christian teacher could plausibly reject." Anna N. Williams, *The Divine Sense: The Intellect in Patristic Theology* (New York: Cambridge University Press, 2007), 66–67.

8. In Dostoyevsky's fictionalized encounter, Father Paisy tells young novice Alyosha: "Secular learning, having united itself into a great power, has studied all the celestial things that were bequeathed to us in the Holy Books, and after the cruel analysis of scholars of this world there remains of all the earlier holiness absolutely nothing at all. But their study was conducted piecemeal, and they missed the whole; indeed, such blindness is positively worthy of marvel. Whereas the whole stands right before their eyes immovably as ever, and the gates of hell shall not prevail against it." Fyodor M. Dostoyevsky, *The Brothers Karamazov: A Novel in Four Parts and an Epilogue*, trans. David McDuff, 2nd ed. (London: Penguin Books, 2003), 225–26.

9. See Aquinas's unnecessary speculations in *Summa theologiae* IIIa, q. 3, art. 5–7 on "whether each of the divine Persons could have assumed human nature," "whether several divine Persons can assume one and the same individual nature," or even "two human natures," when, in fact, revelation affirms that only the Son took on one human nature, while the Father and the Spirit did not become incarnate.

10. For example, he maintained that "Catholicism is *rationalist* and *immanentist* [i.e., empirical], while Orthodoxy is *mystical* and *transcendentalist*. The rationalism

of Catholicism has its source in Roman positivism." Dumitru Staniloae, *Natiune si Crestinism*, ed. Constantin Schifirnet (Bucharest: Elion, 2003), 19.

11. Roberson, "Contemporary Romanian Orthodox Ecclesiology" 49.

12. Roberson, "Dumitru Staniloae on Christian Unity," 117. Roberson refers here to Dumitru Staniloae, "In problema intercomuniunii" (On the Issue of Intercommunion), *Ortodoxia* 23, no. 4 (1971): 583–84.

13. Roberson, "Dumitru Staniloae on Christian Unity," 113. Roberson refers here to Ioanichie Balan, ed., *Convorbiri Duhovnicesti* (Spiritual conversations), vol. 2 (Roman: Editura Episcopiei Romanului si Husilor, 1988), 92–93.

14. Gheorghe F. Anghelescu and Ioan I. Ica Jr., "Parintele Prof. Acad. Dumitru Staniloae: Bibliografie Sistematica," in *Persoana si Comuniune: Prinos de Cinstire Parintelui Profesor Academician Dumitru Staniloae la implinirea varstei de 90 de ani*, ed. Ioan I. Ica jr. and Mircea Pacurariu (Sibiu: Editura Arhiepiscopiei Ortodoxe Sibiu, 1993). See also *Bibliografia Parintelui Academician Profesor Dr. Dumitru Staniloae* (Bucharest, EIBMBOR, 1993).

15. Dumitru Staniloae, *Teologia Dogmatica Ortodoxa*, 2nd ed., vol. 2 (Bucharest: EIBMBOR, 1997), 176. Translated in English as *The Experience of God: Orthodox Dogmatic Theology*, vol. 2, *The World: Creation and Deification*, trans. Ioan Ionita (Brookline, Mass.: Holy Cross Orthodox Press, 2005).

16. Ibid., 121.

17. Turcescu, introduction to *Dumitru Staniloae: Tradition and Modernity in Theology*, ed. Lucian Turcescu (Iasi, Romania: Center for Romanian Studies, 2002), 7. For a description of Staniloae as a "neo-Orthodox" theologian writing a "neopatristic" synthesis, see also Maciej Bielawski, *Parintele Dumitru Staniloae, o viziune filocalica despre lume*, trans. Ioan I. Ica Jr., Dogmatica (Sibiu: Deisis, 1998), 74–77.

18. Louth, "The Orthodox Dogmatic Theology of Dumitru Staniloae," *Modern Theology* 13, no. 2 (1997): 254, 58.

19. Dumitru Staniloae, *Chipul evanghelic al lui Iisus Hristos* (The evangelical image of Jesus Christ) (Sibiu: Editura Centrului Mitropolitan Sibiu, 1991).

20. Dumitru Staniloae, *Filocalia sau Culegere din scrierile Sfintilor Parinti care arata cum se poate omul curati, lumina si desavirsi*, 4th ed., 12 vols. (Bucharest: Harisma-Humanitas, 1993–).

21. For example, Staniloae considered that the iconodules of the eighth century could have explained better the relationship between Christ and the icon, and how the veneration passes on to the prototype, had they had the benefits of a fully explicit theology and terminology of the uncreated energies. Dumitru Staniloae, *Spiritualitate si comuniune in Liturghia Ortodoxa* (Spirituality and communion in the orthodox liturgy) (Craiova: Editura Mitropoliei Olteniei, 1986), 65. See also Dumitru Staniloae, *The Experience of God: Revelation and Knowledge of the Triune God*, trans. Ioan Ionita and Robert Barringer, 2nd ed., vol. 1 (Brookline, Mass.: Holy Cross Orthodox Press, 1998), 252.

22. Staniloae, *Teologia Dogmatica Ortodoxa* (Orthodox dogmatic theology), 2nd ed., vol. 1 (Bucharest: EIBMBOR, 1996), 7. This passage was not included in the English translation. There is no doubt among scholars who have studied Staniloae's theology that Maximus the Confessor was the Church Father who inspired him the most (Louth, "Staniloae's Dogmatics," 257). Staniloae also relied heavily on Pseudo-Dionysius the Areopagite (see Gheorghe Dragulin, "Pseudo-Dionysios the Areopagite in Dumitru Staniloae's Theology," in Turcescu, *Dumitru Staniloae*), Athanasius of Alexandria, John Chrysostom, Gregory of Nyssa, Gregory of Nazianzen, Basil the Great, John Chrysostom, John of Damascus, and Gregory Palamas, to name a few.

23. Louth writes about Staniloae's thought: "One of the sources of Orthodox theology comes into its own: that is the liturgical ceremonies of the Orthodox Church, not just the texts, but also what takes place, what is expressed through what is done." Louth, "Staniloae's Dogmatics," 264.

24. His daughter, Lidia, writes: "The extreme suffering he underwent was an experience that brought him even closer to God. . . . He passed through that hell with a luminous smile on his lips, and with confidence that God gives us hardships to purify us so that we might obtain the future life, a reality that presupposes effort and a powerful will." Lidia Staniloae, "Remembering My Father," in Turcescu, *Dumitru Staniloae*, 21. For more details on Staniloae's life, see Lidia Staniloae, *Lumina faptei din lumina cuvantului: impreuna cu tatal meu*, Dumitru Staniloae (Bucuresti: Humanitas, 2000).

25. Préface to Dumitru Staniloae, *Prière de Jésus et expérience de Saint Esprit, Théophanie* (Paris: Desclée De Brouwer, 1981), 11.

26. Staniloae and M.A. Costa de Beauregard, *Ose comprendre que je t'aime* (Paris: Editions du Cerf, 1983), 28.

27. Lucian Turcescu, "Eucharistic Ecclesiology or Open Sobornicity?," in Turcescu, *Dumitru Staniloae*. In the same volume, Roberson analyzes "open sobornicity" and its value for promoting Christian unity. Roberson, "Dumitru Staniloae on Christian Unity," 120–22.

28. On the contributions of Ernst Käsemann and Raymond Brown in this sense, as well as another description of the same development within the WCC, including the Fourth World Conference of Faith and Order, Montreal (1963), see Michael Kinnamon, *The Vision of the Ecumenical Movement and How It Has Been Impoverished by Its Friends* (St. Louis: Chalice Press, 2003), 55ff.

29. To give just one example, Staniloae admitted that, at times, Orthodoxy has fallen into the temptation to emphasize either ordained or universal priesthood over the other. This is why, for the Orthodox, unity in diversity, or "sobornicity must be more than a theory; it must be a practice."

30. Dumitru Staniloae, "Sobornicitate deschisa," (Open sobornicity) *Ortodoxia* 23, no. 2 (1971): 171.

31. See the same idea in Dumitru Staniloae, "Coordonatele ecumenismului din punct de vedere Ortodox" (The coordinates of ecumenism from the orthodox perspective), *Ortodoxia* 19, no. 4 (1967): 517–18.

32. Staniloae, "Open Sobornicity," 178.

33. Staniloae, *Theology and the Church*, 221–22.

34. Ibid., 217.

35. These exercises form a true communion, albeit a lesser one than the Eucharistic communion. Staniloae did not explain the historic origin for his terminological choice of "spiritual intercommunion." It is probably related to Origen's use of "spiritual communion" as a designation of the benefits of attending the Divine Liturgy and partaking of God's words, even when not receiving the Eucharist (in Num. 16:9, in Matt. 11:14). See a repudiation of Origen's concept in Nicolas Afanassieff, *The Church of the Holy Spirit*, trans. Vitaly Permiakov (South Bend, Ind: Notre Dame University Press, 2007), 57, 287.

36. Dumitru Staniloae, "Teologia Euharistiei" (The theology of the Eucharist), *Ortodoxia* 21, no. 3 (1969): 361.

37. Louth, "Staniloae's Dogmatics," 259.

38. Staniloae used the Romanian word *arhiereu*, which means "bishop" or literally, "high priest." However, in accordance with common English usage, I translate it as "priest."

39. John Calvin, *Institutes of the Christian Religion*, ed. John T. McNeill, trans. Ford Lewis Battles, vol. 1 (Louisville, Ky.: Westminster John Knox Press, 2006), 494. Chapter 15 in Book 2 of the first volume is entitled, "To Know the Purpose for Which Christ Was Sent by the Father, and What He Conferred upon Us, We Must Look above All at Three Things in Him: The Prophetic Office, Kingship, and Priesthood."

40. Without any exegesis, or mentioning the texts that do not explicitly state that Jesus is King, Prophet, Priest, here are some of the most relevant examples from the Gospels and the Letter to the Hebrews:

Jesus is King: Mt 21:5; Lk 19:38; Jn 12:13, 15. Parables that make reference to Jesus as King: Mt 22:2–14; 25:31–46, etc. Jesus is "King of Israel": Jn 1:49. "King of the Jews": Mt 2:2; 27:11, 29, 37, 42; Mk 15:2, 9, 12, 18, 26, 32; Lk 23:3, 37, 38; Jn 18:33, 37 twice, 39; 19:3, 19, 21 twice.

Jesus is Prophet: Mt 21:11, 46; Lk 4:24, 44; 7:16; 24:19; Jn 4:19; 6:14; 7:40; 9:17.

Jesus is Priest or "high priest": Heb 2:17; 3:1; 4:14, 15; 5:1, 5, 6, 10; 6:20; 7:11, 15, 16, 17, 21 twice, 26; 8:1, 3; 9:11; 10:21. Jesus "holds his priesthood permanently": Heb 7:24.

There are also patristic examples with this sense. Macarius affirmed: "Spiritual men, who are anointed with the heavenly unction, become Christs according to grace, so that they too are kings, priests, and prophets of heavenly mysteries." *Homily* 27:4, *PG* 34:696BC, *Homily* 17:1, *PG* 34:624BC, quoted in Paul Evdokimov, *The Sacrament of Love: The Nuptial Mystery in the Light of the Orthodox Tradition*, trans. Anthony P. Gythiel and Victoria Steadman (Crestwood, N.Y.: St. Vladimir's Seminary Press, 1985), 88. Maximus the Confessor stressed that Joachim (Virgin Mary's father) and Joseph were descendants of David, whose tribe was intermingled with that of Judah, so the kingly and priestly tribes have been intermingled; hence Christ is both Priest and King because he is both God and human (Saint Maximus the Confessor, *Viata Fecioarei Maria* [The life of Virgin Mary], trans. Ioan Ica Jr. [Sibiu: Deisis, 1999], 7). Moreover, in Calvin's above-mentioned chapter, the third footnote makes reference to Thomas Aquinas's *Summa theologiae* IIIa q. 22, art. 1, rp 3, which reads: "Wherefore, as to others, one is a lawgiver [i.e., prophet], another is a priest, another is king; but all these concur in Christ as the fount of all grace."

These examples are not meant to challenge the fact that Calvin was the first to stress Christ's threefold office as clearly and emphatically as he did.

41. According to Staniloae, Christ was Prophet, Priest, and King in all the stages of his mission on earth: "Jesus's three offices . . . always coexist together even though, in each stage [of Jesus's life], one of them is more prominent. When he was teaching as prophet, Jesus was also performing miracles as king, and through teaching, he was exercising a certain kingly power on the souls. He also taught through his Passion. And from his death to his second coming, even though his kingly office is more prominent, shining in his heavenly glory and exercising a greater dominion over the souls, he also continues to teach through the Holy Spirit and to sacrifice himself in the Eucharist or to intervene to the Father as priest forever." Dumitru Staniloae, *Iisus Hristos sau restaurarea omului* (Jesus Christ or the restoration of humankind), 2nd ed. (Craiova: Editura Omniscop, 1993), 347–48. Staniloae did not mean to discard completely Bulgakov's assertion that certain events in Jesus's life correspond to one of the offices, since Staniloae organized the second part of his book, *Iisus Hristos sau restaurarea omului* (Jesus Christ or the restoration of humankind), according to the three offices.

42. Dumitru Staniloae, "Temeiurile teologice ale ierarhiei si ale sinodalitatii" (The theological foundations of hierarchy and synodality), *Studii Teologice* 22, no. 3–4 (1970): 167–68.

43. The Greek term for sacrament is *mystērion* and, beginning with Tertullian, it has been translated into Latin as *sacramentum*; hence the common usage of the word sacrament in the Western world, both Protestant and Catholic. Some English-speaking Orthodox theologians prefer *mysteries*, while others are comfortable with *sacrament*. I translate Staniloae's Romanian term, *taina* with *sacrament*. However, when I occasionally use translations other than mine, I respect their use of *mystery*. Staniloae would most likely be neutral in the debate on

whether to use a term of Greek origin, or one with a Latin root, since the Romanian *taina* comes from the Slavonic *taina*, which means mystery.

44. Louth, "Staniloae's Dogmatics," 259–60.

45. Staniloae, *Dogmatics* 3, 118–35.

46. Staniloae, "Numarul Tainelor, raporturile intre ele si problema Tainelor din afara Bisericii" (The number of the sacraments, their relationships, and the problem of the sacraments outside the Church), *Ortodoxia* 8, no. 2 (1956): 192.

47. Leijssen places this development even earlier: "This process of acknowledgment culminated in the theology of Peter Lombard (1095–1160) and, further, in the official doctrine of the church as established in the councils of Florence (1439) and Trent (1547). Scholastic theology had a clear definition of the sacrament as 'a visible sign of an invisible grace.'" Lambert J. Leijssen, *With the Silent Glimmer of God's Spirit: A Postmodern Look at the Sacraments*, trans. Marie Baird (New York: Paulist Press, 2006), 19. However, the date that is generally accepted for the official establishment of the number seven for the sacraments is 1547, with the first canon of the Council of Trent, as a reaction against Luther who challenged Catholic sacramental theology.

48. Staniloae rightly identifies the role of Pope Alexander III and Peter Lombard in the development of the doctrine and adds the name of the monk Job of Iasi to Paleologos's role in the Eastern adoption. Staniloae, "Number of the Sacraments," 191.

49. Ware, *The Orthodox Church*, new ed. (London: Penguin Books, 1997), 275.

50. See for example, *The Ecclesiastical Hierarchy* II, IV in Pseudo-Dionysius the Areopagite, *Pseudo-Dionysius: The Complete Works*, trans. Colm Luibheid and Paul Rorem, The Classics of Western Spirituality (New York: Paulist Press, 1987), 208, 32. Staniloae was no stranger to Dionysius, whose works he translated and commented upon extensively, adopting his theological ethos. Gheorghe Dragulin actually praised Staniloae precisely for his Dionysian approach to sacraments. Pseudo-Dionysius the Areopagite, *Sfântul Dionisie Areopagitul: Opere complete si Scoliile Sfântului Maxim Marturisitorul*, trans. Dumitru Staniloae (Bucharest: Paideia, 1996), 130. See Dragulin, "Pseudo-Dionysios the Areopagite in Dumitru Staniloae's Theology," 80.

51. This is also the case of persons who, although initially Orthodox, subsequently embraced other religions but eventually came back to Orthodoxy.

52. Having said that, Staniloae did not separate Baptism and Chrismation totally, especially given their unity together with the Eucharist in the early rites of initiation. For a historical and theological analysis, see Staniloae, "Number of the Sacraments," 202–03.

53. Dumitru Staniloae, "Din aspectul Sacramental al Bisericii" (Of the sacramental aspect of the Church), *Studii Teologice* 18, no. 9–10 (1966): 531–32. See

also Dumitru Staniloae, "Transparenta Bisericii in viata Sacramentala" (The transparence of the Church in sacramental Life), *Ortodoxia* 22, no. 4 (1970): 501–16. Moreover, Staniloae affirms that "The divine life, the divine energies of the Trinity, present in the humanity of the Son and descended to us through the Holy Spirit, overflow into human beings through the sacraments. Their purpose is to transform gradually the existence of the faithful according to the image of the Human-Christ." Staniloae, "Number of the Sacraments," 195.

54. Louth, "Staniloae's Dogmatics," (Reprint 2002), 60.

55. Andrew Louth, "What Is Theology? What Is Orthodox Theology?," *St. Vladimir's Theological Quarterly* 51, no. 4 (2007): 435–44.

56. Staniloae, *Theology and the Church*, 214–15.

57. I translate the Romanian *ierurgii* as "sacramentals" (or as Aquinas used it in Latin, *sacramentalia*—Summa I–II, Q. cviii, a. 2 ad 2um; III, Q. lxv, a. 1 ad 8um), which refers to Church services other than the seven sacraments. Ware is one of the English-speaking Orthodox theologians who uses this term, in Ware, *The Orthodox Church*, 276.

58. The "Pastoral Statement on Orthodox-Roman Catholic Marriages" (1990) recommends "that when an Orthodox and Catholic marry there be only one liturgical ceremony in which either one or both priests are present, with the rite being that of the officiating priest . . . [and] that such marriages be recorded in the registries of both churches." John Borelli and John H. Erickson, eds., *The Quest for Unity: Orthodox and Catholics in Dialogue* (Crestwood, N.Y.: St. Vladimir's Seminary Press, 1996) 239–43.

59. Staniloae, "Number of the Sacraments," 215.

60. Andrew Louth, review of Aristotle Papanikolaou, "Being with God: Trinity, Apophaticism, and Divine-Human Communion," *St. Vladimir's Theological Quarterly* 51, no. 4 (2007): 447.

61. To give just one example, in his Trinitarian theology, Barth prefers "modes of being" to "persons." Karl Barth, *Church Dogmatics: The Doctrine of the Word of God*, trans. G.W. Bromiley, 2nd ed., vol. 1 (Edinburgh: T&T Clark, 1999), 299.

Contributors

Radu Bordeianu is an associate professor at Duquesne University in Pittsburgh, Pennsylvannia, and an Orthodox priest. His research focuses on ecumenical ecclesiologies, especially the dialogue between the Orthodox and Catholic churches. He is particularly engaged with the ecclesiology of the Romanian Orthodox theologian Dumitru Staniloae, placing special emphasis on Staniloae's contribution in ecumenical discussions on the Church. His book, *Dumitru Staniloae: An Ecumenical Ecclesiology* has been published by Continuum (2011) and he serves as president of the Orthodox Theological Society in America (OTSA).

Sarah Coakley is Norris-Hulse Professor of Divinity at the University of Cambridge, and was previously Mallinckrodt Professor of Divinity at Harvard University. She is a philosopher of religion and systematic theology who also has keen interests in patristic thought. Her publications include *Powers and Submissions* (Oxford: Blackwell, 2002); the first of her four-volume systematic theology, *God, Sexuality and the Self* (Cambridge: Cambridge University Press, 2013); and her recent Gifford Lectures, *Sacrifice Regained* (Aberdeen University, online, 2012).

George E. Demacopoulos is professor of theology and director and cofounder of the Orthodox Christian Studies Center at Fordham University. He specializes in the history of Christianity in late antiquity and the middle ages. His monographs include *The Invention of Peter: Apostolic Discourse and Papal Authority in Late Antiquity* (Philadelphia: University of Pennsylvania Press, 2013) and *Five Models of Spiritual Direction in the Early Church* (Notre Dame, Ind.: University of Notre Dame Press, 2007).

Effie Fokas is a research fellow at the Hellenic Foundation for European and Foreign Policy (ELIAMEP), leading a project entitled "Pluralism and Religious Freedom in Orthodox Countries in Europe." She was founding director of the London School of Economics Forum on Religion and is currently research associate of the LSE Hellenic Observatory. Her publications include *Islam in Europe: Diversity, Identity and Influence*, co-edited with Aziz Al-Azmeh (Cambridge: Cambridge University Press, 2007) and *Religious America, Secular Europe? A Theme and Variations*, co-authored with Peter Berger and Grace Davie (Aldershot, U.K.: Ashgate Press, 2008).

Paul Gavrilyuk is associate professor of historical theology at the University of St Thomas, Saint Paul, Minnesota. He is the author of *The Suffering of the Impassible God: The Dialectics of Patristic Thought* (Oxford: Oxford University Press, 2004; Spanish ed. 2012) and *Histoire du catéchuménat dans l'église ancienne* (Paris: Cerf, 2007). He also coedited with Sarah Coakley, *The Spiritual Senses: Perceiving God in Western Christianity* (Cambridge: Cambridge University Press, 2012).

Pantelis Kalaitzidis is the director of the Volos Academy for Theological Studies, Volos, Greece, a church-related institution focusing mainly on contemporary issues of Eastern Orthodoxy. He is currently a lecturer at Hellenic Open University and the University of Thessaly, Greece, as well as a visiting professor at St. Sergius Theological Institute, Paris, he has also been a visiting scholar and visiting research fellow at Holy Cross Greek Orthodox School of Theology, Princeton Theological Seminary, and Princeton University. He serves as editor of the series Doxa & Praxis: Exploring Orthodox Theology, from WCC Publications, Geneva. His research interests lie especially in the the eschatological dimension of Christianity, the dialogues between Orthodox Christianity and modernity, theology and modern literature, religion and multiculturalism, religious nationalism and fundamentalism in the Orthodox context, and postmodern hermeneutics of patristics. His last book, *Orthodoxy and Political Theology* has been published by WCC Publications (Geneva, 2012).

Tia Kolbaba is an associate professor in the Department of Religion at Rutgers University. Her work focuses on Byzantine Orthodox perceptions of the Latin West. She is the author of two books: *The Byzantine Lists: Errors of the Latins* (Champaign, Ill.: University of Illinois Press, 2000) and *Inventing Latin Heretics: The Byzantines and the Filioque in the Ninth Century* (Kalamazoo, Mich.: Medieval Institute Publications, 2008).

John Panteleimon Manoussakis is assistant professor of philosophy and the Edward Bennett Williams Fellow at the College of the Holy Cross as well as an honorary fellow in theology and philosophy at the Australian Catholic University. He has edited five volumes, authored two books—among which is *God after Metaphysics* (Bloomington: Indiana University Press, 2007)—and written over twenty articles on the phenomenology of religion and the contemporary philosophical appropriation of patristic theology.

Aristotle Papanikolaou is Archbishop Demetrios Chair of Orthodox Theology and Culture and cofounder of the Orthodox Christian Studies Center at Fordham University. His on-going research interests include contemporary Orthodox theology (nineteenth and twentieth centuries) and trinitarian theology. His current research agenda relates to theological anthropology, and specifically explores the relevancy of truth telling (confession) for understanding what it means to be human.

Basilio Petrà, of Greek origin, born in 1946, a priest of the diocese of Prato (Italy), is professor of (Roman Catholic) moral theology at the Theological Faculty of Central Italy, Florence, and professor of (Eastern) moral theology at the Pontifical Oriental Institute, Rome. Among his major publications are *Tra cielo e terra: Introduzione alla teologia morale ortodossa contemporanea* (Bologna: EDB, 1992); *La Chiesa dei Padri Breve introduzione all'Ortodossia*, 2a ed. riv. (Bologna: EDB, 2007); *L'etica ortodossa. Storia, fonti, identità* (Assisi: Cittadella Editrice, 2010). He has translated several of Yannaras's books into Italian.

Marcus Plested is the academic director of the Institute for Orthodox Christian Studies (Cambridge Theological Federation) and affiliated lecturer in the Faculty of Divinity of the University of Cambridge. He is the author of *The Macarian Legacy* (Oxford: Oxford University Press, 2004) and *Orthodox Readings of Aquinas* (Oxford: Oxford University Press, 2012). His research centres on patristic, Byzantine, and modern Orthodox theology with special reference to East-West relations.

Elizabeth Prodromou is affiliate scholar at the Center for European Studies at Harvard University, where she is co-chair of the Southeastern Europe Study Group. She received her PhD in political science from the Massachusetts Institute of Technology (1993). She completed diplomatic service (2004–12) for the United States of America, serving as vice chair of the United States Commission on International Religious Freedom. Her published scholarship has appeared in journals such as *Social Compass, European Journal of Political Research, Journal of the American Academy of Religion, The Brandywine Review, Harvard International Review, Orbis,* and *Survival,* as well as in numerous edited volumes in English, Greek, and Bulgarian. She is coeditor and contributor to *Thinking through Faith: Perspectives from Orthodox Christian Scholars* (Crestwood, N.Y.: St. Vladimir's Seminary Press, 2008). She has held teaching appointments at Boston University and Princeton University.

Norman Russell, an honorary research fellow at St. Stephen's House, Oxford, also teaches at Heythrop College, London, and the Institute for Orthodox Christian Studies, Cambridge. His publications include *The Doctrine of Deification in the Greek Patristic Tradition* (New York: Oxford University Press, 2006) and a number of translations of modern Greek theologians.

Vera Shevzov is professor of religion at Smith College. Her book, *Russian Orthodoxy on the Eve of Revolution* (New York: Oxford University Press, 2004), was awarded the Frank S. and Elizabeth D. Brewer Prize of the American Society of Church History. She is currently completing a book on the image of Mary in late imperial and contemporary Russia.

Robert Taft, S.J., is an American Jesuit priest and archimandrite of the Byzantine rite and an expert and author of numerous books and essay on eastern Christian liturgy. He taught for thirty-eight years at the Pontifical Oriental Institute in Rome until his retirement in 2008. He is also the founder of the Societas Orientalium Liturgiarum.

Dr. Lucian Turcescu is professor and chair of the Department of Theological Studies at Concordia University, Montreal, Canada. He has published in several areas, including early Christianity, religion and politics, and ecumenism. His most recent books include *Church, State, and Democracy in Expanding Europe* (Oxford: Oxford University Press, 2011) and *Religion and Politics in Post-Communist Romania* (Oxford: Oxford University Press, 2007).

INDEX

1204, 8, 28, 34, 160

Abramtsov, David F., 24
Aeterni Patris, 126
Aksakov, Konstantin, 83, 300n53
Aleksy II, Patriarch, 225–26
Allatius, Leo, 78, 81
alterity: immutable, 199; and Orthodoxy, 195–97, 201, 203, 206
Ambrose of Milan, 3
anerastos, 166
Angelikoudes, 67
anthropology, 88, 123, 129, 177, 194, 198, 242
antichrist, 163, 226
antinomic, 14, 133, 313
antipapism, 4, 229, 237
apophaticism/apophatism, 14–16, 66, 70, 119, 132–40, 159–62, 168–70, 179–80, 198, 206, 241–43, 251–53, 310n6, 316n70
Aquinas, Thomas, 58–70, 108, 123, 126, 155, 165. *See also* Thomism
Arapasu, Teoctist, 213
Arian, 4, 46, 47, 276n6, 277n12
Aristotle, 7, 64, 65, 67, 68, 69, 117, 151, 172, 218

Armenians, 33, 45, 49–57, 75, 279n27
Augustine of Hippo, Saint, 4, 13, 15–16, 65, 115–16, 123, 145, 155, 256, 258n26, 259n38, 306n45

Babylonian captivity, 102, 143, 151
Balkanism, 204, 237
Barreto, Patriarch, 27
Barth, Karl, 123, 130, 156, 312n22, 355n61
Berdiaev, Nikolai, 84, 103, 104, 106, 112, 305n28, 308n63
Berger, Peter, 181, 182, 184, 187, 331n28
Berlin Wall, 193
Bethlehem, Council of, 74
Bhabha, Homi, 18–19, 257n20, 259n44, 260n49, 260n50
binary, 1–2, 6, 194, 195, 196, 206, 209
Brzezinski, Zbigniew, 205
Bukharev, Feodor, 87
Bukharev, Archimandrite, 94, 95
Bulgakov, Sergius, 14, 15, 16, 60–61, 102–3, 109, 112, 120, 128, 130, 164, 247, 248, 282, 307n98, 353n41
Bulgaria, 35–36, 222–23
Byzantine Commonwealth, 200, 296n6

ORTHODOX CHRISTIANITY AND CONTEMPORARY THOUGHT

SERIES EDITORS
George E. Demacopoulos and Aristotle Papanikolaou

Ecumenical Patriarch Bartholomew, *In the World, Yet Not of the World: Social and Global Initiatives of Ecumenical Patriarch Bartholomew.* Edited by John Chryssavgis. Foreword by José Manuel Barroso.

Ecumenical Patriarch Bartholomew, *Speaking the Truth in Love: Theological and Spiritual Exhortations of Ecumenical Patriarch Bartholomew.* Edited by John Chryssavgis. Foreword by Dr. Rowan Williams, Archbishop of Canterbury.

Ecumenical Patriarch Bartholomew, *On Earth as in Heaven: Ecological Vision and Initiatives of Ecumenical Patriarch Bartholomew.* Edited by John Chryssavgis. Foreword by His Royal Highness the Duke of Edinburgh.

George E. Demacopoulos and Aristotle Papanikolaou (eds.), *Orthodox Constructions of the West.*

John Chryssavgis and Bruce V. Foltz (eds.), *Toward an Ecology of Transfiguration: Orthodox Christian Perspectives on Environment, Nature, and Creation.* Prefatory Letter by Ecumenical Patriarch Bartholomew. Foreword by Bill McKibben.